# WUTHERING HEIGHTS

AUTHORITATIVE TEXT

BACKGROUNDS

CRITICISM

⋙ ⋘

THIRD EDITION

➤➤ A NORTON CRITICAL EDITION ➤➤

*EMILY BRONTË*

# WUTHERING HEIGHTS

AUTHORITATIVE TEXT
BACKGROUNDS
CRITICISM

➤➤ ➤➤

THIRD EDITION

*Edited by*

WILLIAM M. SALE, JR.

LATE OF CORNELL UNIVERSITY

and

RICHARD J. DUNN

UNIVERSITY OF WASHINGTON

W • W • NORTON & COMPANY

*New York • London*

Library of Congress Cataloging-in-Publication Data

Brontë, Emily, 1818–1848.
    Wuthering Heights : an authoritative text, selected poems, with
essays in criticism / Emily Brontë ; edited by William M. Sale, Jr.
and Richard J. Dunn. — 3rd ed.
        p.    cm. — (A Norton critical edition)
    Bibliography: p.
    ISBN 0-393-95760-8
    1. Brontë, Emily, 1818–1848. Wuthering heights.    I. Sale,
William Merritt, 1899–    . II. Dunn, Richard J., 1938–
III. Brontë, Emily, 1818–1848. Poems. Selections. 1989.
IV. Title.
PR4172.W7    1989
823'.8—dc19        88-8543

W. W. Norton & Company, Inc., 500 Fifth Avenue, New York, N.Y. 10110
W. W. Norton & Company Ltd., 10 Coptic Street, London, WC1A 1PU

2 3 4 5 6 7 8 9 0

# Contents

Preface to the Third Edition     vii
Preface to the First Edition     xi

The Text of *Wuthering Heights*     1

    Textual Commentary · By William M. Sale, Jr.     257

Backgrounds

    Poems from the 1850 *Wuthering Heights*     267
      [Charlotte Brontë] · Selections     267
       Stanzas     269
       The Bluebell     271
       Stanzas     272
       "Shall Earth no more inspire thee"     275
       The Night Wind     276
       "Aye, there it is!"     277
       Love and Friendship     278
       The Elder's Rebuke     278
       The Wanderer from the Fold     279
       Warning and Reply     281
       Last Words     282
       The Lady to Her Guitar     282
       The Two Children     283
       The Visionary     285
       Encouragement     286
       Stanzas     287
       No Coward Soul     287

      William M. Sale, Jr. · Emily Brontë's
      History of Gondal     289

    Emily Brontë's Diary     295
      November 24, 1834     295
      June 26, 1837     296
      July 30, 1841     296
      July 30, 1845     297

Contemporary Reception                                          299
    Emily Brontë's First Edition Reviews                        299
        *Atlas*                                                 299
        *Douglas Jerrold's Weekly Newspaper*                    301
        *Examiner*                                              302
        *Britannia*                                             305
        Unidentified Review                                     308
        *Palladium*                                             309
    [Charlotte Brontë] · Biographical Notice of Ellis
        and Acton Bell (1850)                                   313
    [Charlotte Brontë] · Editor's Preface to the New Edition
        of *Wuthering Heights* (1850)                           319
    Reviews of the 1850 Edition of *Wuthering Heights*          323
        *Examiner*                                              323
        *Leader*                                                325
        *Athenaeum*                                             327

Criticism

    Charles Percy Sanger · The Structure of
        *Wuthering Heights*                                     331
    A. Stuart Daley · The Moons and Almanacs of
        *Wuthering Heights*                                     336
    A. Stuart Daley · A Chronology of *Wuthering Heights*       349
    Carol Jacobs · At the Threshold of Interpretation           353
    Nancy Armstrong · Emily Brontë In and Out of Her Time       365
    J. Hillis Miller · *Wuthering Heights:* Repetition and the
        "Uncanny"                                               378

Selected Bibliography                                           395

# Preface to the Third Edition

The presence now of *Wuthering Heights* in most listings of great English novels would have been difficult to predict when it appeared in 1847, because initial response to Emily Brontë's strange work was often negative. At first there was considerable confusion about whether this was a book by the same hand that produced *Jane Eyre* and whether it was the work of a woman or a man. Thomas Newby, Emily's publisher, himself furthered the mis-impressions that *Wuthering Heights* and Anne Brontë's *Agnes Grey*, which appeared together in three volumes, were the work of one writer. Small wonder that when preparing a second edition after her sisters' deaths Charlotte Brontë took responsibility for setting straight the facts of authorship and publication and for countering what she could of the negative reaction. As she said in her preface to the 1850 edition of *Wuthering Heights*, she thought an interpreter ought to have stood between her sister and the world, and clearly that was the role she assumed in reissuing the novel with a biograph-ical statement, preface, and selection of her sister's poetry. Charlotte's in-tervention in itself did not assure the gradually increasing value *Wuthering Heights* acquired in its rise to a position among the classics of English fiction, but along with the interest in the Brontës that was stimulated by Elizabeth Gaskell's 1855 biography of Charlotte, the 1850 edition of *Wuthering Heights* established the grounds upon which the novel would be evaluated by gen-erations of readers, and it called attention to a selection of Emily's poetry.

A critical edition of *Wuthering Heights* allows us to have the novel both as it first appeared and as it was reprinted under Charlotte's particular di-rection. Although she made a number of changes, which are fully described in William M. Sale's textual notes and in Juliet Barker's notes to the poems, the effect of these on our understanding of the novel surely is less than that of the arguments Charlotte makes in the biographical note and preface. So that we may have those statements in the context of the nineteenth-century reception, I have placed the 1850 introductory material among the early reviews. Charlotte's remarks were motivated by reviewers of the first edition, and her opinions affected subsequent reviewers and critics. As J. Hillis Miller notes, thanks to Charlotte "the novel comes wrapped in layers of prefatory material," and it is therefore often "difficult to be sure where the margin of the introductions ends and where the novel 'proper' begins." By separating the introductory material but by preserving it as part of the influential early reception of *Wuthering Heights*, this Norton edition lets readers enter the novel directly as it appeared to its first readers and then to follow the history of its popular and critical reception.

The first and second editions of the Norton *Wuthering Heights* included samples from the five reviews found in Emily Brontë's desk. This edition expands those samples and adds also reviews of the 1850 edition. Apart from her poems and several school exercises in French, little other than her novel remains of Emily's writing, but this edition includes four brief diary entries that give glimpses of contentment, good humor, and continuing interest in the imaginary world of the Gondals as well as some information about the comings and goings of the Brontës. The final diary piece looks forward to the period when Emily wrote *Wuthering Heights*. Still, it has little to suggest the power of the forthcoming novel, although Emily does note that she has "plenty of work on hands, and writing, and am altogether full of business." But as Sidney Biddell remarked in 1883, "Knowledge is denied to us, and we have still to learn how Emily Brontë came to write *Wuthering Heights*, the hidden spring within her that at last found vent in that awful book. . . . Such work may ultimately result from years of toil and thought, but suddenly without preparation or effort, inspiration can alone account." Although Biddell is responding to an unreliable early biography by Mary Robinson, his wonderment echoes that of Charlotte Brontë, who concluded her 1850 preface insisting that the sculptor of this novel worked "from no model but the vision of his meditations."

Because A. Stuart Daley has made important corrections to Charles Percy Sanger's long-accepted chronology of the story, this edition retains only Sanger's explanations of the family trees and of Heathcliff's manipulation of the inheritances. Daley's "The Moons and Almanacs of *Wuthering Heights*" provides a detailed account of the novel's chronology.

The critical essays by Carol Jacobs, Nancy Armstrong, and J. Hillis Miller are all new selections for this edition. As have a number of previous commentators, Jacobs recognizes the problematic roles of Lockwood and Nelly Dean as narrators, the importance of dreams and visions, and the "fundamental estrangement that *Wuthering Heights* imposes on narrator and characters alike" as she considers various ways by which the novel "speaks of its own textuality." Nancy Armstrong's "Emily Brontë In and Out of Her Time" finds *Wuthering Heights* to be "an essentially disjunctive novel," posing questions in one set of literary conventions that cannot be answered by another convention. J. Hillis Miller thinks that the best readings of the novel are those "which best account for the heterogeneity of the text, its presentation of a definite group of possible meanings which are systematically interconnected, determined by the text, but logically incompatible." Therefore, he finds it necessary to free the novel from the multiple, but restricted, interpretations of Charlotte's preface and the hundreds of commentaries it inspired. There is not, Miller insists, "a single secret truth about *Wuthering Heights*," and thus his essay, like those by Jacobs and Armstrong, resists the reductive as it respects this as an "over-rich" text, ever open to the process of interpretation.

In preparing this third edition, I am indebted especially to Dr. Juliet Barker, to the Brontë Society, to the scholars who kindly assisted in determining how best to accommodate their longer essays for this volume, to John Benedict and Carol Stiles Bemis of Norton for their encouragement and patience, to the family of the late William M. Sale, and, for special assistance, to Susan Dunn.

RICHARD J. DUNN

Seattle, Washington

# Preface to the First Edition

*Wuthering Heights* was first published in December 1847. Emily Brontë died a year later, and the second edition, revised by her sister Charlotte, did not appear until December 1850. Charlotte Brontë had recognized that revision was required, since the first edition abounded in errors and inconsistencies, for many of which Emily's printer was responsible. But in trying to do justice to her sister's novel, she assumed privileges that now seem unwarranted. Therefore, it seems desirable to return to the first edition as a point of departure. My intention, like Charlotte's, is to provide a readable text, but at the same time to supply for the reader with a more special interest something other than the assurance that editions have been "collated." I have therefore noted all the substantive changes that I have made from the first edition (Notes to the Text, pp. 259–64), and I have indicated in Appendix I the departures made from that edition with respect to spelling and capitalization. Only the incredibly chaotic punctuation and such obvious errors as *to* for *two*, *who's* for *whose*, *Linton's* for *Lintons* have been corrected silently. When a change in punctuation is made to resolve an ambiguity in meaning, the original punctuation is recorded in the textual notes. In order to make clear the responsibilities of a modern editor, I have provided in a section following the text (pp. 257–59) a full account of the difficulties that Emily Brontë met with in the printing and publishing of her novel. To the best of my knowledge, this is the first time that such an account has been provided.

I have glossed at the foot of the appropriate pages those words of the Yorkshire dialect that I think the modern reader may have difficulty in understanding, and I have provided a few notes explaining other matters. This glossary seems to me to be long overdue, and the need in no satisfactory way supplied by Charlotte Brontë's occasional replacing of a word of dialect by its equivalent in standard English. Charlotte justified her changes by saying that Emily's orthography exactly rendered "the Yorkshire dialect to a Yorkshire ear," but "Southerns must find it unintelligible."[1] But she herself was so familiar with the dialect that she never really knew when a "Southern" needed help. Emily is no expert in reproducing dialect, but she is surprisingly good. Hers is at least a literary convention preferable to the hit-or-miss mixture of dialect and standard English which Charlotte produced.

\* \* \*

WILLIAM M. SALE, JR.

Ithaca, N.Y.

1. *The Brontës: Their Lives, Friendships and Correspondence*, Oxford, Shakespeare Head Press, ed. Wise and Symington, 4 vols., 1932, III, 165.

# The Text of
# Wuthering Heights

# Wuthering Heights

## Chapter I

1801——I have just returned from a visit to my landlord—the solitary neighbour that I shall be troubled with. This is certainly a beautiful country! In all England, I do not believe that I could have fixed on a situation so completely removed from the stir of society. A perfect misanthropist's heaven—and Mr. Heathcliff and I are such a suitable pair to divide the desolation between us. A capital fellow! He little imagined how my heart warmed towards him when I beheld his black eyes withdraw so suspiciously under their brows, as I rode up, and when his fingers sheltered themselves, with a jealous resolution, still further in his waistcoat, as I announced my name.

"Mr. Heathcliff?" I said.

A nod was the answer.

"Mr. Lockwood, your new tenant, sir. I do myself the honour of calling as soon as possible after my arrival, to express the hope that I have not inconvenienced you by my perseverance in soliciting the occupation of Thrushcross Grange: I heard, yesterday, you had had some thoughts—"

"Thrushcross Grange is my own, sir," he interrupted, wincing, "I should not allow any one to inconvenience me, if I could hinder it—walk in!"

The "walk in," was uttered with closed teeth and expressed the sentiment, "Go to the Deuce!". Even the gate over which he leant manifested no sympathizing movement to the words, and I think that circumstance determined me to accept the invitation: I felt interested in a man who seemed more exaggeratedly reserved than myself.

When he saw my horse's breast fairly pushing the barrier, he did pull out his hand to unchain it, and then sullenly preceded me up the causeway, calling, as we entered the court—

"Joseph, take Mr. Lockwood's horse; and bring up some wine."

"Here we have the whole establishment of domestics, I suppose," was the reflection, suggested by this compound order. "No wonder the grass grows up between the flags, and cattle are the only hedge-cutters."

Joseph was an elderly, nay, an old man, very old, perhaps, though hale and sinewy.

"The Lord help us!" he soliloquized in an undertone of peevish displeasure, while relieving me of my horse: looking, meantime, in my face so sourly that I charitably conjectured he must have need of divine aid to digest his dinner, and his pious ejaculation had no reference to my unexpected advent.

Wuthering Heights is the name of Mr. Heathcliff's dwelling. "Wuthering" being a significant provincial adjective, descriptive of the atmospheric tumult to which its station is exposed in stormy weather. Pure, bracing ventilation they must have up there, at all times, indeed: one may guess the power of the north wind, blowing over the edge, by the excessive slant of a few stunted firs at the end of the house; and by a range of gaunt thorns all stretching their limbs one way, as if craving alms of the sun. Happily, the architect had foresight to build it strong: the narrow windows are deeply set in the wall, and the corners defended with large jutting stones.

Before passing the threshold, I paused to admire a quantity of grotesque carving lavished over the front, and especially about the principal door, above which, among a wilderness of crumbling griffins and shameless little boys, I detected the date "1500," and the name "Hareton Earnshaw." I would have made a few comments, and requested a short history of the place from the surly owner, but his attitude at the door appeared to demand my speedy entrance, or complete departure, and I had no desire to aggravate his impatience, previous to inspecting the penetralium.

One step brought us into the family sitting-room, without any introductory lobby or passage: they call it here "the house" preeminently. It includes kitchen and parlour, generally, but I believe at Wuthering Heights the kitchen is forced to retreat altogether into another quarter; at least I distinguished a chatter of tongues, and a clatter of culinary utensils deep within; and I observed no signs of roasting, boiling, or baking about the huge fire-place; nor any glitter of copper saucepans and tin cullenders on the walls. One end, indeed, reflected splendidly both light and heat from ranks of immense pewter dishes, interspersed with silver jugs and tankards, towering row after row, in a vast oak dresser, to the very roof. The latter had never been underdrawn: its entire anatomy lay bare to an inquiring eye, except where a frame of wood laden with oatcakes, and clusters of legs of beef, mutton, and ham, concealed it. Above the chimney were sundry villanous old guns, and a couple of horse-pistols, and, by way of ornament, three gaudily-painted canisters disposed along its ledge. The floor was of smooth, white stone; the chairs, high-backed, primitive structures, painted green, one or two heavy black ones lurking in the shade. In an arch under the dresser, reposed a huge, liver-coloured bitch pointer surrounded by a swarm of squealing puppies, and other dogs haunted other recesses.

The apartment and furniture would have been nothing extraordinary as belonging to a homely, northern farmer, with a stubborn countenance, and stalwart limbs set out to advantage in knee-breeches and gaiters. Such an individual, seated in his arm-chair, his mug of ale frothing on the round table before him, is to be seen in any circuit of five or six miles among these hills, if you go at the right time, after dinner. But Mr. Heathcliff forms a singular contrast to his abode and style of living. He is a dark-skinned gypsy in aspect, in dress and manners a gentleman, that is, as much a gentleman as many a country squire: rather slovenly, perhaps, yet not looking amiss with his negligence, because he has an erect and handsome figure—and rather morose. Possibly, some people might suspect him of a degree of under-bred pride; I have a sympathetic chord within that tells me it is nothing of the sort: I know, by instinct, his reserve springs from an aversion to showy displays of feeling—to manifestations of mutual kindliness. He'll love and hate, equally under cover, and esteem it a species of impertinence to be loved or hated again—No, I'm running on too fast—I bestow my own attributes over-liberally on him. Mr. Heathcliff may have entirely dissimilar reasons for keeping his hand out of the way when he meets a would-be acquaintance, to those which actuate me. Let me hope my constitution is almost peculiar: my dear mother used to say I should never have a comfortable home, and only last summer I proved myself perfectly unworthy of one.

While enjoying a month of fine weather at the sea-coast, I was thrown into the company of a most fascinating creature, a real goddess in my eyes, as long as she took no notice of me. I "never told my love" vocally; still, if looks have language, the merest idiot might have guessed I was over head and ears: she understood me at last, and looked a return—the sweetest of all imaginable looks. And what did I do? I confess it with shame—shrunk icily into myself, like a snail; at every glance retired colder and farther; till, finally, the poor innocent was led to doubt her own senses, and, overwhelmed with confusion at her supposed mistake, persuaded her mamma to decamp.

By this curious turn of disposition I have gained the reputation of deliberate heartlessness, how undeserved, I alone can appreciate.

I took a seat at the end of the hearthstone opposite that towards which my landlord advanced, and filled up an interval of silence by attempting to caress the canine mother, who had left her nursery and was sneaking wolfishly to the back of my legs, her lip curled up, and her white teeth watering for a snatch.

My caress provoked a long, guttural gnarl.

"You'd better let the dog alone," growled Mr. Heathcliff in unison, checking fiercer demonstrations with a punch of his foot. "She's not accustomed to be spoiled—not kept for a pet."

Then, striding to a side-door, he shouted again—

"Joseph!"

Joseph mumbled indistinctly in the depths of the cellar, but gave no intimation of ascending; so his master dived down to him, leaving me *vis-à-vis* the ruffianly bitch and a pair of grim, shaggy sheep dogs, who shared with her a jealous guardianship over all my movements.

Not anxious to come in contact with their fangs, I sat still; but, imagining they would scarcely understand tacit insults, I unfortunately indulged in winking and making faces at the trio, and some turn of my physiognomy so irritated madam, that she suddenly broke into a fury and leapt on my knees. I flung her back, and hastened to interpose the table between us. This proceeding roused the whole hive. Half-a-dozen four-footed fiends, of various sizes and ages, issued from hidden dens to the common centre. I felt my heels and coat-laps peculiar subjects of assault; and, parrying off the larger combatants as effectually as I could with the poker, I was constrained to demand, aloud, assistance from some of the household in re-establishing peace.

Mr. Heathcliff and his man climbed the cellar steps with vexatious phlegm. I don't think they moved one second faster than usual, though the hearth was an absolute tempest of worrying and yelping.

Happily, an inhabitant of the kitchen made more dispatch; a lusty dame, with tucked-up gown, bare arms, and fire-flushed cheeks, rushed into the midst of us flourishing a frying-pan; and used that weapon, and her tongue, to such purpose, that the storm subsided magically, and she only remained, heaving like a sea after a high wind, when her master entered on the scene.

"What the devil is the matter?" he asked, eyeing me in a manner that I could ill endure after this inhospitable treatment.

"What the devil, indeed!" I muttered. "The herd of possessed swine could have had no worse spirits in them than those animals of yours, sir. You might as well leave a stranger with a brood of tigers!"

"They won't meddle with persons who touch nothing," he remarked, putting the bottle before me, and restoring the displaced table. "The dogs do right to be vigilant. Take a glass of wine?"

"No, thank you."

"Not bitten, are you?"

"If I had been, I would have set my signet on the biter."

Heathcliff's countenance relaxed into a grin.

"Come, come," he said, "you are flurried, Mr. Lockwood. Here, take a little wine. Guests are so exceedingly rare in this house that I and my dogs, I am willing to own, hardly know how to receive them. Your health, sir!"

I bowed and returned the pledge, beginning to perceive that it would be foolish to sit sulking for the misbehaviour of a pack of curs: besides, I felt loath to yield the fellow further amusement, at my expense, since his humour took that turn.

He—probably swayed by prudential considerations of the folly of offending a good tenant—relaxed a little, in the laconic style of chipping off his pronouns and auxiliary verbs, and introduced what he supposed would be a subject of interest to me, a discourse on the advantages and disadvantages of my present place of retirement.

I found him very intelligent on the topics we touched; and, before I went home, I was encouraged so far as to volunteer another visit to-morrow.

He evidently wished no repetition of my intrusion. I shall go, notwithstanding. It is astonishing how sociable I feel myself compared with him.

## Chapter II

Yesterday afternoon set in misty and cold. I had half a mind to spend it by my study fire, instead of wading through heath and mud to Wuthering Heights.

On coming up from dinner, however (N. B. I dine between twelve and one o'clock; the housekeeper, a matronly lady taken as a fixture along with the house, could not, or would not comprehend my request that I might be served at five.)—on mounting the stairs with this lazy intention, and stepping into the room, I saw a servant-girl on her knees, surrounded by brushes and coal-scuttles, and raising an infernal dust as she extinguished the flames with heaps of cinders. This spectacle drove me back immediately; I took my hat, and, after a four miles' walk, arrived at Heathcliff's garden gate just in time to escape the first feathery flakes of a snow shower.

On that bleak hill-top the earth was hard with a black frost, and the air made me shiver through every limb. Being unable to remove the chain, I jumped over, and, running up the flagged causeway bordered with straggling gooseberry bushes, knocked vainly for admittance, till my knuckles tingled and the dogs howled.

"Wretched inmates!" I ejaculated, mentally, "you deserve perpetual isolation from your species for your churlish inhospitality. At least, I would not keep my doors barred in the day time. I don't care—I will get in!"

So resolved, I grasped the latch and shook it vehemently. Vinegar-faced Joseph projected his head from a round window of the barn.

"Whet are ye for?" he shouted. "T' maister's dahn i' t'fowld. Goa rahnd by th' end ut' laith, if yah went tuh spake tull him."[1]

"Is there nobody inside to open the door?" I hallooed, responsively.

"They's nobbut t' missis; and shoo'll nut oppen't an ye mak yer flaysome dins till neeght."[2]

"Why? cannot you tell her who I am, eh, Joseph?"

"Nor-ne me![3] Aw'll hae noa hend wi't," muttered the head vanishing.

The snow began to drive thickly. I seized the handle to essay another trial, when a young man, without coat, and shouldering a pitchfork, appeared in the yard behind. He hailed me to follow him, and, after marching through a washhouse and a paved area containing a coal-shed, pump, and pigeon cote, we at length arrived in the large, warm, cheerful apartment where I was formerly received.

It glowed delightfully in the radiance of an immense fire, compounded of coal, peat, and wood; and near the table, laid for a plentiful evening meal, I was pleased to observe the "missis," an individual whose existence I had never previously suspected.

I bowed and waited, thinking she would bid me take a seat. She looked at me, leaning back in her chair, and remained motionless and mute.

"Rough weather!" I remarked. "I'm afraid, Mrs. Heathcliff, the door must bear the consequence of your servants' leisure attendance: I had hard work to make them hear me!"

She never opened her mouth. I stared—she stared also. At any rate, she kept her eyes on me, in a cool, regardless manner, exceedingly embarrassing and disagreeable.

"Sit down," said the young man, gruffly. "He'll be in soon."

I obeyed; and hemmed, and called the villain Juno, who deigned, at this second interview, to move the extreme tip of her tail, in token of owning my acquaintance.

"A beautiful animal!" I commenced again. "Do you intend parting with the little ones, madam?"

"They are not mine," said the amiable hostess more repellingly than Heathcliff himself could have replied.

"Ah, your favourites are among these!" I continued, turning to an obscure cushion full of something like cats.

1. See pp. 262–63 for some general comments on Emily Brontë's transcription of dialect; *t'fowld*: the fold; *ut' laith*: of the barn.

2. *Nobbut*; only; *shoo'll*: she'll; *flaysome*: terrible.
3. *Nor-ne me*; not me.

"A strange choice of favourites," she observed scornfully.

Unluckily, it was a heap of dead rabbits. I hemmed once more, and drew closer to the hearth, repeating my comment on the wildness of the evening.

"You should not have come out," she said, rising and reaching from the chimney-piece two of the painted canisters.

Her position before was sheltered from the light; now, I had a distinct view of her whole figure and countenance. She was slender, and apparently scarcely past girlhood: an admirable form, and the most exquisite little face that I have ever had the pleasure of beholding: small features, very fair; flaxen ringlets, or rather golden, hanging loose on her delicate neck; and eyes—had they been agreeable in expression, they would have been irresistible. Fortunately for my susceptible heart, the only sentiment they evinced hovered between scorn and a kind of desperation, singularly unnatural to be detected there.

The canisters were almost out of her reach; I made a motion to aid her; she turned upon me as a miser might turn if any one attempted to assist him in counting his gold.

"I don't want your help," she snapped, "I can get them for myself."

"I beg your pardon," I hastened to reply.

"Were you asked to tea?" she demanded, tying an apron over her neat black frock, and standing with a spoonful of the leaf poised over the pot.

"I shall be glad to have a cup," I answered.

"Were you asked?" she repeated.

"No," I said, half smiling. "You are the proper person to ask me."

She flung the tea back, spoon and all, and resumed her chair in a pet, her forehead corrugated, and her red under-lip pushed out, like a child's, ready to cry.

Meanwhile, the young man had slung onto his person a decidedly shabby upper garment, and, erecting himself before the blaze, looked down on me from the corner of his eyes, for all the world as if there were some mortal feud unavenged between us. I began to doubt whether he were a servant or not; his dress and speech were both rude, entirely devoid of the superiority observable in Mr. and Mrs. Heathcliff; his thick, brown curls were rough and uncultivated, his whiskers encroached bearishly over his cheeks, and his hands were embrowned like those of a common labourer. Still his bearing was free, almost haughty, and he showed none of a domestic's assiduity in attending on the lady of the house.

In the absence of clear proofs of his condition, I deemed it best to abstain from noticing his curious conduct, and, five minutes afterwards, the entrance of Heathcliff relieved me, in some measure, from my uncomfortable state.

"You see, sir, I am come according to promise!" I exclaimed, assuming the cheerful; "and I fear I shall be weather-bound for half an hour, if you can afford me shelter during that space."

"Half an hour?" he said, shaking the white flakes from his clothes; "I wonder you should select the thick of a snow-storm to ramble about in. Do you know that you run a risk of being lost in the marshes? People familiar with these moors often miss their road on such evenings, and, I can tell you, there is no chance of a change at present."

"Perhaps I can get a guide among your lads, and he might stay at the Grange till morning—could you spare me one?"

"No, I could not."

"Oh, indeed! Well, then, I must trust to my own sagacity."

"Umph."

"Are you going to mak th' tea?" demanded he of the shabby coat, shifting his ferocious gaze from me to the young lady.

"Is *he* to have any?" she asked, appealing to Heathcliff.

"Get it ready, will you?" was the answer, uttered so savagely that I started. The tone in which the words were said revealed a genuine bad nature. I no longer felt inclined to call Heathcliff a capital fellow.

When the preparations were finished, he invited me with—

"Now, sir, bring forward your chair." And we all, including the rustic youth, drew round the table, an austere silence prevailing while we discussed our meal.

I thought, if I had caused the cloud, it was my duty to make an effort to dispel it. They could not every day sit so grim and taciturn, and it was impossible, however ill-tempered they might be, that the universal scowl they wore was their every day countenance.

"It is strange," I began in the interval of swallowing one cup of tea and receiving another, "it is strange how custom can mould our tastes and ideas; many could not imagine the existence of happiness in a life of such complete exile from the world as you spend, Mr. Heathcliff; yet, I'll venture to say, that, surrounded by your family, and with your amiable lady as the presiding genius over your home and heart—"

"My amiable lady!" he interrupted, with an almost diabolical sneer on his face. "Where is she—my amiable lady?"

"Mrs. Heathcliff, your wife, I mean."

"Well, yes—Oh! you would intimate that her spirit has taken the post of ministering angel, and guards the fortunes of Wuthering Heights, even when her body is gone. Is that it?"

Perceiving myself in a blunder, I attempted to correct it. I might have seen there was too great a disparity between the ages of the parties to make it likely that they were man and wife. One was about forty, a period of mental vigour at which men seldom cherish the delusion of being married for love, by girls: that dream is reserved for the solace of our declining years. The other did not look seventeen.

Then it flashed upon me—"The clown at my elbow, who is drinking his tea out of a basin and eating his bread with unwashed hands, may be her husband. Heathcliff, junior, of course. Here is the consequence of being buried alive: she has thrown herself away upon that boor, from sheer ignorance that better individuals existed! A sad pity—I must beware how I cause her to regret her choice."

The last reflection may seem conceited; it was not. My neighbour struck me as bordering on repulsive. I knew, through experience, that I was tolerably attractive.

"Mrs. Heathcliff is my daughter-in-law," said Heathcliff, corroborating my surmise. He turned, as he spoke, a peculiar look in her direction, a look of hatred, unless he has a most perverse set of facial muscles that will not, like those of other people, interpret the language of his soul.

"Ah, certainly—I see now; you are the favoured possessor of the beneficent fairy," I remarked, turning to my neighbour.

This was worse than before: the youth grew crimson, and clenched his fist with every appearance of a meditated assault. But he seemed to recollect himself, presently, and smothered the storm in a brutal curse, muttered on my behalf, which, however, I took care not to notice.

"Unhappy in your conjectures, sir!" observed my host; "we neither of us have the privilege of owning your good fairy; her mate is dead. I said she was my daughter-in-law, therefore, she must have married my son."

"And this young man is—"

"Not my son, assuredly!"

Heathcliff smiled again, as if it were rather too bold a jest to attribute the paternity of that bear to him.

"My name is Hareton Earnshaw," growled the other; "and I'd counsel you to respect it!"

"I have shown no disrespect," was my reply, laughing internally at the dignity with which he announced himself.

He fixed his eye on me longer than I cared to return the stare, for fear I might be tempted either to box his ears, or render my hilarity audible. I began to feel unmistakably out of place in that pleasant family circle. The dismal spiritual atmosphere overcame, and more than neutralized the glowing physical comforts round me; and I resolved to be cautious how I ventured under those rafters a third time.

The business of eating being concluded, and no one uttering a word of sociable conversation, I approached a window to examine the weather.

A sorrowful sight I saw: dark night coming down prematurely, and sky and hills mingled in one bitter whirl of wind and suffocating snow.

"I don't think it possible for me to get home now, without a guide," I could not help exclaiming. "The roads will be buried already; and, if they were bare, I could scarcely distinguish a foot in advance."

"Hareton, drive those dozen sheep into the barn porch. They'll be covered if left in the fold all night; and put a plank before them," said Heathcliff.

"How must I do?" I continued, with rising irritation.

There was no reply to my question; and, on looking round, I saw only Joseph bringing in a pail of porridge for the dogs, and Mrs. Heathcliff, leaning over the fire, diverting herself with burning a bundle of matches which had fallen from the chimney-piece as she restored the tea-canister to its place.

The former, when he had deposited his burden, took a critical survey of the room, and, in cracked tones, grated out—

"Aw woonder hagh yah can faishion tuh stand thear i' idleness un war, when all on 'em's goan aght! Bud yah're a nowt, and it's noa use talking—yah'll niver mend uh yer ill ways; bud goa raight tuh t' divil, like yer mother afore ye!"[4]

I imagined, for a moment, that this piece of eloquence was addressed to me; and, sufficiently enraged, stepped towards the aged rascal with an intention of kicking him out of the door.

Mrs. Heathcliff, however, checked me by her answer.

"You scandalous old hypocrite!" she replied. "Are you not afraid of being carried away bodily, whenever you mention the devil's name? I warn you to refrain from provoking me, or I'll ask your abduction as a special favour. Stop, look here, Joseph," she continued, taking a long, dark book from a shelf. "I'll show you how far I've progressed in the Black Art—I shall soon be competent to make a clear house of it. The red cow didn't die by chance; and your rheumatism can hardly be reckoned among providential visitations!"

"Oh, wicked, wicked!" gasped the elder, "may the Lord deliver us from evil!"

"No, reprobate! you are a castaway—be off, or I'll hurt you seriously! I'll have you all modelled in wax and clay; and the first who passes the limits I fix, shall—I'll not say what he shall be done to—

4. *Faishion:* bring yourself; *un war:* and worse; *yah're a nowt:* you're a nothing.

but, you'll see! Go, I'm looking at you!"

The little witch put a mock malignity into her beautiful eyes, and Joseph, trembling with sincere horror, hurried out praying and ejaculating "wicked" as he went.

I thought her conduct must be prompted by a species of dreary fun; and, now that we were alone, I endeavoured to interest her in my distress.

"Mrs. Heathcliff," I said, earnestly, "you must excuse me for troubling you—I presume, because, with that face, I'm sure you cannot help being good-hearted. Do point out some landmarks by which I may know my way home. I have no more idea how to get there than you would have how to get to London!"

"Take the road you came," she answered, ensconcing herself in a chair, with a candle, and the long book open before her. "It is brief advice, but as sound as I can give."

"Then, if you hear of me being discovered dead in a bog, or a pit full of snow, your conscience won't whisper that it is partly your fault?"

"How so? I cannot escort you. They wouldn't let me go to the end of the garden-wall."

"*You!* I should be sorry to ask you to cross the threshold, for my convenience, on such a night," I cried. "I want you to *tell* me my way, not to *show* it; or else to persuade Mr. Heathcliff to give me a guide."

"Who? There is himself, Earnshaw, Zillah, Joseph, and I. Which would you have?"

"Are there no boys at the farm?"

"No, those are all."

"Then it follows that I am compelled to stay."

"That you may settle with your host. I have nothing to do with it."

"I hope it will be a lesson to you, to make no more rash journeys on these hills," cried Heathcliff's stern voice from the kitchen entrance. "As to staying here, I don't keep accommodations for visitors; you must share a bed with Hareton, or Joseph, if you do."

"I can sleep on a chair in this room," I replied.

"No, no! A stranger is a stranger, be he rich or poor—it will not suit me to permit any one the range of the place while I am off guard!" said the unmannerly wretch.

With this insult my patience was at an end. I uttered an expression of disgust, and pushed past him into the yard, running against Earnshaw in my haste. It was so dark that I could not see the means of exit, and, as I wandered round, I heard another specimen of their civil behaviour amongst each other.

At first, the young man appeared about to befriend me.

"I'll go with him as far as the park," he said.

"You'll go with him to hell!" exclaimed his master, or whatever relation he bore. "And who is to look after the horses, eh?"

"A man's life is of more consequence than one evening's neglect of the horses; somebody must go," murmured Mrs. Heathcliff, more kindly than I expected.

"Not at your command!" retorted Hareton. "If you set store on him, you'd better be quiet."

"Then I hope his ghost will haunt you; and I hope Mr. Heathcliff will never get another tenant, till the Grange is a ruin!" she answered sharply.

"Hearken, hearken, shoo's[5] cursing on em!" muttered Joseph, towards whom I had been steering.

He sat within earshot, milking the cows by the aid of a lantern which I seized unceremoniously, and, calling out that I would send it back on the morrow, rushed to the nearest postern.

"Maister, maister, he's staling t' lantern!" shouted the ancient, pursuing my retreat. "Hey, Gnasher! Hey, dog! Hey, Wolf, holld him, holld him!"

On opening the little door, two hairy monsters flew at my throat, bearing me down and extinguishing the light, while a mingled guffaw, from Heathcliff and Hareton, put the copestone on my rage and humiliation.

Fortunately, the beasts seemed more bent on stretching their paws, and yawning and flourishing their tails, than devouring me alive; but they would suffer no resurrection, and I was forced to lie till their malignant masters pleased to deliver me: then hatless, and trembling with wrath, I ordered the miscreants to let me out—on their peril to keep me one minute longer—with several incoherent threats of retaliation that, in their indefinite depth of virulency, smacked of King Lear.

The vehemence of my agitation brought on a copious bleeding at the nose, and still Heathcliff laughed, and still I scolded. I don't know what would have concluded the scene had there not been one person at hand rather more rational than myself, and more benevolent than my entertainer. This was Zillah, the stout housewife, who at length issued forth to inquire into the nature of the uproar. She thought that some of them had been laying violent hands on me, and, not daring to attack her master, she turned her vocal artillery against the younger scoundrel.

"Well, Mr. Earnshaw," she cried, "I wonder what you'll have agait[6] next! Are we going to murder folk on our very door-stones? I see this house will never do for me—look at t' poor lad, he's fair choking! Wisht, wisht![7] you mun'n't go on so—come in, and I'll

5. She's.
6. A-going.
7. Hush.

cure that. There now, hold ye still."

With these words she suddenly splashed a pint of icy water down my neck, and pulled me into the kitchen. Mr. Heathcliff followed, his accidental merriment expiring quickly in his habitual moroseness.

I was sick exceedingly, and dizzy and faint; and thus compelled, perforce, to accept lodgings under his roof. He told Zillah to give me a glass of brandy, and then passed on to the inner room, while she condoled with me on my sorry predicament, and having obeyed his orders, whereby I was somewhat revived, ushered me to bed.

### Chapter III

While leading the way upstairs, she recommended that I should hide the candle, and not make a noise, for her master had an odd notion about the chamber she would put me in, and never let anybody lodge there willingly.

I asked the reason.

She did not know, she answered; she had only lived there a year or two; and they had so many queer goings on, she could not begin to be curious.

Too stupified to be curious myself, I fastened my door and glanced round for the bed. The whole furniture consisted of a chair, a clothes-press, and a large oak case, with squares cut out near the top, resembling coach windows.

Having approached this structure, I looked inside, and perceived it to be a singular sort of old-fashioned couch, very conveniently designed to obviate the necessity for every member of the family having a room to himself. In fact, it formed a little closet, and the ledge of a window, which it enclosed, served as a table.

I slid back the panelled sides, got in with my light, pulled them together again, and felt secure against the vigilance of Heathcliff, and every one else.

The ledge, where I placed my candle, had a few mildewed books piled up in one corner; and it was covered with writing scratched on the paint. This writing, however, was nothing but a name repeated in all kinds of characters, large and small—*Catherine Earnshaw*, here and there varied to *Catherine Heathcliff*, and then again to *Catherine Linton*.

In vapid listlessness I leant my head against the window, and continued spelling over Catherine Earnshaw—Heathcliff—Linton, till my eyes closed; but they had not rested five minutes when a glare of white letters started from the dark, as vivid as spectres—the air swarmed with Catherines; and rousing myself to dispel the obtrusive name, I discovered my candle wick reclining on one of the antique volumes, and perfuming the place with an odour of roasted calf-skin.

I snuffed it off, and, very ill at ease under the influence of cold and lingering nausea, sat up, and spread open the injured tome on my knee. It was a Testament, in lean type, and smelling dreadfully musty: a fly-leaf bore the inscription—"Catherine Earnshaw, her book," and a date some quarter of a century back.

I shut it, and took up another, and another, till I had examined all. Catherine's library was select, and its state of dilapidation proved it to have been well used, though not altogether for a legitimate purpose; scarcely one chapter had escaped a pen and ink commentary—at least, the appearance of one—covering every morsel of blank that the printer had left.

Some were detached sentences; other parts took the form of a regular diary, scrawled in an unformed, childish hand. At the top of an extra page, quite a treasure probably when first lighted on, I was greatly amused to behold an excellent caricature of my friend Joseph, rudely yet powerfully sketched.

An immediate interest kindled within me for the unknown Catherine, and I began, forthwith, to decypher her faded hieroglyphics.

"An awful Sunday!" commenced the paragraph beneath. "I wish my father were back again. Hindley is a detestable substitute—his conduct to Heathcliff is atrocious—H. and I are going to rebel—we took our initiatory step this evening.

"All day had been flooding with rain; we could not go to church, so Joseph must needs get up a congregation in the garret; and, while Hindley and his wife basked downstairs before a comfortable fire—doing anything but reading their Bibles, I'll answer for it—Heathcliff, myself, and the unhappy plough-boy were commanded to take our Prayer-books, and mount. We were ranged in a row, on a sack of corn, groaning and shivering, and hoping that Joseph would shiver too, so that he might give us a short homily for his own sake. A vain idea! The service lasted precisely three hours; and yet my brother had the face to exclaim, when he saw us descending—

" 'What, done already?'

"On Sunday evenings we used to be permitted to play, if we did not make much noise; now a mere titter is sufficient to send us into corners!

" 'You forget you have a master here,' says the tyrant. 'I'll demolish the first who puts me out of temper! I insist on perfect sobriety and silence. Oh, boy! was that you? Frances, darling, pull his hair as you go by; I heard him snap his fingers.'

"Frances pulled his hair heartily; and then went and seated herself on her husband's knee, and there they were, like two babies, kissing and talking nonsense by the hour—foolish palaver that we should be ashamed of.

"We made ourselves as snug as our means allowed in the arch of the dresser. I had just fastened our pinafores together, and hung them up for a curtain, when in comes Joseph, on an errand from the stables. He tears down my handywork, boxes my ears, and croaks—

" 'T' maister nobbut just buried, and Sabbath nut oe'red, und t'sahnd uh't gospel still i' yer lugs, and yah darr be laiking! shame on ye! sit ye dahn, ill childer! they's good books eneugh if ye'll read 'em; sit ye dahn, and think uh yer sowls!' [1]

"Saying this, he compelled us so to square our positions that we might receive, from the far-off fire, a dull ray to show us the text of the lumber he thrust upon us.

"I could not bear the employment. I took my dingy volume by the scroop,[2] and hurled it into the dog-kennel, vowing I hated a good book.

"Heathcliff kicked his to the same place.

"Then there was a hubbub!

" 'Maister Hindley!' shouted our chaplain. 'Maister, coom hither! Miss Cathy's riven th' back off "Th' Helmet uh Salvation," un' Heathcliff's pawsed his fit intuh t' first part uh "T' Brooad Way to Destruction!" It's fair flaysome ut yah let 'em goa on this gait.[3] Ech! th' owd man ud uh laced 'em properly—bud he's goan!'

"Hindley hurried up from his paradise on the hearth, and seizing one of us by the collar, and the other by the arm, hurled both into the back-kitchen, where, Joseph asseverated, 'owd Nick' would fetch us as sure as we were living; and, so comforted, we each sought a separate nook to await his advent.

"I reached this book, and a pot of ink from a shelf, and pushed the house-door ajar to give me light, and I have got the time on with writing for twenty minutes; but my companion is impatient and proposes that we should appropriate the dairy woman's cloak, and have a scamper on the moors, under its shelter. A pleasant suggestion—and then, if the surly old man come in, he may believe his prophesy verified—we cannot be damper, or colder, in the rain than we are here."

I suppose Catherine fulfilled her project, for the next sentence took up another subject; she waxed lachrymose.

"How little did I dream that Hindley would ever make me cry so!" she wrote. "My head aches, till I cannot keep it on the pillow;

1. *Nobbut:* only; *oe'red:* gone by, got past; *t'sahnd:* the sound; *lugs:* ears; *darr be laiking:* dare be playing; *ill childer:* bad children.

2. The back of the cover of a book.

3. *Riven:* torn; *pawsed his fit:* made a hole with his foot; *flaysome:* terrible; *gait:* way.

and still I can't give over. Poor Heathcliff! Hindley calls him a vagabond, and won't let him sit with us, nor eat with us any more; and, he says, he and I must not play together, and threatens to turn him out of the house if we break his orders.

"He has been blaming our father (how dared he?) for treating H. too liberally; and swears he will reduce him to his right place—"

I began to nod drowsily over the dim page; my eye wandered from manuscript to print. I saw a red ornamented title—"Seventy Times Seven, and the First of the Seventy-First. A Pious Discourse delivered by the Reverend Jabes Branderham, in the Chapel of Gimmerden Sough." And while I was, half consciously, worrying my brain to guess what Jabes Branderham would make of his subject, I sank back in bed, and fell asleep.

Alas, for the effects of bad tea and bad temper! what else could it be that made me pass such a terrible night? I don't remember another that I can at all compare with it since I was capable of suffering.

I began to dream, almost before I ceased to be sensible of my locality. I thought it was morning, and I had set out on my way home, with Joseph for a guide. The snow lay yards deep in our road; and, as we floundered on, my companion wearied me with constant reproaches that I had not brought a pilgrim's staff, telling me I could never get into the house without one, and boastfully flourishing a heavy-headed cudgel, which I understood to be so denominated.

For a moment I considered it absurd that I should need such a weapon to gain admittance into my own residence. Then, a new idea flashed across me. I was not going there; we were journeying to hear the famous Jabes Branderham preach from the text— "Seventy Times Seven"; and either Joseph, the preacher, or I had committed the "First of the Seventy-First," and were to be publicly exposed and excommunicated.[4]

We came to the chapel. I have passed it really in my walks, twice or thrice; it lies in a hollow, between two hills—an elevated hollow, near a swamp, whose peaty moisture is said to answer all the purposes of embalming on the few corpses deposited there. The roof has been kept whole hitherto, but, as the clergyman's stipend is only twenty pounds per annum, and a house with two rooms, threatening speedily to determine into one, no clergyman will undertake the duties of pastor, especially as it is currently reported that his flock would rather let him starve than increase the living by one penny from their own pockets. However, in my dream, Jabes had a full and attentive congregation: and he preached— good God—what a sermon! Divided into *four hundred and ninety*

4. Matthew 18.21–35.

parts, each fully equal to an ordinary address from the pulpit, and each discussing a separate sin! Where he searched for them, I cannot tell; he had his private manner of interpreting the phrase, and it seemed necessary the brother should sin different sins on every occasion.

They were of the most curious character—odd trangressions that I never imagined previously.

Oh, how weary I grew. How I writhed, and yawned, and nodded, and revived! How I pinched and pricked myself, and rubbed my eyes, and stood up, and sat down again, and nudged Joseph to inform me if he would *ever* have done!

I was condemned to hear all out; finally, he reached the "*First of the Seventy-First*." At that crisis, a sudden inspiration descended on me; I was moved to rise and denounce Jabes Branderham as the sinner of the sin that no Christian need pardon.

"Sir," I exclaimed, "sitting here, within these four walls, at one stretch, I have endured and forgiven the four hundred and ninety heads of your discourse. Seventy times seven times have I plucked up my hat and been about to depart—Seventy times seven times have you preposterously forced me to resume my seat. The four hundred and ninety-first is too much. Fellow martyrs, have at him! Drag him down, and crush him to atoms, that the place which knows him may know him no more!"

"*Thou art the Man!*" cried Jabes, after a solemn pause, leaning over his cushion. "Seventy times seven times didst thou gapingly contort thy visage—seventy times seven did I take counsel with my soul—Lo, this is human weakness; this also may be absolved! The First of the Seventy-First is come. Brethren, execute upon him the judgment written! such honour have all His saints!"

With that concluding word, the whole assembly, exalting their pilgrim's staves, rushed round me in a body, and I, having no weapon to raise in self-defence, commenced grappling with Joseph, my nearest and most ferocious assailant, for his. In the confluence of the multitude, several clubs crossed; blows, aimed at me, fell on other sconces. Presently the whole chapel resounded with rappings and counter-rappings. Every man's hand was against his neighbour; and Branderham, unwilling to remain idle, poured forth his zeal in a shower of loud taps on the boards of the pulpit, which responded so smartly that, at last, to my unspeakable relief, they woke me.

And what was it that had suggested the tremendous tumult, what had played Jabes's part in the row? Merely the branch of a fir tree that touched my lattice, as the blast wailed by, and rattled its dry cones against the panes!

I listened doubtingly an instant; detected the disturber, then turned and dozed, and dreamt again; if possible, still more dis-agreebly than before.

This time, I remembered I was lying in the oak closet, and I heard distinctly the gusty wind, and the driving of the snow; I heard, also, the fir-bough repeat its teasing sound, and ascribed it to the right cause; but it annoyed me so much, that I resolved to silence it, if possible; and, I thought, I rose and endeavoured to unhasp the casement. The hook was soldered into the staple, a circumstance observed by me when awake, but forgotten.

"I must stop it, nevertheless!" I muttered, knocking my knuckles through the glass, and stretching an arm out to seize the importu-nate branch: instead of which, my fingers closed on the fingers of a little, ice-cold hand!

The intense horror of nightmare came over me; I tried to draw back my arm, but the hand clung to it, and a most melancholy voice sobbed—

"Let me in—let me in!"

"Who are you?" I asked, struggling, meanwhile, to disengage myself.

"Catherine Linton," it replied, shiveringly (why did I think of *Linton?* I had read *Earnshaw* twenty times for Linton). "I'm come home, I'd lost my way on the moor!"

As it spoke, I discerned, obscurely, a child's face looking through the window. Terror made me cruel; and, finding it useless to at-tempt shaking the creature off, I pulled its wrist on to the broken pane, and rubbed it to and fro till the blood ran down and soaked the bed-clothes: still it wailed, "Let me in!" and maintained its tenacious gripe, almost maddening me with fear.

"How can I?" I said at length. "Let *me* go, if you want me to let you in!"

The fingers relaxed, I snatched mine through the hole, hurriedly piled the books up in a pyramid against it, and stopped my ears to exclude the lamentable prayer.

I seemed to keep them closed above a quarter of an hour, yet, the instant I listened again, there was the doleful cry moaning on!

"Begone!" I shouted, "I'll never let you in, not if you beg for twenty years!"

"It's twenty years," mourned the voice, "twenty years, I've been a waif for twenty years!"

Thereat began a feeble scratching outside, and the pile of books moved as if thrust forward.

I tried to jump up, but could not stir a limb; and so yelled aloud, in a frenzy of fright.

To my confusion, I discovered the yell was not ideal. Hasty footsteps approached my chamber door; somebody pushed it open, with a vigorous hand, and a light glimmered through the squares at the top of the bed. I sat shuddering yet, and wiping the perspiration from my forehead: the intruder appeared to hesitate, and muttered to himself.

At last, he said in a half-whisper, plainly not expecting an answer—

"Is any one here?"

I considered it best to confess my presence, for I knew Heathcliff's accents, and feared he might search further, if I kept quiet.

With this intention, I turned and opened the panels. I shall not soon forget the effect my action produced.

Heathcliff stood near the entrance, in his shirt and trousers, with a candle dripping over his fingers, and his face as white as the wall behind him. The first creak of the oak startled him like an electric shock: the light leaped from his hold to a distance of some feet, and his agitation was so extreme that he could hardly pick it up.

"It is only your guest, sir," I called out, desirous to spare him the humiliation of exposing his cowardice further. "I had the misfortune to scream in my sleep, owing to a frightful nightmare. I'm sorry I disturbed you."

"Oh, God confound you, Mr. Lockwood! I wish you were at the—" commenced my host, setting the candle on a chair, because he found it impossible to hold it steady.

"And who showed you up to this room?" he continued, crushing his nails into his palms, and grinding his teeth to subdue the maxillary convulsions. "Who was it? I've a good mind to turn them out of the house this moment!"

"It was your servant, Zillah," I replied, flinging myself on to the floor, and rapidly resuming my garments. "I should not care if you did, Mr. Heathcliff; she richly deserves it. I suppose that she wanted to get another proof that the place was haunted, at my expense. Well, it is—swarming with ghosts and goblins! You have reason in shutting it up, I assure you. No one will thank you for a doze in such a den!"

"What do you mean?" asked Heathcliff, "and what are you doing? Lie down and finish out the night, since you *are* here; but, for heaven's sake! don't repeat that horrid noise. Nothing could excuse it, unless you were having your throat cut!"

"If the little fiend had got in at the window, she probably would have strangled me!" I returned. "I'm not going to endure the persecutions of your hospitable ancestors again. Was not the Reverend Jabes Branderham akin to you on the mother's side? And that minx, Catherine Linton, or Earnshaw, or however she was called—she must have been a changeling—wicked little soul! She told me she had been walking the earth these twenty years: a just punishment for her mortal transgressions, I've no doubt!"

Scarcely were these words uttered, when I recollected the association of Heathcliff's with Catherine's name in the book, which had completely slipped from my memory till thus awakened. I blushed at my inconsideration; but, without showing further consciousness of the offence, I hastened to add—

"The truth is, sir, I passed the first part of the night in—" here, I stopped afresh—I was about to say "perusing those old volumes;" then it would have revealed my knowledge of their written, as well as their printed contents; so, correcting myself, I went on—"in spelling over the name scratched on that window-ledge. A monotonous occupation, calculated to set me asleep, like counting, or—"

"What *can* you mean by talking in this way to *me!*" thundered Heathcliff with savage vehemence. "How—how *dare* you, under my roof—God! he's mad to speak so!" And he struck his forehead with rage.

I did not know whether to resent this language, or pursue my explanation; but he seemed so powerfully affected that I took pity and proceeded with my dreams, affirming I had never heard the appellation of "Catherine Linton" before, but reading it often over produced an impression which personified itself when I had no longer my imagination under control.

Heathcliff gradually fell back into the shelter of the bed as I spoke, finally sitting down almost concealed behind it. I guessed, however, by his irregular and intercepted breathing, that he struggled to vanquish an access of violent emotion.

Not liking to show him that I heard the conflict, I continued my toilette rather noisily, looked at my watch, and soliloquized on the length of the night—

"Not three o'clock yet! I could have taken oath it had been six. Time stagnates here—we must surely have retired to rest at eight!"

"Always at nine in winter, and always rise at four," said my host, suppressing a groan, and, as I fancied, by the motion of his shadow's arm, dashing a tear from his eyes.

"Mr. Lockwood," he added, "you may go into my room; you'll only be in the way, coming downstairs so early; and your childish outcry has sent sleep to the devil for me."

"And for me, too," I replied. "I'll walk in the yard till daylight, and then I'll be off; and you need not dread a repetition of my intrusion. I am now quite cured of seeking pleasure in society, be it country or town. A sensible man ought to find sufficient company in himself."

"Delightful company!" muttered Heathcliff. "Take the candle, and go where you please. I shall join you directly. Keep out of the yard, though; the dogs are unchained, and the house—Juno mounts sentinel there, and—nay, you can only ramble about the steps and passages. But, away with you! I'll come in two minutes."

I obeyed, so far as to quit the chamber; when, ignorant where the narrow lobbies led, I stood still, and was witness, involuntarily, to a piece of superstition on the part of my landlord, which belied, oddly, his apparent sense.

He got on to the bed and wrenched open the lattice, bursting, as he pulled at it, into an uncontrollable passion of tears.

"Come in! come in!" he sobbed. "Cathy, do come. Oh, do— *once* more! Oh! my heart's darling, hear me *this* time—Catherine, at last!"

The spectre showed a spectre's ordinary caprice; it gave no sign of being; but the snow and wind whirled wildly through, even reaching my station, and blowing out the light.

There was such anguish in the gush of grief that accompanied this raving, that my compassion made me overlook its folly, and I drew off, half angry to have listened at all, and vexed at having related my ridiculous nightmare, since it produced that agony, though *why*, was beyond my comprehension.

I descended cautiously to the lower regions and landed in the back-kitchen, where a gleam of fire, raked compactly together, enabled me to rekindle my candle.

Nothing was stirring except a brindled, grey cat, which crept from the ashes and saluted me with a querulous mew.

Two benches, shaped in sections of a circle, nearly enclosed the hearth; on one of these I stretched myself, and Grimalkin mounted the other. We were both of us nodding, ere any one invaded our retreat; and then it was Joseph shuffling down a wooden ladder that vanished in the roof, through a trap: the ascent to his garret, I suppose.

He cast a sinister look at the little flame which I had enticed to play between the ribs, swept the cat from its elevation, and bestowing himself in the vacancy, commenced the operation of stuffing a three-inch pipe with tobacco; my presence in his sanctum was evidently esteemed a piece of impudence too shameful for remark. He silently applied the tube to his lips, folded his arms, and puffed away.

I let him enjoy the luxury, unannoyed; and after sucking out the last wreath, and heaving a profound sigh, he got up, and departed as solemnly as he came.

A more elastic footstep entered next, and now I opened my mouth for a "good morning," but closed it again, the salutation unachieved; for Hareton Earnshaw was performing his orisons, *sotto voce*, in a series of curses directed against every object he touched, while he rummaged a corner for a spade or shovel to dig through the drifts. He glanced over the back of the bench, dilating his nostrils, and thought as little of exchanging civilities with me as with my companion, the cat.

I guessed by his preparations that egress was allowed, and leaving my hard couch, made a movement to follow him. He noticed this, and thrust at an inner door with the end of his spade, intimating by an inarticulate sound, that there was the place where I must go, if I changed my locality.

It opened into the house, where the females were already astir, Zillah, urging flakes of flame up the chimney with a colossal bellows, and Mrs. Heathcliff, kneeling on the hearth, reading a book by the aid of the blaze.

She held her hand interposed between the furnace-heat and her eyes, and seemed absorbed in her occupation; desisting from it only to chide the servant for covering her with sparks, or to push away a dog, now and then, that snoozled its nose over-forwardly into her face.

I was surprised to see Heathcliff there also. He stood by the fire, his back towards me, just finishing a stormy scene to poor Zillah, who ever and anon interrupted her labour to pluck up the corner of her apron, and heave an indignant groan.

"And you, you worthless—" he broke out as I entered, turning to his daughter-in-law, and employing an epithet as harmless as duck, or sheep, but generally represented by a dash—"there you are at your idle tricks again! The rest of them do earn their bread —you live on my charity! Put your trash away, and find something to do. You shall pay me for the plague of having you eternally in my sight—do you hear, damnable jade?"

"I'll put my trash away, because you can make me, if I refuse," answered the young lady, closing her book, and throwing it on a chair. "But I'll not do anything, though you should swear your tongue out, except what I please!"

Heathcliff lifted his hand, and the speaker sprang to a safer distance, obviously acquainted with its weight.

Having no desire to be entertained by a cat and dog combat, I stepped forward briskly, as if eager to partake the warmth of the hearth, and innocent of any knowledge of the interrupted dispute. Each had enough decorum to suspend further hostilities: Heathcliff placed his fists, out of temptation, in his pockets; Mrs. Heathcliff curled her lip and walked to a seat far off, where she kept her word by playing the part of a statue during the remainder of my stay.

That was not long. I declined joining their breakfast, and, at the first gleam of dawn, took an opportunity of escaping into the free air, now clear and still, and cold as impalpable ice.

My landlord hallooed for me to stop, ere I reached the bottom of the garden, and offered to accompany me across the moor. It was well he did, for the whole hill-back was one billowy, white ocean, the swells and falls not indicating corresponding rises and depressions in the ground: many pits, at least, were filled to a level; and entire ranges of mounds, the refuse of the quarries, blotted from the chart which my yesterday's walk left pictured in my mind.

I had remarked on one side of the road, at intervals of six or seven yards, a line of upright stones, continued through the whole length of the barren: these were erected, and daubed with lime, on purpose to serve as guides in the dark, and also, when a fall, like the present, confounded the deep swamps on either hand with the firmer path: but, excepting a dirty dot pointing up here and there, all traces of their existence had vanished; and my companion found it necessary to warn me frequently to steer to the right or left, when I imagined I was following, correctly, the windings of the road.

We exchanged little conversation, and he halted at the entrance of Thrushcross park, saying, I could make no error there. Our adieux were limited to a hasty bow, and then I pushed forward, trusting to my own resources, for the porter's lodge is untenanted as yet.

The distance from the gate to the Grange is two miles: I believe I managed to make it four, what with losing myself among the trees, and sinking up to the neck in snow, a predicament which only those who have experienced it can appreciate. At any rate, whatever were my wanderings, the clock chimed twelve as I entered the house; and that gave exactly an hour for every mile of the usual way from Wuthering Heights.

My human fixture and her satellites rushed to welcome me; exclaiming, tumultuously, they had completely given me up: everybody conjectured that I perished last night; and they were wondering how they must set about the search for my remains.

I bid them be quiet, now that they saw me returned, and, benumbed to my very heart, I dragged upstairs, whence, after putting on dry clothes, and pacing to and fro thirty or forty minutes, to restore the animal heat, I am adjourned to my study, feeble as a kitten, almost too much so to enjoy the cheerful fire and smoking coffee which the servant has prepared for my refreshment.

## Chapter IV

What vain weather-cocks we are! I, who had determined to hold myself independent of all social intercourse, and thanked my stars that, at length, I had lighted on a spot where it was next to impracticable—I, weak wretch, after maintaining till dusk a struggle with low spirits and solitude, was finally compelled to strike my colours; and, under pretence of gaining information concerning the necessities of my establishment, I desired Mrs. Dean, when she brought in supper, to sit down while I ate it, hoping sincerely she would prove a regular gossip, and either rouse me to animation, or lull me to sleep by her talk.

"You have lived here a considerable time," I commenced; "did you not say sixteen years?"

"Eighteen, sir; I came, when the mistress was married, to wait on her; after she died, the master retained me for his house-keeper."

"Indeed."

There ensued a pause. She was not a gossip, I feared, unless about her own affairs, and those could hardly interest me.

However, having studied for an interval, with a fist on either knee, and a cloud of meditation over her ruddy countenance, she ejaculated—

"Ah, times are greatly changed since then!"

"Yes," I remarked, "you've seen a good many alterations, I suppose?"

"I have: and troubles too," she said.

"Oh, I'll turn the talk on my landlord's family!" I thought to myself. "A good subject to start—and that pretty girl-widow, I should like to know her history: whether she be a native of the country, or, as is more probable, an exotic that the surly *indigenae* will not recognise for kin."

With this intention I asked Mrs. Dean why Heathcliff let Thrushcross Grange, and preferred living in a situation and residence so much inferior.

"Is he not rich enough to keep the estate in good order?" I enquired.

"Rich, sir!" she returned. "He has, nobody knows what money, and every year it increases. Yes, yes, he's rich enough to live in a finer house than this, but he's very near—close-handed; and, if he had meant to flit to Thrushcross Grange, as soon as he heard of a good tenant he could not have borne to miss the chance of getting a few hundreds more. It is strange people should be so greedy, when they are alone in the world!"

"He had a son, it seems?"

"Yes, he had one—he is dead."

"And that young lady, Mrs. Heathcliff, is his widow?"

"Yes."

"Where did she come from originally?"

"Why, sir, she is my late master's daughter; Catherine Linton was her maiden name. I nursed her, poor thing! I did wish Mr.

Heathcliff would remove here, and then we might have been to-gether again."

"What, Catherine Linton!" I exclaimed, astonished. But a minute's reflection convinced me it was not my ghostly Catherine. "Then," I continued, "my predecessor's name was Linton?"

"It was."

"And who is that Earnshaw, Hareton Earnshaw, who lives with Mr. Heathcliff? are they relations?"

"No; he is the late Mrs. Linton's nephew."

"The young lady's cousin, then?"

"Yes; and her husband was her cousin also—one, on the mother's —the other, on the father's side. Heathcliff married Mr. Linton's sister."

"I see the house at Wuthering Heights has 'Earnshaw' carved over the front door. Are they an old family?"

"Very old, sir; and Hareton is the last of them, as our Miss Cathy is of us—I mean, of the Lintons. Have you been to Wuther-ing Heights? I beg pardon for asking; but I should like to hear how she is!"

"Mrs. Heathcliff? She looked very well, and very handsome; yet, I think, not very happy."

"Oh dear, I don't wonder! And how did you like the master?"

"A rough fellow, rather, Mrs. Dean. Is not that his character?"

"Rough as a saw-edge, and hard as whinstone! The less you med-dle with him the better."

"He must have had some ups and downs in life to make him such a churl. Do you know anything of his history?"

"It's a cuckoo's, sir—I know all about it, except where he was born, and who were his parents, and how he got his money, at first. And Hareton has been cast out like an unfledged dunnock! The unfortunate lad is the only one, in all this parish, that does not guess how he has been cheated!"

"Well, Mrs. Dean, it will be a charitable deed to tell me some-thing of my neighbours—I feel I shall not rest, if I go to bed; so, be good enough to sit and chat an hour."

"Oh, certainly, sir! I'll just fetch a little sewing, and then I'll sit as long as you please. But you've caught cold; I saw you shiver-ing, and you must have some gruel to drive it out."

The worthy woman bustled off; and I crouched nearer the fire; my head felt hot, and the rest of me chill: moreover, I was ex-cited, almost to a pitch of foolishness, through my nerves and brain. This caused me to feel, not uncomfortable, but rather fear-ful, as I am still, of serious effects from the incidents of today and yesterday.

She returned presently, bringing a smoking basin, and a basket of work; and, having placed the former on the hob, drew in her seat, evidently pleased to find me so companionable.

———

Before I came to live here, she commenced, waiting no further invitation to her story, I was almost always at Wuthering Heights, because my mother had nursed Mr. Hindley Earnshaw, that was Hareton's father, and I got used to playing with the children. I ran errands too, and helped to make hay, and hung about the farm ready for anything that anybody would set me to.

One fine summer morning—it was the beginning of harvest, I remember—Mr. Earnshaw, the old master, came downstairs, dressed for a journey; and, after he had told Joseph what was to be done during the day, he turned to Hindley, and Cathy, and me—for I sat eating my porridge with them—and he said, speaking to his son—

"Now, my bonny man, I'm going to Liverpool, to-day. What shall I bring you? You may choose what you like; only let it be little, for I shall walk there and back; sixty miles each way, that is a long spell!"

Hindley named a fiddle, and then he asked Miss Cathy; she was hardly six years old, but she could ride any horse in the stable, and she chose a whip.

He did not forget me, for he had a kind heart, though he was rather severe, sometimes. He promised to bring me a pocketful of apples and pears, and then he kissed his children good-bye, and set off.

It seemed a long while to us all—the three days of his absence —and often did little Cathy ask when he would be home. Mrs. Earnshaw expected him by supper-time, on the third evening; and she put the meal off hour after hour; there were no signs of his coming, however, and at last the children got tired of running down to the gate to look. Then it grew dark; she would have had them to bed, but they begged sadly to be allowed to stay up; and, just about eleven o'clock, the door-latch was raised quietly and in stept the master. He threw himself into a chair, laughing and groaning, and bid them all stand off, for he was nearly killed—he would not have such another walk for the three kingdoms.

"And at the end of it, to be flighted[1] to death!" he said, opening his great coat, which he held bundled up in his arms, "See here, wife; I was never so beaten with anything in my life; but you must e'en take it as a gift of God, though it's as dark almost as if it came from the devil."

We crowded round, and, over Miss Cathy's head, I had a peep

1. Frightened.

at a dirty, ragged, black-haired child; big enough both to walk and talk—indeed, its face looked older than Catherine's—yet, when it was set on its feet, it only stared round, and repeated over and over again some gibberish that nobody could understand. I was frightened, and Mrs. Earnshaw was ready to fling it out of doors: she did fly up—asking how he could fashion to bring that gipsy brat into the house, when they had their own bairns to feed and fend for? What he meant to do with it, and whether he were mad?

The master tried to explain the matter; but he was really half dead with fatigue, and all that I could make out, amongst her scolding, was a tale of his seeing it starving, and houseless, and as good as dumb in the streets of Liverpool, where he picked it up and inquired for its owner. Not a soul knew to whom it belonged, he said, and his money and time being both limited, he thought it better to take it home with him at once, than run into vain expenses there; because he was determined he would not leave it as he found it.

Well, the conclusion was that my mistress grumbled herself calm; and Mr. Earnshaw told me to wash it, and give it clean things, and let it sleep with the children.

Hindley and Cathy contented themselves with looking and listening till peace was restored; then, both began searching their father's pockets for the presents he had promised them. The former was a boy of fourteen, but when he drew out what had been a fiddle, crushed to morsels in the great coat, he blubbered aloud, and Cathy, when she learnt the master had lost her whip in attending on the stranger, showed her humour by grinning and spitting at the stupid little thing, earning for her pains a sound blow from her father to teach her cleaner manners.

They entirely refused to have it in bed with them, or even in their room, and I had no more sense, so I put it on the landing of the stairs, hoping it might be gone on the morrow. By chance, or else attracted by hearing his voice, it crept to Mr. Earnshaw's door and there he found it on quitting his chamber. Inquiries were made as to how it got there; I was obliged to confess, and in recompense for my cowardice and inhumanity was sent out of the house.

This was Heathcliff's first introduction to the family. On coming back a few days afterwards, for I did not consider my banishment perpetual, I found they had christened him "Heathcliff"; it was the name of a son who died in childhood, and it has served him ever since, both for Christian and surname.

Miss Cathy and he were now very thick; but Hindley hated him, and to say the truth I did the same; and we plagued and went on with him shamefully, for I wasn't reasonable enough to

feel my injustice, and the mistress never put in a word on his behalf when she saw him wronged.

He seemed a sullen, patient child, hardened, perhaps, to ill-
treatment: he would stand Hindley's blows without winking or
shedding a tear, and my pinches moved him only to draw in a
breath, and open his eyes as if he had hurt himself by accident,
and nobody was to blame.

This endurance made old Earnshaw furious when he discovered
his son persecuting the poor, fatherless child, as he called him.
He took to Heathcliff strangely, believing all he said (for that
matter, he said precious little, and generally the truth) and petting
him up far above Cathy, who was too mischievous and wayward
for a favourite.

So, from the very beginning, he bred bad feeling in the house;
and at Mrs. Earnshaw's death, which happened in less than two
years after, the young master had learnt to regard his father as an
oppressor rather than a friend, and Heathcliff as a usurper of his
parent's affections and his privileges, and he grew bitter with
brooding over these injuries.

I sympathised a while, but, when the children fell ill of the
measles and I had to tend them, and take on me the cares of a
woman at once, I changed my ideas. Heathcliff was dangerously
sick, and while he lay at the worst he would have me constantly
by his pillow; I suppose he felt I did a good deal for him, and he
hadn't wit to guess that I was compelled to do it. However, I will
say this, he was the quietest child that ever nurse watched over.
The difference between him and the others forced me to be less
partial. Cathy and her brother harassed me terribly; *he* was as
uncomplaining as a lamb, though hardness, not gentleness, made
him give little trouble.

He got through, and the doctor affirmed it was in a great measure owing to me, and praised me for my care. I was vain of his
commendations, and softened towards the being by whose means
I earned them, and thus Hindley lost his last ally; still I couldn't
dote on Heathcliff, and I wondered often what my master saw to
admire so much in the sullen boy who never, to my recollection,
repaid his indulgence by any sign of gratitude. He was not insolent
to his benefactor; he was simply insensible, though knowing perfectly the hold he had on his heart, and conscious he had only
to speak and all the house would be obliged to bend to his wishes.

As an instance, I remember Mr. Earnshaw once bought a couple
of colts at the parish fair, and gave the lads each one. Heathcliff
took the handsomest, but it soon fell lame, and when he discovered it, he said to Hindley—

"You must exchange horses with me; I don't like mine, and if you won't I shall tell your father of the three thrashings you've given me this week, and show him my arm, which is black to the shoulder."

Hindley put out his tongue, and cuffed him over the ears.

"You'd better do it at once," he persisted, escaping to the porch (they were in the stable); "you will have to, and if I speak of these blows, you'll get them again with interest."

"Off, dog!" cried Hindley, threatening him with an iron weight, used for weighing potatoes and hay.

"Throw it," he replied, standing still, "and then I'll tell how you boasted that you would turn me out of doors as soon as he died, and see whether he will not turn you out directly."

Hindley threw it, hitting him on the breast, and down he fell, but staggered up immediately, breathless and white, and had not I prevented it, he would have gone just so to the master, and got full revenge by letting his condition plead for him, intimating who had caused it.

"Take my colt, gipsy, then!" said young Earnshaw. "And I pray that he may break your neck; take him, and be damned, you beggarly interloper! and wheedle my father out of all he has, only afterwards show him what you are, imp of Satan—And take that, I hope he'll kick out your brains!"

Heathcliff had gone to loose the beast, and shift it to his own stall. He was passing behind it, when Hindley finished his speech by knocking him under its feet, and without stopping to examine whether his hopes were fulfilled, ran away as fast as he could.

I was surprised to witness how coolly the child gathered himself up, and went on with his intention, exchanging saddles and all, and then sitting down on a bundle of hay to overcome the qualm which the violent blow occasioned, before he entered the house.

I persuaded him easily to let me lay the blame of his bruises on the horse; he minded little what tale was told since he had what he wanted. He complained so seldom, indeed, of such stirs as these, that I really thought him not vindictive—I was deceived completely, as you will hear.

## Chapter V

In the course of time, Mr. Earnshaw began to fail. He had been active and healthy, yet his strength left him suddenly; and when he was confined to the chimney-corner he grew grievously irritable. A nothing vexed him, and suspected slights of his authority nearly threw him into fits.

This was especially to be remarked if any one attempted to impose upon, or domineer over, his favourite: he was painfully jealous lest a word should be spoken amiss to him, seeming to have got into his head the notion that, because he liked Heathcliff, all hated, and longed to do him an ill-turn.

It was a disadvantage to the lad, for the kinder among us did not wish to fret the master, so we humoured his partiality; and that humouring was rich nourishment to the child's pride and black tempers. Still it became in a manner necessary; twice, or thrice, Hindley's manifestations of scorn, while his father was near, roused the old man to a fury. He seized his stick to strike him, and shook with rage that he could not do it.

At last, our curate (we had a curate then who made the living answer by teaching the little Lintons and Earnshaws, and farming his bit of land himself) he advised that the young man should be sent to college, and Mr. Earnshaw agreed, though with a heavy spirit, for he said—

"Hindley was naught, and would never thrive as where he wandered."

I hoped heartily we should have peace now. It hurt me to think the master should be made uncomfortable by his own good deed. I fancied the discontent of age and disease arose from his family disagreements, as he would have it that it did; really, you know, sir, it was in his sinking frame.

We might have got on tolerably, notwithstanding, but for two people, Miss Cathy and Joseph, the servant; you saw him, I dare say, up yonder. He was, and is yet, most likely, the wearisomest, self-righteous pharisee that ever ransacked a Bible to rake the promises to himself, and fling the curses on his neighbours. By his knack of sermonizing and pious discoursing, he contrived to make a great impression on Mr. Earnshaw, and the more feeble the master became, the more influence he gained.

He was relentless in worrying him about his soul's concerns, and about ruling his children rigidly. He encouraged him to regard Hindley as a reprobate; and, night after night, he regularly grumbled out a long string of tales against Heathcliff and Catherine; always minding to flatter Earnshaw's weakness by heaping the heaviest blame on the last.

Certainly, she had ways with her such as I never saw a child take up before; and she put all of us past our patience fifty times and oftener in a day: from the hour she came downstairs, till the hour she went to bed, we had not a minute's security that she wouldn't be in mischief. Her spirits were always at high-water mark, her tongue always going—singing, laughing, and plaguing everybody who would not do the same. A wild, wicked slip she was —but she had the bonniest eye, and sweetest smile, and lightest foot in the parish; and, after all, I believe she meant no harm; for when once she made you cry in good earnest, it seldom happened that she would not keep you company, and oblige you to be quiet that you might comfort her.

She was much too fond of Heathcliff. The greatest punishment we could invent for her was to keep her separate from him: yet she got chided more than any of us on his account.

In play, she liked, exceedingly, to act the little mistress; using her hands freely, and commanding her companions: she did so to me, but I would not bear slapping and ordering; and so I let her know.

Now, Mr. Earnshaw did not understand jokes from his children: he had always been strict and grave with them; and Catherine, on her part, had no idea why her father should be crosser and less patient in his ailing condition, than he was in his prime.

His peevish reproofs wakened in her a naughty delight to provoke him; she was never so happy as when we were all scolding her at once, and she defying us with her bold, saucy look, and her ready words; turning Joseph's religious curses into ridicule, baiting me, and doing just what her father hated most, showing how her pretended insolence, which he thought real, had more power over Heathcliff than his kindness; how the boy would do *her* bidding in anything, and *his* only when it suited his own inclination.

After behaving as badly as possible all day, she sometimes came fondling to make it up at night.

"Nay, Cathy," the old man would say, "I cannot love thee; thou'rt worse than thy brother. Go, say thy prayers, child, and ask God's pardon. I doubt thy mother and I must rue that we ever reared thee!"

That made her cry, at first; and then, being repulsed continually hardened her, and she laughed if I told her to say she was sorry for her faults, and beg to be forgiven.

But the hour came, at last, that ended Mr. Earnshaw's troubles on earth. He died quietly in his chair one October evening, seated by the fire-side.

A high wind blustered round the house, and roared in the chimney: it sounded wild and stormy, yet it was not cold, and we were all together—I, a little removed from the hearth, busy at my knitting, and Joseph reading his Bible near the table (for the servants generally sat in the house then, after their work was done). Miss Cathy had been sick, and that made her still; she leant against her father's knee, and Heathcliff was lying on the floor with his head in her lap.

I remember the master, before he fell into a doze, stroking her bonny hair—it pleased him rarely[1] to see her gentle—and saying—

"Why canst thou not always be a good lass, Cathy?"

And she turned her face up to his, and laughed, and answered—

"Why cannot you always be a good man, father?"

But as soon as she saw him vexed again, she kissed his hand, and said she would sing him to sleep. She began singing very low, till his fingers dropped from hers, and his head sank on his breast. Then I told her to hush, and not stir, for fear she should wake him. We all kept as mute as mice a full half-hour, and should have done so longer, only Joseph, having finished his chapter, got up and said that he must rouse the master for prayers and bed. He stepped forward, and called him by name, and touched his shoulder, but he would not move—so he took the candle and looked at him.

I thought there was something wrong as he set down the light; and seizing the children each by an arm, whispered them to "frame[2] upstairs, and make little din—they might pray alone that evening—he had summut to do."

"I shall bid father good-night first," said Catherine, putting her arms round his neck, before we could hinder her.

The poor thing discovered her loss directly—she screamed out—

"Oh, he's dead, Heathcliff! he's dead!"

And they both set up a heart-breaking cry.

I joined my wail to theirs, loud and bitter; but Joseph asked what we could be thinking of to roar in that way over a saint in heaven.

He told me to put on my cloak and run to Gimmerton for the doctor and the parson. I could not guess the use that either would be of, then. However, I went, through wind and rain, and brought one, the doctor, back with me; the other said he would come in the morning.

Leaving Joseph to explain matters, I ran to the children's room; their door was ajar, I saw they had never laid down, though it was past midnight; but they were calmer, and did not need me to console them. The little souls were comforting each other with better thoughts than I could have hit on; no parson in the world ever pictured heaven so beautifully as they did, in their innocent talk; and, while I sobbed and listened, I could not help wishing we were all there safe together.

1. Exceedingly.    2. Go.

*Chapter* VI

Mr. Hindley came home to the funeral; and—a thing that amazed us, and set the neighbours gossipping right and left—he brought a wife with him.

What she was, and where she was born he never informed us; probably, she had neither money nor name to recommend her, or he would scarcely have kept the union from his father.

She was not one that would have disturbed the house much on her own account. Every object she saw, the moment she crossed the threshold, appeared to delight her; and every circumstance that took place about her, except the preparing for the burial, and the presence of the mourners.

I thought she was half silly, from her behaviour while that went on; she ran into her chamber, and made me come with her, though I should have been dressing the children; and there she sat shivering and clasping her hands, and asking repeatedly—

"Are they gone yet?"

Then she began describing with hysterical emotion the effect it produced on her to see black; and started, and trembled, and, at last, fell a weeping—and when I asked what was the matter? answered, she didn't know; but she felt so afraid of dying!

I imagined her as little likely to die as myself. She was rather thin, but young, and fresh complexioned, and her eyes sparkled as bright as diamonds. I did remark, to be sure, that mounting the stairs made her breathe very quick, that the least sudden noise set her all in a quiver, and that she coughed troublesomely sometimes: but I knew nothing of what these symptoms portended, and had no impulse to sympathize with her. We don't in general take to foreigners here, Mr. Lockwood, unless they take to us first.

Young Earnshaw was altered considerably in the three years of his absence. He had grown sparer, and lost his colour, and spoke and dressed quite differently; and, on the very day of his return, he told Joseph and me we must thenceforth quarter ourselves in the back-kitchen, and leave the house for him. Indeed, he would have carpeted and papered a small spare room for a parlour; but his wife expressed such pleasure at the white floor, and huge glowing fire-place, at the pewter dishes, and delf-case, and dog-kennel, and the wide space there was to move about in, where they usually sat, that he thought it unnecessary to her comfort, and so dropped the intention.

She expressed pleasure, too, at finding a sister among her new acquaintance; and she prattled to Catherine, and kissed her, and ran about with her, and gave her quantities of presents, at the beginning. Her affection tired very soon, however, and when she grew peevish, Hindley became tyrannical. A few words from her, evincing a dislike to Heathcliff, were enough to rouse in him all his old hatred of the boy. He drove him from their company to the servants, deprived him of the instructions of the curate, and insisted that he should labour out of doors instead, compelling him to do so, as hard as any other lad on the farm.

Heathcliff bore his degradation pretty well at first, because Cathy taught him what she learnt, and worked or played with him in the fields. They both promised fair to grow up as rude as savages, the young master being entirely negligent how they behaved, and what they did, so they kept clear of him. He would not even have seen after their going to church on Sundays, only Joseph and the curate reprimanded his carelessness when they absented themselves, and that reminded him to order Heathcliff a flogging, and Catherine a fast from dinner or supper.

But it was one of their chief amusements to run away to the moors in the morning and remain there all day, and the after-punishment grew a mere thing to laugh at. The curate might set as many chapters as he pleased for Catherine to get by heart, and Joseph might thrash Heathcliff till his arm ached; they forgot everything the minute they were together again, at least the minute they had contrived some naughty plan of revenge; and many a time I've cried to myself to watch them growing more reckless daily, and I not daring to speak a syllable for fear of losing the small power I still retained over the unfriended creatures.

One Sunday evening, it chanced that they were banished from the sitting-room, for making a noise, or a light offence of the kind, and when I went to call them to supper, I could discover them nowhere.

We searched the house, above and below, and the yard and stables; they were invisible; and, at last, Hindley in a passion told us to bolt the doors, and swore nobody should let them in that night.

The household went to bed; and I, too anxious to lie down, opened my lattice and put my head out to hearken, though it rained, determined to admit them in spite of the prohibition, should they return.

In a while, I distinguished steps coming up the road, and the light of a lantern glimmered through the gate.

I threw a shawl over my head and ran to prevent them from waking Mr. Earnshaw by knocking. There was Heathcliff, by himself; it gave me a start to see him alone.

"Where is Miss Catherine?" I cried hurriedly. "No accident, I hope?"

"At Thrushcross Grange," he answered, "and I would have been there too, but they had not the manners to ask me to stay."

"Well, you will catch it!" I said, "you'll never be content till you're sent about your business. What in the world led you wandering to Thrushcross Grange?"

"Let me get off my wet clothes, and I'll tell you all about it, Nelly," he replied.

I bid him beware of rousing the master, and while he undressed, and I waited to put out the candle, he continued—

"Cathy and I escaped from the wash-house to have a ramble at liberty, and getting a glimpse of the Grange lights, we thought we would just go and see whether the Lintons passed their Sunday evenings standing shivering in corners, while their father and mother sat eating and drinking, and singing and laughing, and burning their eyes out before the fire. Do you think they do? Or reading sermons, and being catechised by their man-servant, and set to learn a column of Scripture names, if they don't answer properly?"

"Probably not," I responded. "They are good children, no doubt, and don't deserve the treatment you receive, for your bad conduct."

"Don't you cant, Nelly," he said. "Nonsense! We ran from the top of the Heights to the park, without stopping—Catherine completely beaten in the race, because she was barefoot. You'll have to seek for her shoes in the bog to-morrow. We crept through a broken hedge, groped our way up the path, and planted ourselves on a flower-plot under the drawing-room window. The light came from thence; they had not put up the shutters, and the curtains were only half closed. Both of us were able to look in by standing on the basement, and clinging to the ledge, and we saw—ah! it was beautiful—a splendid place carpeted with crimson, and crimson-covered chairs and tables, and a pure white ceiling bordered by gold, a shower of glass-drops hanging in silver chains from the centre, and shimmering with little soft tapers. Old Mr. and Mrs. Linton were not there. Edgar and his sister had it entirely to themselves; shouldn't they have been happy? We should have thought ourselves in heaven! And now, guess what your good children were doing? Isabella—I believe she is eleven, a year younger than Cathy—lay screaming at the farther end of the room, shrieking as if witches were running red hot needles into her. Edgar stood on the hearth weeping silently, and in the middle of the table sat a little dog shaking its paw and yelping, which, from their mutual accusations, we understood they had nearly pulled in two between them. The idiots! That was their pleasure! to quarrel who should hold a heap of warm hair, and each begin to cry because both, after struggling to get it, refused to take it. We laughed outright at the petted things, we did despise them! When would you catch me wishing to have what Catherine wanted? or find us by ourselves, seeking entertainment in yelling, and sobbing, and rolling on the ground, divided by the whole room? I'd not exchange, for a thousand lives, my condition here, for Edgar Linton's at Thrushcross Grange—not if I might have the privilege of flinging Joseph off the highest gable, and painting the house-front with Hindley's blood!"

"Hush, hush!" I interrupted. "Still you have not told me, Heathcliff, how Catherine is left behind?"

"I told you we laughed," he answered. "The Lintons heard us, and with one accord, they shot like arrows to the door; there was silence, and then a cry, 'Oh, mamma, mamma! Oh, papa! Oh, mamma, come here. Oh, papa, oh!' They really did howl out, something in that way. We made frightful noises to terrify them still more, and then we dropped off the ledge, because somebody was drawing the bars, and we felt we had better flee. I had Cathy by the hand, and was urging her on, when all at once she fell down.

" 'Run, Heathcliff, run!' she whispered. 'They have let the bull-dog loose, and he holds me!'

"The devil had seized her ankle, Nelly; I heard his abominable snorting. She did not yell out—no! She would have scorned to do it, if she had been spitted on the horns of a mad cow. I did, though; I vociferated curses enough to annihilate any fiend in Christendom, and I got a stone and trust it between his jaws, and tried with all my might to cram it down his throat. A beast of a servant came up with a lantern, at last, shouting—

" 'Keep fast, Skulker, keep fast!'

"He changed his note, however, when he saw Skulker's game. The dog was throttled off, his huge, purple tongue hanging half a foot out of his mouth, and his pendant lips streaming with bloody slaver.

"The man took Cathy up; she was sick, not from fear, I'm certain, but from pain. He carried her in; I followed, grumbling execrations and vengeance.

" 'What prey, Robert?' hallooed Linton from the entrance.

" 'Skulker has caught a little girl, sir,' he replied, 'and there's a lad here,' he added, making a clutch at me, 'who looks an out-and-outer! Very like, the robbers were for putting them through the window, to open the doors to the gang after all were asleep, that they might murder us at their ease. Hold your tongue, you foul-mouthed thief, you! you shall go to the gallows for this. Mr.

Linton, sir, don't lay by your gun!'

" 'No, no, Robert!' said the old fool. 'The rascals knew that yesterday was my rent-day; they thought to have me cleverly. Come in; I'll furnish them a reception. There, John, fasten the chain. Give Skulker some water, Jenny. To beard a magistrate in his strong-hold, and on the Sabbath, too! Where will their insolence stop? Oh, my dear Mary, look here! Don't be afraid, it is but a boy—yet the villain scowls so plainly in his face, would it not be a kindness to the country to hang him at once, before he shows his nature in acts, as well as features?'

"He pulled me under the chandelier, and Mrs. Linton placed her spectacles on her nose and raised her hands in horror. The cowardly children crept nearer also, Isabella lisping—

" 'Frightful thing! Put him in the cellar, papa. He's exactly like the son of the fortune-teller that stole my tame pheasant. Isn't he, Edgar?'

"While they examined me, Cathy came round; she heard the last speech, and laughed. Edgar Linton, after an inquisitive stare, collected sufficient wit to recognise her. They see us at church, you know, though we seldom meet them elsewhere.

" 'That's Miss Earnshaw!' he whispered to his mother, 'and look how Skulker has bitten her—how her foot bleeds!'

" 'Miss Earnshaw? Nonsense!' cried the dame, 'Miss Earnshaw scouring the country with a gipsy! And yet, my dear, the child is in mourning—surely it is—and she may be lamed for life!'

" 'What culpable carelessness in her brother!' exclaimed Mr. Linton, turning from me to Catherine. 'I've understood from Shielders' (that was the curate, sir) 'that he lets her grow up in absolute heathenism. But who is this? Where did she pick up this companion? Oho! I declare he is that strange acquisition my late neighbour made in his journey to Liverpool—a little Lascar, or an American or Spanish castaway.'

" 'A wicked boy, at all events,' remarked the old lady, 'and quite unfit for a decent house! Did you notice his language, Linton? I'm shocked that my children should have heard it.'

"I recommenced cursing—don't be angry, Nelly—and so Robert was ordered to take me off. I refused to go without Cathy; he dragged me into the garden, pushed the lantern into my hand, assured me that Mr. Earnshaw should be informed of my behaviour, and bidding me march directly, secured the door again.

"The curtains were still looped up at one corner; and I resumed my station as spy, because, if Catherine had wished to return, I intended shattering their great glass panes to a million fragments, unless they let her out.

"She sat on the sofa quietly. Mrs. Linton took off the grey cloak of the dairy maid which we had borrowed for our excursion, shaking her head, and expostulating with her, I suppose; she was a young lady and they made a distinction between her treatment and mine. Then the woman servant brought a basin of warm water, and washed her feet; and Mr. Linton mixed a tumbler of negus, and Isabella emptied a plateful of cakes into her lap, and Edgar stood gaping at a distance. Afterwards, they dried and combed her beautiful hair, and gave her a pair of enormous slippers, and wheeled her to the fire, and I left her, as merry as she could be, dividing her food between the little dog and Skulker whose nose she pinched as he ate; and kindling a spark of spirit in the vacant blue eyes of the Lintons—a dim reflection from her own enchanting face. I saw they were full of stupid admiration; she is so immeasurably superior to them—to everybody on earth, is she not, Nelly?"

"There will more come of this business than you reckon on," I answered, covering him up and extinguishing the light. "You are incurable, Heathcliff, and Mr. Hindley will have to proceed to extremities, see if he won't."

My words came truer than I desired. The luckless adventure made Earnshaw furious. And then Mr. Linton, to mend matters, paid us a visit himself on the morrow; and read the young master such a lecture on the road he guided his family, that he was stirred to look about him, in earnest.

Heathcliff received no flogging, but he was told that the first word he spoke to Miss Catherine should ensure a dismissal; and Mrs. Earnshaw undertook to keep her sister-in-law in due restraint, when she returned home; employing art, not force—with force she would have found it impossible.

## Chapter VII

Cathy stayed at Thrushcross Grange five weeks, till Christmas. By that time her ankle was thoroughly cured, and her manners much improved. The mistress visited her often, in the interval, and commenced her plan of reform by trying to raise her self-respect with fine clothes and flattery, which she took readily: so that, instead of a wild, hatless little savage jumping into the house, and rushing to squeeze us all breathless, there alighted from a handsome black pony a very dignified person with brown ringlets falling from the cover of a feathered beaver, and a long cloth habit which she was obliged to hold up with both hands that she might sail in.

Hindley lifted her from her horse, exclaiming delightedly—

"Why, Cathy, you are quite a beauty! I should scarcely have

known you—you look like a lady now. Isabella Linton is not to be compared with her, is she, Frances?"

"Isabella has not her natural advantages," replied his wife, "but she must mind and not grow wild again here. Ellen, help Miss Catherine off with her things. Stay, dear, you will disarrange your curls—let me untie your hat."

I removed the habit, and there shone forth beneath, a grand plaid silk frock, white trousers, and burnished shoes; and, while her eyes sparkled joyfully when the dogs came bounding up to welcome her, she dare hardly touch them lest they should fawn upon her splendid garments.

She kissed me gently—I was all flour making the Christmas cake, and it would not have done to give me a hug—and then she looked round for Heathcliff. Mr. and Mrs. Earnshaw watched anxiously their meeting, thinking it would enable them to judge, in some measure, what grounds they had for hoping to succeed in separating the two friends.

Heathcliff was hard to discover, at first. If he were careless and uncared for, before Catherine's absence, he had been ten times more so, since.

Nobody but I even did him the kindness to call him a dirty boy, and bid him wash himself, once a week; and children of his age seldom have a natural pleasure in soap and water. Therefore, not to mention his clothes, which had seen three months' service in mire and dust, and his thick uncombed hair, the surface of his face and hands was dismally beclouded. He might well skulk behind the settle, on beholding such a bright, graceful damsel enter the house, instead of a rough-headed counterpart of himself, as he expected.

"Is Heathcliff not here?" she demanded, pulling off her gloves, and displaying fingers wonderfully whitened with doing nothing, and staying indoors.

"Heathcliff, you may come forward," cried Mr. Hindley, enjoying his discomfiture and gratified to see what a forbidding young blackguard he would be compelled to present himself. "You may come and wish Miss Catherine welcome, like the other servants."

Cathy, catching a glimpse of her friend in his concealment, flew to embrace him; she bestowed seven or eight kisses on his cheek within the second, and then stopped, and drawing back, burst into a laugh, exclaiming—

"Why, how very black and cross you look! and how—how funny and grim! But that's because I'm used to Edgar and Isabella Linton. Well, Heathcliff, have you forgotten me?"

She had some reason to put the question, for shame and pride threw double gloom over his countenance, and kept him immovable.

"Shake hands, Heathcliff," said Mr. Earnshaw, condescendingly; "once in a way, that is permitted."

"I shall not!" replied the boy, finding his tongue at last, "I shall not stand to be laughed at, I shall not bear it!"

And he would have broken from the circle, but Miss Cathy seized him again.

"I did not mean to laugh at you," she said, "I could not hinder myself. Heathcliff, shake hands, at least! What are you sulky for? It was only that you looked odd. If you wash your face and brush your hair, it will be all right. But you are so dirty!"

She gazed concernedly at the dusky fingers she held in her own, and also at her dress, which she feared had gained no embellishment from its contact with his.

"You needn't have touched me!" he answered, following her eye and snatching away his hand. "I shall be as dirty as I please, and I like to be dirty, and I will be dirty."

With that he dashed head foremost out of the room, amid the merriment of the master and mistress, and to the serious disturbance of Catherine, who could not comprehend how her remarks should have produced such an exhibition of bad temper.

After playing lady's maid to the new-comer, and putting my cakes in the oven, and making the house and kitchen cheerful with great fires befitting Christmas eve, I prepared to sit down and amuse myself by singing carols, all alone, regardless of Joseph's affirmations that he considered the merry tunes I chose as next door to songs.

He had retired to private prayer in his chamber, and Mr. and Mrs. Earnshaw were engaging Missy's attention by sundry gay trifles bought for her to present to the little Lintons, as an acknowledgment of their kindness.

They had invited them to spend the morrow at Wuthering Heights, and the invitation had been accepted, on one condition: Mrs. Linton begged that her darlings might be kept carefully apart from that "naughty, swearing boy."

Under these circumstances I remained solitary. I smelt the rich scent of the heating spices; and admired the shining kitchen utensils, the polished clock, decked in holly, the silver mugs ranged on a tray ready to be filled with mulled ale for supper; and, above all, the speckless purity of my particular care—the scoured and well-swept floor.

I gave due inward applause to every object, and then I remembered how old Earnshaw used to come in when all was tidied, and call me a cant lass,[1] and slip a shilling into my hand, as a

---

1. Lively girl.

Christmas box; and from that I went on to think of his fondness for Heathcliff, and his dread lest he should suffer neglect after death had removed him; and that naturally led me to consider the poor lad's situation now, and from singing I changed my mind to crying. It struck me soon, however, there would be more sense in endeavouring to repair some of his wrongs than shedding tears over them. I got up and walked into the court to seek him.

He was not far; I found him smoothing the glossy coat of the new pony in the stable, and feeding the other beasts, according to custom.

"Make haste, Heathcliff!" I said, "the kitchen is so comfortable —and Joseph is upstairs; make haste, and let me dress you smart before Miss Cathy comes out, and then you can sit together, with the whole hearth to yourselves, and have a long chatter till bed-time."

He proceeded with his task and never turned his head towards me.

"Come—are you coming?" I continued. "There's a little cake for each of you, nearly enough; and you'll need half an hour's donning."

I waited five minutes, but getting no answer left him. Catherine supped with her brother and sister-in-law: Joseph and I joined at an unsociable meal seasoned with reproofs on one side and sauciness on the other. His cake and cheese remained on the table all night for the fairies. He managed to continue work till nine o'clock, and then marched dumb and dour to his chamber.

Cathy sat up late, having a world of things to order for the reception of her new friends: she came into the kitchen, once, to speak to her old one, but he was gone, and she only stayed to ask what was the matter with him, and then went back.

In the morning, he rose early; and, as it was a holiday, carried his ill-humour onto the moors, not re-appearing till the family were departed for church. Fasting and reflection seemed to have brought him to a better spirit. He hung about me for a while, and having screwed up his courage, exclaimed abruptly—

"Nelly, make me decent, I'm going to be good."

"High time, Heathcliff," I said, "you *have* grieved Catherine; she's sorry she ever came home, I dare say! It looks as if you envied her, because she is more thought of than you."

The notion of *envying* Catherine was incomprehensible to him, but the notion of grieving her he understood clearly enough.

"Did she say she was grieved?" he inquired, looking very serious.

"She cried when I told her you were off again this morning."

"Well, *I* cried last night," he returned, "and I had more reason to cry than she."

"Yes, you had the reason of going to bed with a proud heart and an empty stomach," said I. "Proud people breed sad sorrows for themselves. But, if you be ashamed of your touchiness, you must ask pardon, mind, when she comes in. You must go up and offer to kiss her, and say—you know best what to say, only do it heartily, and not as if you thought her converted into a stranger by her grand dress. And now, though I have dinner to get ready, I'll steal time to arrange you so that Edgar Linton shall look quite a doll beside you: and that he does. You are younger, and yet, I'll be bound, you are taller and twice as broad across the shoulders—you could knock him down in a twinkling. Don't you feel that you could?"

Heathcliff's face brightened a moment; then it was overcast afresh, and he sighed.

"But, Nelly, if I knocked him down twenty times, that wouldn't make him less handsome, or me more so. I wish I had light hair and a fair skin, and was dressed and behaved as well, and had a chance of being as rich as he will be!"

"And cried for mamma, at every turn," I added, "and trembled if a country lad heaved his fist against you, and sat at home all day for a shower of rain. O, Heathcliff, you are showing a poor spirit! Come to the glass, and I'll let you see what you should wish. Do you mark those two lines between your eyes; and those thick brows, that instead of rising arched, sink in the middle; and that couple of black fiends, so deeply buried, who never open their windows boldly, but lurk glinting under them, like devil's spies? Wish and learn to smooth away the surly wrinkles, to raise your lids frankly, and change the fiends to confident, innocent angels, suspecting and doubting nothing, and always seeing friends where they are not sure of foes. Don't get the expression of a vicious cur that appears to know the kicks it gets are its desert, and yet hates all the world, as well as the kicker, for what it suffers."

"In other words, I must wish for Edgar Linton's great blue eyes, and even forehead," he replied. "I do—and that won't help me to them."

"A good heart will help you to a bonny face, my lad," I continued, "if you were a regular black; and a bad one will turn the bonniest into something worse than ugly. And now that we've done washing, and combing, and sulking—tell me whether you don't think yourself rather handsome? I'll tell you, I do. You're fit for a prince in disguise. Who knows but your father was Emperor of China, and your mother an Indian queen, each of them able to buy up, with one week's income, Wuthering Heights and Thrushcross Grange together? And you were kidnapped by wicked sailors, and brought to England. Were I in your place, I would frame high notions of my birth; and the thoughts of what I was should give me courage and dignity to support the oppressions of a little farmer!"

So I chattered on; and Heathcliff gradually lost his frown, and began to look quite pleasant, when, all at once, our conversation was interrupted by a rumbling sound moving up the road and entering the court. He ran to the window, and I to the door, just in time to behold the two Lintons descend from the family carriage, smothered in cloaks and furs, and the Earnshaws dismount from their horses—they often rode to church in winter. Catherine took a hand of each of the children, and brought them into the house, and set them before the fire, which quickly put colour into their white faces.

I urged my companion to hasten now, and show his amiable humour, and he willingly obeyed; but ill luck would have it that, as he opened the door leading from the kitchen on one side, Hindley opened it on the other. They met, and the master, irritated at seeing him clean and cheerful, or, perhaps, eager to keep his promise to Mrs. Linton, shoved him back with a sudden thrust, and angrily bade Joseph "keep the fellow out of the room —send him into the garret till dinner is over. He'll be cramming his fingers in the tarts, and stealing the fruit, if left alone with them a minute."

"Nay, sir," I could not avoid answering, "he'll touch nothing, not he—and, I suppose, he must have his share of the dainties as well as we."

"He shall have his share of my hand, if I catch him downstairs again till dark," cried Hindley. "Begone, you vagabond! What! you are attempting the coxcomb, are you? Wait till I get hold of those elegant locks—see if I won't pull them a bit longer!"

"They are long enough already," observed Master Linton, peeping from the door-way; "I wonder they don't make his head ache. It's like a colt's mane over his eyes!"

He ventured this remark without any intention to insult; but Heathcliff's violent nature was not prepared to endure the appearance of impertinence from one whom he seemed to hate, even then, as a rival. He seized a tureen of hot apple-sauce, the first thing that came under his gripe, and dashed it full against the speaker's face and neck—who instantly commenced a lament that brought Isabella and Catherine hurrying to the place.

Mr. Earnshaw snatched up the culprit directly and conveyed him to his chamber, where, doubtless, he administered a rough remedy to cool the fit of passion, for he reappeared red and breathless. I got the dishcloth, and, rather spitefully, scrubbed Edgar's nose and mouth, affirming it served him right for meddling. His sister began weeping to go home, and Cathy stood by, confounded, blushing for all.

"You should not have spoken to him!" she expostulated with Master Linton. "He was in a bad temper, and now you've spoilt your visit, and he'll be flogged—I hate him to be flogged! I can't eat my dinner. Why did you speak to him, Edgar?"

"I didn't," sobbed the youth, escaping from my hands, and finishing the remainder of the purification with his cambric pocket-handkerchief. "I promised mamma that I wouldn't say one word to him, and I didn't!"

"Well, don't cry!" replied Catherine, contemptuously. "You're not killed. Don't make more mischief—my brother is coming—be quiet! Give over, Isabella! Has anybody hurt *you?*"

"There, there, children—to your seats!" cried Hindley, bustling in. "That brute of a lad has warmed me nicely. Next time, Master Edgar, take the law into your own fists—it will give you an appetite!"

The little party recovered its equanimity at sight of the fragrant feast. They were hungry after their ride, and easily consoled, since no real harm had befallen them.

Mr. Earnshaw carved bountiful platefuls; and the mistress made them merry with lively talk. I waited behind her chair, and was pained to behold Catherine, with dry eyes and an indifferent air, commence cutting up the wing of a goose before her.

"An unfeeling child," I thought to myself, "how lightly she dismisses her old playmate's troubles. I could not have imagined her to be so selfish."

She lifted a mouthful to her lips; then she set it down again: her cheeks flushed, and the tears gushed over them. She slipped her fork to the floor, and hastily dived under the cloth to conceal her emotion. I did not call her unfeeling long, for I perceived she was in purgatory throughout the day, and wearying to find an opportunity of getting by herself, or paying a visit to Heathcliff, who had been locked up by the master, as I discovered on endeavouring to introduce to him a private mess of victuals.

In the evening we had a dance. Cathy begged that he might be liberated then, as Isabella Linton had no partner; her entreaties were vain, and I was appointed to supply the deficiency.

We got rid of all gloom in the excitement of the exercise, and our pleasure was increased by the arrival of the Gimmerton band, mustering fifteen strong: a trumpet, a trombone, clarionets, bassoons, French horns, and a bass viol, besides singers. They go the rounds of all the respectable houses, and receive contributions every Christmas, and we esteemed it a first-rate treat to hear them.

After the usual carols had been sung, we set them to songs

and glees. Mrs. Earnshaw loved the music, and so they gave us plenty.

Catherine loved it too; but she said it sounded sweetest at the top of the steps, and she went up in the dark; I followed. They shut the house door below, never noting our absence, the place was so full of people. She made no stay at the stairs' head, but mounted farther, to the garret where Heathcliff was confined, and called him. He stubbornly declined answering for a while; she persevered, and finally persuaded him to hold communion with her through the boards.

I let the poor things converse unmolested, till I supposed the songs were going to cease, and the singers to get some refreshment: then, I clambered up the ladder to warn her.

Instead of finding her outside, I heard her voice within. The little monkey had crept by the skylight of one garret, along the roof, into the skylight of the other, and it was with the utmost difficulty I could coax her out again.

When she did come, Heathcliff came with her; and she insisted that I should take him into the kitchen, as my fellow-servant had gone to a neighbour's to be removed from the sound of our "devil's psalmody," as it pleased him to call it.

I told them I intended, by no means, to encourage their tricks; but as the prisoner had never broken his fast since yesterday's dinner, I would wink at his cheating Mr. Hindley that once.

He went down; I set him a stool by the fire, and offered him a quantity of good things; but he was sick and could eat little, and my attempts to entertain him were thrown away. He leant his two elbows on his knees, and his chin on his hands, and remained wrapt in dumb meditation. On my inquiring the subject of his thoughts, he answered gravely—

"I'm trying to settle how I shall pay Hindley back. I don't care how long I wait, if I can only do it, at last. I hope he will not die before I do!"

"For shame, Heathcliff!" said I. "It is for God to punish wicked people; we should learn to forgive."

"No, God won't have the satisfaction that I shall," he returned. "I only wish I knew the best way! Let me alone, and I'll plan it out: while I'm thinking of that, I don't feel pain."

But, Mr. Lockwood, I forget these tales cannot divert you. I'm annoyed how I should dream of chattering on at such a rate; and your gruel cold, and you nodding for bed! I could have told Heathcliff's history, all that you need hear, in half-a-dozen words.

Thus interrupting herself, the housekeeper rose, and proceeded to lay aside her sewing; but I felt incapable of moving from the hearth, and I was very far from nodding.

"Sit still, Mrs. Dean," I cried, "do sit still, another half hour! You've done just right to tell the story leisurely. That is the method I like; and you must finish in the same style. I am interested in every character you have mentioned, more or less."

"The clock is on the stroke of eleven, sir."

"No matter—I'm not accustomed to go to bed in the long hours. One or two is early enough for a person who lies till ten."

"You shouldn't lie till ten. There's the very prime of the morning gone long before that time. A person who has not done one half his day's work by ten o'clock runs a chance of leaving the other half undone."

"Nevertheless, Mrs. Dean, resume your chair; because to-morrow I intend lengthening the night till afternoon. I prognosticate for myself an obstinate cold, at least."

"I hope not, sir. Well, you must allow me to leap over some three years; during that space Mrs. Earnshaw—"

"No, no, I'll allow nothing of the sort! Are you acquainted with the mood of mind in which, if you were seated alone, and the cat licking its kitten on the rug before you, you would watch the operation so intently that puss's neglect of one ear would put you seriously out of temper?"

"A terribly lazy mood, I should say."

"On the contrary, a tiresomely active one. It is mine, at present, and, therefore, continue minutely. I perceive that people in these regions acquire over people in towns the value that a spider in a dungeon does over a spider in a cottage, to their various occupants; and yet the deepened attraction is not entirely owing to the situation of the looker-on. They *do* live more in earnest, more in themselves, and less in surface change, and frivolous external things. I could fancy a love for life here almost possible; and I was a fixed unbeliever in any love of a year's standing. One state resembles setting a hungry man down to a single dish on which he may concentrate his entire appetite, and do it justice; the other, introducing him to a table laid out by French cooks. He can perhaps extract as much enjoyment from the whole, but each part is a mere atom in his regard and remembrance."

"Oh! here we are the same as anywhere else, when you get to know us," observed Mrs. Dean, somewhat puzzled at my speech.

"Excuse me," I responded; "you, my good friend, are a striking evidence against that assertion. Excepting a few provincialisms of slight consequence, you have no marks of the manners that I am habituated to consider as peculiar to your class. I am sure you have thought a great deal more than the generality of servants think. You have been compelled to cultivate your reflective faculties, for want of occasions for frittering your life away in silly trifles."

Mrs. Dean laughed.

"I certainly esteem myself a steady, reasonable kind of body," she said, "not exactly from living among the hills and seeing one set of faces, and one series of actions, from year's end to year's end; but I have undergone sharp discipline which has taught me wisdom; and then, I have read more than you would fancy, Mr. Lockwood. You could not open a book in this library that I have not looked into, and got something out of also, unless it be that range of Greek and Latin, and that of French—and those I know one from another: it is as much as you can expect of a poor man's daughter."

"However, if I am to follow my story in true gossip's fashion, I had better go on; and instead of leaping three years, I will be content to pass to the next summer—the summer of 1778, that is, nearly twenty-three years ago."

## Chapter VIII

On the morning of a fine June day, my first bonny little nursling, and the last of the ancient Earnshaw stock, was born.

We were busy with the hay in a far-away field, when the girl that usually brought our breakfasts came running, an hour too soon, across the meadow and up the lane, calling me as she ran.

"Oh, such a grand bairn!" she panted out. "The finest lad that ever breathed! But the doctor says missis must go; he says she's been in a consumption these many months. I heard him tell Mr. Hindley: and now she has nothing to keep her, and she'll be dead before winter. You must come home directly. You're to nurse it, Nelly—to feed it with sugar and milk, and take care of it, day and night. I wish I were you, because it will be all yours when there is no missis!"

"But is she very ill?" I asked, flinging down my rake, and tying my bonnet.

"I guess she is; yet she looks bravely," replied the girl, "and she talks as if she thought of living to see it grow a man. She's out of her head for joy, it's such a beauty! If I were her, I'm certain I should not die. I should get better at the bare sight of it, in spite of Kenneth. I was fairly mad at him. Dame Archer brought the cherub down to master, in the house, and his face just began to light up, when the old croaker steps forward, and, says he—'Earn- shaw, it's a blessing your wife has been spared to leave you this son. When she came, I felt convinced we shouldn't keep her long; and now, I must tell you, the winter will probably finish her. Don't take on, and fret about it too much, it can't be helped. And besides, you should have known better than to choose such a rush of a lass!' "[1]

"And what did the master answer?" I enquired.

"I think he swore—but I didn't mind him, I was straining tc see the bairn," and she began again to describe it rapturously. I, as zealous as herself, hurried eagerly home to admire, on my part, though I was very sad for Hindley's sake; he had room in his heart only for two idols—his wife and himself: he doted on both, and adored one, and I couldn't conceive how he would bear the loss.

When we got to Wuthering Heights, there he stood at the front door; and, as I passed in, I asked, how was the baby?

"Nearly ready to run about, Nell!" he replied, putting on a cheerful smile.

"And the mistress?" I ventured to inquire, "the doctor says she's—"

"Damn the doctor!" he interrupted, reddening. "Frances is quite right—she'll be perfectly well by this time next week. Are you going upstairs? will you tell her that I'll come, if she'll promise not to talk? I left her because she would not hold her tongue; and she must—tell her Mr. Kenneth says she must be quiet."

I delivered this message to Mrs. Earnshaw; she seemed in flighty spirits, and replied merrily—

"I hardly spoke a word, Ellen, and there he has gone out twice, crying. Well, say I promise I won't speak; but that does not bind me not to laugh at him!"

Poor soul! Till within a week of her death that gay heart never failed her; and her husband persisted doggedly, nay, furiously, in affirming her health improved every day. When Kenneth warned him that his medicines were useless at that stage of the malady, and he needn't put him to further expense by attending her, he retorted—

"I know you need not—she's well—she does not want any more attendance from you! She never was in a consumption. It was a fever; and it is gone—her pulse is as slow as mine now, and her cheek as cool."

He told his wife the same story, and she seemed to believe him; but one night, while leaning on his shoulder, in the act of saying she thought she should be able to get up to-morrow, a fit of coughing took her—a very slight one. He raised her in his arms; she put her two hands about his neck, her face changed, and she was dead.

As the girl had anticipated, the child Hareton fell wholly into my hands. Mr. Earnshaw, provided he saw him healthy, and never heard him cry, was contented, as far as regarded him. For

1. *Rush of a lass:* slender, delicate, like a rush.

himself, he grew desperate; his sorrow was of that kind that will not lament. He neither wept nor prayed—he cursed and defied—execrated God and man, and gave himself up to reckless dissipation.

The servants could not bear his tyrannical and evil conduct long: Joseph and I were the only two that would stay. I had not the heart to leave my charge; and besides, you know, I had been his foster sister, and excused his behaviour more readily than a stranger would.

Joseph remained to hector over tenants and labourers, and because it was his vocation to be where there was plenty of wickedness to reprove.

The master's bad ways and bad companions formed a pretty example for Catherine and Heathcliff. His treatment of the latter was enough to make a fiend of a saint. And, truly, it appeared as if the lad *were* possessed of something diabolical at that period. He delighted to witness Hindley degrading himself past redemption; and became daily more notable for savage sullenness and ferocity.

I could not half tell what an infernal house we had. The curate dropped calling, and nobody decent came near us, at last, unless Edgar Linton's visits to Miss Cathy might be an exception. At fifteen she was the queen of the country-side; she had no peer, and she did turn out a haughty, headstrong creature! I own I did not like her after her infancy was past; and I vexed her frequently by trying to bring down her arrogance; she never took an aversion to me, though. She had a wondrous constancy to old attachments; even Heathcliff kept his hold on her affections unalterably, and young Linton, with all his superiority, found it difficult to make an equally deep impression.

He was my late master; that is his portrait over the fireplace. It used to hang on one side, and his wife's on the other; but hers has been removed, or else you might see something of what she was. Can you make that out?

Mrs. Dean raised the candle, and I discerned a soft-featured face, exceedingly resembling the young lady at the Heights, but more pensive and amiable in expression. It formed a sweet picture. The long light hair curled slightly on the temple; the eyes were large and serious; the figure almost too graceful. I did not marvel how Catherine Earnshaw could forget her first friend for such an individual. I marvelled much how he, with a mind to correspond with his person, could fancy my idea of Catherine Earnshaw.

"A very agreeable portrait," I observed to the housekeeper. "Is it like?"

"Yes," she answered; "but he looked better when he was animated; that is his every day countenance; he wanted spirit in general."

Catherine had kept up her acquaintance with the Lintons since her five weeks' residence among them; and as she had no temptation to show her rough side in their company, and had the sense to be ashamed of being rude where she experienced such invariable courtesy, she imposed unwittingly on the old lady and gentleman, by her ingenious cordiality; gained the admiration of Isabella, and the heart and soul of her brother—acquisitions that flattered her from the first, for she was full of ambition, and led her to adopt a double character without exactly intending to deceive anyone.

In the place where she heard Heathcliff termed a "vulgar young ruffian," and "worse than a brute," she took care not to act like him; but at home she had small inclination to practise politeness that would only be laughed at, and restrain an unruly nature when it would bring her neither credit nor praise.

Mr. Edgar seldom mustered courage to visit Wuthering Heights openly. He had a terror of Earnshaw's reputation, and shrunk from encountering him, and yet he was always received with our best attempts at civility: the master himself avoided offending him, knowing why he came, and if he could not be gracious, kept out of the way. I rather think his appearance there was distasteful to Catherine; she was not artful, never played the coquette, and had evidently an objection to her two friends meeting at all; for when Heathcliff expressed contempt of Linton, in his presence, she could not half coincide, as she did in his absence; and when Linton evinced disgust and antipathy to Heathcliff, she dare not treat his sentiments with indifference, as if depreciation of her playmate were of scarcely any consequence to her.

I've had many a laugh at her perplexities and untold troubles, which she vainly strove to hide from my mockery. That sounds ill-natured—but she was so proud, it became really impossible to pity her distresses, till she should be chastened into more humility.

She did bring herself, finally, to confess, and confide in me. There was not a soul else that she might fashion into an adviser.

Mr. Hindley had gone from home, one afternoon, and Heathcliff presumed to give himself a holiday on the strength of it. He had reached the age of sixteen then, I think, and without having bad features or being deficient in intellect, he contrived to convey an impression of inward and outward repulsiveness that his present aspect retains no traces of.

In the first place, he had, by that time, lost the benefit of his early education: continual hard work, begun soon and concluded late, had extinguished any curiosity he once possessed in pursuit of knowledge, and any love for books or learning. His childhood's sense of superiority, instilled into him by the favours of old Mr. Earnshaw, was faded away. He struggled long to keep up an equality with Catherine in her studies and yielded with poignant though silent regret: but he yielded completely; and there was no prevailing on him to take a step in the way of moving upward, when he found he must, necessarily, sink beneath his former level. Then personal appearance sympathised with mental deterioration; he acquired a slouching gait, and ignoble look; his naturally reserved disposition was exaggerated into an almost idiotic excess of unsociable moroseness; and he took a grim pleasure, apparently, in exciting the aversion rather than the esteem of his few acquaintance.

Catherine and he were constant companions still, at his seasons of respite from labour; but he had ceased to express his fondness for her in words, and recoiled with angry suspicion from her girlish caresses, as if conscious there could be no gratification in lavishing such marks of affection on him. On the before-named occasion he came into the house to announce his intention of doing nothing, while I was assisting Miss Cathy to arrange her dress: she had not reckoned on his taking it into his head to be idle, and imagining she would have the whole place to herself, she managed, by some means, to inform Mr. Edgar of her brother's absence, and was then preparing to receive him.

"Cathy, are you busy, this afternoon?" asked Heathcliff. "Are you going anywhere?"

"No, it is raining," she answered.

"Why have you that silk frock on, then?" he said. "Nobody coming here, I hope?"

"Not that I know of," stammered Miss, "but you should be in the field now, Heathcliff. It is an hour past dinner time; I thought you were gone."

"Hindley does not often free us from his accursed presence," observed the boy. "I'll not work any more to-day, I'll stay with you."

"O, but Joseph will tell," she suggested. "You'd better go!"

"Joseph is loading lime on the farther side of Pennistow Crag; it will take him till dark, and he'll never know."

So saying he lounged to the fire, and sat down. Catherine reflected an instant, with knitted brows—she found it needful to smooth the way for an intrusion.

"Isabella and Edgar Linton talked of calling this afternoon," she said, at the conclusion of a minute's silence. "As it rains, I hardly expect them; but they may come, and if they do, you run the risk of being scolded for no good."

"Order Ellen to say you are engaged, Cathy," he persisted. "Don't turn me out for those pitiful, silly friends of yours! I'm on the point, sometimes, of complaining that they—but I'll not—"

"That they what?" cried Catherine, gazing at him with a troubled countenance. "Oh, Nelly!" she added petulantly, jerking her head away from my hands, "you've combed my hair quite out of curl! That's enough, let me alone. What are you on the point of complaining about, Heathcliff?"

"Nothing—only look at the almanack on that wall." He pointed to a framed sheet hanging near the window, and continued—

"The crosses are for the evenings you have spent with the Lintons, the dots for those spent with me. Do you see? I've marked every day."

"Yes—very foolish; as if I took notice!" replied Catherine in a peevish tone. "And where is the sense of that?"

"To show that I *do* take notice," said Heathcliff.

"And should I always be sitting with you?" she demanded, growing more irritated. "What good do I get? What do you talk about? You might be dumb or a baby for anything you say to amuse me, or for anything you do, either!"

"You never told me before that I talked too little, or that you disliked my company, Cathy!" exclaimed Heathcliff in much agitation.

"It is no company at all, when people know nothing and say nothing," she muttered.

Her companion rose up, but he hadn't time to express his feelings further, for a horse's feet were heard on the flags, and, having knocked gently, young Linton entered, his face brilliant with delight at the unexpected summons he had received.

Doubtless Catherine marked the difference between her friends as one came in, and the other went out. The contrast resembled what you see in exchanging a bleak, hilly, coal country, for a beautiful fertile valley; and his voice and greeting were as opposite as his aspect. He had a sweet, low manner of speaking, and pronounced his words as you do: that's less gruff than we talk here, and softer.

"I'm not come too soon, am I?" he said, casting a look at me. I had begun to wipe the plate, and tidy some drawers at the far end in the dresser.

"No," answered Catherine. "What are you doing there, Nelly?"

"My work, Miss," I replied. (Mr. Hindley had given me directions to make a third party in any private visits Linton chose to pay.)

She stepped behind me and whispered crossly, "Take yourself and your dusters off; when company are in the house, servants don't commence scouring and cleaning in the room where they are!"

"It's a good opportunity, now that master is away," I answered aloud: "he hates me to be fidgetting over these things in his presence. I'm sure Mr. Edgar will excuse me."

"I hate you to be fidgetting in *my* presence," exclaimed the young lady imperiously, not allowing her guest time to speak. She had failed to recover her equanimity since the little dispute with Heathcliff.

"I'm sorry for it, Miss Catherine!" was my response; and I proceeded assiduously with my occupation.

She, supposing Edgar could not see her, snatched the cloth from my hand, and pinched me, with a prolonged wrench, very spitefully on the arm.

I've said I did not love her, and rather relished mortifying her vanity, now and then; besides, she hurt me extremely, so I started up from my knees, and screamed out—

"O, Miss, that's a nasty trick! you have no right to nip me, and I'm not going to bear it!"

"I didn't touch you, you lying creature!" cried she, her fingers tingling to repeat the act, and her ears red with rage. She never had power to conceal her passion, it always set her whole complexion in a blaze.

"What's that, then?" I retorted, showing a decided purple witness to refute her.

She stamped her foot, wavered a moment, and then, irresistibly impelled by the naughty spirit within her, slapped me on the cheek a stinging blow that filled both eyes with water.

"Catherine, love! Catherine!" interposed Linton, greatly shocked at the double fault of falsehood and violence which his idol had committed.

"Leave the room, Ellen!" she repeated, trembling all over.

Little Hareton, who followed me everywhere, and was sitting near me on the floor, at seeing my tears commenced crying himself, and sobbed out complaints against "wicked Aunt Cathy," which drew her fury on to his unlucky head: she seized his shoulders, and shook him till the poor child waxed livid, and Edgar thoughtlessly laid hold of her hands to deliver him. In an instant one was wrung free, and the astonished young man felt it applied over his own ear in a way that could not be mistaken for jest.

He drew back in consternation. I lifted Hareton in my arms, and walked off to the kitchen with him, leaving the door of communication open, for I was curious to watch how they would settle their disagreement.

The insulted visitor moved to the spot where he had laid his hat, pale and with a quivering lip.

"That's right!" I said to myself. "Take warning and begone! It's a kindness to let you have a glimpse of her genuine disposition."

"Where are you going?" demanded Catherine, advancing to the door.

He swerved aside and attempted to pass.

"You must not go!" she exclaimed energetically.

"I must and shall!" he replied in a subdued voice.

"No," she persisted, grasping the handle; "not yet, Edgar Linton —sit down; you shall not leave me in that temper. I should be miserable all night, and I won't be miserable for you!"

"Can I stay after you have struck me?" asked Linton.

Catherine was mute.

"You've made me afraid, and ashamed of you," he continued; "I'll not come here again!"

Her eyes began to glisten and her lids to twinkle.

"And you told a deliberate untruth!" he said.

"I didn't!" she cried, recovering her speech. "I did nothing deliberately—Well, go, if you please—get away! And now I'll cry— I'll cry myself sick!"

She dropped down on her knees by a chair and set to weeping in serious earnest.

Edgar persevered in his resolution as far as the court; there he lingered. I resolved to encourage him.

"Miss is dreadfully wayward, sir!" I called out. "As bad as any marred child[2] —you'd better be riding home, or else she will be sick, only to grieve us."

The soft thing looked askance through the window: he possessed the power to depart, as much as a cat possesses the power to leave a mouse half killed, or a bird half eaten.

Ah, I thought, there will be no saving him—He's doomed, and flies to his fate!

And so it was; he turned abruptly, hastened into the house again, shut the door behind him; and, when I went in a while after to inform them that Earnshaw had come home rabid drunk, ready to pull the old place about our ears (his ordinary frame of mind in that condition), I saw the quarrel had merely effected a closer intimacy—had broken the outworks of youthful timidity, and enabled them to forsake the disguise of friendship, and confess themselves lovers.

Intelligence of Mr. Hindley's arrival drove Linton speedily to his horse, and Catherine to her chamber. I went to hide little Hareton, and to take the shot out of the master's fowling piece, which he was fond of playing with in his insane excitement, to the hazard of the lives of any who provoked, or even attracted his notice too much; and I had hit upon the plan of removing it, that he might do less mischief, if he did go the length of firing the gun.

2. Spoiled child.

## Chapter IX

He entered, vociferating oaths dreadful to hear; and caught me in the act of stowing his son away in the kitchen cupboard. Hareton was impressed with a wholesome terror of encountering either his wild beast's fondness or his madman's rage; for in one he ran a chance of being squeezed and kissed to death, and in the other of being flung into the fire, or dashed against the wall; and the poor thing remained perfectly quiet wherever I chose to put him.

"There, I've found it out at last!" cried Hindley, pulling me back by the skin of the neck, like a dog. "By heaven and hell, you've sworn between you to murder that child! I know how it is, now, that he is always out of my way. But, with the help of Satan, I shall make you swallow the carving knife, Nelly! You needn't laugh; for I've just crammed Kenneth, head-downmost, in the Blackhorse marsh; and two is the same as one—and I want to kill some of you, I shall have no rest till I do!"

"But I don't like the carving knife, Mr. Hindley," I answered; "it has been cutting red herrings. I'd rather be shot, if you please."

"You'd rather be damned!" he said, "and so you shall. No law in England can hinder a man from keeping his house decent, and mine's abominable! open your mouth."

He held the knife in his hand, and pushed its point between my teeth: but, for my part, I was never much afraid of his vagaries. I spat out, and affirmed it tasted detestably—I would not take it on any account.

"Oh!" said he, releasing me, "I see that hideous little villain is not Hareton: I beg your pardon, Nell. If it be, he deserves flaying alive for not running to welcome me, and for screaming as if I were a goblin. Unnatural cub, come hither! I'll teach thee to impose on a good-hearted, deluded father. Now, don't you think the lad would be handsomer cropped? It makes a dog fiercer, and I love something fierce—get me a scissors—something fierce and trim! Besides, it's infernal affectation—devilish conceit it is—to cherish our ears: we're asses enough without them. Hush, child, hush! well, then, it is my darling! wisht,[1] dry thy eyes—there's a joy; kiss me; what! it won't? kiss me, Hareton! Damn thee, kiss me! By God, as if I would rear such a monster! As sure as I'm living, I'll break the brat's neck."

Poor Hareton was squalling and kicking in his father's arms with all his might, and redoubled his yells when he carried him upstairs and lifted him over the banister. I cried out that he would frighten the child into fits, and ran to rescue him.

As I reached them, Hindley leant forward on the rails to listen

1. Be quiet.

to a noise below, almost forgetting what he had in his hands.

"Who is that?" he asked, hearing some one approaching the stair's foot.

I leant forward also, for the purpose of signing to Heathcliff, whose step I recognized, not to come further; and, at the instant when my eye quitted Hareton, he gave a sudden spring, delivered himself from the careless grasp that held him, and fell.

There was scarcely time to experience a thrill of horror before we saw that the little wretch was safe. Heathcliff arrived underneath just at the critical moment; by a natural impulse, he arrested his descent, and setting him on his feet, looked up to discover the author of the accident.

A miser who has parted with a lucky lottery ticket for five shillings, and finds next day he has lost in the bargain five thousand pounds, could not show a blanker countenance than he did on beholding the figure of Mr. Earnshaw above. It expressed, plainer than words could do, the intensest anguish at having made himself the instrument of thwarting his own revenge. Had it been dark, I dare say, he would have tried to remedy the mistake by smashing Hareton's skull on the steps; but we witnessed his salvation; and I was presently below with my precious charge pressed to my heart.

Hindley descended more leisurely, sobered and abashed.

"It is your fault, Ellen," he said, "you should have kept him out of sight; you should have taken him from me! Is he injured anywhere?"

"Injured!" I cried angrily, "If he's not killed, he'll be an idiot! Oh! I wonder his mother does not rise from her grave to see how you use him. You're worse than a heathen—treating your own flesh and blood in that manner!"

He attempted to touch the child, who, on finding himself with me, sobbed off his terror directly. At the first finger his father laid on him, however, he shrieked again louder than before, and struggled as if he would go into convulsions.

"You shall not meddle with him!" I continued, "He hates you —they all hate you—that's the truth! A happy family you have; and a pretty state you're come to!"

"I shall come to a prettier, yet, Nelly!" laughed the misguided man, recovering his hardness. "At present, convey yourself and him away. And, hark you, Heathcliff! clear you too, quite from my reach and hearing. I wouldn't murder you to-night, unless, perhaps, I set the house on fire; but that's as my fancy goes—"

While saying this he took a pint bottle of brandy from the dresser, and poured some into a tumbler.

"Nay, don't!" I entreated, "Mr. Hindley, do take warning. Have mercy on this unfortunate boy, if you care nothing for yourself!"

"Any one will do better for him than I shall," he answered.

"Have mercy on your own soul!" I said, endeavouring to snatch the glass from his hand.

"Not I! on the contrary, I shall have great pleasure in sending it to perdition, to punish its Maker," exclaimed the blasphemer. "Here's to its hearty damnation!"

He drank the spirits, and impatiently bade us go; terminating his command with a sequel of horrid imprecations, too bad to repeat or remember.

"It's a pity he cannot kill himself with drink," observed Heathcliff, muttering an echo of curses back when the door was shut. "He's doing his very utmost; but his constitution defies him. Mr. Kenneth says he would wager his mare, that he'll outlive any man on this side Gimmerton, and go to the grave a hoary sinner; unless some happy chance out of the common course befall him."

I went into the kitchen and sat down to lull my little lamb to sleep. Heathcliff, as I thought, walked through to the barn. It turned out, afterwards, that he only got as far as the other side the settle, when he flung himself on a bench by the wall, removed from the fire, and remained silent.

I was rocking Hareton on my knee, and humming a song that began—

"It was far in the night, and the bairnies grat,
The mither beneath the mools heard that,"[2]

when Miss Cathy, who had listened to the hubbub from her room, put her head in, and whispered—

"Are you alone, Nelly?"

"Yes, Miss," I replied.

She entered and approached the hearth. I, supposing she was going to say something, looked up. The expression of her face seemed disturbed and anxious. Her lips were half asunder as if she meant to speak; and she drew a breath, but it escaped in a sigh, instead of a sentence.

I resumed my song, not having forgotten her recent behaviour.

"Where's Heathcliff?" she said, interrupting me.

"About his work in the stable," was my answer.

He did not contradict me; perhaps he had fallen into a doze.

There followed another long pause, during which I perceived a drop or two trickle from Catherine's cheek to the flags.

Is she sorry for her shameful conduct? I asked myself. That will be a novelty, but she may come to the point as she will—I shan't help her!

No, she felt small trouble regarding any subject, save her own

2. *Bairnies grat:* little ones wept; *mools:* earth of a grave.

concerns.

"Oh, dear!" she cried at last. "I'm very unhappy!"

"A pity," observed I. "You're hard to please—so many friends and so few cares, and can't make yourself content!"

"Nelly, will you keep a secret for me?" she pursued, kneeling down by me, and lifting her winsome eyes to my face with that sort of look which turns off bad temper, even when one has all the right in the world to indulge it.

"Is it worth keeping?" I inquired, less sulkily.

"Yes, and it worries me, and I must let it out! I want to know what I should do. To-day, Edgar Linton has asked me to marry him, and I've given him an answer. Now, before I tell you whether it was a consent, or denial, you tell me which it ought to have been."

"Really, Miss Catherine, how can I know?" I replied. "To be sure, considering the exhibition you performed in his presence this afternoon, I might say it would be wise to refuse him: since he asked you after that, he must either be hopelessly stupid or a venturesome fool."

"If you talk so, I won't tell you any more," she returned, pee-vishly, rising to her feet, "I accepted him, Nelly. Be quick, and say whether I was wrong!"

"You accepted him? then, what good is it discussing the matter? You have pledged your word, and cannot retract."

"But, say whether I should have done so—do!" she exclaimed in an irritated tone, chafing her hands together, and frowning.

"There are many things to be considered before that question can be answered properly," I said sententiously. "First and fore-most, do you love Mr. Edgar?"

"Who can help it? Of course I do," she answered.

Then I put her through the following catechism: for a girl of twenty-two, it was not injudicious.

"Why do you love him, Miss Cathy?"

"Nonsense, I do—that's sufficient."

"By no means; you must say why."

"Well, because he is handsome, and pleasant to be with."

"Bad," was my commentary.

"And because he is young and cheerful."

"Bad, still."

"And because he loves me."

"Indifferent, coming there."

"And he will be rich, and I shall like to be the greatest woman of the neighbourhood, and I shall be proud of having such a hus-band."

"Worst of all! And now, say how you love him."

"As everybody loves—You're silly, Nelly."

"Not at all—Answer."

"I love the ground under his feet, and the air over his head, and everything he touches, and every word he says—I love all his looks, and all his actions, and him entirely, and altogether. There now!"

"And why?"

"Nay—you are making a jest of it; it is exceedingly ill-natured! It's no jest to me!" said the young lady, scowling, and turning her face to the fire.

"I'm very far from jesting, Miss Catherine," I replied. "You love Mr. Edgar, because he is handsome, and young, and cheerful, and rich, and loves you. The last, however, goes for nothing. You would love him without that, probably; and with it, you wouldn't, unless he possessed the four former attractions."

"No, to be sure not: I should only pity him—hate him, perhaps, if he were ugly, and a clown."

"But there are several other handsome, rich young men in the world; handsomer, possibly, and richer than he is. What should hinder you from loving them?"

"If there be any, they are out of my way. I've seen none like Edgar."

"You may see some; and he won't always be handsome, and young, and may not always be rich."

"He is now; and I have only to do with the present. I wish you would speak rationally."

"Well, that settles it—if you have only to do with the present, marry Mr. Linton."

"I don't want your permission for that—I *shall* marry him; and yet you have not told me whether I'm right."

"Perfectly right; if people be right to marry only for the present. And now, let us hear what you are unhappy about. Your brother will be pleased; the old lady and gentleman will not object, I think; you will escape from a disorderly, comfortless home into a wealthy, respectable one; and you love Edgar, and Edgar loves you. All seems smooth and easy—where is the obstacle?"

"*Here!* and *here!*" replied Catherine, striking one hand on her forehead, and the other on her breast. "In whichever place the soul lives—in my soul, and in my heart, I'm convinced I'm wrong!"

"That's very strange! I cannot make it out."

"It's my secret; but if you will not mock at me, I'll explain it; I can't do it distinctly, but I'll give you a feeling of how I feel."

She seated herself by me again: her countenance grew sadder and graver, and her clasped hands trembled.

"Nelly, do you never dream queer dreams?" she said, suddenly, after some minutes' reflection.

"Yes, now and then," I answered.

"And so do I. I've dreamt in my life dreams that have stayed with me ever after, and changed my ideas; they've gone through and through me, like wine through water, and altered the colour of my mind. And this is one—I'm going to tell it—but take care not to smile at any part of it."

"Oh! don't, Miss Catherine!" I cried. "We're dismal enough without conjuring up ghosts and visions to perplex us. Come, come, be merry, and like yourself! Look at little Hareton—*he's* dreaming nothing dreary. How sweetly he smiles in his sleep!"

"Yes; and how sweetly his father curses in his solitude! You remember him, I dare say, when he was just such another as that chubby thing—nearly as young and innocent. However, Nelly, I shall oblige you to listen—it's not long; and I've no power to be merry to-night."

"I won't hear it, I won't hear it!" I repeated, hastily.

I was superstitious about dreams then, and am still; and Catherine had an unusual gloom in her aspect, that made me dread something from which I might shape a prophecy, and foresee a fearful catastrophe.

She was vexed, but she did not proceed. Apparently taking up another subject, she recommenced in a short time.

"If I were in heaven, Nelly, I should be extremely miserable."

"Because you are not fit to go there," I answered. "All sinners would be miserable in heaven."

"But it is not for that. I dreamt, once, that I was there."

"I tell you I won't harken to your dreams, Miss Catherine! I'll go to bed," I interrupted again.

She laughed, and held me down, for I made a motion to leave my chair.

"This is nothing," cried she; "I was only going to say that heaven did not seem to be my home; and I broke my heart with weeping to come back to earth; and the angels were so angry that they flung me out, into the middle of the heath on the top of Wuthering Heights; where I woke sobbing for joy. That will do to explain my secret, as well as the other. I've no more business to marry Edgar Linton than I have to be in heaven; and if the wicked man in there had not brought Heathcliff so low, I shouldn't have thought of it. It would degrade me to marry Heathcliff now; so he shall never know how I love him; and that, not because he's handsome, Nelly, but because he's more myself than I am. Whatever our souls are made of, his and mine are the same, and Linton's is as different as a moonbeam from lightning, or frost from fire."

Ere this speech ended, I became sensible of Heathcliff's presence. Having noticed a slight movement, I turned my head, and saw him rise from the bench, and steal out, noiselessly. He had listened till he heard Catherine say it would degrade her to marry him, and then he stayed to hear no farther.

My companion, sitting on the ground, was prevented by the back of the settle from remarking his presence or departure; but I started, and bade her hush!

"Why?" she asked, gazing nervously round.

"Joseph is here," I answered, catching, opportunely, the roll of his cartwheels up the road; "and Heathcliff will come in with him. I'm not sure whether he were not at the door this moment."

"Oh, he couldn't overhear me at the door!" said she. "Give me Hareton, while you get the supper, and when it is ready ask me to sup with you. I want to cheat my uncomfortable conscience, and be convinced that Heathcliff has no notion of these things. He has not, has he? He does not know what being in love is?"

"I see no reason that he should not know, as well as you," I returned; "and if *you* are his choice, he'll be the most unfortunate creature that ever was born! As soon as you become Mrs. Linton, he loses friend, and love, and all! Have you considered how you'll bear the separation, and how he'll bear to be quite deserted in the world? Because, Miss Catherine—"

"He quite deserted! we separated!" she exclaimed, with an accent of indignation. "Who is to separate us, pray? They'll meet the fate of Milo![3] Not as long as I live, Ellen—for no mortal creature. Every Linton on the face of the earth might melt into nothing, before I could consent to forsake Heathcliff. Oh, that's not what I intend—that's not what I mean! I shouldn't be Mrs. Linton were such a price demanded! He'll be as much to me as he has been all his lifetime. Edgar must shake off his antipathy, and tolerate him, at least. He will when he learns my true feelings towards him. Nelly, I see now, you think me a selfish wretch, but, did it never strike you that if Heathcliff and I married, we should be beggars? whereas, if I marry Linton, I can aid Heathcliff to rise, and place him out of my brother's power."

"With your husband's money, Miss Catherine?" I asked. "You'll find him not so pliable as you calculate upon: and, though I'm hardly a judge, I think that's the worst motive you've given yet for being the wife of young Linton."

"It is not," retorted she, "it is the best! The others were the satisfaction of my whims; and for Edgar's sake, too, to satisfy him. This is for the sake of one who comprehends in his person my feelings to Edgar and myself. I cannot express it; but surely you and everybody have a notion that there is, or should be, an exist-

3. An athlete of Crotona, who, caught by the tree he was trying to split, was eaten up by wild beasts.

ence of yours beyond you. What were the use of my creation if I were entirely contained here? My great miseries in this world have been Heathcliff's miseries, and I watched and felt each from the beginning; my great thought in living is himself. If all else perished, and *he* remained, I should still continue to be; and, if all else remained, and he were annihilated, the Universe would turn to a mighty stranger. I should not seem a part of it. My love for Linton is like the foliage in the woods. Time will change it, I'm well aware, as winter changes the trees. My love for Heathcliff resembles the eternal rocks beneath—a source of little visible delight, but necessary. Nelly, I *am* Heathcliff—he's always, always in my mind —not as a pleasure, any more than I am always a pleasure to myself—but as my own being—so, don't talk of our separation again—it is impracticable; and—"

She paused, and hid her face in the folds of my gown; but I jerked it forcibly away. I was out of patience with her folly!

"If I can make any sense of your nonsense, Miss," I said, "it only goes to convince me that you are ignorant of the duties you undertake in marrying; or else that you are a wicked, unprincipled girl. But trouble me with no more secrets. I'll not promise to keep them."

"You'll keep that?" she asked, eagerly.

"No, I'll not promise," I repeated.

She was about to insist, when the entrance of Joseph finished our conversation; and Catherine removed her seat to a corner, and nursed Hareton, while I made the supper.

After it was cooked, my fellow servant and I began to quarrel who should carry some to Mr. Hindley; and we didn't settle it till all was nearly cold. Then we came to the agreement that we would let him ask, if he wanted any, for we feared particularly to go into his presence when he had been some time alone.

"Und hah isn't that nowt comed in frough th' field, be this time? What is he abaht? girt eedle seeght!"[4] demanded the old man, looking round for Heathcliff.

"I'll call him," I replied. "He's in the barn, I've no doubt."

I went and called, but got no answer. On returning, I whispered to Catherine that he had heard a good part of what she said, I was sure; and told how I saw him quit the kitchen just as she complained of her brother's conduct regarding him.

She jumped up in a fine fright, flung Hareton onto the settle, and ran to seek for her friend herself, not taking leisure to consider why she was so flurried, or how her talk would have affected him.

She was absent such a while that Joseph proposed we should

4. "And how isn't that nothing come in from the field by this time?"; *Girt eedle seeght:* great idle sight.

wait no longer. He cunningly conjectured they were staying away in order to avoid hearing his protracted blessing. They were "ill eneugh for ony fahl manners," he affirmed. And, on their behalf, he added that night a special prayer to the usual quarter of an hour's supplication before meat, and would have tacked another to the end of the grace, had not his young mistress broken in upon him with a hurried command that he must run down the road, and, wherever Heathcliff had rambled, find and make him re-enter directly!

"I want to speak to him, and I *must*, before I go upstairs," she said. "And the gate is open, he is somewhere out of hearing; for he would not reply, though I shouted at the top of the fold as loud as I could."

Joseph objected at first; she was too much in earnest, however, to suffer contradiction; and at last he placed his hat on his head, and walked grumbling forth.

Meantime, Catherine paced up and down the floor, exclaiming—

"I wonder where he is—I wonder where he *can* be! What did I say, Nelly? I've forgotten. Was he vexed at my bad humour this afternoon? Dear! tell me what I've said to grieve him. I do wish he'd come. I do wish he would!"

"What a noise for nothing!" I cried, though rather uneasy myself. "What a trifle scares you! It's surely no great cause of alarm that Heathcliff should take a moonlight saunter on the moors, or even lie too sulky to speak to us, in the hay-loft. I'll engage he's lurking there. See if I don't ferret him out!"

I departed to renew my search; its result was disappointment, and Joseph's quest ended in the same.

"Yon lad gets war un war!" observed he on re-entering. "He's left th' yate ut t' full swing, and Miss's pony has trodden dahn two rigs uh corn, un plottered through, raight o'er intuh t' meadow! Hahsomdiver, t' maister 'ull play t' divil to-morn, and he'll do weel. He's patience itsseln wi' sich careless, offald craters—patience itsseln, he is! Bud he'll nut be soa allus—yah's see, all on ye! Yah mumn't drive him aht uf his heead fur nowt!"[5]

"Have you found Heathcliff, you ass?" interrupted Catherine. "Have you been looking for him, as I ordered?"

"Aw sud more likker look for th' horse," he replied. "It 'ud be tuh more sense. Bud Aw can look for norther horse, nur man uf a neeght loike this—as black as t' chimbley![6] und Hathecliff's noan t' chap tuh coom ut *maw* whistle—happen he'll be less hard uh hearing wi' *ye!*"

5. *War un war:* worse and worse; *yate:* gate; *rigs:* ridges; *plottered:* scrambled; *hahsomdiver:* howsoever; *offald:* worthless, good-for-nothing.

6. *Sud:* should; *likker:* comparative of like; *norther . . . nur:* neither . . . nor; *neeght:* night.

It *was* a very dark evening for summer: the clouds appeared in-clined to thunder, and I said we had better all sit down; the ap-proaching rain would be certain to bring him home without further trouble.

However, Catherine would not be persuaded into tranquillity. She kept wandering to and fro, from the gate to the door, in a state of agitation which permitted no repose; and at length took up a permanent situation on one side of the wall, near the road, where, heedless of my expostulations, and the growling thunder, and the great drops that began to plash around her, she remained, calling at intervals, and then listening, and then crying outright. She beat Hareton, or any child, at a good, passionate fit of crying.

About midnight, while we still sat up, the storm came rattling over the Heights in full fury. There was a violent wind, as well as thunder, and either one or the other split a tree off at the corner of the building; a huge bough fell across the roof, and knocked down a portion of the east chimney-stack, sending a clatter of stones and soot into the kitchen fire.

We thought a bolt had fallen in the middle of us, and Joseph swung onto his knees, beseeching the Lord to remember the Pa-triarchs Noah and Lot; and, as in former times, spare the righteous, though he smote the ungodly. I felt some sentiment that it must be a judgment on us also. The Jonah, in my mind, was Mr. Earn-shaw, and I shook the handle of his den that I might ascertain if he were yet living. He replied audibly enough, in a fashion which made my companion vociferate more clamorously than before that a wide distinction might be drawn between saints like himself, and sinners like his master. But the uproar passed away in twenty minutes, leaving us all unharmed, excepting Cathy, who got thor-oughly drenched for her obstinacy in refusing to take shelter, and standing bonnetless and shawlless to catch as much water as she could with her hair and clothes.

She came in and lay down on the settle, all soaked as she was, turning her face to the back, and putting her hands before it.

"Well, Miss!" I exclaimed, touching her shoulder; "you are not bent on getting your death, are you? Do you know what o'clock it is? Half-past twelve. Come! come to bed; there's no use waiting longer on that foolish boy—he'll be gone to Gimmerton, and he'll stay there now. He guesses we shouldn't wake[7] for him till this late hour; at least, he guesses that only Mr. Hindley would be up; and he'd rather avoid having the door opened by the master."

"Nay, nay, he's noan at Gimmerton!" said Joseph. "Aw's niver wonder, bud he's at t' bothom uf a bog-hoile.[8] This visitation worn't for nowt, und Aw wod hev ye tuh look aht, Miss—yah muh

7. Wait up.                     8. Bottom of a bog-hole.

be t' next. Thank Hivin for all! All warks togither for gooid tuh them as is chozzen and piked aht froo' th' rubbidge![9] Yah knaw whet t' Scripture ses—"

And he began quoting several texts; referring us to the chapters and verses where we might find them.

I, having vainly begged the wilful girl to rise and remove her wet things, left him preaching and her shivering, and betook myself to bed with little Hareton, who slept as fast as if every one had been sleeping round him.

I heard Joseph read on a while afterwards; then I distinguished his slow step on the ladder, and then I dropt asleep.

Coming down somewhat later than usual, I saw, by the sunbeams piercing the chinks of the shutters, Miss Catherine still seated near the fire-place. The house door was ajar, too; light entered from its unclosed windows; Hindley had come out, and stood on the kitchen hearth, haggard and drowsy.

"What ails you, Cathy?" he was saying when I entered; "you look as dismal as a drowned whelp. Why are you so damp and pale, child?"

"I've been wet," she answered reluctantly, "and I'm cold, that's all."

"Oh, she is naughty!" I cried, perceiving the master to be tolerably sober. "She got steeped in the shower of yesterday evening, and there she has sat the night through, and I couldn't prevail on her to stir."

Mr. Earnshaw stared at us in surprise. "The night through," he repeated. "What kept her up, not fear of the thunder, surely? That was over, hours since."

Neither of us wished to mention Heathcliff's absence, as long as we could conceal it; so I replied, I didn't know how she took it into her head to sit up; and she said nothing.

The morning was fresh and cool; I threw back the lattice, and presently the room filled with sweet scents from the garden; but Catherine called peevishly to me—

"Ellen, shut the window. I'm starving!" And her teeth chattered as she shrunk closer to the almost extinguished embers.

"She's ill," said Hindley, taking her wrist, "I suppose that's the reason she would not go to bed. Damn it! I don't want to be troubled with more sickness here. What took you into the rain?"

"Running after t'lads, as usuald!" croaked Joseph, catching an opportunity, from our hesitation, to thrust in his evil tongue. "If Aw wur yah, maister, Aw'd just slam t'boards i' their faces all on 'em, gentle and simple! Never a day ut yah're off, but yon cat uh Linton comes sneaking hither; and Miss Nelly shoo's a fine

9. Picked out from the rubbish.

lass! shoo sits watching for ye i' t'kitchen; and as yah're in at one door, he's aht at t'other; und, then, wer grand lady goes a coorting uf hor side![1] It's bonny behaviour, lurking amang t'flields, after twelve ut' night, wi that fahl, flaysome divil uf a gipsy, Heathcliff! They think *Aw'm* blind; but Aw'm noan, nowt ut t'soart! Aw seed young Linton, boath coming and going, and Aw seed *yah*" (directing his discourse to me), "yah gooid fur nowt, slattenly witch! nip up und bolt intuh th' hahs, t' minute yah heard t'maister's horse fit clatter up t' road."[2]

"Silence, eavesdropper!" cried Catherine. "None of your insolence before me! Edgar Linton came yesterday, by chance, Hindley; and it was *I* who told him to be off, because I knew you would not like to have met him as you were."

"You lie, Cathy, no doubt," answered her brother, "and you are a confounded simpleton! But never mind Linton, at present. Tell me, were you not with Heathcliff last night? Speak the truth, now. You need not be afraid of harming him: though I hate him as much as ever, he did me a good turn a short time since, that will make my conscience tender of breaking his neck. To prevent it, I shall send him about his business this very morning; and after he's gone, I'd advise you all to look sharp, I shall only have the more humour for you!"

"I never saw Heathcliff last night," answered Catherine, beginning to sob bitterly: "and if you do turn him out of doors, I'll go with him. But, perhaps, you'll never have an opportunity—perhaps, he's gone." Here she burst into uncontrollable grief, and the remainder of her words were inarticulate.

Hindley lavished on her a torrent of scornful abuse, and bid her get to her room immediately, or she shouldn't cry for nothing! I obliged her to obey; and I shall never forget what a scene she acted, when we reached her chamber. It terrified me. I thought she was going mad, and I begged Joseph to run for the doctor.

It proved the commencement of delirium; Mr. Kenneth, as soon as he saw her, pronounced her dangerously ill; she had a fever.

He bled her, and he told me to let her live on whey and watergruel, and take care she did not throw herself downstairs, or out of the window; and then he left, for he had enough to do in the parish where two or three miles was the ordinary distance between cottage and cottage.

Though I cannot say I made a gentle nurse, and Joseph and the master were no better; and though our patient was as wearisome and headstrong as a patient could be, she weathered it through.

Old Mrs. Linton paid us several visits, to be sure, and set things

1. *T'boards:* the doors; *cat:* a term of contempt; *shoo's:* she's; *wer grand lady:* our grand lady.

2. *Nowt ut t'soart:* nothing of the sort; *slattenly:* slovenly; *hahs:* house; *horse fit:* horse feet.

to rights, and scolded and ordered us all; and when Catherine was convalescent, she insisted on conveying her to Thrushcross Grange: for which deliverance we were very grateful. But the poor dame had reason to repent of her kindness; she and her husband both took the fever, and died within a few days of each other.

Our young lady returned to us, saucier and more passionate, and haughtier than ever. Heathcliff had never been heard of since the' evening of the thunder-storm, and, one day, I had the misfortune, when she had provoked me exceedingly, to lay the blame of his disappearance on her (where indeed it belonged, as she well knew). From that period, for several months, she ceased to hold any communication with me, save in the relation of a mere servant. Joseph fell under a ban also; he *would* speak his mind, and lecture her all the same as if she were a little girl; and she esteemed herself a woman, and our mistress, and thought that her recent illness gave her a claim to be treated with consideration. Then the doctor had said that she would not bear crossing much, she ought to have her own way; and it was nothing less than murder, in her eyes, for any one to presume to stand up and contradict her.

From Mr. Earnshaw and his companions she kept aloof; and tutored by Kenneth, and serious threats of a fit that often attended her rages, her brother allowed her whatever she pleased to demand, and generally avoided aggravating her fiery temper. He was rather *too* indulgent in humouring her caprices; not from affection, but from pride, he wished earnestly to see her bring honour to the family by an alliance with the Lintons, and, as long as she let him alone, she might trample us like slaves for ought he cared!

Edgar Linton, as multitudes have been before and will be after him, was infatuated; and believed himself the happiest man alive on the day he led her to Gimmerton chapel, three years subsequent to his father's death.

Much against my inclination, I was persuaded to leave Wuthering Heights and accompany her here. Little Hareton was nearly five years old, and I had just begun to teach him his letters. We made a sad parting, but Catherine's tears were more powerful than ours. When I refused to go, and when she found her entreaties did not move me, she went lamenting to her husband and brother. The former offered me munificent wages; the latter ordered me to pack up. He wanted no women in the house, he said, now that there was no mistress; and as to Hareton, the curate should take him in hand, by and by. And so I had but one choice left, to do as I was ordered. I told the master he got rid of all decent people only to run to ruin a little faster; I kissed Hareton good-bye; and, since then, he has been a stranger, and it's very queer to think it, but I've no doubt he has completely forgotten all about Ellen

Dean and that he was ever more than all the world to her, and she to him!

At this point of the housekeeper's story, she chanced to glance towards the time-piece over the chimney; and was in amazement on seeing the minute-hand measure half-past one. She would not hear of staying a second longer. In truth, I felt rather disposed to defer the sequel of her narrative myself: and now that she is vanished to her rest, and I have meditated for another hour or two, I shall summon courage to go, also, in spite of aching laziness of head and limbs.

## Chapter X

A charming introduction to a hermit's life! Four weeks' torture, tossing and sickness! Oh, these bleak winds, and bitter, northern skies, and impassable roads, and dilatory country surgeons! And, oh, this dearth of the human physiognomy, and, worse than all, the terrible intimation of Kenneth that I need not expect to be out of doors till spring!

Mr. Heathcliff has just honoured me with a call. About seven days ago he sent me a brace of grouse—the last of the season. Scoundrel! He is not altogether guiltless in this illness of mine; and that I had a great mind to tell him. But, alas! how could I offend a man who was charitable enough to sit at my bedside a good hour, and talk on some other subject than pills and draughts, blisters and leeches?

This is quite an easy interval. I am too weak to read, yet I feel as if I could enjoy something interesting. Why not have up Mrs. Dean to finish her tale? I can recollect its chief incidents, as far as she had gone. Yes, I remember her hero had run off, and never been heard of for three years; and the heroine was married. I'll ring; she'll be delighted to find me capable of talking cheerfully.

Mrs. Dean came.

"It wants twenty minutes, sir, to taking the medicine," she commenced.

"Away, away with it!" I replied; "I desire to have—"

"The doctor says you must drop the powders."

"With all my heart! Don't interrupt me. Come and take your seat here. Keep your fingers from that bitter phalanx of vials. Draw your knitting out of your pocket—that will do—now continue the history of Mr. Heathcliff, from where you left off, to the present day. Did he finish his education on the Continent, and come back a gentleman? or did he get a sizer's place at college? or escape to America, and earn honours by drawing blood from his foster country? or make a fortune more promptly, on the English highways?"

"He may have done a little in all these vocations, Mr. Lockwood; but I couldn't give my word for any. I stated before that I didn't know how he gained his money; neither am I aware of the means he took to raise his mind from the savage ignorance into which it was sunk; but, with your leave, I'll proceed in my own fashion, if you think it will amuse and not weary you. Are you feeling better this morning?"

"Much."

"That's good news."

I got Miss Catherine and myself to Thrushcross Grange; and to my agreeable disappointment, she behaved infinitely better than I dared to expect. She seemed almost over-fond of Mr. Linton; and even to his sister, she showed plenty of affection. They were both very attentive to her comfort, certainly. It was not the thorn bending to the honeysuckles, but the honeysuckles embracing the thorn. There were no mutual concessions; one stood erect, and the others yielded; and who *can* be ill-natured and bad-tempered, when they encounter neither opposition nor indifference?

I observed that Mr. Edgar had a deep-rooted fear of ruffling her humour. He concealed it from her; but if ever he heard me answer sharply, or saw any other servant grow cloudy at some imperious order of hers, he would show his trouble by a frown of displeasure that never darkened on his own account. He, many a time, spoke sternly to me about my pertness; and averred that the stab of a knife could not inflict a worse pang than he suffered at seeing his lady vexed.

Not to grieve a kind master, I learnt to be less touchy; and, for the space of half a year, the gunpowder lay as harmless as sand, because no fire came near to explode it. Catherine had seasons of gloom and silence, now and then: they were respected with sympathizing silence by her husband, who ascribed them to an alteration in her constitution, produced by her perilous illness, as she was never subject to depression of spirits before. The return of sunshine was welcomed by answering sunshine from him. I believe I may assert that they were really in possession of deep and growing happiness.

It ended. Well, we *must* be for ourselves in the long run; the mild and generous are only more justly selfish than the domineering; and it ended when circumstances caused each to feel that the one's interest was not the chief consideration in the other's thoughts.

On a mellow evening in September, I was coming from the garden with a heavy basket of apples which I had been gathering.

It had got dusk, and the moon looked over the high wall of the court, causing undefined shadows to lurk in the corners of the numerous projecting portions of the building. I set my burden on the house steps by the kitchen door, and lingered to rest and draw in a few more breaths of the soft, sweet air; my eyes were on the moon, and my back to the entrance, when I heard a voice behind me say—

"Nelly, is that you?"

It was a deep voice, and foreign in tone; yet there was something in the manner of pronouncing my name which made it sound familiar. I turned about to discover who spoke, fearfully, for the doors were shut, and I had seen nobody on approaching the steps.

Something stirred in the porch; and moving nearer, I distinguished a tall man dressed in dark clothes, with dark face and hair. He leant against the side, and held his fingers on the latch, as if intending to open for himself.

"Who can it be?" I thought. "Mr. Earnshaw? Oh, no! The voice has no resemblance to his."

"I have waited here an hour," he resumed, while I continued staring; "and the whole of that time all round has been as still as death. I dared not enter. You do not know me? Look, I'm not a stranger!"

A ray fell on his features; the cheeks were sallow, and half covered with black whiskers; the brows lowering, the eyes deep set and singular. I remembered the eyes.

"What!" I cried, uncertain whether to regard him as a worldly visitor, and I raised my hands in amazement. "What! you come back? Is it really you? Is it?"

"Yes, Heathcliff," he replied, glancing from me up to the windows, which reflected a score of glittering moons, but showed no lights from within. "Are they at home—where is she? Nelly, you are not glad—you needn't be so disturbed. Is she here? Speak! I want to have one word with her—your mistress. Go, and say some person from Gimmerton desires to see her."

"How will she take it?" I exclaimed. "What will she do? The surprise bewilders me—it will put her out of her head! And you *are* Heathcliff? But altered! Nay, there's no comprehending it. Have you been for a soldier?"

"Go, and carry my message," he interrupted impatiently; "I'm in hell till you do!"

He lifted the latch, and I entered; but when I got to the parlour where Mr. and Mrs. Linton were, I could not persuade myself to proceed.

At length, I resolved on making an excuse to ask if they would have the candles lighted, and I opened the door.

They sat together in a window whose lattice lay back against the wall, and displayed, beyond the garden trees and the wild green park, the valley of Gimmerton, with a long line of mist winding nearly to its top (for very soon after you pass the chapel, as you may have noticed, the sough that runs from the marshes joins a beck which follows the bend of the glen). Wuthering Heights rose above this silvery vapour; but our old house was invisible—it rather dips down on the other side.

Both the room and its occupants, and the scene they gazed on, looked wondrously peaceful. I shrank reluctantly from performing my errand, and was actually going away, leaving it unsaid, after having put my question about the candles, when a sense of my folly compelled me to return, and mutter—

"A person from Gimmerton wishes to see you, ma'am."

"What does he want?" asked Mrs. Linton.

"I did not question him," I answered.

"Well, close the curtains, Nelly," she said; "and bring up tea. I'll be back again directly."

She quitted the apartment; Mr. Edgar inquired carelessly, who it was?

"Some one the mistress does not expect," I replied. "That Heathcliff, you recollect him, sir, who used to live at Mr. Earnshaw's."

"What, the gipsy—the plough-boy?" he cried. "Why did you not say so to Catherine?"

"Hush! you must not call him by those names, master," I said. "She'd be sadly grieved to hear you. She was nearly heart-broken when he ran off; I guess his return will make a jubilee to her."

Mr. Linton walked to a window on the other side of the room that overlooked the court. He unfastened it, and leant out. I suppose they were below, for he exclaimed, quickly—

"Don't stand there, love! Bring the person in, if it be any one particular."

Ere long, I heard the click of the latch, and Catherine flew upstairs, breathless and wild, too excited to show gladness; indeed, by her face, you would rather have surmised an awful calamity.

"Oh, Edgar, Edgar!" she panted, flinging her arms round his neck. "Oh, Edgar, darling! Heathcliff's come back—he is!" And she tightened her embrace to a squeeze.

"Well, well," cried her husband, crossly, "don't strangle me for that! He never struck me as such a marvellous treasure. There is no need to be frantic!"

"I know you didn't like him," she answered, repressing a little the intensity of her delight. "Yet, for my sake, you must be friends now. Shall I tell him to come up?"

"Here?" he said, "into the parlour?"

"Where else?" she asked.

He looked vexed, and suggested the kitchen as a more suitable place for him.

Mrs. Linton eyed him with a droll expression—half angry, half laughing at his fastidiousness.

"No," she added, after a while; "I cannot sit in the kitchen. Set two tables here, Ellen; one for your master and Miss Isabella, being gentry; the other for Heathcliff and myself, being of the lower orders. Will that please you, dear? Or must I have a fire lighted elsewhere? If so, give directions. I'll run down and secure my guest. I'm afraid the joy is too great to be real!"

She was about to dart off again; but Edgar arrested her.

"*You* bid him step up," he said, addressing me; "and, Catherine, try to be glad, without being absurd! The whole household need not witness the sight of your welcoming a runaway servant as a brother."

I descended and found Heathcliff waiting under the porch, evidently anticipating an invitation to enter. He followed my guidance without waste of words, and I ushered him into the presence of the master and mistress, whose flushed cheeks betrayed signs of warm talking. But the lady's glowed with another feeling when her friend appeared at the door; she sprang forward, took both his hands, and led him to Linton; and then she seized Linton's reluctant fingers and crushed them into his.

Now fully revealed by the fire and candlelight, I was amazed, more than ever, to behold the transformation of Heathcliff. He had grown a tall, athletic, well-formed man, beside whom my master seemed quite slender and youth-like. His upright carriage suggested the idea of his having been in the army. His countenance was much older in expression and decision of feature than Mr. Linton's; it looked intelligent, and retained no marks of former degradation. A half-civilized ferocity lurked yet in the depressed brows and eyes full of black fire, but it was subdued; and his manner was even dignified, quite divested of roughness, though too stern for grace.

My master's surprise equalled or exceeded mine: he remained for a minute at a loss how to address the ploughboy, as he had called him. Heathcliff dropped his slight hand, and stood looking at him coolly till he chose to speak.

"Sit down, sir," he said, at length. "Mrs. Linton, recalling old times, would have me give you a cordial reception, and, of course, I am gratified when anything occurs to please her."

"And I also," answered Heathcliff, "especially if it be anything in which I have a part. I shall stay an hour or two willingly."

He took a seat opposite Catherine, who kept her gaze fixed on him as if she feared he would vanish were she to remove it. He

did not raise his to her often; a quick glance now and then sufficed;
but it flashed back, each time more confidently, the undisguised
delight he drank from hers.

They were too much absorbed in their mutual joy to suffer embarrassment. Not so Mr. Edgar; he grew pale with pure annoyance,
a feeling that reached its climax when his lady rose, and stepping
across the rug, seized Heathcliff's hands again, and laughed like
one beside herself.

"I shall think it a dream to-morrow!" she cried. "I shall not be
able to believe that I have seen, and touched, and spoken to you
once more—and yet, cruel Heathcliff! you don't deserve this welcome. To be absent and silent for three years, and never to think
of me!"

"A little more than you have thought of me!" he murmured. "I
heard of your marriage, Cathy, not long since; and, while waiting
in the yard below, I meditated this plan: just to have one glimpse
of your face, a stare of surprise, perhaps, and pretended pleasure;
afterwards settle my score with Hindley; and then prevent the law
by doing execution on myself. Your welcome has put these ideas
out of my mind; but beware of meeting me with another aspect
next time! Nay, you'll not drive me off again. You were really sorry
for me, were you? Well, there was cause. I've fought through a
bitter life since I last heard your voice, and you must forgive me,
for I struggled only for you."

"Catherine, unless we are to have cold tea, please to come to
the table," interrupted Linton, striving to preserve his ordinary
tone, and a due measure of politeness. "Mr. Heathcliff will have
a long walk, wherever he may lodge to-night; and I'm thirsty."

She took her post before the urn; and Miss Isabella came, summoned by the bell; then, having handed their chairs forward, I left
the room.

The meal hardly endured ten minutes. Catherine's cup was never
filled, she could neither eat nor drink. Edgar had made a slop in
his saucer, and scarcely swallowed a mouthful.

Their guest did not protract his stay that evening above an hour
longer. I asked, as he departed, if he went to Gimmerton?

"No, to Wuthering Heights," he answered, "Mr. Earnshaw invited me when I called this morning."

Mr. Earnshaw invited *him!* and *he* called on Mr. Earnshaw! I
pondered this sentence painfully after he was gone. Is he turning
out a bit of a hypocrite, and coming into the country to work
mischief under a cloak? I mused—I had a presentiment, in the
bottom of my heart, that he had better have remained away.

About the middle of the night, I was wakened from my first nap
by Mrs. Linton gliding into my chamber, taking a seat on my

bed-side, and pulling me by the hair to rouse me.

"I cannot rest, Ellen," she said by way of apology. "And I want some living creature to keep me company in my happiness! Edgar is sulky, because I'm glad of a thing that does not interest him. He refuses to open his mouth, except to utter pettish, silly speeches; and he affirmed I was cruel and selfish for wishing to talk when he was so sick and sleepy. He always contrives to be sick at the least cross! I gave a few sentences of commendation to Heathcliff, and he, either for a headache or a pang of envy, began to cry: so I got up and left him."

"What use is it praising Heathcliff to him?" I answered. "As lads they had an aversion to each other, and Heathcliff would hate just as much to hear him praised—it's human nature. Let Mr. Linton alone about him, unless you would like an open quarrel between them."

"But does it not show great weakness?" pursued she. "I'm not envious: I never feel hurt at the brightness of Isabella's yellow hair, and the whiteness of her skin; at her dainty elegance, and the fondness all the family exhibit for her. Even you, Nelly, if we have a dispute sometimes, you back Isabella, at once; and I yield like a foolish mother—I call her a darling, and flatter her into a good temper. It pleases her brother to see us cordial, and that pleases me. But they are very much alike; they are spoiled children, and fancy the world was made for their accommodation; and, though I humour both, I think a smart chastisement might improve them, all the same."

"You're mistaken, Mrs. Linton," said I. "They humour you: I know what there would be to do if they did not! You can well afford to indulge their passing whims, as long as their business is to anticipate all your desires. You may, however, fall out, at last, over something of equal consequence to both sides; and then those you term weak are very capable of being as obstinate as you!"

"And then we shall fight to the death, shan't we, Nelly?" she returned laughing. "No! I tell you, I have such faith in Linton's love that I believe I might kill him, and he wouldn't wish to retaliate."

I advised her to value him the more for his affection.

"I do," she answered, "but he needn't resort to whining for trifles. It is childish; and, instead of melting into tears because I said that Heathcliff was now worthy of any one's regard, and it would honour the first gentleman in the country to be his friend, he ought to have said it for me, and been delighted from sympathy. He must get accustomed to him, and he may as well like him. Considering how Heathcliff has reason to object to him, I'm sure he behaved excellently!"

"What do you think of his going to Wuthering Heights?" I inquired. "He is reformed in every respect, apparently—quite a Christian—offering the right hand of fellowship to his enemies all round!"

"He explained it," she replied. "I wondered as much as you. He said he called to gather information concerning me, from you, supposing you resided there still; and Joseph told Hindley, who came out and fell to questioning him of what he had been doing, and how he had been living; and finally, desired him to walk in. There were some persons sitting at cards; Heathcliff joined them; my brother lost some money to him; and, finding him plentifully supplied, he requested that he would come again in the evening, to which he consented. Hindley is too reckless to select his acquaintance prudently; he doesn't trouble himself to reflect on the causes he might have for mistrusting one whom he has basely injured. But Heathcliff affirms his principal reason for resuming a connection with his ancient persecutor is a wish to install himself in quarters at walking distance from the Grange, and an attachment to the house where we lived together, and likewise a hope that I shall have more opportunities of seeing him there than I could have if he settled in Gimmerton. He means to offer liberal payment for permission to lodge at the Heights; and doubtless my brother's covetousness will prompt him to accept the terms; he was always greedy, though what he grasps with one hand, he flings away with the other."

"It's a nice place for a young man to fix his dwelling in!" said I. "Have you no fear of the consequences, Mrs. Linton?"

"None for my friend," she replied. "His strong head will keep him from danger; a little for Hindley, but he can't be made morally worse than he is; and I stand between him and bodily harm. The event of this evening has reconciled me to God and humanity! I had risen in angry rebellion against providence. Oh, I've endured very, very bitter misery, Nelly! If that creature knew how bitter, he'd be ashamed to cloud its removal with idle petulance. It was kindness for him which induced me to bear it alone: had I expressed the agony I frequently felt, he would have been taught to long for its alleviation as ardently as I. However, it's over, and I'll take no revenge on his folly; I can afford to suffer anything, hereafter! Should the meanest thing alive slap me on the cheek, I'd not only turn the other, but I'd ask pardon for provoking it; and, as a proof, I'll go make my peace with Edgar instantly. Goodnight—I'm an angel!"

In this self-complacent conviction she departed; and the success of her fulfilled resolution was obvious on the morrow: Mr. Linton had not only abjured his peevishness (though his spirits seemed still subdued by Catherine's exuberance of vivacity), but he ventured no objection to her taking Isabella with her to Wuthering Heights in the afternoon; and she rewarded him with such a summer of sweetness and affection in return, as made the house a paradise for several days; both master and servants profiting from the perpetual sunshine.

Heathcliff—Mr. Heathcliff I should say in future—used the liberty of visiting at Thrushcross Grange cautiously, at first: he seemed estimating how far its owner would bear his intrusion. Catherine, also, deemed it judicious to moderate her expressions of pleasure in receiving him; and he gradually established his right to be expected.

He retained a great deal of the reserve for which his boyhood was remarkable, and that served to repress all startling demonstrations of feeling. My master's uneasiness experienced a lull, and further circumstances diverted it into another channel for a space.

His new source of trouble sprang from the not anticipated misfortune of Isabella Linton evincing a sudden and irresistible attraction towards the tolerated guest. She was at that time a charming young lady of eighteen; infantile in manners, though possessed of keen wit, keen feelings, and a keen temper, too, if irritated. Her brother, who loved her tenderly, was appalled at this fantastic preference. Leaving aside the degradation of an alliance with a nameless man, and the possible fact that his property, in default of heirs male, might pass into such a one's power, he had sense to comprehend Heathcliff's disposition—to know that, though his exterior was altered, his mind was unchangeable, and unchanged. And he dreaded that mind; it revolted him; he shrank forebodingly from the idea of committing Isabella to its keeping.

He would have recoiled still more had he been aware that her attachment rose unsolicited, and was bestowed where it awakened no reciprocation of sentiment; for the minute he discovered its existence, he laid the blame on Heathcliff's deliberate designing.

We had all remarked, during some time, that Miss Linton fretted and pined over something. She grew cross and wearisome, snapping at and teasing Catherine continually, at the imminent risk of exhausting her limited patience. We excused her to a certain extent, on the plea of ill health—she was dwindling and fading before our eyes. But one day, when she had been peculiarly wayward, rejecting her breakfast, complaining that the servants did not do what she told them; that the mistress would allow her to be nothing in the house, and Edgar neglected her; that she had caught a cold with the doors being left open, and we let the parlour fire go out on purpose to vex her; with a hundred yet more frivolous accusations, Mrs. Linton peremptorily insisted that she should get to bed; and, having scolded her heartily, threatened to send for the doctor.

Mention of Kenneth caused her to exclaim, instantly, that her health was perfect, and it was only Catherine's harshness which made her unhappy.

"How can you say I am harsh, you naughty fondling?" cried the mistress, amazed at the unreasonable assertion. "You are surely losing your reason. When have I been harsh, tell me?"

"Yesterday," sobbed Isabella, "and now!"

"Yesterday!" said her sister-in-law. "On what occasion?"

"In our walk along the moor; you told me to ramble where I pleased, while you sauntered on with Mr. Heathcliff!"

"And that's your notion of harshness?" said Catherine, laughing. "It was no hint that your company was superfluous; we didn't care whether you kept with us or not; I merely thought Heathcliff's talk would have nothing entertaining for your ears."

"Oh, no," wept the young lady; "you wished me away, because you knew I liked to be there!"

"Is she sane?" asked Mrs. Linton, appealing to me. "I'll repeat our conversation, word for word, Isabella; and you point out any charm it could have had for you."

"I don't mind the conversation," she answered. "I wanted to be with—"

"Well!" said Catherine, perceiving her hesitate to complete the sentence.

"With him; and I won't be always sent off!" she continued, kindling up. "You are a dog in the manger, Cathy, and desire no one to be loved but yourself!"

"You are an impertinent little monkey!" exclaimed Mrs. Linton, in surprise. "But I'll not believe this idiocy! It is impossible that you can covet the admiration of Heathcliff—that you can consider him an agreeable person! I hope I have misunderstood you, Isabella?"

"No, you have not," said the infatuated girl. "I love him more than ever you loved Edgar; and he might love me if you would let him!"

"I wouldn't be you for a kingdom, then!" Catherine declared, emphatically—and she seemed to speak sincerely. "Nelly, help me to convince her of her madness. Tell her what Heathcliff is—an unreclaimed creature, without refinement, without cultivation; an arid wilderness of furze and whinstone. I'd as soon put that little canary into the park on a winter's day as recommend you to bestow your heart on him! It is deplorable ignorance of his character, child, and nothing else, which makes that dream enter your head. Pray don't imagine that he conceals depths of benevolence and affection beneath a stern exterior! He's not a rough diamond—a pearl-containing oyster of a rustic; he's a fierce, pitiless, wolfish man. I never say to him, 'Let this or that enemy alone, because it would be ungenerous or cruel to harm them'; I say, 'Let them alone, because *I* should hate them to be wronged': and he'd crush you, like a sparrow's egg, Isabella, if he found you a troublesome charge. I know he couldn't love a Linton; and yet he'd be quite capable of marrying your fortune and expectations. Avarice is growing with him a besetting sin. There's my picture; and I'm his friend—so much so, that had he thought seriously to catch you, I should, perhaps, have held my tongue, and let you fall into his trap."

Miss Linton regarded her sister-in-law with indignation.

"For shame! for shame!" she repeated, angrily. "You are worse than twenty foes, you poisonous friend!"

"Ah! you won't believe me, then?" said Catherine. "You think I speak from wicked selfishness?"

"I'm certain you do," retorted Isabella; "and I shudder at you!"

"Good!" cried the other. "Try for yourself, if that be your spirit; I have done, and yield the argument to your saucy insolence."

"And I must suffer for her egotism!" she sobbed, as Mrs. Linton left the room. "All, all is against me; she has blighted my single consolation. But she uttered falsehoods, didn't she? Mr. Heathcliff is not a fiend; he has an honourable soul, and a true one, or how could he remember her?"

"Banish him from your thoughts, Miss," I said. "He's a bird of bad omen; no mate for you. Mrs. Linton spoke strongly, and yet I can't contradict her. She is better acquainted with his heart than I, or any one besides; and she never would represent him as worse than he is. Honest people don't hide their deeds. How has he been living? how has he got rich? why is he staying at Wuthering Heights, the house of a man whom he abhors? They say Mr. Earnshaw is worse and worse since he came. They sit up all night together continually; and Hindley has been borrowing money on his land, and does nothing but play and drink: I heard only a week ago—it was Joseph who told me—I met him at Gimmerton."

" 'Nelly,' he said, 'we's hae a Crahnr's 'quest enah, at ahr folks. One on 'em's a'most getten his finger cut off wi' hauding t'other froo' sticking hisseln loike a cawlf. That's maister, yah knaw, ut's soa up uh going tuh t'grand 'sizes. He's noan feard uh t' Bench uh judges, norther Paul, nur Peter, nur John, nor Mathew, nor noan on 'em, nut he! He fair like's—he langs tuh set his brazened face agean 'em! And yon bonny lad Heathcliff, yah mind, he's a

rare un! He cau girn a laugh,[1] as weel's onybody at a raight divil's
jest. Does he niver say nowt of his fine living amang us, when he
goas tuh t' Grange? This is t' way on't—up at sun-dahn; dice,
brandy, cloised shutters, und can'le lught till next day, at nooin
—then, t'fooil gangs banning un raving tuh his cham'er, makking
dacent fowks dig thur fingers i' thur lugs fur varry shaume; un'
the' knave, wah, he carn cahnt his brass, un ate, un' sleep, un'
off tuh his neighbour's tuh gossip wi' t' wife. I' course, he tells
Dame Catherine hah hor father's goold runs intuh his pocket, and
her fathur's son gallops dahn t' broad road, while he flees afore tuh
oppen t' pikes.'[2] Now, Miss Linton, Joseph is an old rascal, but
no liar; and, if his account of Heathcliff's conduct be true, you
would never think of desiring such a husband, would you?"

"You are leagued with the rest, Ellen!" she replied. "I'll not
listen to your slanders. What malevolence you must have to wish
to convince me that there is no happiness in the world!"

Whether she would have got over this fancy if left to herself,
or persevered in nursing it perpetually, I cannot say; she had little
time to reflect. The day after, there was a justice-meeting at the
next town; my master was obliged to attend; and Mr. Heathcliff,
aware of his absence, called rather earlier than usual.

Catherine and Isabella were sitting in the library, on hostile
terms, but silent. The latter, alarmed at her recent indiscretion,
and the disclosure she had made of her secret feelings in a transient
fit of passion; the former, on mature consideration, really offended
with her companion; and, if she laughed again at her pertness,
inclined to make it no laughing matter to *her*.

She did laugh as she saw Heathcliff pass the window. I was
sweeping the hearth, and I noticed a mischievous smile on her
lips. Isabella, absorbed in her meditations, or a book, remained
till the door opened, and it was too late to attempt an escape,
which she would gladly have done had it been practicable.

"Come in, that's right!" exclaimed the mistress, gaily, pulling a
chair to the fire. "Here are two people sadly in need of a third
to thaw the ice between them, and you are the very one we
should both of us choose. Heathcliff, I'm proud to show you, at
last, somebody that dotes on you more than myself. I expect you
to feel flattered. Nay, it's not Nelly; don't look at her! My poor
little sister-in-law is breaking her heart by mere contemplation of

---

1. *Crahnr's 'quest:* coroner's inquest; *enah:*
soon; *hauding:* holding; *soa:* therefore; *t'grand 'sizes:* the grand assizes
(sessions of court in English counties);
*girn a laugh:* show the teeth in laughing.

2. *Sun-dahn:* sundown; *lught:* light; *gangs
banning:* goes cursing; *lugs:* ears;
*wah, he carn cahnt his brass:* why,
he can count his money; *oppen t'
pikes:* open the tollgates (i.e., hasten
him to his ruin).

your physical and moral beauty. It lies in your own power to be Edgar's brother! No, no, Isabella, you shan't run off," she continued, arresting, with feigned playfulness, the confounded girl who had risen indignantly. "We were quarrelling like cats about you, Heathcliff; and I was fairly beaten in protestations of devotion and admiration; and, moreover, I was informed that if I would but have the manners to stand aside, my rival, as she will have herself to be, would shoot a shaft into your soul that would fix you for ever, and send my image into eternal oblivion!"

"Catherine," said Isabella, calling up her dignity, and disdaining to struggle from the tight grasp that held her, "I'd thank you to adhere to the truth and not slander me, even in joke! Mr. Heathcliff, be kind enough to bid this friend of yours release me: she forgets that you and I are not intimate acquaintances, and what amuses her is painful to me beyond expression."

As the guest answered nothing, but took his seat, and looked thoroughly indifferent what sentiments she cherished concerning him, she turned, and whispered an earnest appeal for liberty to her tormentor.

"By no means!" cried Mrs. Linton in answer. "I won't be named a dog in the manger again. You *shall* stay: now then, Heathcliff, why don't you evince satisfaction at my pleasant news? Isabella swears that the love Edgar has for me is nothing to that she entertains for you. I'm sure she made some speech of the kind, did she not, Ellen? And she has fasted ever since the day before yesterday's walk, from sorrow and rage that I despatched her out of your society, under the idea of its being unacceptable."

"I think you belie her," said Heathcliff, twisting his chair to face them. "She wishes to be out of my society now, at any rate!"

And he stared hard at the object of discourse, as one might do at a strange repulsive animal, a centipede from the Indies, for instance, which curiosity leads one to examine in spite of the aversion it raises.

The poor thing couldn't bear that; she grew white and red in rapid succession, and, while tears beaded her lashes, bent the strength of her small fingers to loosen the firm clutch of Catherine, and perceiving that as fast as she raised one finger off her arm, another closed down, and she could not remove the whole together, she began to make use of her nails, and their sharpness presently ornamented the detainer's with crescents of red.

"There's a tigress!" exclaimed Mrs. Linton, setting her free, and shaking her hand with pain. "Begone, for God's sake, and hide your vixen face! How foolish to reveal those talons to *him*. Can't you fancy the conclusions he'll draw? Look, Heathcliff! they are instruments that will do execution—you must beware of your eyes."

"I'd wrench them off her fingers, if they ever menaced me," he answered brutally, when the door had closed after her. "But what did you mean by teasing the creature in that manner, Cathy? You were not speaking the truth, were you?"

"I assure you I was," she returned. "She has been pining for your sake several weeks; and raving about you this morning, and pouring forth a deluge of abuse, because I represented your failings in a plain light for the purpose of mitigating her adoration. But don't notice it further. I wished to punish her sauciness, that's all. I like her too well, my dear Heathcliff, to let you absolutely seize and devour her up."

"And I like her too ill to attempt it," said he, "except in a very ghoulish fashion. You'd hear of odd things, if I lived alone with that mawkish, waxen face; the most ordinary would be painting on its white the colours of the rainbow, and turning the blue eyes black, every day or two; they detestably resemble Linton's."

"Delectably," observed Catherine. "They are dove's eyes— angel's!"

"She's her brother's heir, is she not?" he asked, after a brief silence.

"I should be sorry to think so," returned his companion. "Half-a-dozen nephews shall erase her title, please Heaven! Abstract your mind from the subject, at present. You are too prone to covet your neighbour's goods: remember *this* neighbour's goods are mine."

"If they were *mine*, they would be none the less that," said Heathcliff, "but though Isabella Linton may be silly, she is scarcely mad; and, in short, we'll dismiss the matter, as you advise."

From their tongues, they did dismiss it; and Catherine, probably, from her thoughts. The other, I felt certain, recalled it often in the course of the evening; I saw him smile to himself—grin rather—and lapse into ominous musing whenever Mrs. Linton had occasion to be absent from the apartment.

I determined to watch his movements. My heart invariably cleaved to the master's, in preference to Catherine's side; with reason, I imagined, for he was kind, and trustful, and honourable: and she—she could not be called the *opposite*, yet she seemed to allow herself such wide latitude that I had little faith in her principles, and still less sympathy for her feelings. I wanted something to happen which might have the effect of freeing both Wuthering Heights and the Grange of Mr. Heathcliff, quietly, leaving us as we had been prior to his advent. His visits were a continual nightmare to me; and, I suspected, to my master also. His abode at the Heights was an oppression past explaining. I felt that God had forsaken the stray sheep there to its own wicked wanderings, and an evil beast prowled between it and the fold, waiting his time to spring and destroy.

## Chapter XI

Sometimes, while meditating on these things in solitude, I've got up in a sudden terror, and put on my bonnet to go see how all was at the farm; I've persuaded my conscience that it was a duty to warn him how people talked regarding his ways; and then I've recollected his confirmed bad habits, and, hopeless of benefiting him, have flinched from re-entering the dismal house, doubting if I could bear to be taken at my word.

One time I passed the old gate, going out of my way, on a journey to Gimmerton. It was about the period that my narrative has reached—a bright, frosty afternoon, the ground bare, and the road hard and dry.

I came to a stone where the highway branches off on to the moor at your left hand; a rough sand-pillar, with the letters W. H. cut on its north side, on the east, G., and on the south-west, T. G. It serves as guide-post to the Grange, and Heights, and village.

The sun shone yellow on its grey head, reminding me of summer; and I cannot say why, but all at once, a gush of child's sensations flowed into my heart. Hindley and I held it a favourite spot twenty years before.

I gazed long at the weather-worn block; and, stooping down, perceived a hole near the bottom still full of snail-shells and pebbles, which we were fond of storing there with more perishable things; and, as fresh as reality, it appeared that I beheld my early playmate seated on the withered turf, his dark, square head bent forward, and his little hand scooping out the earth with a piece of slate.

"Poor Hindley!" I exclaimed, involuntarily.

I started—my bodily eye was cheated into a momentary belief that the child lifted its face and stared straight into mine! It vanished in a twinkling; but, immediately, I felt an irresistible yearning to be at the Heights. Superstition urged me to comply with this impulse. Supposing he should be dead! I thought—or should die soon!—supposing it were a sign of death!

The nearer I got to the house the more agitated I grew; and on catching sight of it, I trembled every limb. The apparition had outstripped me; it stood looking through the gate. That was my first idea on observing an elf-locked, brown-eyed boy setting his ruddy countenance against the bars. Further reflection suggested this must be Hareton, *my* Hareton, not altered greatly since I left him, ten months since.

"God bless thee, darling!" I cried, forgetting instantaneously my foolish fears. "Hareton, it's Nelly—Nelly, thy nurse."

He retreated out of arm's length, and picked up a large flint.

"I am come to see thy father, Hareton," I added, guessing from the action that Nelly, if she lived in his memory at all, was not recognised as one with me.

He raised his missile to hurl it; I commenced a soothing speech, but could not stay his hand. The stone struck my bonnet; and then ensued, from the stammering lips of the little fellow, a string of curses, which, whether he comprehended them or not, were delivered with practised emphasis, and distorted his baby features into a shocking expression of malignity.

You may be certain this grieved more than angered me. Fit to cry, I took an orange from my pocket, and offered it to propitiate him.

He hesitated, and then snatched it from my hold, as if he fancied I only intended to tempt and disappoint him.

I showed another, keeping it out of his reach.

"Who has taught you those fine words, my barn,"[1] I inquired. "The curate?"

"Damn the curate, and thee! Gie me that," he replied.

"Tell us where you got your lessons, and you shall have it," said I. "Who's your master?"

"Devil daddy," was his answer.

"And what do you learn from Daddy?" I continued.

He jumped at the fruit; I raised it higher. "What does he teach you?" I asked.

"Naught," said he, "but to keep out of his gait.[2] Daddy cannot bide me, because I swear at him."

"Ah! and the devil teaches you to swear at Daddy?" I observed.

"Aye—nay," he drawled.

"Who then?"

"Heathcliff."

I asked if he liked Mr. Heathcliff?

"Aye!" he answered again.

Desiring to have his reasons for liking him, I could only gather the sentences—"I known't—he pays Dad back what he gies to me —he curses Daddy for cursing me—he says I mun do as I will."

"And the curate does not teach you to read and write, then?" I pursued.

"No, I was told the curate should have his —— teeth dashed down his —— throat, if he stepped over the threshold. Heathcliff had promised that!"

1. Child (bairn).                    2. Way.

I put the orange in his hand, and bade him tell his father that a woman called Nelly Dean was waiting to speak with him, by the garden gate.

He went up the walk, and entered the house; but, instead of Hindley, Heathcliff appeared on the door stones, and I turned directly and ran down the road as hard as ever I could race, making no halt till I gained the guide post, and feeling as scared as if I had raised a goblin.

This is not much connected with Miss Isabella's affair; except that it urged me to resolve further on mounting vigilant guard, and doing my utmost to check the spread of such bad influence at the Grange, even though I should wake a domestic storm by thwarting Mrs. Linton's pleasure.

The next time Heathcliff came, my young lady chanced to be feeding some pigeons in the court. She had never spoken a word to her sister-in-law for three days; but she had likewise dropped her fretful complaining, and we found it a great comfort.

Heathcliff had not the habit of bestowing a single unnecessary civility on Miss Linton, I knew. Now, as soon as he beheld her, his first precaution was to take a sweeping survey of the house-front. I was standing by the kitchen window, but I drew out of sight. He then stept across the pavement to her, and said something: she seemed embarrassed, and desirous of getting away; to prevent it, he laid his hand on her arm. She averted her face; he apparently put some question which she had no mind to answer. There was another rapid glance at the house, and supposing himself unseen, the scoundrel had the impudence to embrace her.

"Judas! Traitor!" I ejaculated. "You are a hypocrite too, are you? A deliberate deceiver."

"Who is, Nelly?" said Catherine's voice at my elbow. I had been over-intent on watching the pair outside to mark her entrance.

"Your worthless friend!" I answered warmly; "the sneaking rascal yonder. Ah, he has caught a glimpse of us—he is coming in! I wonder will he have the art to find a plausible excuse for making love to Miss, when he told you he hated her?"

Mrs. Linton saw Isabella tear herself free, and run into the garden; and a minute after, Heathcliff opened the door.

I couldn't withhold giving some loose to my indignation; but Catherine angrily insisted on silence, and threatened to order me out of the kitchen, if I dared be so presumptuous as to put in my insolent tongue.

"To hear you, people might think *you* were the mistress!" she cried. "You want setting down in your right place! Heathcliff, what are you about, raising this stir? I said you must let Isabella alone!—I beg you will, unless you are tired of being received here, and wish Linton to draw the bolts against you!"

"God forbid that he should try!" answered the black villain. I detested him just then. "God keep him meek and patient! Every day I grow madder after sending him to heaven!"

"Hush!" said Catherine, shutting the inner door. "Don't vex me. Why have you disregarded my request? Did she come across you on purpose?"

"What is it to you?" he growled. "I have a right to kiss her, if she chooses, and you have no right to object. I'm not *your* husband: *you* needn't be jealous of me!"

"I'm not jealous *of* you," replied the mistress, "I'm jealous *for* you. Clear your face, you shan't scowl at me! If you like Isabella, you shall marry her. But do you like her? Tell the truth, Heathcliff! There, you won't answer. I'm certain you don't!"

"And would Mr. Linton approve of his sister marrying that man?" I inquired.

"Mr. Linton should approve," returned my lady decisively.

"He might spare himself the trouble," said Heathcliff; "I could do as well without his approbation. And as to you, Catherine, I have a mind to speak a few words now, while we are at it. I want you to be aware that I *know* you have treated me infernally—infernally! Do you hear? And if you flatter yourself that I don't perceive it, you are a fool; and if you think I can be consoled by sweet words you are an idiot; and if you fancy I'll suffer unrevenged, I'll convince you of the contrary, in a very little while! Meantime, thank you for telling me your sister-in-law's secret. I swear I'll make the most of it. And stand you aside!"

"What new phase of his character is this?" exclaimed Mrs. Linton, in amazement. "I've treated you infernally—and you'll take revenge! How will you take it, ungrateful brute? How have I treated you infernally?"

"I seek no revenge on you," replied Heathcliff less vehemently. "That's not the plan. The tyrant grinds down his slaves and they don't turn against him, they crush those beneath them. You are welcome to torture me to death for your amusement, only allow me to amuse myself a little in the same style, and refrain from insult, as much as you are able. Having levelled my palace, don't erect a hovel and complacently admire your own charity in giving me that for a home. If I imagined you really wished me to marry Isabella, I'd cut my throat!"

"Oh, the evil is that I am *not* jealous, is it?" cried Catherine. "Well, I won't repeat my offer of a wife: it is as bad as offering Satan a lost soul. Your bliss lies, like his, in inflicting misery. You prove it. Edgar is restored from the ill-temper he gave way to at your coming; I begin to be secure and tranquil; and you, restless to know us at peace, appear resolved on exciting a quarrel. Quarrel with Edgar, if you please, Heathcliff, and deceive his sister; you'll hit on exactly the most efficient method of revenging yourself on me."

The conversation ceased. Mrs. Linton sat down by the fire, flushed and gloomy. The spirit which served her was growing intractable: she could neither lay nor control it. He stood on the hearth, with folded arms, brooding on his evil thoughts; and in this position I left them to seek the master, who was wondering what kept Catherine below so long.

"Ellen," said he, when I entered, "have you seen your mistress?"

"Yes, she's in the kitchen, sir," I answered. "She's sadly put out by Mr. Heathcliff's behaviour: and, indeed, I do think it's time to arrange his visits on another footing. There's harm in being too soft, and now it's come to this—" And I related the scene in the court, and, as near as I dared, the whole subsequent dispute. I fancied it could not be very prejudicial to Mrs. Linton, unless she made it so afterwards, by assuming the defensive for her guest.

Edgar Linton had difficulty in hearing me to the close. His first words revealed that he did not clear his wife of blame.

"This is insufferable!" he exclaimed. "It is disgraceful that she should own him for a friend, and force his company on me! Call me two men out of the hall, Ellen. Catherine shall linger no longer to argue with the low ruffian—I have humoured her enough."

He descended, and bidding the servants wait in the passage, went, followed by me, to the kitchen. Its occupants had recommenced their angry discussion; Mrs. Linton, at least, was scolding with renewed vigour; Heathcliff had moved to the window, and hung his head, somewhat cowed by her violent rating apparently.

He saw the master first, and made a hasty motion that she should be silent; which she obeyed, abruptly, on discovering the reason of his intimation.

"How is this?" said Linton, addressing her; "what notion of propriety must you have to remain here, after the language which has been held to you by that blackguard? I suppose, because it is his ordinary talk, you think nothing of it—you are habituated to his baseness, and, perhaps, imagine I can get used to it too!"

"Have you been listening at the door, Edgar?" asked the mistress, in a tone particularly calculated to provoke her husband, implying both carelessness and contempt of his irritation.

Heathcliff, who had raised his eyes at the former speech, gave a sneering laugh at the latter, on purpose, it seemed, to draw Mr.

Linton's attention to him.

He succeeded; but Edgar did not mean to entertain him with any high flights of passion.

"I have been so far forbearing with you, sir," he said, quietly; "not that I was ignorant of your miserable, degraded character, but I felt you were only partly responsible for that; and Catherine wishing to keep up your acquaintance, I acquiesced—foolishly. Your presence is a moral poison that would contaminate the most virtuous: for that cause, and to prevent worse consequences, I shall deny you, hereafter, admission into this house, and give notice, now, that I require your instant departure. Three minutes' delay will render it involuntary and ignominious."

Heathcliff measured the height and breadth of the speaker with an eye full of derision.

"Cathy, this lamb of yours threatens like a bull!" he said. "It is in danger of splitting its skull against my knuckles. By God, Mr. Linton, I'm mortally sorry that you are not worth knocking down!"

My master glanced towards the passage, and signed me to fetch the men: he had no intention of hazarding a personal encounter.

I obeyed the hint; but Mrs. Linton, suspecting something, followed, and when I attempted to call them, she pulled me back, slammed the door to, and locked it.

"Fair means!" she said, in answer to her husband's look of angry surprise. "If you have not the courage to attack him, make an apology, or allow yourself to be beaten. It will correct you of feigning more valour than you possess. No, I'll swallow the key before you shall get it! I'm delightfully rewarded for my kindness to each! After constant indulgence of one's weak nature, and the other's bad one, I earn, for thanks, two samples of blind ingratitude, stupid to absurdity! Edgar, I was defending you and yours; and I wish Heathcliff may flog you sick, for daring to think an evil thought of me!"

It did not need the medium of a flogging to produce that effect on the master. He tried to wrest the key from Catherine's grasp; and for safety she flung it into the hottest part of the fire; whereupon Mr. Edgar was taken with a nervous trembling, and his countenance grew deadly pale. For his life he could not avert that access of emotion: mingled anguish and humiliation overcame him completely. He leant on the back of a chair, and covered his face.

"Oh, heavens! In old days this would win you knighthood!" exclaimed Mrs. Linton. "We are vanquished! we are vanquished! Heathcliff would as soon lift a finger at you as the king would march his army against a colony of mice. Cheer up, you shan't be hurt! Your type is not a lamb, it's a sucking leveret."

"I wish you joy of the milk-blooded coward, Cathy!" said her friend. "I compliment you on your taste: and that is the slavering, shivering thing you preferred to me! I would not strike him with my fist, but I'd kick him with my foot, and experience considerable satisfaction. Is he weeping, or is he going to faint for fear?"

The fellow approached and gave the chair on which Linton rested a push. He'd better have kept his distance: my master quickly sprang erect, and struck him full on the throat a blow that would have levelled a slighter man.

It took his breath for a minute; and, while he choked, Mr. Linton walked out by the back door into the yard, and from thence, to the front entrance.

"There! you've done with coming here," cried Catherine. "Get away, now; he'll return with a brace of pistols, and half a dozen assistants. If he did overhear us, of course, he'd never forgive you. You've played me an ill turn, Heathcliff! But go—make haste! I'd rather see Edgar at bay than you."

"Do you suppose I'm going with that blow burning in my gullet?" he thundered. "By hell, no! I'll crush his ribs in like a rotten hazel-nut, before I cross the threshold! If I don't floor him now, I shall murder him sometime, so, as you value his existence, let me get at him!"

"He is not coming," I interposed, framing a bit of a lie. "There's the coachman, and the two gardeners; you'll surely not wait to be thrust into the road by them! Each has a bludgeon, and master will, very likely, be watching from the parlour windows to see that they fulfil his orders."

The gardeners and coachman *were* there; but Linton was with them. They had already entered the court. Heathcliff, on second thoughts, resolved to avoid a struggle against three underlings; he seized the poker, smashed the lock from the inner door, and made his escape as they tramped in.

Mrs. Linton, who was very much excited, bid me accompany her upstairs. She did not know my share in contributing to the disturbance, and I was anxious to keep her in ignorance.

"I'm nearly distracted, Nelly!" she exclaimed, throwing herself on the sofa. "A thousand smiths' hammers are beating in my head! Tell Isabella to shun me—this uproar is owing to her; and should she or any one else aggravate my anger at present, I shall get wild. And, Nelly, say to Edgar, if you see him again to-night, that I'm in danger of being seriously ill. I wish it may prove true. He has startled and distressed me shockingly! I want to frighten him. Besides, he might come and begin a string of abuse, or com-

plainings; I'm certain I should recriminate, and God knows where
we should end! Will you do so, my good Nelly? You are aware
that I am no way blameable in this matter. What possessed him
to turn listener? Heathcliff's talk was outrageous, after you left
us; but I could soon have diverted him from Isabella, and the
rest meant nothing. Now, all is dashed wrong by the fool's-craving
to hear evil of self that haunts some people like a demon! Had
Edgar never gathered our conversation, he would never have been
the worse for it. Really, when he opened on me in that unreasonable tone of displeasure, after I had scolded Heathcliff till I was
hoarse for *him*, I did not care, hardly, what they did to each other,
especially as I felt that, however the scene closed, we should all
be driven asunder for nobody knows how long! Well, if I cannot
keep Heathcliff for my friend, if Edgar will be mean and jealous,
I'll try to break their hearts by breaking my own. That will be a
prompt way of finishing all, when I am pushed to extremity! But
it's a deed to be reserved for a forlorn hope; I'd not take Linton
by surprise with it. To this point he has been discreet in dreading
to provoke me; you must represent the peril of quitting that
policy, and remind him of my passionate temper, verging, when
kindled, on frenzy. I wish you could dismiss that apathy out of
your countenance, and look rather more anxious about me!"

The stolidity with which I received these instructions was, no
doubt, rather exasperating, for they were delivered in perfect sincerity; but I believed a person who could plan the turning of her
fits of passion to account, beforehand, might, by exerting her will,
manage to control herself tolerably even while under their influence; and I did not wish to "frighten" her husband, as she
said, and multiply his annoyances for the purpose of serving her
selfishness.

Therefore I said nothing when I met the master coming towards
the parlour; but I took the liberty of turning back to listen whether
they would resume their quarrel together.

He began to speak first.

"Remain where you are, Catherine," he said, without any
anger in his voice, but with much sorrowful despondency. "I shall
not stay. I am neither come to wrangle, nor be reconciled; but I
wish just to learn whether, after this evening's events, you intend
to continue your intimacy with—"

"Oh, for mercy's sake," interrupted the mistress, stamping her
foot, "for mercy's sake, let us hear no more of it now! Your cold
blood cannot be worked into a fever; your veins are full of ice-
water, but mine are boiling, and the sight of such chillness makes
them dance."

"To get rid of me, answer my question," persevered Mr. Linton.

"You *must* answer it; and that violence does not alarm me. I have found that you can be as stoical as any one, when you please. Will you give up Heathcliff hereafter, or will you give up me? It is impossible for you to be *my* friend and *his* at the same time; and I absolutely *require* to know which you choose."

"I require to be let alone!" exclaimed Catherine, furiously. "I demand it! Don't you see I can scarcely stand? Edgar, you—you leave me!"

She rung the bell till it broke with a twang: I entered leisurely. It was enough to try the temper of a saint, such senseless, wicked rages! There she lay dashing her head against the arm of the sofa, and grinding her teeth, so that you might fancy she would crash them to splinters!

Mr. Linton stood looking at her in sudden compunction and fear. He told me to fetch some water. She had no breath for speaking.

I brought a glass full; and, as she would not drink, I sprinkled it on her face. In a few seconds she stretched herself out stiff, and turned up her eyes, while her cheeks, at once blanched and livid, assumed the aspect of death.

Linton looked terrified.

"There is nothing in the world the matter," I whispered. I did not want him to yield, though I could not help being afraid in my heart.

"She has blood on her lips!" he said, shuddering.

"Never mind!" I answered, tartly. And I told him how she had resolved, previous to his coming, on exhibiting a fit of frenzy.

I incautiously gave the account aloud, and she heard me, for she started up—her hair flying over her shoulders, her eyes flashing, the muscles of her neck and arms standing out preternaturally. I made up my mind for broken bones, at least; but she only glared about her for an instant, and then rushed from the room.

The master directed me to follow; I did, to her chamber door; she hindered me from going farther by securing it against me.

As she never offered to descend to breakfast next morning, I went to ask whether she would have some carried up.

"No!" she replied, peremptorily.

The same question was repeated at dinner and tea; and again on the morrow after, and received the same answer.

Mr. Linton, on his part, spent his time in the library, and did not inquire concerning his wife's occupations. Isabella and he had had an hour's interview, during which he tried to elicit from her some sentiment of proper horror for Heathcliff's advances; but he could make nothing of her evasive replies, and was obliged to close the examination unsatisfactorily; adding, however, a solemn warning, that if she were so insane as to encourage that worthless suitor, it would dissolve all bonds of relationship between herself and him.

### *Chapter XII*

While Miss Linton moped about the park and garden, always silent, and almost always in tears; and her brother shut himself up among books that he never opened—wearying, I guessed, with a continual vague expectation that Catherine, repenting her conduct, would come of her own accord to ask pardon, and seek a reconciliation—and while *she* fasted pertinaciously, under the idea, probably, that at every meal, Edgar was ready to choke for her absence, and pride alone held him from running to cast himself at her feet, I went about my household duties, convinced that the Grange had but one sensible soul in its walls, and that lodged in my body.

I wasted no condolences on Miss, nor any expostulations on my mistress, nor did I pay attention to the sighs of my master, who yearned to hear his lady's name, since he might not hear her voice.

I determined they should come about as they pleased for me; and though it was a tiresomely slow process, I began to rejoice at length in a faint dawn of its progress, as I thought at first.

Mrs. Linton, on the third day, unbarred her door; and having finished the water in her pitcher and decanter, desired a renewed supply, and a basin of gruel, for she believed she was dying. That I set down as a speech meant for Edgar's ears; I believed no such thing, so I kept it to myself, and brought her some tea and dry toast.

She ate and drank eagerly; and sank back on her pillow again, clenching her hands and groaning.

"Oh, I will die," she exclaimed, "since no one cares anything about me. I wish I had not taken that."

Then a good while after I heard her murmur—

"No, I'll not die—he'd be glad—he does not love me at all—he would never miss me!"

"Did you want anything, ma'am?" I enquired, still preserving my external composure, in spite of her ghastly countenance and strange exaggerated manner.

"What is that apathetic being doing?" she demanded, pushing the thick entangled locks from her wasted face. "Has he fallen into a lethargy, or is he dead?"

"Neither," replied I; "if you mean Mr. Linton. He's tolerably well, I think, though his studies occupy him rather more than they ought; he is continually among his books, since he has no other society."

I should not have spoken so, if I had known her true condition, but I could not get rid of the notion that she acted a part of her disorder.

"Among his books!" she cried, confounded. "And I dying! I on the brink of the grave! My God! does he know how I'm altered?" continued she, staring at her reflection in a mirror, hanging against the opposite wall. "Is that Catherine Linton? He imagines me in a pet—in play, perhaps. Cannot you inform him that it is frightful earnest? Nelly, if it be not too late, as soon as I learn how he feels, I'll choose between these two: either to starve at once—that would be no punishment unless he had a heart—or to recover and leave the country. Are you speaking the truth about him now? Take care. Is he actually so utterly indifferent for my life?"

"Why, ma'am," I answered, "the master has no idea of your being deranged; and, of course, he does not fear that you will let yourself die of hunger."

"You think not? Cannot you tell him I will?" she returned. "Persuade him—speak of your own mind—say you are certain I will!"

"No, you forget, Mrs. Linton," I suggested, "that you have eaten some food with a relish this evening, and to-morrow you will perceive its good effects."

"If I were only sure it would kill him," she interrupted, "I'd kill myself directly! These three awful nights, I've never closed my lids—and oh, I've been tormented! I've been haunted, Nelly! But I begin to fancy you don't like me. How strange! I thought, though everybody hated and despised each other, they could not avoid loving me—and they have all turned to enemies in a few hours. *They* have, I'm positive; the people *here*. How dreary to meet death, surrounded by their cold faces! Isabella, terrified and repelled, afraid to enter the room, it would be so dreadful to watch Catherine go. And Edgar standing solemnly by to see it over; then offering prayers of thanks to God for restoring peace to his house, and going back to his *books!* What, in the name of all that feels, has he to do with *books*, when I am dying?"

She could not bear the notion which I had put into her head of Mr. Linton's philosophical resignation. Tossing about, she increased her feverish bewilderment to madness, and tore the pillow with her teeth; then raising herself up all burning, desired that I would open the window. We were in the middle of winter, the wind blew strong from the northeast, and I objected.

Both the expressions flitting over her face, and the changes of her moods, began to alarm me terribly; and brought to my recollection her former illness, and the doctor's injunction that she should not be crossed.

A minute previously she was violent; now, supported on one arm, and not noticing my refusal to obey her, she seemed to find child- ish diversion in pulling the feathers from the rents she had just made, and ranging them on the sheet according to their different species: her mind had strayed to other associations.

"That's a turkey's," she murmured to herself; "and this is a wild-duck's; and this is a pigeon's. Ah, they put pigeons' feathers in the pillows—no wonder I couldn't die! Let me take care to throw it on the floor when I lie down. And here is a moor-cock's; and this—I should know it among a thousand—it's a lapwing's. Bonny bird; wheeling over our heads in the middle of the moor. It wanted to get to its nest, for the clouds touched the swells, and it felt rain coming. This feather was picked up from the heath, the bird was not shot; we saw its nest in the winter, full of little skeletons. Heathcliff set a trap over it, and the old ones dare not come. I made him promise he'd never shoot a lapwing after that, and he didn't. Yes, here are more! Did he shoot my lapwings, Nelly? Are they red, any of them? Let me look."

"Give over with that baby-work!" I interrupted, dragging the pillow away, and turning the holes towards the mattress, for she was removing its contents by handfuls. "Lie down and shut your eyes, you're wandering. There's a mess! The down is flying about like snow!"

I went here and there collecting it.

"I see in you, Nelly," she continued, dreamily, "an aged woman —you have grey hair, and bent shoulders. This bed is the fairy cave under Penistone Crag, and you are gathering elf-bolts[1] to hurt our heifers; pretending, while I am near, that they are only locks of wool. That's what you'll come to fifty years hence; I know you are not so now. I'm not wandering: you're mistaken, or else I should believe you really *were* that withered hag, and I should think I *was* under Penistone Crag, and I'm conscious it's night, and there are two candles on the table making the black press shine like jet."

"The black press? where is that?" I asked. "You are talking in your sleep!"

"It's against the wall, as it always is," she replied. "It *does* ap- pear odd—I see a face in it!"

"There is no press in the room, and never was," said I, re- suming my seat, and looping up the curtain that I might watch her.

"Don't *you* see that face?" she enquired, gazing earnestly at the

1. Flint arrowheads.

mirror.

And say what I could, I was incapable of making her comprehend it to be her own; so I rose and covered it with a shawl.

"It's behind there still!" she pursued, anxiously. "And it stirred. Who is it? I hope it will not come out when you are gone! Oh! Nelly, the room is haunted! I'm afraid of being alone!"

I took her hand in mine, and bid her be composed, for a succession of shudders convulsed her frame, and she *would* keep straining her gaze towards the glass.

"There's nobody here!" I insisted. "It was *yourself*, Mrs. Linton; you knew it a while since."

"Myself," she gasped, "and the clock is striking twelve! It's true, then; that's dreadful!"

Her fingers clutched the clothes, and gathered them over her eyes. I attempted to steal to the door with an intention of calling her husband; but I was summoned back by a piercing shriek. The shawl had dropped from the frame.

"Why, what *is* the matter?" cried I. "Who is coward now? Wake up! That is the glass—the mirror, Mrs. Linton; and you see yourself in it, and there am I too, by your side."

Trembling and bewildered, she held me fast, but the horror gradually passed from her countenance; its paleness gave place to a glow of shame.

"Oh, dear! I thought I was at home," she sighed. "I thought I was lying in my chamber at Wuthering Heights. Because I'm weak, my brain got confused, and I screamed unconsciously. Don't say anything; but stay with me. I dread sleeping, my dreams appal me."

"A sound sleep would do you good, ma'am," I answered; "and I hope this suffering will prevent your trying starving again."

"Oh, if I were but in my own bed in the old house!" she went on bitterly, wringing her hands. "And that wind sounding in the firs by the lattice. Do let me feel it—it comes straight down the moor—do let me have one breath!"

To pacify her, I held the casement ajar, a few seconds. A cold blast rushed through; I closed it, and returned to my post.

She lay still now, her face bathed in tears. Exhaustion of body had entirely subdued her spirit; our fiery Catherine was no better than a wailing child!

"How long is it since I shut myself in here?" she asked, suddenly reviving.

"It was Monday evening," I replied, "and this is Thursday night, or rather Friday morning, at present."

"What! of the same week?" she exclaimed. "Only that brief time?"

"Long enough to live on nothing but cold water and ill-temper," observed I.

"Well, it seems a weary number of hours," she muttered doubtfully; "it must be more. I remember being in the parlour after they had quarrelled; and Edgar being cruelly provoking, and me running into this room desperate. As soon as ever I had barred the door, utter blackness overwhelmed me, and I fell on the floor. I couldn't explain to Edgar how certain I felt of having a fit, or going raging mad, if he persisted in teasing me! I had no command of tongue, or brain, and he did not guess my agony, perhaps; it barely left me sense to try to escape from him and his voice. Before I recovered sufficiently to see and hear, it began to be dawn; and, Nelly, I'll tell you what I thought, and what has kept recurring and recurring till I feared for my reason. I thought as I lay there with my head against that table leg, and my eyes dimly discerning the grey square of the window, that I was enclosed in the oak-panelled bed at home; and my heart ached with some great grief which, just waking, I could not recollect. I pondered, and worried myself to discover what it could be; and, most strangely, the whole last seven years of my life grew a blank! I did not recall that they had been at all. I was a child; my father was just buried, and my misery arose from the separation that Hindley had ordered between me and Heathcliff. I was laid alone, for the first time, and, rousing from a dismal doze after a night of weeping, I lifted my hand to push the panels aside: it struck the table-top! I swept it along the carpet, and then memory burst in—my late anguish was swallowed in a paroxysm of despair. I cannot say why I felt so wildly wretched—it must have been temporary derangement, for there is scarcely cause. But, supposing at twelve years old, I had been wrenched from the Heights, and every early association, and my all in all, as Heathcliff was at that time, and been converted at a stroke into Mrs. Linton, the lady of Thrushcross Grange, and the wife of a stranger; an exile, and outcast, thenceforth, from what had been my world. You may fancy a glimpse of the abyss where I grovelled! Shake your head as you will, Nelly, *you* have helped to unsettle me! You should have spoken to Edgar, indeed you should, and compelled him to leave me quiet! Oh, I'm burning! I wish I were out of doors—I wish I were a girl again, half savage, and hardy, and free; and laughing at injuries, not maddening under them! Why am I so changed? why does my blood rush into a hell of tumult at a few words? I'm sure I should be myself were I once among the heather on those hills. Open the window again wide, fasten it open! Quick, why don't you move?"

"Because I won't give you your death of cold," I answered.

"You won't give me a chance of life, you mean," she said sullenly. "However, I'm not helpless yet, I'll open it myself."

And sliding from the bed before I could hinder her, she crossed the room, walking very uncertainly, threw it back, and bent out, careless of the frosty air that cut about her shoulders as keen as a knife.

I entreated, and finally attempted to force her to retire. But I soon found her delirious strength much surpassed mine (she *was* delirious, I became convinced by her subsequent actions, and ravings).

There was no moon, and everything beneath lay in misty darkness; not a light gleamed from any house, far or near; all had been extinguished long ago; and those at Wuthering Heights were never visible—still she asserted she caught their shining.

"Look!" she cried eagerly, "that's my room, with the candle in it, and the trees swaying before it; and the other candle is in Joseph's garret. Joseph sits up late, doesn't he? He's waiting till I come home that he may lock the gate. Well, he'll wait a while yet. It's a rough journey, and a sad heart to travel it; and we must pass by Gimmerton Kirk, to go that journey! We've braved its ghosts often together, and dared each other to stand among the graves and ask them to come. But Heathcliff, if I dare you now, will you venture? If you do, I'll keep you. I'll not lie there by myself; they may bury me twelve feet deep, and throw the church down over me, but I won't rest till you are with me. I never will!"

She paused, and resumed with a strange smile, "He's considering—he'd rather I'd come to him! Find a way, then! not through that Kirkyard. You are slow! Be content, you always followed me!"

Perceiving it vain to argue against her insanity, I was planning how I could reach something to wrap about her, without quitting my hold of herself, for I could not trust her alone by the gaping lattice, when, to my consternation, I heard the rattle of the doorhandle, and Mr. Linton entered. He had only then come from the library; and, in passing through the lobby, had noticed our talking and been attracted by curiosity, or fear, to examine what it signified at that late hour.

"Oh, sir!" I cried, checking the exclamation risen to his lips at the sight which met him, and the bleak atmosphere of the chamber. "My poor mistress is ill, and she quite masters me; I cannot manage her at all; pray, come and persuade her to go to bed. Forget your anger, for she's hard to guide any way but her own."

"Catherine ill?" he said, hastening to us. "Shut the window, Ellen! Catherine! why—"

He was silent; the haggardness of Mrs. Linton's appearance

smote him speechless, and he could only glance from her to me in horrified astonishment.

"She's been fretting here," I continued, "and eating scarcely anything, and never complaining; she would admit none of us till this evening, and so we couldn't inform you of her state, as we were not aware of it ourselves, but it is nothing."

I felt I uttered my explanations awkwardly; the master frowned. "It is nothing, is it, Ellen Dean?" he said sternly. "You shall account more clearly for keeping me ignorant of this!" And he took his wife in his arms, and looked at her with anguish.

At first she gave him no glance of recognition—he was invisible to her abstracted gaze. The delirium was not fixed, however; having weaned her eyes from contemplating the outer darkness, by degrees she centred her attention on him, and discovered who it was that held her.

"Ah! you are come, are you, Edgar Linton?" she said, with angry animation. "You are one of those things that are ever found when least wanted, and when you are wanted, never! I suppose we shall have plenty of lamentations, now—I see we shall—but they can't keep me from my narrow home out yonder, my resting place where I'm bound before spring is over! There it is, not among the Lintons, mind, under the chapel-roof; but in the open air with a head-stone, and you may please yourself, whether you go to them, or come to me!"

"Catherine, what have you done?" commenced the master. "Am I nothing to you, any more? Do you love that wretch, Heath—"

"Hush!" cried Mrs. Linton. "Hush, this moment! You mention that name and I end the matter instantly, by a spring from the window! What you touch at present, you may have; but my soul will be on that hilltop before you lay hands on me again. I don't want you, Edgar; I'm past wanting you. Return to your books. I'm glad you possess a consolation, for all you had in me is gone."

"Her mind wanders, sir," I interposed. "She has been talking nonsense the whole evening; but, let her have quiet and proper attendance, and she'll rally. Hereafter, we must be cautious how we vex her."

"I desire no further advice from you," answered Mr. Linton. "You knew your mistress's nature, and you encouraged me to harass her. And not to give me one hint of how she has been these three days! It was heartless! Months of sickness could not cause such a change!"

I began to defend myself, thinking it too bad to be blamed for another's wicked waywardness!

"I knew Mrs. Linton's nature to be headstrong and domineering," cried I; "but I didn't know that you wished to foster her fierce temper! I didn't know that, to humour her, I should wink at Mr. Heathcliff. I performed the duty of a faithful servant in telling you, and I have got a faithful servant's wages! Well, it will teach me to be careful next time. Next time you may gather intelligence for yourself!"

"The next time you bring a tale to me, you shall quit my service, Ellen Dean," he replied.

"You'd rather hear nothing about it, I suppose, then, Mr. Linton?" said I. "Heathcliff has your permission to come a-courting to Miss, and to drop in at every opportunity your absence offers, on purpose to poison the mistress against you?"

Confused as Catherine was, her wits were alert at applying our conversation.

"Ah! Nelly has played traitor," she exclaimed, passionately. "Nelly is my hidden enemy. You witch! So you do seek elf-bolts to hurt us! Let me go, and I'll make her rue! I'll make her howl a recantation!"

A maniac's fury kindled under her brows; she struggled desperately to disengage herself from Linton's arms. I felt no inclination to tarry the event; and, resolving to seek medical aid on my own responsibility, I quitted the chamber.

In passing the garden to reach the road, at a place where a bridle hook is driven into the wall, I saw something white moved irregularly, evidently by another agent than the wind. Notwithstanding my hurry, I stayed to examine it, lest ever after I should have the conviction impressed on my imagination that it was a creature of the other world.

My surprise and perplexity were great to discover, by touch more than vision, Miss Isabella's springer, Fanny, suspended by a handkerchief, and nearly at its last gasp.

I quickly released the animal, and lifted it into the garden. I had seen it follow its mistress upstairs, when she went to bed, and wondered much how it could have got out there, and what mischievous person had treated it so.

While untying the knot round the hook, it seemed to me that I repeatedly caught the beat of horses' feet galloping at some distance; but there were such a number of things to occupy my reflections that I hardly gave the circumstance a thought, though it was a strange sound, in that place, at two o'clock in the morning.

Mr. Kenneth was fortunately just issuing from his house to see a patient in the village as I came up the street; and my account of Catherine Linton's malady induced him to accompany me back immediately.

He was a plain, rough man; and he made no scruple to speak

his doubts of her surviving this second attack, unless she were more submissive to his directions than she had shown herself before.

"Nelly Dean," said he, "I can't help fancying there's an extra cause for this. What has there been to do at the Grange? We've odd reports up here. A stout, hearty lass like Catherine does not fall ill for a trifle; and that sort of people should not either. It's hard work bringing them through fevers, and such things. How did it begin?"

"The master will inform you," I answered; "but you are acquainted with the Earnshaws' violent dispositions, and Mrs. Linton caps them all. I may say this; it commenced in a quarrel. She was struck during a tempest of passion with a kind of fit. That's her account, at least; for she flew off in the height of it, and locked herself up. Afterwards, she refused to eat, and now she alternately raves and remains in a half dream, knowing those about her, but having her mind filled with all sorts of strange ideas and illusions."

"Mr. Linton will be sorry?" observed Kenneth, interrogatively.

"Sorry? He'll break his heart should anything happen!" I replied. "Don't alarm him more than necessary."

"Well, I told him to beware," said my companion, "and he must bide the consequences of neglecting my warning! Hasn't he been thick with Mr. Heathcliff lately?"

"Heathcliff frequently visits at the Grange," answered I, "though more on the strength of the mistress having known him when a boy, than because the master likes his company. At present, he's discharged from the trouble of calling; owing to some presumptuous aspirations after Miss Linton which he manifested. I hardly think he'll be taken in again."

"And does Miss Linton turn a cold shoulder on him?" was the doctor's next question.

"I'm not in her confidence," returned I, reluctant to continue the subject.

"No, she's a sly one," he remarked, shaking his head. "She keeps her own counsel! But she's a real little fool. I have it from good authority that last night (and a pretty night it was!) she and Heathcliff were walking in the plantation at the back of your house, above two hours; and he pressed her not to go in again, but just mount his horse and away with him! My informant said she could only put him off by pledging her word of honour to be prepared on their first meeting after that: when it was to be, he didn't hear, but you urge Mr. Linton to look sharp!"

This news filled me with fresh fears; I outstripped Kenneth, and ran most of the way back. The little dog was yelping in the garden yet. I spared a minute to open the gate for it, but instead of going to the house door, it coursed up and down snuffing the grass, and would have escaped to the road, had I not seized and conveyed it in with me.

On ascending to Isabella's room, my suspicions were confirmed: it was empty. Had I been a few hours sooner, Mrs. Linton's illness might have arrested her rash step. But what could be done now? There was a bare possibility of overtaking them if pursued instantly. I could not pursue them, however; and I dare not rouse the family, and fill the place with confusion; still less unfold the business to my master, absorbed as he was in his present calamity, and having no heart to spare for a second grief!

I saw nothing for it but to hold my tongue, and suffer matters to take their course; and Kenneth being arrived, I went with a badly composed countenance to announce him.

Catherine lay in a troubled sleep; her husband had succeeded in soothing the access of frenzy; he now hung over her pillow, watching every shade, and every change of her painfully expressive features.

The doctor, on examining the case for himself, spoke hopefully to him of its having a favourable termination, if we could only preserve around her perfect and constant tranquillity. To me, he signified the threatening danger was not so much death, as permanent alienation of intellect.

I did not close my eyes that night, nor did Mr. Linton; indeed, we never went to bed; and the servants were all up long before the usual hour, moving through the house with stealthy tread, and exchanging whispers as they encountered each other in their vocations. Every one was active but Miss Isabella; and they began to remark how sound she slept. Her brother too asked if she had risen, and seemed impatient for her presence, and hurt that she showed so little anxiety for her sister-in-law.

I trembled lest he should send me to call her; but I was spared the pain of being the first proclaimant of her flight. One of the maids, a thoughtless girl, who had been on an early errand to Gimmerton, came panting upstairs, open-mouthed, and dashed into the chamber, crying—

"Oh, dear, dear! What mun[2] we have next? Master, master, our young lady—"

"Hold your noise!" cried I hastily, enraged at her clamorous manner.

"Speak lower, Mary—What is the matter?" said Mr. Linton. "What ails your young lady?"

"She's gone, she's gone! Yon' Heathcliff's run off wi' her!" gasped the girl.

2. Must.

"That is not true!" exclaimed Linton, rising in agitation. "It cannot be—how has the idea entered your head? Ellen Dean, go and seek her—it is incredible—it cannot be."

As he spoke he took the servant to the door, and then repeated his demand to know her reasons for such an assertion.

"Why, I met on the road a lad that fetches milk here," she stammered, "and he asked whether we wern't in trouble at the Grange. I thought he meant for Missis's sickness, so I answered, yes. Then, says he, 'They's somebody gone after 'em, I guess?' I stared. He saw I knew naught about it, and he told how a gentleman and lady had stopped to have a horse's shoe fastened at a blacksmith's shop, two miles out of Gimmerton, not very long after midnight! and how the blacksmith's lass had got up to spy who they were: she knew them both directly. And she noticed the man—Heathcliff it was, she felt certain, nob'dy could mistake him, besides—put a sovereign in her father's hand for payment. The lady had a cloak about her face; but having desired a sup of water, while she drank, it fell back, and she saw her very plain. Heathcliff held both bridles as they rode on, and they set their faces from the village, and went as fast as the rough roads would let them. The lass said nothing to her father, but she told it all over Gimmerton this morning."

I ran and peeped, for form's sake, into Isabella's room: confirming, when I returned, the servant's statement. Mr. Linton had resumed his seat by the bed; on my re-entrance, he raised his eyes, read the meaning of my blank aspect, and dropped them without giving an order, or uttering a word.

"Are we to try any measures for overtaking and bringing her back?" I inquired. "How should we do?"

"She went of her own accord," answered the master; "she had a right to go if she pleased. Trouble me no more about her. Hereafter she is only my sister in name, not because I disown her, but because she has disowned me."

And that was all he said on the subject; he did not make a single inquiry further, or mention her in any way, except directing me to send what property she had in the house to her fresh home, wherever it was, when I knew it.

## Chapter XIII

For two months the fugitives remained absent; in those two months, Mrs. Linton encountered and conquered the worst shock of what was denominated a brain fever. No mother could have nursed an only child more devotedly than Edgar tended her. Day and night, he was watching, and patiently enduring all the annoyances that irritable nerves and a shaken reason could inflict; and, though Kenneth remarked that what he saved from the grave would only recompense his care by forming the source of constant future anxiety—in fact, that his health and strength were being sacrificed to preserve a mere ruin of humanity—he knew no limits in gratitude and joy when Catherine's life was declared out of danger; and hour after hour he would sit beside her, tracing the gradual return to bodily health, and flattering his too sanguine hopes with the illusion that her mind would settle back to its right balance also, and she would soon be entirely her former self.

The first time she left her chamber was at the commencement of the following March. Mr. Linton had put on her pillow, in the morning, a handful of golden crocuses; her eye, long stranger to any gleam of pleasure, caught them in waking, and shone delighted as she gathered them eagerly together.

"These are the earliest flowers at the Heights!" she exclaimed. "They remind me of soft thaw winds, and warm sunshine, and nearly melted snow. Edgar, is there not a south wind, and is not the snow almost gone?"

"The snow is quite gone down here, darling," replied her husband, "and I only see two white spots on the whole range of moors. The sky is blue, and the larks are singing, and the becks and brooks are all brim full. Catherine, last spring at this time, I was longing to have you under this roof; now, I wish you were a mile or two up those hills; the air blows so sweetly, I feel that it would cure you."

"I shall never be there, but once more!" said the invalid; "and then you'll leave me, and I shall remain for ever. Next spring you'll long again to have me under this roof, and you'll look back and think you were happy to-day."

Linton lavished on her the kindest caresses, and tried to cheer her by the fondest words; but, vaguely regarding the flowers, she let the tears collect on her lashes and stream down her cheeks unheeding.

We knew she was really better, and, therefore, decided that long confinement to a single place produced much of this despondency, and it might be partially removed by a change of scene.

The master told me to light a fire in the many-weeks-deserted parlour, and to set an easy-chair in the sunshine by the window; and then he brought her down, and she sat a long while enjoying the genial heat, and, as we expected, revived by the objects round her, which, though familiar, were free from the dreary associations investing her hated sickchamber. By evening, she seemed greatly exhausted; yet no arguments could persuade her to return to that apartment, and I had to arrange the parlour sofa for her bed, till another room could be prepared.

To obviate the fatigue of mounting and descending the stairs, we fitted up this, where you lie at present, on the same floor with the parlour; and she was soon strong enough to move from one to the other, leaning on Edgar's arm.

Ah, I thought myself, she might recover, so waited on as she was. And there was double cause to desire it, for on her existence depended that of another; we cherished the hope that in a little while Mr. Linton's heart would be gladdened, and his lands secured from a stranger's gripe, by the birth of an heir.

I should mention that Isabella sent to her brother, some six weeks from her departure, a short note, announcing her marriage with Heathcliff. It appeared dry and cold; but at the bottom was dotted in with pencil an obscure apology, and an entreaty for kind remembrance and reconciliation, if her proceeding had offended him; asserting that she could not help it then, and being done, she had now no power to repeal it.

Linton did not reply to this, I believe; and, in a fortnight more, I got a long letter, which I considered odd coming from the pen of a bride just out of the honeymoon. I'll read it, for I keep it yet. Any relic of the dead is precious, if they were valued living.

Dear Ellen, it begins.

I came last night to Wuthering Heights, and heard, for the first time, that Catherine has been, and is yet, very ill. I must not write to her, I suppose, and my brother is either too angry or too distressed to answer what I send him. Still, I must write to somebody, and the only choice left me is you.

Inform Edgar that I'd give the world to see his face again—that my heart returned to Thrushcross Grange in twenty-four hours after I left it, and is there at this moment, full of warm feelings for him, and Catherine! *I can't follow it, though*—(those words are underlined)—they need not expect me, and they may draw what conclusions they please; taking care, however, to lay nothing at the door of my weak will or deficient affection.

The remainder of the letter is for yourself alone. I want to ask you two questions: the first is—

How did you contrive to preserve the common sympathies of human nature when you resided here? I cannot recognise any sentiment which those around share with me.

The second question, I have great interest in; it is this—

Is Mr. Heathcliff a man? If so, is he mad? And if not, is he a devil? I shan't tell my reasons for making this inquiry; but I beseech you to explain, if you can, what I have married—that is, when you call to see me; and you must call, Ellen, very soon. Don't write, but come, and bring me something from Edgar.

Now, you shall hear how I have been received in my new home, as I am led to imagine the Heights will be. It is to amuse myself that I dwell on such subjects as the lack of external comforts; they never occupy my thoughts, except at the moment when I miss them. I should laugh and dance for joy, if I found their absence was the total of my miseries, and the rest was an unnatural dream!

The sun set behind the Grange, as we turned on to the moors; by that, I judged it to be six o'clock; and my companion halted half-an-hour, to inspect the park, and the gardens, and, probably, the place itself, as well as he could; so it was dark when we dismounted in the paved yard of the farmhouse, and your old fellow-servant, Joseph, issued out to receive us by the light of a dip candle. He did it with a courtesy that redounded to his credit. His first act was to elevate his torch to a level with my face, squint malignantly, project his under-lip, and turn away.

Then he took the two horses, and led them into the stables; reappearing for the purpose of locking the outer gate, as if we lived in an ancient castle.

Heathcliff stayed to speak to him, and I entered the kitchen— a dingy, untidy hole; I dare say you would not know it, it is so changed since it was in your charge.

By the fire stood a ruffianly child, strong in limb and dirty in garb, with a look of Catherine in his eyes and about his mouth.

"This is Edgar's legal nephew," I reflected—"mine in a manner; I must shake hands, and—yes—I must kiss him. It is right to establish a good understanding at the beginning."

I approached, and, attempting to take his chubby fist, said— "How do you do, my dear?"

He replied in a jargon I did not comprehend.

"Shall you and I be friends, Hareton?" was my next essay at conversation.

An oath, and a threat to set Throttler on me if I did not "frame off,"[1] rewarded my perseverance.

"Hey, Throttler, lad!" whispered the little wretch, rousing a half-bred bull-dog from its lair in a corner. "Now, wilt tuh be ganging?"[2] he asked authoritatively.

Love for my life urged a compliance; I stepped over the threshold to wait till the others should enter. Mr. Heathcliff was nowhere visible; and Joseph, whom I followed to the stables and requested to accompany me in, after staring and muttering to himself, screwed up his nose and replied—

---

1. Be gone.  2. Will you be going?

"Mim! mim! mim! Did iver Christian body hear owt like it? Minching un' munching! Hah can Aw tell whet ye say?"[3]

"I say, I wish you to come with me into the house!" I cried, thinking him deaf, yet highly disgusted at his rudeness.

"Nor nuh me![4] Aw getten summut else to do," he answered, and continued his work, moving his lantern jaws meanwhile, and surveying my dress and countenance (the former a great deal too fine, but the latter, I'm sure, as sad as he could desire) with sovereign contempt.

I walked round the yard, and through a wicket, to another door, at which I took the liberty of knocking, in hopes some more civil servant might shew himself.

After a short suspense, it was opened by a tall, gaunt man, without neckerchief, and otherwise extremely slovenly; his features were lost in masses of shaggy hair that hung on his shoulders; and *his* eyes, too, were like a ghostly Catherine's, with all their beauty annihilated.

"What's your business here?" he demanded, grimly. "Who are you?"

"My name *was* Isabella Linton," I replied. "You've seen me before, sir. I'm lately married to Mr. Heathcliff; and he has brought me here—I suppose by your permission."

"Is he come back, then?" asked the hermit, glaring like a hungry wolf.

"Yes—we came just now," I said; "but he left me by the kitchen door; and when I would have gone in, your little boy played sentinel over the place, and frightened me off by the help of a bull-dog."

"It's well the hellish villain has kept his word!" growled my future host, searching the darkness beyond me in expectation of discovering Heathcliff; and then he indulged in a soliloquy of execrations, and threats of what he would have done had the "fiend" deceived him.

I repented having tried this second entrance, and was almost inclined to slip way before he finished cursing, but ere I could execute that intention, he ordered me in, and shut and re-fastened the door.

There was a great fire, and that was all the light in the huge apartment, whose floor had grown a uniform grey; and the once brilliant pewter dishes, which used to attract my gaze when I was a girl, partook of a similar obscurity, created by tarnish and dust.

I inquired whether I might call the maid, and be conducted to a bed-room? Mr. Earnshaw vouchsafed no answer. He walked up

3. *Owt:* aught; *minching un' munching:* mincing and mouthing.     4. Not me.

and down, with his hands in his pockets, apparently quite forgetting my presence; and his abstraction was evidently so deep, and his whole aspect so misanthropical, that I shrank from disturbing him again.

You'll not be surprised, Ellen, at my feeling particularly cheerless, seated in worse than solitude on that inhospitable hearth, and remembering that four miles distant lay my delightful home, containing the only people I loved on earth; and there might as well be the Atlantic to part us, instead of those four miles: I could not overpass them!

I questioned with myself—where must I turn for comfort? and —mind you don't tell Edgar, or Catherine—above every sorrow beside, this rose pre-eminent—despair at finding nobody who could or would be my ally against Heathcliff!

I had sought shelter at Wuthering Heights, almost gladly, because I was secured by that arrangement from living alone with him; but he knew the people we were coming amongst, and he did not fear their intermeddling.

I sat and thought a doleful time; the clock struck eight, and nine, and still my companion paced to and fro, his head bent on his breast, and perfectly silent, unless a groan or a bitter ejaculation forced itself out at intervals.

I listened to detect a woman's voice in the house, and filled the interim with wild regrets and dismal anticipations, which, at last, spoke audibly in irrepressible sighing and weeping.

I was not aware how openly I grieved, till Earnshaw halted opposite, in his measured walk, and gave me a stare of newly awakened surprise. Taking advantage of his recovered attention, I exclaimed—

"I'm tired with my journey, and I want to go to bed! Where is the maid-servant? Direct me to her, as she won't come to me!"

"We have none," he answered; "you must wait on yourself!"

"Where must I sleep, then?" I sobbed—I was beyond regarding self-respect, weighed down by fatigue and wretchedness.

"Joseph will show you Heathcliff's chamber," said he; "open that door—he's in there."

I was going to obey, but he suddenly arrested me, and added in the strangest tone—

"Be so good as to turn your lock, and draw your bolt—don't omit it!"

"Well!" I said. "But why, Mr. Earnshaw?" I did not relish the notion of deliberately fastening myself in with Heathcliff.

"Look here!" he replied, pulling from his waistcoat a curiously constructed pistol, having a double-edged spring knife attached to the barrel. "That's a great tempter to a desperate man, is it not?

I cannot resist going up with this, every night, and trying his door. If once I find it open, he's done for! I do it invariably, even though the minute before I have been recalling a hundred reasons that should make me refrain: it is some devil that urges me to thwart my own schemes by killing him. You fight against that devil, for love, as long as you may; when the time comes, not all the angels in heaven shall save him!"

I surveyed the weapon inquisitively; a hideous notion struck me. How powerful I should be possessing such an instrument! I took it from his hand, and touched the blade. He looked astonished at the expression my face assumed during a brief second. It was not horror, it was covetousness. He snatched the pistol back, jealously; shut the knife, and returned it to its concealment.

"I don't care if you tell him," said he. "Put him on his guard, and watch for him. You know the terms we are on, I see; his danger does not shock you."

"What has Heathcliff done to you?" I asked. "In what has he wronged you to warrant this appalling hatred? Wouldn't it be wiser to bid him quit the house?"

"No," thundered Earnshaw; "should he offer to leave me, he's a dead man: persuade him to attempt it, and you are a murderess! Am I to lose *all*, without a chance of retrieval? Is Hareton to be a beggar? Oh, damnation! I *will* have it back; and I'll have *his* gold too; and then his blood; and hell shall have his soul! It will be ten times blacker with that guest than ever it was before!"

You've acquainted me, Ellen, with your old master's habits. He is clearly on the verge of madness—he was so last night, at least. I shuddered to be near him, and thought on the servant's ill-bred moroseness as comparatively agreeable.

He now recommenced his moody walk, and I raised the latch, and escaped into the kitchen.

Joseph was bending over the fire, peering into a large pan that swung above it; and a wooden bowl of oatmeal stood on the settle close by. The contents of the pan began to boil, and he turned to plunge his hand into the bowl; I conjectured that this preparation was probably for our supper, and, being hungry, I resolved it should be eatable; so, crying out sharply, "I'*ll* make the porridge!" I removed the vessel out of his reach, and proceeded to take off my hat and riding habit. "Mr. Earnshaw," I continued, "directs me to wait on myself: I will. I'm not going to act the lady among you, for fear I should starve."

"Gooid Lord!" he muttered, sitting down, and stroking his ribbed stockings from the knee to the ankle. "If they's tuh be fresh ortherings—just when Aw getten used tuh two maisters, if Aw mun hev a *mistress* set o'er my heead, it's loike time tuh be flitting. Aw niver *did* think tuh say t' day ut Aw mud lave th' owld place—but Aw daht it's nigh at hend!"[5]

This lamentation drew no notice from me; I went briskly to work, sighing to remember a period when it would have been all merry fun, but compelled speedily to drive off the remembrance. It racked me to recall past happiness, and the greater peril there was of conjuring up its apparition, the quicker the thible[6] ran round, and the faster the handfuls of meal fell into the water.

Joseph beheld my style of cookery with growing indignation.

"Thear!" he ejaculated. "Hareton, thah willut sup thy porridge tuh neeght; they'll be nowt bud lumps as big as maw nave. Thear, agean! Aw'd fling in bowl un all, if Aw wer yah! Thear, pale t' guilp off, un' then yah'll hae done wi't. Bang, bang. It's a marcy t' bothom isn't deaved aht!"[7]

It *was* rather a rough mess, I own, when poured into the basins; four had been provided, and a gallon pitcher of new milk was brought from the dairy, which Hareton seized and commenced drinking and spilling from the expansive lip.

I expostulated, and desired that he should have his in a mug; affirming that I could not taste the liquid treated so dirtily. The old cynic chose to be vastly offended at this nicety; assuring me, repeatedly, that "the barn was every bit as gooid" as I, "and every bit as wollsome,"[8] and wondering how I could fashion to be so conceited; meanwhile, the infant ruffian continued sucking; and glowered up at me defyingly, as he slavered into the jug.

"I shall have my supper in another room," I said. "Have you no place you call a parlour?"

"*Parlour!*" he echoed, sneeringly, "*parlour!* Nay, we've noa *parlours*. If yah dunnut loike wer company,[9] they's maister's; un' if yah dunnut loike maister, they's us."

"Then I shall go upstairs," I answered; "shew me a chamber!"

I put my basin on a tray, and went myself to fetch some more milk.

With great grumblings, the fellow rose and preceded me in my ascent: we mounted to the garrets, he opening a door, now and then, to look into the apartments we passed.

"Here's a rahm," he said, at last, flinging back a cranky board on hinges. "It's weel eneugh tuh ate a few porridge in. They's a pack uh corn i' t' corner, thear, meeterly clane; if yah're feared uh muckying yer grand silk cloes, spread yer hankerchir ut t' top

---

5. *Ortherings:* orders; *flitting:* moving out; *mud lave:* must leave; *daht:* doubt (i.e., don't doubt); *at hend:* at hand.
6. A smooth stick for stirring broth, porridge, etc.
7. *Willut:* will not; *nave:* fist; *pale t' guilp off:* cool the iron pot (of porridge) by taking out a ladleful and dropping it in again; *deaved:* broken violently.
8. *Barn:* child; *wollsome:* healthy.
9. Our company.

on't."[1]

The "rahm" was a kind of lumber-hole smelling strong of malt and grain; various sacks of which articles were piled around, leaving a wide, bare space in the middle.

"Why, man!" I exclaimed, facing him angrily, "this is not a place to sleep in. I wish to see my bed-room."

"*Bed-rume!*" he repeated, in a tone of mockery. "Yah's see all t' *bed-rumes* thear is—yon's mine."

He pointed into the second garret, only differing from the first in being more naked about the walls, and having a large, low, curtainless bed, with an indigo-coloured quilt, at one end.

"What do I want with yours?" I retorted. "I suppose Mr. Heathcliff does not lodge at the top of the house, does he?"

"Oh! it's Maister *Hathecliff's* yah're wenting?" cried he, as if making a new discovery. "Couldn't ye uh said soa, at onst? un then, Aw mud uh telled ye, 'baht all this wark,[2] ut that's just one yah cannut sea—he allas keeps it locked, un' nob'dy iver mells[3] on't but hisseln."

"You've a nice house, Joseph," I could not refrain from observing, "and pleasant inmates; and I think the concentrated essence of all the madness in the world took up its abode in my brain the day I linked my fate with theirs! However, that is not to the present purpose—there are other rooms. For heaven's sake, be quick, and let me settle somewhere!"

He made no reply to this adjuration; only plodding doggedly down the wooden steps, and halting before an apartment which, from that halt and the superior quality of its furniture, I conjectured to be the best one.

There was a carpet, a good one; but the pattern was obliterated by dust; a fire-place hung with cut paper, dropping to pieces; a handsome oak-bedstead with ample crimson curtains of rather expensive material and modern make. But they had evidently experienced rough usage; the valances hung in festoons, wrenched from their rings, and the iron rod supporting them was bent in an arc on one side, causing the drapery to trail upon the floor. The chairs were also damaged, many of them severely; and deep indentations deformed the panels of the walls.

I was endeavouring to gather resolution for entering, and taking possession, when my fool of a guide announced—

"This here is t' maister's."

My supper by this time was cold, my appetite gone, and my patience exhausted. I insisted on being provided instantly with a

---

1. *Rahm:* room; *meeterly clane:* fairly clean; *muckying:* dirtying.
2. *'Baht all this wark:* without all this work.
3. *Mells:* meddles.

place of refuge, and means of repose.

"Whear the divil—" began the religious elder. "The Lord bless us! The Lord forgie us! Whear the *hell* wold ye gang? ye marred, wearisome nowt! Yah seen all bud Hareton's bit uf a cham'er. They's nut another hoile tuh lig dahn in i' th' hahse!"[4]

I was so vexed, I flung my tray and its contents on the ground; and then seated myself at the stairs-head, hid my face in my hands, and cried.

"Ech! ech!" exclaimed Joseph. "Weel done, Miss Cathy! weel done, Miss Cathy! Hahsiver, t' maister sall just tum'le o'er them brocken pots, un' then we's hear summut; we's hear hah it's tuh be. Gooid-fur-nowt madling! yah desarve pining froo this tuh Churstmas, flinging t' precious gifts uh God under fooit i' yer flaysome rages! Bud Aw'm mista'em if yah shew yer sperrit lang. Will Hathecliff bide sich bonny ways, think ye? Aw nobbut wish he muh cotch ye i' that plisky. Aw nobbut wish he may."[5]

And so he went scolding to his den beneath, taking the candle with him, and I remained in the dark.

The period of reflection succeeding this silly action compelled me to admit the necessity of smothering my pride, and choking my wrath, and bestirring myself to remove its effects.

An unexpected aid presently appeared in the shape of Throttler, whom I now recognised as a son of our old Skulker; it had spent its whelphood at the Grange, and was given by my father to Mr. Hindley. I fancy it knew me: it pushed its nose against mine by way of salute, and then hastened to devour the porridge, while I groped from step to step, collecting the shattered earthenware, and drying the spatters of milk from the banister with my pocket-handkerchief.

Our labours were scarcely over when I heard Earnshaw's tread in the passage; my assistant tucked in his tail, and pressed to the wall; I stole into the nearest doorway. The dog's endeavour to avoid him was unsuccessful, as I guessed by a scutter downstairs, and a prolonged, piteous yelping. I had better luck. He passed on, entered his chamber, and shut the door.

Directly after, Joseph came up with Hareton, to put him to bed. I had found shelter in Hareton's room, and the old man, on seeing me, said—

"They's rahm fur boath yah un yer pride, nah, Aw sud think i' th' hahse. It's empty; yah muh hev it all tuh yerseln, un Him[6] as allas maks a third, i' sich ill company!"

Gladly did I take advantage of this intimation; and the minute

4. *Marred, wearisome nowt:* spoiled, wearisome nothing; *hoile:* room; *lig:* lie.

5. *Pining:* starving; *nobbut wish:* only wish; *plisky:* rage.
6. God.

I flung myself into a chair, by the fire, I nodded, and slept.

My slumber was deep and sweet, though over far too soon. Mr. Heathcliff awoke me; he had just come in, and demanded, in his loving manner, what I was doing there?

I told him the cause of my staying up so late—that he had the key of our room in his pocket.

The adjective *our* gave mortal offence. He swore it was not, nor ever should be mine; and he'd—but I'll not repeat his language, nor describe his habitual conduct; he is ingenious and unresting in seeking to gain my abhorrence! I sometimes wonder at him with an intensity that deadens my fear: yet, I assure you, a tiger or a venomous serpent could not rouse terror in me equal to that which he wakens. He told me of Catherine's illness, and accused my brother of causing it; promising that I should be Edgar's proxy in suffering, till he could get a hold of him.

I do hate him—I am wretched—I have been a fool! Beware of uttering one breath of this to any one at the Grange. I shall expect you every day—don't disappoint me!

Isabella.

## Chapter XIV

As soon as I had perused this epistle, I went to the master, and informed him that his sister had arrived at the Heights, and sent me a letter expressing her sorrow for Mrs. Linton's situation, and her ardent desire to see him; with a wish that he would transmit to her, as early as possible, some token of forgiveness by me.

"Forgiveness!" said Linton. "I have nothing to forgive her, Ellen. You may call at Wuthering Heights this afternoon, if you like, and say that I am not *angry*, but I'm *sorry* to have lost her: especially as I can never think she'll be happy. It is out of the question my going to see her, however; we are eternally divided; and should she really wish to oblige me, let her persuade the villain she has married to leave the country."

"And you won't write her a little note, sir?" I asked, imploringly.

"No," he answered. "It is needless. My communication with Heathcliff's family shall be as sparing as his with mine. It shall not exist!"

Mr. Edgar's coldness depressed me exceedingly; and all the way from the Grange I puzzled my brains how to put more heart into what he said, when I repeated it; and how to soften his refusal of even a few lines to console Isabella.

I dare say she had been on the watch for me since morning: I saw her looking through the lattice, as I came up the garden causeway, and I nodded to her; but she drew back, as if afraid of being observed.

I entered without knocking. There never was such a dreary, dismal scene as the formerly cheerful house presented! I must confess that, if I had been in the young lady's place, I would, at least, have swept the hearth and wiped the tables with a duster. But she already partook of the pervading spirit of neglect which encompassed her. Her pretty face was wan and listless; her hair uncurled, some locks hanging lankly down, and some carelessly twisted round her head. Probably she had not touched her dress since yester evening.

Hindley was not there. Mr. Heathcliff sat at a table, turning over some papers in his pocket-book; but he rose when I appeared, asked me how I did, quite friendly, and offered me a chair.

He was the only thing there that seemed decent, and I thought he never looked better. So much had circumstances altered their positions, that he would certainly have struck a stranger as a born and bred gentleman, and his wife as a thorough little slattern!

She came forward eagerly to greet me; and held out one hand to take the expected letter.

I shook my head. She wouldn't understand the hint, but followed me to a sideboard, where I went to lay my bonnet, and importuned me in a whisper to give her directly what I had brought.

Heathcliff guessed the meaning of her manœuvres, and said—

"If you have got anything for Isabella, as no doubt you have, Nelly, give it to her. You needn't make a secret of it; we have no secrets between us."

"Oh, I have nothing," I replied, thinking it best to speak the truth at once. "My master bid me tell his sister that she must not expect either a letter or a visit from him at present. He sends his love, ma'am, and his wishes for your happiness, and his pardon for the grief you have occasioned; but he thinks that after this time, his household, and the household here, should drop intercommunication, as nothing good could come of keeping it up."

Mrs. Heathcliff's lip quivered slightly, and she returned to her seat in the window. Her husband took his stand on the hearthstone, near me, and began to put questions concerning Catherine.

I told him as much as I thought proper of her illness, and he extorted from me, by cross-examination, most of the facts connected with its origin.

I blamed her, as she deserved, for bringing it all on herself; and ended by hoping that he would follow Mr. Linton's example, and avoid future interference with his family, for good or evil.

"Mrs. Linton is now just recovering," I said; "she'll never be like she was, but her life is spared, and if you really have a regard for her, you'll shun crossing her way again. Nay, you'll move out of this country entirely; and that you may not regret it, I'll inform you Catherine Linton is as different now from your old friend Catherine Earnshaw, as that young lady is different from me! Her appearance is changed greatly, her character much more so; and the person who is compelled, of necessity, to be her companion, will only sustain his affection hereafter by the remembrance of what she once was, by common humanity, and a sense of duty!"

"That is quite possible," remarked Heathcliff, forcing himself to seem calm, "quite possible that your master should have nothing but common humanity, and a sense of duty to fall back upon. But do you imagine that I shall leave Catherine to his *duty* and *humanity*? and can you compare my feelings respecting Catherine, to his? Before you leave this house, I must exact a promise from you, that you'll get me an interview with her: consent, or refuse, I *will* see her! What do you say?"

"I say, Mr. Heathcliff," I replied, "you must not—you never shall, through my means. Another encounter between you and the master would kill her altogether!"

"With your aid that may be avoided," he continued, "and should there be danger of such an event—should he be the cause of adding a single trouble more to her existence—why, I think, I shall be justified in going to extremes! I wish you had sincerity enough to tell me whether Catherine would suffer greatly from his loss. The fear that she would restrains me: and there you see the distinction between our feelings. Had he been in my place, and I in his, though I hated him with a hatred that turned my life to gall, I never would have raised a hand against him. You may look incredulous, if you please! I never would have banished him from her society, as long as she desired his. The moment her regard ceased, I would have torn his heart out, and drank his blood! But, till then—if you don't believe me, you don't know me—till then, I would have died by inches before I touched a single hair of his head!"

"And yet," I interrupted, "you have no scruples in completely ruining all hopes of her perfect restoration, by thrusting yourself into her remembrance, now, when she has nearly forgotten you, and involving her in a new tumult of discord and distress."

"You suppose she has nearly forgotten me?" he said. "Oh, Nelly! you know she has not! You know as well as I do, that for every thought she spends on Linton, she spends a thousand on me! At a most miserable period of my life, I had a notion of the kind; it haunted me on my return to the neighbourhood last summer, but only her own assurance could make me admit the horrible idea again. And then, Linton would be nothing, nor Hindley, nor all the dreams that ever I dreamt. Two words would comprehend my future—*death* and *hell*; existence, after losing her, would be hell.

"Yet I was a fool to fancy for a moment that she valued Edgar Linton's attachment more than mine. If he loved with all the powers of his puny being, he couldn't love as much in eighty years as I could in a day. And Catherine has a heart as deep as I have; the sea could be as readily contained in that horse-trough, as her whole affection be monopolized by him. Tush! He is scarcely a degree dearer to her than her dog, or her horse. It is not in him to be loved like me: how can she love in him what he has not?"

"Catherine and Edgar are as fond of each other as any two people can be!" cried Isabella, with sudden vivacity. "No one has a right to talk in that manner, and I won't hear my brother depreciated in silence!"

"Your brother is wondrous fond of you too, isn't he?" observed Heathcliff scornfully. "He turns you adrift on the world with surprising alacrity."

"He is not aware of what I suffer," she replied. "I didn't tell him that."

"You have been telling him something, then—you have written, have you?"

"To say that I was married, I did write—you saw the note."

"And nothing since?"

"No."

"My young lady is looking sadly the worse for her change of condition," I remarked. "Somebody's love comes short in her case, obviously—whose I may guess; but, perhaps, I shouldn't say."

"I should guess it was her own," said Heathcliff. "She degenerates into a mere slut! She is tired of trying to please me, uncommonly early. You'd hardly credit it, but the very morrow of our wedding, she was weeping to go home. However, she'll suit this house so much the better for not being over nice, and I'll take care she does not disgrace me by rambling abroad."

"Well, sir," returned I, "I hope you'll consider that Mrs. Heathcliff is accustomed to be looked after and waited on; and that she has been brought up like an only daughter, whom every one was ready to serve. You must let her have a maid to keep things tidy about her, and you must treat her kindly. Whatever be your notion of Mr. Edgar, you cannot doubt that she has a capacity for strong attachments, or she wouldn't have abandoned the elegancies, and comforts, and friends of her former home, to fix contentedly, in such a wilderness as this, with you."

"She abandoned them under a delusion," he answered, "picturing in me a hero of romance, and expecting unlimited indulgences from my chivalrous devotion. I can hardly regard her in the light of a rational creature, so obstinately has she persisted in forming a fabulous notion of my character, and acting on the false impressions she cherished. But, at last, I think she begins to know me. I don't perceive the silly smiles and grimaces that provoked me at first; and the senseless incapability of discerning that I was in earnest when I gave her my opinion of her infatuation, and herself. It was a marvellous effort of perspicacity to discover that I did not love her. I believed, at one time, no lessons could teach her that! And yet it is poorly learnt; for this morning she announced, as a piece of appalling intelligence, that I had actually succeeded in making her hate me! A positive labour of Hercules, I assure you! If it be achieved, I have cause to return thanks. Can I trust your assertion, Isabella? Are you sure you hate me? If I let you alone for half-a-day, won't you come sighing and wheedling to me again? I dare say she would rather I had seemed all tenderness before you; it wounds her vanity, to have the truth exposed. But I don't care who knows that the passion was wholly on one side, and I never told her a lie about it. She cannot accuse me of showing one bit of deceitful softness. The first thing she saw me do, on coming out of the Grange, was to hang up her little dog; and when she pleaded for it the first words I uttered were a wish that I had the hanging of every being belonging to her, except one: possibly she took that exception for herself. But no brutality disgusted her. I suppose she has an innate admiration of it, if only her precious person were secure from injury! Now, was it not the depth of absurdity—of genuine idiocy—for that pitiful, slavish, mean-minded brach[1] to dream that I could love her? Tell your master, Nelly, that I never, in all my life, met with such an abject thing as she is. She even disgraces the name of Linton; and I've sometimes relented, from pure lack of invention, in my experiments on what she could endure, and still creep shamefully cringing back! But tell him, also, to set his fraternal and magisterial heart at ease, that I keep strictly within the limits of the law. I have avoided, up to this period, giving her the slightest right to claim a separation; and, what's more, she'd thank nobody for dividing us. If she desired to go she might: the nuisance of her presence outweighs the gratification to be derived from tormenting her!"

"Mr. Heathcliff," said I, "this is the talk of a madman, and your wife, most likely, is convinced you are mad; and, for that reason, she has borne with you hitherto: but now that you say she may go, she'll doubtless avail herself of the permission. You are not so bewitched, ma'am, are you, as to remain with him of your own accord?"

"Take care, Ellen!" answered Isabella, her eyes sparkling irefully; there was no misdoubting by their expression, the full success of

1. Bitch-hound.

her partner's endeavours to make himself detested. "Don't put faith in a single word he speaks. He's a lying fiend, a monster, and not a human being! I've been told I might leave him before; and I've made the attempt, but I dare not repeat it! Only, Ellen, promise you'll not mention a syllable of his infamous conversation to my brother or Catherine. Whatever he may pretend, he wishes to provoke Edgar to desperation: he says he has married me on purpose to obtain power over him; and he shan't obtain it —I'll die first! I just hope, I pray, that he may forget his diabolical prudence, and kill me! The single pleasure I can imagine is to die, or to see him dead!"

"There—that will do for the present!" said Heathcliff. "If you are called upon in a court of law, you'll remember her language, Nelly! And take a good look at that countenance—she's near the point which would suit me. No, you're not fit to be your own guardian, Isabella, now; and I, being your legal protector, must retain you in my custody, however distasteful the obligation may be. Go upstairs; I have something to say to Ellen Dean in private. That's not the way—upstairs, I tell you! Why, this is the road upstairs, child!"

He seized, and thrust her from the room; and returned muttering—

"I have no pity! I have no pity! The more the worms writhe, the more I yearn to crush out their entrails! It is a moral teething, and I grind with greater energy, in proportion to the increase of pain."

"Do you understand what the word pity means?" I said, hastening to resume my bonnet. "Did you ever feel a touch of it in your life?"

"Put that down!" he interrupted, perceiving my intention to depart. "You are not going yet. Come here now, Nelly: I must either persuade or compel you to aid me in fulfilling my determination to see Catherine, and that without delay. I swear that I meditate no harm; I don't desire to cause any disturbance, or to exasperate or insult Mr. Linton; I only wish to hear from herself how she is, and why she has been ill; and to ask if anything that I could do would be of use to her. Last night, I was in the Grange garden six hours, and I'll return there to-night; and every night I'll haunt the place, and every day, till I find an opportunity of entering. If Edgar Linton meets me, I shall not hesitate to knock him down, and give him enough to ensure his quiescence while I stay. If his servants oppose me, I shall threaten them off with these pistols. But wouldn't it be better to prevent my coming in contact with them, or their master? And you could do it so easily! I'd warn you when I came, and then you might let me in unobserved, as soon as she was alone, and watch till I departed, your conscience quite calm: you would be hindering mischief."

I protested against playing that treacherous part in my employer's house; and besides, I urged the cruelty and selfishness of his destroying Mrs. Linton's tranquillity, for his satisfaction.

"The commonest occurrence startles her painfully," I said. "She's all nerves, and she couldn't bear the surprise, I'm positive. Don't persist, sir! or else, I shall be obliged to inform my master of your designs, and he'll take measures to secure his house and its inmates from any such unwarrantable intrusions!"

"In that case, I'll take measures to secure you, woman!" exclaimed Heathcliff; "you shall not leave Wuthering Heights till to-morrow morning. It is a foolish story to assert that Catherine could not bear to see me; and as to surprising her, I don't desire it: you must prepare her—ask her if I may come. You say she never mentions my name, and that I am never mentioned to her. To whom should she mention me if I am a forbidden topic in the house? She thinks you are all spies for her husband. Oh, I've no doubt she's in hell among you! I guess by her silence, as much as any thing, what she feels. You say she is often restless, and anxious-looking—is that a proof of tranquillity? You talk of her mind being unsettled. How the devil could it be otherwise, in her frightful isolation. And that insipid, paltry creature attending her from *duty* and *humanity!* From *pity* and *charity!* He might as well plant an oak in a flowerpot, and expect it to thrive, as imagine he can restore her to vigour in the soil of his shallow cares! Let us settle it at once; will you stay here, and am I to fight my way to Catherine over Linton and his footmen? Or will you be my friend, as you have been hitherto, and do what I request? Decide! Because there is no reason for my lingering another minute, if you persist in your stubborn ill-nature!"

Well, Mr. Lockwood, I argued and complained, and flatly refused him fifty times; but in the long run he forced me to an agreement. I engaged to carry a letter from him to my mistress; and should she consent, I promised to let him have intelligence of Linton's next absence from home, when he might come, and get in as he was able. I wouldn't be there, and my fellow servants should be equally out of the way.

Was it right or wrong? I fear it was wrong, though expedient. I thought I prevented another explosion by my compliance; and I thought, too, it might create a favourable crisis in Catherine's mental illness: and then I remembered Mr. Edgar's stern rebuke of my carrying tales; and I tried to smooth away all disquietude on the subject, by affirming, with frequent iteration, that that betrayal of trust, if it merited so harsh an appellation, should be the last.

Notwithstanding, my journey homeward was sadder than my journey thither; and many misgivings I had, ere I could prevail on myself to put the missive into Mrs. Linton's hand.

But here is Kenneth; I'll go down, and tell him how much better you are. My history is *dree*[2] as we say, and will serve to wile away another morning.

Dree, and dreary! I reflected as the good woman descended to receive the doctor; and not exactly of the kind which I should have chosen to amuse me. But never mind! I'll extract wholesome medicines from Mrs. Dean's bitter herbs; and firstly, let me beware of the fascination that lurks in Catherine Heathcliff's brilliant eyes. I should be in a curious taking if I surrendered my heart to that young person, and the daughter turned out a second edition of the mother!

## Chapter XV

Another week over—and I am so many days nearer health, and spring! I have now heard all my neighbour's history, at different sittings, as the housekeeper could spare time from more important occupations. I'll continue it in her own words, only a little condensed. She is, on the whole, a very fair narrator and I don't think I could improve her style.

In the evening, she said, the evening of my visit to the Heights, I knew, as well as if I saw him, that Mr. Heathcliff was about the place; and I shunned going out, because I still carried his letter in my pocket, and didn't want to be threatened, or teased any more.

I had made up my mind not to give it till my master went somewhere, as I could not guess how its receipt would affect Catherine. The consequence was, that it did not reach her before the lapse of three days. The fourth was Sunday, and I brought it into her room after the family were gone to church.

There was a man-servant left to keep the house with me, and we generally made a practice of locking the doors during the hours of service; but on that occasion the weather was so warm and pleasant that I set them wide open, and, to fulfil my engagement, as I knew who would be coming, I told my companion that the mistress wished very much for some oranges, and he must run over to the village and get a few, to be paid for on the morrow. He departed, and I went upstairs.

Mrs. Linton sat in a loose, white dress, with a light shawl over her shoulders, in the recess of the open window, as usual. Her thick, long hair had been partly removed at the beginning of her

2. Sad.

illness, and now she wore it simply combed in its natural tresses over her temples and neck. Her appearance was altered, as I had told Heathcliff, but when she was calm, there seemed unearthly beauty in the change.

The flash of her eyes had been succeeded by a dreamy and melancholy softness; they no longer gave the impression of looking at the objects around her; they appeared always to gaze beyond, and far beyond—you would have said out of this world. Then, the paleness of her face—its haggard aspect having vanished as she recovered flesh—and the peculiar expression arising from her mental state, though painfully suggestive of their causes, added to the touching interest which she wakened, and—invariably to me, I know, and to any person who saw her, I should think—refuted more tangible proofs of convalescence and stamped her as one doomed to decay.

A book lay spread on the sill before her, and the scarcely perceptible wind fluttered its leaves at intervals. I believe Linton had laid it there, for she never endeavoured to divert herself with reading, or occupation of any kind, and he would spend many an hour in trying to entice her attention to some subject which had formerly been her amusement.

She was conscious of his aim, and in her better moods endured his efforts placidly, only showing their uselessness by now and then suppressing a wearied sigh, and checking him at last with the saddest of smiles and kisses. At other times, she would turn petulantly away, and hide her face in her hands, or even push him off angrily; and then he took care to let her alone, for he was certain of doing no good.

Gimmerton chapel bells were still ringing; and the full, mellow flow of the beck in the valley came soothingly on the ear. It was a sweet substitute for the yet absent murmur of the summer foliage, which drowned that music about the Grange when the trees were in leaf. At Wuthering Heights it always sounded on quiet days, following a great thaw or a season of steady rain; and of Wuthering Heights, Catherine was thinking as she listened—that is, if she thought, or listened, at all—but she had the vague, distant look I mentioned before, which expressed no recognition of material things either by ear or eye.

"There's a letter for you, Mrs. Linton," I said, gently inserting it in one hand that rested on her knee. "You must read it immediately, because it wants an answer. Shall I break the seal?"

"Yes," she answered, without altering the direction of her eyes. I opened it—it was very short.

"Now," I continued, "read it."

She drew away her hand, and let it fall. I replaced it in her lap, and stood waiting till it should please her to glance down; but that movement was so long delayed that at last I resumed—

"Must I read it, ma'am? It is from Mr. Heathcliff."

There was a start, and a troubled gleam of recollection, and a struggle to arrange her ideas. She lifted the letter, and seemed to peruse it; and when she came to the signature she sighed; yet still I found she had not gathered its import, for, upon my desiring to hear her reply, she merely pointed to the name, and gazed at me with mournful and questioning eagerness.

"Well, he wishes to see you," said I, guessing her need of an interpreter. "He's in the garden by this time, and impatient to know what answer I shall bring."

As I spoke, I observed a large dog, lying on the sunny grass beneath, raise its ears, as if about to bark, and then smoothing them back, announce by a wag of the tail that some one approached whom it did not consider a stranger.

Mrs. Linton bent forward, and listened breathlessly. The minute after, a step traversed the hall; the open house was too tempting for Heathcliff to resist walking in: most likely he supposed that I was inclined to shirk my promise, and so resolved to trust to his own audacity.

With straining eagerness Catherine gazed towards the entrance of her chamber. He did not hit the right room directly; she motioned me to admit him; but he found it out, ere I could reach the door, and in a stride or two was at her side, and had her grasped in his arms.

He neither spoke, nor loosed his hold, for some five minutes, during which period he bestowed more kisses than ever he gave in his life before, I dare say; but then my mistress had kissed him first, and I plainly saw that he could hardly bear, for downright agony, to look into her face! The same conviction had stricken him as me, from the instant he beheld her, that there was no prospect of ultimate recovery there—she was fated, sure to die.

"Oh, Cathy! Oh, my life! how can I bear it?" was the first sentence he uttered, in a tone that did not seek to disguise his despair.

And now he stared at her so earnestly that I thought the very intensity of his gaze would bring tears into his eyes; but they burned with anguish, they did not melt.

"What now?" said Catherine, leaning back, and returning his look with a suddenly clouded brow: her humour was a mere vane for constantly varying caprices. "You and Edgar have broken my heart, Heathcliff! And you both come to bewail the deed to me, as if *you* were the people to be pitied! I shall not pity you, not I. You have killed me—and thriven on it, I think. How strong you are! How many years do you mean to live after I am gone?"

Heathcliff had knelt on one knee to embrace her; he attempted to rise, but she seized his hair, and kept him down.

"I wish I could hold you," she continued, bitterly, "till we were both dead! I shouldn't care what you suffered. I care nothing for your sufferings. Why shouldn't you suffer? I do! Will you forget me—will you be happy when I am in the earth? Will you say twenty years hence, 'That's the grave of Catherine Earnshaw. I loved her long ago, and was wretched to lose her; but it is past. I've loved many others since—my children are dearer to me than she was, and, at death, I shall not rejoice that I am going to her, I shall be sorry that I must leave them!' Will you say so, Heathcliff?"

"Don't torture me till I'm as mad as yourself," cried he, wrenching his head free, and grinding his teeth.

The two, to a cool spectator, made a strange and fearful picture. Well might Catherine deem that heaven would be a land of exile to her, unless, with her mortal body, she cast away her mortal character also. Her present countenance had a wild vindictiveness in its white cheek, and a bloodless lip and scintillating eye; and she retained in her closed fingers a portion of the locks she had been grasping. As to her companion, while raising himself with one hand, he had taken her arm with the other; and so inadequate was his stock of gentleness to the requirements of her condition, that on his letting go, I saw four distinct impressions left blue in the colourless skin.

"Are you possessed with a devil," he pursued, savagely, "to talk in that manner to me, when you are dying? Do you reflect that all those words will be branded in my memory, and eating deeper eternally, after you have left me? You know you lie to say I have killed you; and, Catherine, you know that I could as soon forget you as my existence! Is it not sufficient for your infernal selfishness, that while you are at peace I shall writhe in the torments of hell?"

"I shall not be at peace," moaned Catherine, recalled to a sense of physical weakness by the violent, unequal throbbing of her heart, which beat visibly and audibly under this excess of agitation.

She said nothing further till the paroxysm was over; then she continued, more kindly—

"I'm not wishing you greater torment than I have, Heathcliff! I only wish us never to be parted—and should a word of mine distress you hereafter, think I feel the same distress underground, and for my own sake, forgive me! Come here and kneel down again! You never harmed me in your life. Nay, if you nurse anger, that will be worse to remember than my harsh words! Won't you come here again? Do!"

Heathcliff went to the back of her chair, and leant over, but not so far as to let her see his face, which was livid with emotion. She bent round to look at him; he would not permit it; turning abruptly, he walked to the fire-place, where he stood, silent, with his back towards us.

Mrs. Linton's glance followed him suspiciously: every movement woke a new sentiment in her. After a pause, and a prolonged gaze, she resumed, addressing me in accents of indignant disappointment—

"Oh, you see, Nelly! he would not relent a moment, to keep me out of the grave! *That* is how I'm loved! Well, never mind! That is not *my* Heathcliff. I shall love mine yet; and take him with me—he's in my soul. And," added she, musingly, "the thing that irks me most is this shattered prison, after all. I'm tired, tired of being enclosed here. I'm wearying to escape into that glorious world, and to be always there; not seeing it dimly through tears, and yearning for it through the walls of an aching heart; but really with it, and in it. Nelly, you think you are better and more fortunate than I; in full health and strength. You are sorry for me—very soon that will be altered. I shall be sorry for *you*. I shall be incomparably beyond and above you all. I *wonder* he won't be near me!" She went on to herself. "I thought he wished it. Heathcliff, dear! you should not be sullen now. Do come to me, Heathcliff."

In her eagerness she rose and supported herself on the arm of the chair. At that earnest appeal, he turned to her, looking absolutely desperate. His eyes wide, and wet at last, flashed fiercely on her; his breast heaved convulsively. An instant they held asunder; and then how they met I hardly saw, but Catherine made a spring, and he caught her, and they were locked in an embrace from which I thought my mistress would never be released alive. In fact, to my eyes, she seemed directly insensible. He flung himself into the nearest seat, and on my approaching hurriedly to ascertain if she had fainted, he gnashed at me, and foamed like a mad dog, and gathered her to him with greedy jealousy. I did not feel as if I were in the company of a creature of my own species; it appeared that he would not understand, though I spoke to him; so I stood off, and held my tongue, in great perplexity.

A movement of Catherine's relieved me a little presently: she put up her hand to clasp his neck, and bring her cheek to his, as he held her; while he, in return, covering her with frantic caresses, said wildly—

"You teach me now how cruel you've been—cruel and false. *Why* did you despise me? *Why* did you betray your own heart, Cathy? I have not one word of comfort. You deserve this. You have killed yourself. Yes, you may kiss me, and cry; and wring out my kisses and tears. They'll blight you—they'll damn you. You loved me—then what *right* had you to leave me? What right —answer me—for the poor fancy you felt for Linton? Because misery, and degradation, and death, and nothing that God or Satan could inflict would have parted us, *you*, of your own will, did it. I have not broken your heart—*you* have broken it—and in breaking it, you have broken mine. So much the worse for me, that I am strong. Do I want to live? What kind of living will it be when you—oh, God! would *you* like to live with your soul in the grave?"

"Let me alone. Let me alone," sobbed Catherine. "If I've done wrong, I'm dying for it. It is enough! You left me too; but I won't upbraid you! I forgive you. Forgive me!"

"It is hard to forgive, and to look at those eyes, and feel those wasted hands," he answered. "Kiss me again; and don't let me see your eyes! I forgive what you have done to me. I love *my* murderer—but *yours!* How can I?"

They were silent—their faces hid against each other, and washed by each other's tears. At least, I suppose the weeping was on both sides; as it seemed Heathcliff *could* weep on a great occasion like this.

I grew very uncomfortable, meanwhile; for the afternoon wore fast away, the man whom I had sent off returned from his errand, and I could distinguish, by the shine of the westering sun up the valley, a concourse thickening outside Gimmerton chapel porch.

"Service is over," I announced. "My master will be here in half-an-hour."

Heathcliff groaned a curse, and strained Catherine closer—she never moved.

Ere long I perceived a group of the servants passing up the road towards the kitchen wing. Mr. Linton was not far behind; he opened the gate himself, and sauntered slowly up, probably enjoying the lovely afternoon that breathed as soft as summer.

"Now he is here," I exclaimed. "For heaven's sake, hurry down! You'll not meet any one on the front stairs. Do be quick; and stay among the trees till he is fairly in."

"I must go, Cathy," said Heathcliff, seeking to extricate himself from his companion's arms. "But, if I live, I'll see you again before you are asleep. I won't stray five yards from your window."

"You must not go!" she answered, holding him as firmly as her strength allowed. "You shall not, I tell you."

"For one hour," he pleaded, earnestly.

"Not for one minute," she replied.

"I *must*—Linton will be up immediately," persisted the alarmed intruder.

He would have risen, and unfixed her fingers by the act—she clung fast, gasping; there was mad resolution in her face.

"No!" she shrieked. "Oh, don't, don't go. It is the last time! Edgar will not hurt us. Heathcliff, I shall die! I shall die!"

"Damn the fool. There he is," cried Heathcliff, sinking back into his seat. "Hush, my darling! Hush, hush, Catherine! I'll stay. If he shot me so, I'd expire with a blessing on my lips."

And there they were fast again. I heard my master mounting the stairs—the cold sweat ran from my forehead; I was horrified.

"Are you going to listen to her ravings?" I said, passionately. "She does not know what she says. Will you ruin her, because she has not wit to help herself? Get up! You could be free instantly. That is the most diabolical deed that ever you did. We are all done for—master, mistress, and servant."

I wrung my hands, and cried out; and Mr. Linton hastened his step at the noise. In the midst of my agitation, I was sincerely glad to observe that Catherine's arms had fallen relaxed, and her head hung down.

"She's fainted or dead," I thought, "so much the better. Far better that she should be dead, than lingering a burden and a misery-maker to all about her."

Edgar sprang to his unbidden guest, blanched with astonishment and rage. What he meant to do, I cannot tell; however, the other stopped all demonstrations, at once, by placing the lifeless-looking form in his arms.

"Look there," he said. "Unless you be a fiend, help her first—then you shall speak to me!"

He walked into the parlour, and sat down. Mr. Linton summoned me, and with great difficulty, and after resorting to many means, we managed to restore her to sensation; but she was all bewildered; she sighed, and moaned, and knew nobody. Edgar, in his anxiety for her, forgot her hated friend. I did not. I went at the earliest opportunity, and besought him to depart, affirming that Catherine was better, and he should hear from me in the morning, how she passed the night.

"I shall not refuse to go out of doors," he answered; "but I shall stay in the garden; and, Nelly, mind you keep your word to-morrow. I shall be under those larch trees. Mind! or I pay another visit, whether Linton be in or not."

He sent a rapid glance through the half-open door of the chamber, and ascertaining that what I stated was apparently true, delivered the house of his luckless presence.

## Chapter XVI

About twelve o'clock that night was born the Catherine you saw at Wuthering Heights, a puny, seven months' child; and two hours after, the mother died, having never recovered sufficient consciousness to miss Heathcliff, or know Edgar.

The latter's distraction at his bereavement is a subject too painful to be dwelt on; its after effects showed how deep the sorrow sunk.

A great addition, in my eyes, was his being left without an heir. I bemoaned that, as I gazed on the feeble orphan; and I mentally abused old Linton for—what was only natural partiality—the securing his estate to his own daughter, instead of his son's.

An unwelcomed infant it was, poor thing! It might have wailed out of life, and nobody cared a morsel, during those first hours of existence. We redeemed the neglect afterwards; but its beginning was as friendless as its end is likely to be.

Next morning—bright and cheerful out of doors—stole softened in through the blinds of the silent room, and suffused the couch and its occupant with a mellow, tender glow.

Edgar Linton had his head laid on the pillow, and his eyes shut. His young and fair features were almost as death-like as those of the form beside him, and almost as fixed; but *his* was the hush of exhausted anguish, and *hers* of perfect peace. Her brow smooth, her lids closed, her lips wearing the expression of a smile. No angel in heaven could be more beautiful than she appeared; and I partook of the infinite calm in which she lay. My mind was never in a holier frame than while I gazed on that untroubled image of Divine rest. I instinctively echoed the words she had uttered, a few hours before. "Incomparably beyond, and above us all! Whether still on earth or now in heaven, her spirit is at home with God!"

I don't know if it be a peculiarity in me, but I am seldom otherwise than happy while watching in the chamber of death, should no frenzied or despairing mourner share the duty with me. I see a repose that neither earth nor hell can break; and I feel an assurance of the endless and shadowless hereafter—the Eternity they have entered—where life is boundless in its duration, and love in its sympathy, and joy in its fulness. I noticed on that occasion how much selfishness there is even in a love like Mr. Linton's, when he so regretted Catherine's blessed release!

To be sure, one might have doubted, after the wayward and impatient existence she had led, whether she merited a haven of peace at last. One might doubt in seasons of cold reflection, but not then, in the presence of her corpse. It asserted its own tranquillity, which seemed a pledge of equal quiet to its former inhabitant.

"Do you believe such people *are* happy in the other world, sir? I'd give a great deal to know."

I declined answering Mrs. Dean's question, which struck me as something heterodox. She proceeded—

"Retracing the course of Catherine Linton, I fear we have no right to think she is: but we'll leave her with her Maker."

The master looked asleep, and I ventured soon after sunrise to quit the room and steal out to the pure, refreshing air. The servants thought me gone to shake off the drowsiness of my protracted watch; in reality, my chief motive was seeing Mr. Heathcliff. If he had remained among the larches all night, he would have heard nothing of the stir at the Grange, unless, perhaps, he might catch the gallop of the messenger going to Gimmerton. If he had come nearer, he would probably be aware, from the lights flitting to and fro, and the opening and shutting of the outer doors, that all was not right within.

I wished, yet feared, to find him. I felt the terrible news must be told, and I longed to get it over, but *how* to do it I did not know.

He was there—at least a few yards further in the park; leant against an old ash tree, his hat off, and his hair soaked with the dew that had gathered on the budded branches, and fell pattering round him. He had been standing a long time in that position, for I saw a pair of ousels passing and repassing scarcely three feet from him, busy in building their nest, and regarding his proximity no more than that of a piece of timber. They flew off at my approach, and he raised his eyes and spoke—

"She's dead!" he said; "I've not waited for you to learn that. Put your handkerchief away—don't snivel before me. Damn you all! she wants none of *your* tears!"

I was weeping as much for him as her: we do sometimes pity creatures that have none of the feeling either for themselves or others; and when I first looked into his face, I perceived that he had got intelligence of the catastrophe; and a foolish notion struck me that his heart was quelled and he prayed, because his lips moved and his gaze was bent on the ground.

"Yes, she's dead!" I answered, checking my sobs and drying my cheeks. "Gone to heaven, I hope, where we may, everyone, join her, if we take due warning, and leave our evil ways to follow good!"

"Did *she* take due warning, then?" asked Heathcliff, attempting a sneer. "Did she die like a saint? Come, give me a true history of the event. How did—"

He endeavoured to pronounce the name, but could not manage it; and compressing his mouth, he held a silent combat with his inward agony, defying, meanwhile, my sympathy with an unflinching, ferocious stare.

"How did she die?" he resumed, at last—fain, notwithstanding his hardihood, to have a support behind him, for, after the struggle, he trembled, in spite of himself, to his very finger-ends.

"Poor wretch!" I thought; "you have a heart and nerves the same as your brother men! Why should you be so anxious to conceal them? Your pride cannot blind God! You tempt Him to wring them, till He forces a cry of humiliation!"

"Quietly as a lamb!" I answered, aloud. "She drew a sigh, and stretched herself, like a child reviving, and sinking again to sleep; and five minutes after I felt one little pulse at her heart, and nothing more!"

"And—and did she ever mention me?" he asked, hesitating, as if he dreaded the answer to his question would introduce details that he could not bear to hear.

"Her senses never returned—she recognised nobody from the time you left her," I said. "She lies with a sweet smile on her face; and her latest ideas wandered back to pleasant early days. Her life closed in a gentle dream—may she wake as kindly in the other world!"

"May she wake in torment!" he cried, with frightful vehemence, stamping his foot, and groaning in a sudden paroxysm of ungovernable passion. "Why, she's a liar to the end! Where is she? Not *there*—not in heaven—not perished—where? Oh! you said you cared nothing for my sufferings! And I pray one prayer—I repeat it till my tongue stiffens—Catherine Earnshaw, may you not rest, as long as I am living! You said I killed you—haunt me, then! The murdered *do* haunt their murderers, I believe. I know that ghosts *have* wandered on earth. Be with me always—take any form—drive me mad! only *do* not leave me in this abyss, where I cannot find you! Oh, God! it is unutterable! I *cannot* live without my life! I *cannot* live without my soul!"

He dashed his head against the knotted trunk; and, lifting up his eyes, howled, not like a man, but like a savage beast getting goaded to death with knives and spears.

I observed several splashes of blood about the bark of the tree, and his hand and forehead were both stained; probably the scene I witnessed was a repetition of others acted during the night. It hardly moved my compassion—it appalled me; still I felt reluctant to quit him so. But the moment he recollected himself enough to notice me watching, he thundered a command for me to go, and I obeyed. He was beyond my skill to quiet or console!

Mrs. Linton's funeral was appointed to take place on the Friday following her decease; and till then her coffin remained uncovered, and strewn with flowers and scented leaves, in the great drawing-room. Linton spent his days and nights there, a sleepless guardian; and—a circumstance concealed from all but me—Heathcliff spent his nights, at least, outside, equally a stranger to repose.

I held no communication with him; still I was conscious of his design to enter, if he could; and on the Tuesday, a little after dark, when my master, from sheer fatigue, had been compelled to retire a couple of hours, I went and opened one of the windows, moved by his perseverance to give him a chance of bestowing on the fading image of his idol one final adieu.

He did not omit to avail himself of the opportunity, cautiously and briefly—too cautiously to betray his presence by the slightest noise; indeed, I shouldn't have discovered that he had been there, except for the disarrangement of the drapery about the corpse's face, and for observing on the floor a curl of light hair, fastened with a silver thread, which, on examination, I ascertained to have been taken from a locket hung round Catherine's neck. Heathcliff had opened the trinket and cast out its contents, replacing them by a black lock of his own. I twisted the two, and enclosed them together.

Mr. Earnshaw was, of course, invited to attend the remains of his sister to the grave; he sent no excuse, but he never came; so that besides her husband, the mourners were wholly composed of tenants and servants. Isabella was not asked.

The place of Catherine's interment, to the surprise of the villagers, was neither in the chapel, under the carved monument of the Lintons, nor yet by the tombs of her own relations, outside. It was dug on a green slope, in a corner of the kirkyard, where the wall is so low that heath and bilberry plants have climbed over it from the moor; and peat mould almost buries it. Her husband lies in the same spot, now; and they have each a simple headstone above, and a plain grey block at their feet, to mark the graves.

## Chapter XVII

That Friday made the last of our fine days, for a month. In the evening, the weather broke; the wind shifted from south to northeast, and brought rain first, and then sleet and snow.

On the morrow one could hardly imagine that there had been three weeks of summer: the primroses and crocuses were hidden under wintry drifts; the larks were silent, the young leaves of the early trees smitten and blackened. And dreary, and chill, and dismal that morrow did creep over! My master kept his room. I took possession of the lonely parlour, converting it into a nursery; and there I was sitting, with the moaning doll of a child laid on my knee, rocking it to and fro, and watching, meanwhile, the still driving flakes build up the uncurtained window, when the door opened, and some person entered, out of breath and laughing!

My anger was greater than my astonishment for a minute; I supposed it one of the maids, and I cried—

"Have done! How dare you show your giddiness here? What would Mr. Linton say if he heard you?"

"Excuse me!" answered a familiar voice, "but I know Edgar is in bed, and I cannot stop myself."

With that, the speaker came forward to the fire, panting and holding her hand to her side.

"I have run the whole way from Wuthering Heights!" she continued, after a pause. "Except where I've flown. I couldn't count the number of falls I've had. Oh, I'm aching all over! Don't be alarmed. There shall be an explanation as soon as I can give it— only just have the goodness to step out and order the carriage to take me on to Gimmerton, and tell a servant to seek up a few clothes in my wardrobe."

The intruder was Mrs. Heathcliff. She certainly seemed in no laughing predicament: her hair streamed on her shoulders, dripping with snow and water; she was dressed in the girlish dress she commonly wore, befitting her age more than her position—a low frock, with short sleeves, and nothing on either head or neck. The frock was of light silk, and clung to her with wet; and her feet were protected merely by thin slippers; add to this a deep cut under one ear, which only the cold prevented from bleeding profusely, a white face scratched and bruised, and a frame hardly able to support itself through fatigue, and you may fancy my first fright was not much allayed when I had leisure to examine her.

"My dear young lady," I exclaimed, "I'll stir nowhere, and hear nothing, till you have removed every article of your clothes, and put on dry things; and certainly you shall not go to Gimmerton to-night; so it is needless to order the carriage."

"Certainly, I shall," she said; "walking or riding; yet I've no objection to dress myself decently; and—ah, see how it flows down my neck now! The fire does make it smart."

She insisted on my fulfilling her directions, before she would let me touch her; and not till after the coachman had been instructed to get ready, and a maid set to pack up some necessary attire, did I obtain her consent for binding the wound and helping to change her garments.

"Now, Ellen," she said, when my task was finished, and she was seated in an easy chair on the hearth, with a cup of tea before her, "you sit down opposite me, and put poor Catherine's baby away—I don't like to see it! You mustn't think I care little for Catherine, because I behaved so foolishly on entering. I've cried too, bitterly—yes, more than any one else has reason to cry. We parted unreconciled, you remember, and I shan't forgive myself. But for all that, I was not going to sympathise with him— the brute beast! O, give me the poker! This is the last thing of his I have about me." She slipped the gold ring from her third finger, and threw it on the floor. "I'll smash it!" she continued, striking with childish spite. "And then I'll burn it!" and she took and dropped the misused article among the coals. "There! he shall buy another, if he gets me back again. He'd be capable of coming to seek me, to tease Edgar—I dare not stay, lest that notion should possess his wicked head! And besides, Edgar has not been kind, has he? And I won't come suing for his assistance; nor will I bring him into more trouble. Necessity compelled me to seek shelter here; though, if I had not learnt he was out of the way, I'd have halted at the kitchen, washed my face, warmed myself, got you to bring what I wanted, and departed again to anywhere out of the reach of my accursed—of that incarnate goblin! Ah, he was in such a fury! If he had caught me! It's a pity Earnshaw is not his match in strength—I wouldn't have run till I'd seen him all but demolished, had Hindley been able to do it!"

"Well, don't talk so fast, Miss!" I interrupted, "you'll disorder the handkerchief I have tied round your face, and make the cut bleed again. Drink your tea, and take breath and give over laughing. Laughter is sadly out of place under this roof, and in your condition!"

"An undeniable truth," she replied. "Listen to that child! It maintains a constant wail—send it out of my hearing, for an hour; I shan't stay any longer."

I rang the bell, and committed it to a servant's care; and then I inquired what had urged her to escape from Wuthering Heights in such an unlikely plight, and where she meant to go, as she refused remaining with us.

"I ought, and I wish to remain," answered she, "to cheer Edgar and take care of the baby, for two things, and because the Grange is my right home. But I tell you, he wouldn't let me! Do you think he could bear to see me grow fat and merry; and could bear to think that we were tranquil, and not resolve on poisoning our comfort? Now, I have the satisfaction of being sure that he detests me to the point of its annoying him seriously to have me within ear-shot, or eye-sight. I notice, when I enter his presence, the muscles of his countenance are involuntarily distorted into an expression of hatred; partly arising from his knowledge of the good causes I have to feel that sentiment for him, and partly from original aversion. It is strong enough to make me feel pretty certain that he would not chase me over England, supposing I contrived a clear escape; and therefore I must get quite away. I've recovered from my first desire to be killed by him. I'd rather he'd kill himself! He has extinguished my love effectually, and so I'm at my ease. I can recollect yet how I loved him; and can dimly imagine that I could still be loving him, if—no, no! Even if he had doted on me, the devilish nature would have revealed its existence somehow. Catherine had an awfully perverted taste to esteem him so dearly, knowing him so well. Monster! would that he could be blotted out of creation, and out of my memory!"

"Hush, hush! He's a human being," I said. "Be more charitable; there are worse men than he is yet!"

"He's not a human being," she retorted; "and he has no claim on my charity. I gave him my heart, and he took and pinched it to death; and flung it back to me. People feel with their hearts, Ellen, and since he has destroyed mine, I have not power to feel for him, and I would not, though he groaned from this to his dying day, and wept tears of blood for Catherine! No, indeed, indeed, I wouldn't!" And here Isabella began to cry; but, immediately dashing the water from her lashes, she recommenced.

"You asked, what has driven me to flight at last? I was compelled to attempt it, because I had succeeded in rousing his rage a pitch above his malignity. Pulling out the nerves with red hot pincers requires more coolness than knocking on the head. He was worked up to forget the fiendish prudence he boasted of, and proceeded to murderous violence. I experienced pleasure in being able to exasperate him: the sense of pleasure woke my instinct of self-preservation, so I fairly broke free, and if ever I come into his hands again he is welcome to a signal revenge.

"Yesterday, you know, Mr. Earnshaw should have been at the funeral. He kept himself sober for the purpose—tolerably sober; not going to bed mad at six o'clock and getting up drunk at twelve. Consequently, he rose, in suicidal low spirits, as fit for the church as for a dance; and instead, he sat down by the fire and swallowed gin or brandy by tumblerfuls.

"Heathcliff—I shudder to name him!—has been a stranger in the house from last Sunday till to-day. Whether the angels have fed him, or his kin beneath, I cannot tell; but he has not eaten a meal with us for nearly a week. He has just come home at dawn, and gone upstairs to his chamber; locking himself in—as

if anybody dreamt of coveting his company! There he has continued, praying like a Methodist; only the deity he implored is
senseless dust and ashes; and God, when addressed, was curiously
confounded with his own black father! After concluding these
precious orisons—and they lasted generally till he grew hoarse,
and his voice was strangled in his throat—he would be off again;
always straight down to the Grange! I wonder Edgar did not send
for a constable, and give him into custody! For me, grieved as I
was about Catherine, it was impossible to avoid regarding this
season of deliverance from degrading oppression as a holiday.

"I recovered spirits sufficient to hear Joseph's eternal lectures
without weeping; and to move up and down the house, less with
the foot of a frightened thief than formerly. You wouldn't think
that I should cry at anything Joseph could say, but he and Hareton
are detestable companions. I'd rather sit with Hindley, and hear
his awful talk, than with 't' little maister,' and his staunch sup-
porter, that odious old man!

"When Heathcliff is in, I'm often obliged to seek the kitchen and
their society, or starve among the damp, uninhabited chambers;
when he is not, as was the case this week, I establish a table and
chair at one corner of the house fire, and never mind how Mr. Earnshaw may occupy himself; and he does not interfere with my arrangements. He is quieter now than he used to be, if no one provokes
him; more sullen and depressed, and less furious. Joseph affirms he's
sure he's an altered man; that the Lord has touched his heart, and
he is saved 'so as by fire.' I'm puzzled to detect signs of the favourable change, but it is not my business.

"Yester-evening, I sat in my nook reading some old books till late
on towards twelve. It seemed so dismal to go upstairs, with the wild
snow blowing outside, and my thoughts continually reverting to the
kirkyard and the new made grave! I dared hardly lift my eyes from
the page before me, that melancholy scene so instantly usurped its
place.

"Hindley sat opposite, his head leant on his hand, perhaps meditating on the same subject. He had ceased drinking at a point below
irrationality, and had neither stirred nor spoken during two or three
hours. There was no sound through the house but the moaning
wind which shook the windows every now and then, the faint crack-
ling of the coals, and the click of my snuffers as I removed at intervals the long wick of the candle. Hareton and Joseph were probably
fast asleep in bed. It was very, very sad, and while I read, I sighed,
for it seemed as if all joy had vanished from the world, never to be
restored.

"The doleful silence was broken at length by the sound of the
kitchen latch. Heathcliff had returned from his watch earlier than

usual, owing, I suppose, to the sudden storm.

"That entrance was fastened, and we heard him coming round to get in by the other. I rose with an irrepressible expression of what I felt on my lips, which induced my companion, who had been staring towards the door, to turn and look at me.

" 'I'll keep him out five minutes,' he exclaimed. 'You won't object?'

" 'No, you may keep him out the whole night, for me,' I answered. 'Do! put the key in the lock, and draw the bolts.'

"Earnshaw accomplished this ere his guest reached the front; he then came and brought his chair to the other side of my table, leaning over it, and searching in my eyes for a sympathy with the burning hate that gleamed from his: as he both looked and felt like an assassin, he couldn't exactly find that; but he discovered enough to encourage him to speak.

" 'You and I,' he said, 'have each a great debt to settle with the man out yonder! If we were neither of us cowards, we might combine to discharge it. Are you as soft as your brother? Are you willing to endure to the last, and not once attempt a repayment?'

" 'I'm weary of enduring now,' I replied, 'and I'd be glad of a retaliation that wouldn't recoil on myself; but treachery and violence are spears pointed at both ends—they wound those who resort to them, worse than their enemies.'

" 'Treachery and violence are a just return for treachery and violence!' cried Hindley. 'Mrs. Heathcliff, I'll ask you to do nothing but sit still and be dumb. Tell me now, can you? I'm sure you would have as much pleasure as I in witnessing the conclusion of the fiend's existence; he'll be *your* death unless you overreach him —and he'll be *my* ruin. Damn the hellish villain! He knocks at the door as if he were master here already! Promise to hold your tongue, and before that clock strikes—it wants three minutes of one—you're a free woman!'

"He took the implements which I described to you in my letter from his breast, and would have turned down the candle. I snatched it away, however, and seized his arm.

" 'I'll not hold my tongue!' I said; 'you mustn't touch him. Let the door remain shut and be quiet!'

" 'No! I've formed my resolution, and by God, I'll execute it!' cried the desperate being. 'I'll do you a kindness in spite of yourself, and Hareton justice! And you needn't trouble your head to screen me; Catherine is gone. Nobody alive would regret me, or be ashamed, though I cut my throat this minute—and it's time to make an end!'

"I might as well have struggled with a bear, or reasoned with a lunatic. The only resource left me was to run to a lattice, and warn his intended victim of the fate which awaited him.

"'You'd better seek shelter somewhere else to-night!' I exclaimed in a rather triumphant tone. 'Mr. Earnshaw has a mind to shoot you, if you persist in endeavouring to enter.'

"'You'd better open the door, you—' he answered, addressing me by some elegant term that I don't care to repeat.

"'I shall not meddle in the matter,' I retorted again. 'Come in, and get shot, if you please! I've done my duty.'

"With that I shut the window, and returned to my place by the fire, having too small a stock of hypocrisy at my command to pretend any anxiety for the danger that menaced him.

"Earnshaw swore passionately at me, affirming that I loved the villain yet, and calling me all sorts of names for the base spirit I evinced. And I, in my secret heart (and conscience never reproached me) thought what a blessing it would be for *him*, should Heathcliff put him out of misery; and what a blessing for *me*, should he send Heathcliff to his right abode! As I sat nursing these reflections, the casement behind me was banged on to the floor by a blow from the latter individual, and his black countenance looked blightingly through. The stanchions stood too close to suffer his shoulders to follow, and I smiled, exulting in my fancied security. His hair and clothes were whitened with snow, and his sharp cannibal teeth, revealed by cold and wrath, gleamed through the dark.

"'Isabella, let me in, or I'll make you repent!' he 'girned,'[1] as Joseph calls it.

"'I cannot commit murder,' I replied. 'Mr. Hindley stands sentinel with a knife and loaded pistol.'

"'Let me in by the kitchen door!' he said.

"'Hindley will be there before me,' I answered. 'And that's a poor love of yours that cannot bear a shower of snow! We were left at peace in our beds as long as the summer moon shone, but the moment a blast of winter returns, you must run for shelter! Heathcliff, if I were you, I'd go stretch myself over her grave and die like a faithful dog. The world is surely not worth living in now, is it? You had distinctly impressed on me the idea that Catherine was the whole joy of your life. I can't imagine how you think of surviving her loss.'

"'He's there, is he?' exclaimed my companion, rushing to the gap. 'If I can get my arm out I can hit him!'

"I'm afraid, Ellen, you'll set me down as really wicked; but you don't know all, so don't judge! I wouldn't have aided or abetted an attempt on even *his* life, for anything. Wish that he were dead, I must; and therefore I was fearfully disappointed, and

1. Snarled.

unnerved by terror for the consequences of my taunting speech, when he flung himself on Earnshaw's weapon and wrenched it from his grasp.

"The charge exploded, and the knife, in springing back, closed into its owner's wrist. Heathcliff pulled it away by main force, slitting up the flesh as it passed on, and thrust it dripping into his pocket. He then took a stone, struck down the division between two windows, and sprung in. His adversary had fallen senseless with excessive pain and the flow of blood that gushed from an artery, or a large vein.

"The ruffian kicked and trampled on him, and dashed his head repeatedly against the flags, holding me with one hand, meantime, to prevent me summoning Joseph.

"He exerted preter-human self-denial in abstaining from finishing him completely; but getting out of breath, he finally desisted, and dragged the apparently inanimate body onto the settle.

"There he tore off the sleeve of Earnshaw's coat, and bound up the wound with brutal roughness, spitting and cursing during the operation, as energetically as he had kicked before.

"Being at liberty, I lost no time in seeking the old servant, who, having gathered by degrees the purport of my hasty tale, hurried below, gasping, as he descended the steps two at once.

" 'Whet is thur tuh do, nah? whet is thur tuh do, nah?'

" 'There's this to do,' thundered Heathcliff, 'that your master's mad; and should he last another month, I'll have him to an asylum. And how the devil did you come to fasten me out, you toothless hound? Don't stand muttering and mumbling there. Come, I'm not going to nurse him. Wash that stuff away; and mind the sparks of your candle—it is more than half brandy!'

" 'Und soa, yah been murthering on him!' exclaimed Joseph, lifting his hands and eyes in horror. 'If iver Aw seed a seeght loike this! May the Lord—'

"Heathcliff gave him a push onto his knees in the middle of the blood, and flung a towel to him; but instead of proceeding to dry it up, he joined his hands, and began a prayer which excited my laughter from its odd phraseology. I was in the condition of mind to be shocked at nothing; in fact, I was as reckless as some malefactors show themselves at the foot of the gallows.

" 'Oh, I forgot you,' said the tyrant. 'You shall do that. Down with you. And you conspire with him against me, do you, viper? There, that is work fit for you!'

"He shook me till my teeth rattled, and pitched me beside Joseph, who steadily concluded his supplications and then rose, vowing he would set off for the Grange directly. Mr. Linton was a magistrate, and though he had fifty wives dead, he should inquire into this.

"He was so obstinate in his resolution that Heathcliff deemed it expedient to compel from my lips a recapitulation of what had taken place; standing over me, heaving with malevolence, as I reluctantly delivered the account in answer to his questions.

"It required a great deal of labour to satisfy the old man that Heathcliff was not the aggressor; especially with my hardly wrung replies. However, Mr. Earnshaw soon convinced him that he was alive still; he hastened to administer a dose of spirits, and by their succour his master presently regained motion and consciousness.

"Heathcliff, aware that his opponent was ignorant of the treatment received while insensible, called him deliriously intoxicated; and said he should not notice his atrocious conduct further, but advised him to get to bed. To my joy, he left us after giving this judicious counsel, and Hindley stretched himself on the hearthstone. I departed to my own room, marvelling that I had escaped so easily.

"This morning, when I came down, about half-an-hour before noon, Mr. Earnshaw was sitting by the fire, deadly sick; his evil genius, almost as gaunt and ghastly, leant against the chimney. Neither appeared inclined to dine, and having waited till all was cold on the table, I commenced alone.

"Nothing hindered me from eating heartily; and I experienced a certain sense of satisfaction and superiority, as, at intervals, I cast a look towards my silent companions, and felt the comfort of a quiet conscience within me.

"After I had done, I ventured on the unusual liberty of drawing near the fire, going round Earnshaw's seat, and kneeling in the corner beside him.

"Heathcliff did not glance my way, and I gazed up and contemplated his features almost as confidently as if they had been turned to stone. His forehead, that I once thought so manly, and that I now think so diabolical, was shaded with a heavy cloud; his basilisk eyes were nearly quenched by sleeplessness, and weeping, perhaps, for the lashes were wet then; his lips devoid of their ferocious sneer, and sealed in an expression of unspeakable sadness. Had it been another, I would have covered my face in the presence of such grief. In *his* case, I was gratified; and ignoble as it seems to insult a fallen enemy, I couldn't miss this chance of sticking in a dart; his weakness was the only time when I could taste the delight of paying wrong for wrong."

"Fie, fie, Miss!" I interrupted. "One might suppose you had never opened a Bible in your life. If God afflict your enemies, surely that ought to suffice you. It is both mean and presumptuous to add your torture to his!"

"In general, I'll allow that it would be, Ellen," she continued. "But what misery laid on Heathcliff could content me, unless I have a hand in it? I'd rather he suffered *less*, if I might cause his sufferings and he might *know* that I was the cause. Oh, I owe him so much. On only one condition can I hope to forgive him. It is, if I may take an eye for an eye, a tooth for a tooth; for every wrench of agony, return a wrench, reduce him to my level. As he was the first to injure, make him the first to implore pardon; and then—why then, Ellen, I might show you some generosity. But it is utterly impossible I can ever be revenged, and therefore I cannot forgive him. Hindley wanted some water, and I handed him a glass, and asked him how he was.

" 'Not as ill as I wish,' he replied. 'But leaving out my arm, every inch of me is as sore as if I had been fighting with a legion of imps!'

" 'Yes, no wonder,' was my next remark. 'Catherine used to boast that she stood between you and bodily harm: she meant that certain persons would not hurt you, for fear of offending her. It's well people don't *really* rise from their grave, or, last night, she might have witnessed a repulsive scene! Are not you bruised, and cut over your chest and shoulders?'

" 'I can't say,' he answered; 'but what do you mean? Did he dare to strike me when I was down?'

" 'He trampled on, and kicked you, and dashed you on the ground,' I whispered. 'And his mouth watered to tear you with his teeth; because he's only half a man—not so much.'

"Mr. Earnshaw looked up, like me, to the countenance of our mutual foe, who, absorbed in his anguish, seemed insensible to anything around him; the longer he stood, the plainer his reflections revealed their blackness through his features.

" 'Oh, if God would but give me strength to strangle him in my last agony, I'd go to hell with joy,' groaned the impatient man, writhing to rise, and sinking back in despair, convinced of his inadequacy for the struggle.

" 'Nay, it's enough that he has murdered one of you,' I observed aloud. 'At the Grange, every one knows your sister would have been living now, had it not been for Mr. Heathcliff. After all, it is preferable to be hated than loved by him. When I recollect how happy we were—how happy Catherine was before he came—I'm fit to curse the day.'

"Most likely, Heathcliff noticed more the truth of what was said, than the spirit of the person who said it. His attention was roused, I saw, for his eyes rained down tears among the ashes, and he drew his breath in suffocating sighs.

"I stared full at him, and laughed scornfully. The clouded windows of hell flashed a moment towards me; the fiend which usually looked out, however, was so dimmed and drowned that I did not fear to hazard another sound of derision.

" 'Get up, and begone out of my sight,' said the mourner.

"I guessed he uttered those words, at least, though his voice was hardly intelligible.

" 'I beg your pardon,' I replied. 'But I loved Catherine too; and her brother requires attendance which, for her sake, I shall supply. Now that she's dead, I see her in Hindley; Hindley has exactly her eyes, if you had not tried to gouge them out and made them black and red, and her—'

" 'Get up, wretched idiot, before I stamp you to death!' he cried, making a movement that caused me to make one also.

" 'But then,' I continued, holding myself ready to flee, 'if poor Catherine had trusted you, and assumed the ridiculous, contemptible, degrading title of Mrs. Heathcliff, she would soon have presented a similar picture! *She* wouldn't have borne your abominable behaviour quietly; her detestation and disgust must have found voice.'

"The back of the settle and Earnshaw's person interposed between me and him; so instead of endeavouring to reach me, he snatched a dinner knife from the table and flung it at my head. It struck beneath my ear, and stopped the sentence I was uttering; but, pulling it out, I sprang to the door and delivered another which I hope went a little deeper than his missile.

"The last glimpse I caught of him was a furious rush on his part, checked by the embrace of his host; and both fell locked together on the hearth.

"In my flight through the kitchen I bid Joseph speed to his master; I knocked over Hareton, who was hanging a litter of puppies from a chair-back in the doorway; and, blest as a soul escaped from purgatory, I bounded, leaped, and flew down the steep road; then, quitting its windings, shot direct across the moor, rolling over banks, and wading through marshes; precipitating myself, in fact, towards the beacon light of the Grange. And far rather would I be condemned to a perpetual dwelling in the infernal regions, than even for one night abide beneath the roof of Wuthering Heights again."

Isabella ceased speaking, and took a drink of tea; then she rose, and bidding me put on her bonnet and a great shawl I had brought, and turning a deaf ear to my entreaties for her to remain another hour, she stepped onto a chair, kissed Edgar's and Catherine's portraits, bestowed a similar salute on me, and descended to the carriage accompanied by Fanny, who yelped wild with joy at recovering her mistress. She was driven away, never to revisit this neighbourhood;

but a regular correspondence was established between her and my master when things were more settled.

I believe her new abode was in the south, near London; there she had a son born, a few months subsequent to her escape. He was christened Linton, and, from the first, she reported him to be an ailing, peevish creature.

Mr. Heathcliff, meeting me one day in the village, inquired where she lived. I refused to tell. He remarked that it was not of any moment, only she must beware of coming to her brother; she should not be with him, if he had to keep her himself.

Though I would give no information, he discovered, through some of the other servants, both her place of residence and the existence of the child. Still he didn't molest her; for which forbearance she might thank his aversion, I suppose.

He often asked about the infant, when he saw me; and on hearing its name, smiled grimly, and observed—

"They wish me to hate it too, do they?"

"I don't think they wish you to know any thing about it," I answered.

"But I'll have it," he said, "when I want it. They may reckon on that!"

Fortunately, its mother died before the time arrived, some thirteen years after the decease of Catherine, when Linton was twelve, or a little more.

On the day succeeding Isabella's unexpected visit, I had no opportunity of speaking to my master: he shunned conversation, and was fit for discussing nothing. When I could get him to listen, I saw it pleased him that his sister had left her husband, whom he abhorred with an intensity which the mildness of his nature would scarcely seem to allow. So deep and sensitive was his aversion, that he refrained from going anywhere where he was likely to see or hear of Heathcliff. Grief, and that together, transformed him into a complete hermit: he threw up his office of magistrate, ceased even to attend church, avoided the village on all occasions, and spent a life of entire seclusion within the limits of his park and grounds, only varied by solitary rambles on the moors, and visits to the grave of his wife, mostly at evening, or early morning before other wanderers were abroad.

But he was too good to be thoroughly unhappy long. *He* didn't pray for Catherine's soul to haunt him. Time brought resignation, and a melancholy sweeter than common joy. He recalled her memory with ardent, tender love, and hopeful aspiring to the better world, where, he doubted not, she was gone.

And he had earthly consolation and affections, also. For a few days, I said, he seemed regardless of the puny successor to the departed: that coldness melted as fast as snow in April, and ere the tiny thing could stammer a word or totter a step, it wielded a despot's sceptre in his heart.

It was named Catherine, but he never called it the name in full, as he had never called the first Catherine short, probably because Heathcliff had a habit of doing so. The little one was always Cathy; it formed to him a distinction from the mother, and yet, a connection with her; and his attachment sprang from its relation to her, far more than from its being his own.

I used to draw a comparison between him and Hindley Earnshaw, and perplex myself to explain satisfactorily why their conduct was so opposite in similar circumstances. They had both been fond husbands, and were both attached to their children; and I could not see how they shouldn't both have taken the same road, for good or evil. But, I thought in my mind, Hindley, with apparently the stronger head, has shown himself sadly the worse and the weaker man. When his ship struck, the captain abandoned his post; and the crew, instead of trying to save her, rushed into riot and confusion, leaving no hope for their luckless vessel. Linton, on the contrary, displayed the true courage of a loyal and faithful soul: he trusted God; and God comforted him. One hoped, and the other despaired: they chose their own lots, and were righteously doomed to endure them.

But you'll not want to hear my moralizing, Mr. Lockwood: you'll judge as well as I can, all these things; at least, you'll think you will, and that's the same.

The end of Earnshaw was what might have been expected; it followed fast on his sister's: there were scarcely six months between them. We, at the Grange, never got a very succinct account of his state preceding it; all that I did learn was on occasion of going to aid in the preparations for the funeral. Mr. Kenneth came to announce the event to my master.

"Well, Nelly," said he, riding into the yard one morning, too early not to alarm me with an instant presentiment of bad news. "It's yours and my turn to go into mourning at present. Who's given us the slip now, do you think?"

"Who?" I asked in a flurry.

"Why, guess!" he returned, dismounting, and slinging his bridle on a hook by the door. "And nip up the corner of your apron; I'm certain you'll need it."

"Not Mr. Heathcliff, surely?" I exclaimed.

"What! would you have tears for him?" said the doctor. "No, Heathcliff's a tough young fellow; he looks blooming to-day—I've just seen him. He's rapidly regaining flesh since he lost his better half."

"Who is it, then, Mr. Kenneth?" I repeated impatiently.

"Hindley Earnshaw! Your old friend Hindley," he replied, "and my wicked gossip; though he's been too wild for me this long while. There! I said we should draw water. But cheer up! He died true to his character, drunk as a lord. Poor lad; I'm sorry, too. One can't help missing an old companion, though he had the worst tricks with him that ever man imagined, and has done me many a rascally turn. He's barely twenty-seven, it seems; that's your own age; who would have thought you were born in one year!"

I confess this blow was greater to me than the shock of Mrs. Linton's death: ancient associations lingered round my heart; I sat down in the porch and wept as for a blood relation, desiring Kenneth to get another servant to introduce him to the master.

I could not hinder myself from pondering on the question— "Had he had fair play?" Whatever I did, that idea would bother me: it was so tiresomely pertinacious that I resolved on requesting leave to go to Wuthering Heights, and assist in the last duties to the dead. Mr. Linton was extremely reluctant to consent, but I pleaded eloquently for the friendless condition in which he lay; and I said my old master and foster brother had a claim on my services as strong as his own. Besides, I reminded him that the child, Hareton, was his wife's nephew, and, in the absence of nearer kin, he ought to act as its guardian; and he ought to and must inquire how the property was left, and look over the concerns of his brother-in-law.

He was unfit for attending to such matters then, but he bid me speak to his lawyer; and at length permitted me to go. His lawyer had been Earnshaw's also: I called at the village, and asked him to accompany me. He shook his head, and advised that Heathcliff should be let alone, affirming, if the truth were known, Hareton would be found little else than a beggar.

"His father died in debt," he said; "the whole property is mortgaged, and the sole chance for the natural heir is to allow him an opportunity of creating some interest in the creditor's heart, that he may be inclined to deal leniently towards him."

When I reached the Heights, I explained that I had come to see everything carried on decently, and Joseph, who appeared in sufficient distress, expressed satisfaction at my presence. Mr. Heathcliff said he did not perceive that I was wanted, but I might stay and order the arrangements for the funeral, if I chose.

"Correctly," he remarked, "that fool's body should be buried at the cross-roads, without ceremony of any kind. I happened to leave him ten minutes, yesterday afternoon; and, in that interval, he fastened the two doors of the house against me, and he has spent the night in drinking himself to death deliberately! We broke in this morning, for we heard him snorting like a horse; and there he was, laid over the settle: flaying and scalping would not have wakened him. I sent for Kenneth, and he came; but not till the beast had changed into carrion: he was both dead and cold and stark; and so you'll allow, it was useless making more stir about him!"

The old servant confirmed this statement, but muttered—

"Aw'd rayther he'd goan hisseln fur t'doctor! Aw sud uh taen tent uh t'maister better nur him—un he warn't deead when Aw left, nowt uh t'soart!"[2]

I insisted on the funeral being respectable. Mr. Heathcliff said I might have my own way there too; only, he desired me to remember that the money for the whole affair came out of his pocket.

He maintained a hard, careless deportment, indicative of neither joy nor sorrow; if anything, it expressed a flinty gratification at a piece of difficult work successfully executed. I observed once, indeed, something like exultation in his aspect: it was just when the people were bearing the coffin from the house. He had the hypocrisy to represent a mourner; and previous to following with Hareton, he lifted the unfortunate child on to the table and muttered, with peculiar gusto—

"Now, my bonny lad, you are *mine!* And we'll see if one tree won't grow as crooked as another, with the same wind to twist it!"

The unsuspecting thing was pleased at this speech; he played with Heathcliff's whiskers, and stroked his cheek, but I divined its meaning and observed tartly—

"That boy must go back with me to Thrushcross Grange, sir. There is nothing in the world less yours than he is!"

"Does Linton say so?" he demanded.

"Of course—he has ordered me to take him," I replied.

"Well," said the scoundrel, "we'll not argue the subject now; but I have a fancy to try my hand at rearing a young one, so intimate to your master that I must supply the place of this with my own, if he attempt to remove it. I don't engage to let Hareton go, undisputed; but I'll be pretty sure to make the other come! Remember to tell him."

This hint was enough to bind our hands. I repeated its substance on my return, and Edgar Linton, little interested at the commencement, spoke no more of interfering. I'm not aware that he could have done it to any purpose, had he been ever so willing.

The guest was now the master of Wuthering Heights: he held firm possession, and proved to the attorney, who, in his turn, proved it to Mr. Linton, that Earnshaw had mortgaged every yard of land he owned for cash to supply his mania for gaming; and he,

2. *Sud uh taen tent:* should have taken care; *nur him:* than him; *nowt uh t'soart:* nothing of the sort.

Heathcliff, was the mortgagee.

In that manner, Hareton, who should now be the first gentleman in the neighbourhood, was reduced to a state of complete dependence on his father's inveterate enemy; and lives in his own house as a servant deprived of the advantage of wages, and quite unable to right himself, because of his friendlessness, and his ignorance that he has been wronged.

## Chapter XVIII

The twelve years, continued Mrs. Dean, following that dismal period, were the happiest of my life: my greatest troubles, in their passage, rose from our little lady's trifling illnesses, which she had to experience in common with all children, rich and poor.

For the rest, after the first six months, she grew like a larch, and could walk and talk too, in her own way, before the heath blossomed a second time over Mrs. Linton's dust.

She was the most winning thing that ever brought sunshine into a desolate house—a real beauty in face, with the Earnshaws' handsome dark eyes, but the Lintons' fair skin, and small features, and yellow curling hair. Her spirit was high, though not rough, and qualified by a heart sensitive and lively to excess in its affections. That capacity for intense attachments reminded me of her mother; still she did not resemble her, for she could be soft and mild as a dove, and she had a gentle voice, and pensive expression: her anger was never furious; her love never fierce; it was deep and tender.

However, it must be acknowledged, she had faults to foil her gifts. A propensity to be saucy was one; and a perverse will that indulged children invariably acquire, whether they be good tempered or cross. If a servant chanced to vex her, it was always: "I shall tell papa!" And if he reproved her, even by a look, you would have thought it a heartbreaking business: I don't believe he ever did speak a harsh word to her.

He took her education entirely on himself, and made it an amusement. Fortunately, curiosity and a quick intellect urged her into an apt scholar; she learnt rapidly and eagerly, and did honour to his teaching.

Till she reached the age of thirteen, she had not once been beyond the range of the park by herself. Mr. Linton would take her with him a mile or so outside, on rare occasions; but he trusted her to no one else. Gimmerton was an unsubstantial name in her ears; the chapel, the only building she had approached or entered, except her own home. Wuthering Heights and Mr. Heathcliff did not exist for her; she was a perfect recluse, and, apparently, perfectly contented. Sometimes, indeed, while surveying the country from her nursery window, she would observe—

"Ellen, how long will it be before I can walk to the top of those hills? I wonder what lies on the other side—is it the sea?"

"No, Miss Cathy," I would answer, "it is hills again just like these."

"And what are those golden rocks like, when you stand under them?" she once asked.

The abrupt descent of Penistone Crags particularly attracted her notice, especially when the setting sun shone on it and the topmost heights, and the whole extent of landscape besides lay in shadow.

I explained that they were bare masses of stone, with hardly enough earth in their clefts to nourish a stunted tree.

"And why are they bright so long after it is evening here?" she pursued.

"Because they are a great deal higher up than we are," replied I; "you could not climb them, they are too high and steep. In winter the frost is always there before it comes to us; and, deep into summer, I have found snow under that black hollow on the north-east side!"

"Oh, you have been on them!" she cried, gleefully. "Then I can go, too, when I am a woman. Has papa been, Ellen?"

"Papa would tell you, Miss," I answered, hastily, "that they are not worth the trouble of visiting. The moors, where you ramble with him, are much nicer; and Thrushcross park is the finest place in the world."

"But I know the park, and I don't know those," she murmured to herself. "And I should delight to look round me from the brow of that tallest point—my little pony, Minny, shall take me some time."

One of the maids mentioning the Fairy cave quite turned her head with a desire to fulfil this project; she teased Mr. Linton about it; and he promised she should have the journey when she got older. But Miss Catherine measured her age by months, and—

"Now, am I old enough to go to Penistone Crags?" was the constant question in her mouth.

The road thither wound close by Wuthering Heights. Edgar had not the heart to pass it; so she received as constantly the answer—

"Not yet, love, not yet."

I said Mrs. Heathcliff lived above a dozen years after quitting her husband. Her family were of a delicate constitution: she and Edgar both lacked the ruddy health that you will generally meet in these parts. What her last illness was, I am not certain; I conjecture they died of the same thing, a kind of fever, slow at its commencement, but incurable, and rapidly consuming life towards the close.

She wrote to inform her brother of the probable conclusion of a four months' indisposition under which she had suffered; and entreated him to come to her, if possible, for she had much to settle, and she wished to bid him adieu, and deliver Linton safely into his hands. Her hope was, that Linton might be left with him, as he had been with her; his father, she would fain convince herself, had no desire to assume the burden of his maintenance or education.

My master hesitated not a moment in complying with her request; reluctant as he was to leave home at ordinary calls, he flew to answer this; commending Catherine to my peculiar vigilance in his absence, with reiterated orders that she must not wander out of the park, even under my escort: he did not calculate on her going unaccompanied.

He was away three weeks: the first day or two, my charge sat in a corner of the library, too sad for either reading or playing: in that quiet state she caused me little trouble; but it was succeeded by an interval of impatient, fretful weariness; and being too busy, and too old then, to run up and down amusing her, I hit on a method by which she might entertain herself.

I used to send her on her travels round the grounds—now on foot, and now on a pony; indulging her with a patient audience of all her real and imaginary adventures, when she returned.

The summer shone in full prime; and she took such a taste for this solitary rambling that she often contrived to remain out from breakfast till tea; and then the evenings were spent in recounting her fanciful tales. I did not fear her breaking bounds, because the gates were generally locked, and I thought she would scarcely venture forth alone, if they had stood wide open.

Unluckily, my confidence proved misplaced. Catherine came to me, one morning, at eight o'clock, and said she was that day an Arabian merchant, going to cross the Desert with his caravan; and I must give her plenty of provision for herself and beasts, a horse and three camels, personated by a large hound and a couple of pointers.

I got together good store of dainties, and slung them in a basket on one side of the saddle; and she sprang up as gay as a fairy, sheltered by her wide-brimmed hat and gauze veil from the July sun, and trotted off with a merry laugh, mocking my cautious counsel to avoid galloping, and come back early.

The naughty thing never made her appearance at tea. One traveller, the hound, being an old dog and fond of its ease, returned; but neither Cathy, nor the pony, nor the two pointers were visible in any direction; and I despatched emissaries down this path, and that path, and, at last, went wandering in search of her myself.

There was a labourer working at a fence round a plantation, on the borders of the grounds. I enquired of him if he had seen our young lady.

"I saw her at morn," he replied; "she would have me to cut her a hazel switch, and then she leapt her galloway[1] over the hedge yonder, where it is lowest, and galloped out of sight."

You may guess how I felt at hearing this news. It struck me directly she must have started for Penistone Crags.

"What will become of her?" I ejaculated, pushing through a gap which the man was repairing, and making straight to the high road.

I walked as if for a wager, mile after mile, till a turn brought me in view of the Heights, but no Catherine could I detect, far or near.

The Crags lie about a mile and a half beyond Mr. Heathcliff's place, and that is four from the Grange, so I began to fear night would fall ere I could reach them.

"And what if she should have slipped in, clambering among them," I reflected, "and been killed, or broken some of her bones?"

My suspense was truly painful; and, at first, it gave me delightful relief to observe, in hurrying by the farm-house, Charlie, the fiercest of the pointers, lying under a window, with swelled head and bleeding ear.

I opened the wicket and ran to the door, knocking vehemently for admittance. A woman whom I knew, and who formerly lived at Gimmerton, answered: she had been servant there since the death of Mr Earnshaw.

"Ah," said she, "you are come a seeking your little mistress! don't be frightened. She's here safe—but I'm glad it isn't the master."

"He is not at home then, is he?" I panted, quite breathless with quick walking and alarm.

"No, no," she replied, "both he and Joseph are off, and I think they won't return this hour or more. Step in and rest you a bit."

I entered, and beheld my stray lamb seated on the hearth, rocking herself in a little chair that had been her mother's, when a child. Her hat was hung against the wall, and she seemed perfectly at home, laughing and chattering, in the best spirits imaginable, to Hareton, now a great, strong lad of eighteen, who stared at her with considerable curiosity and astonishment; comprehending precious little of the fluent succession of remarks and questions which her tongue never ceased pouring forth.

"Very well, Miss," I exclaimed, concealing my joy under an

1. One of a small but strong breed of horses peculiar to Galloway.

angry countenance. "This is your last ride, till papa comes back. I'll not trust you over the threshold again, you naughty, naughty girl."

"Aha, Ellen!" she cried gaily, jumping up, and running to my side. "I shall have a pretty story to tell to-night—and so you've found me out. Have you ever been here in your life before?"

"Put that hat on, and home at once," said I. "I'm dreadfully grieved at you, Miss Cathy, you've done extremely wrong! It's no use pouting and crying; that won't repay the trouble I've had, scouring the country after you. To think how Mr. Linton charged me to keep you in; and you stealing off so; it shows you are a cunning little fox, and nobody will put faith in you any more."

"What have I done?" sobbed she, instantly checked. "Papa charged me nothing: he'll not scold me, Ellen—he's never cross, like you!"

"Come, come!" I repeated. "I'll tie the riband. Now, let us have no petulance. Oh, for shame. You thirteen years old, and such a baby!"

This exclamation was caused by her pushing the hat from her head, and retreating to the chimney out of my reach.

"Nay," said the servant, "don't be hard on the bonny lass, Mrs. Dean. We made her stop—she'd fain have ridden forwards, afeard you should be uneasy. Hareton offered to go with her, and I thought he should. It's a wild road over the hills."

Hareton, during the discussion, stood with his hands in his pockets, too awkward to speak, though he looked as if he did not relish my intrusion.

"How long am I to wait?" I continued, disregarding the woman's interference. "It will be dark in ten minutes. Where is the pony, Miss Cathy? And where is Phœnix? I shall leave you, unless you be quick, so please yourself."

"The pony is in the yard," she replied, "and Phœnix is shut in there. He's bitten—and so is Charlie. I was going to tell you all about it; but you are in a bad temper, and don't deserve to hear."

I picked up her hat, and approached to reinstate it; but perceiving that the people of the house took her part, she commenced capering round the room; and, on my giving chase, ran like a mouse, over and under and behind the furniture, rendering it ridiculous for me to pursue.

Hareton and the woman laughed, and she joined them, and waxed more impertinent still; till I cried, in great irritation—

"Well, Miss Cathy, if you were aware whose house this is, you'd be glad enough to get out."

"It's *your* father's, isn't it?" said she, turning to Hareton.

"Nay," he replied, looking down, and blushing bashfully.

He could not stand a steady gaze from her eyes, though they were just his own.

"Whose, then—your master's?" she asked.

He coloured deeper, with a different feeling, muttered an oath, and turned away.

"Who is his master?" continued the tiresome girl, appealing to me. "He talked about 'our house,' and 'our folk.' I thought he had been the owner's son. And he never said, Miss; he should have done, shouldn't he, if he's a servant?"

Hareton grew black as a thunder-cloud, at this childish speech. I silently shook my questioner, and, at last, succeeded in equipping her for departure.

"Now, get my horse," she said, addressing her unknown kinsman as she would one of the stable-boys at the Grange. "And you may come with me. I want to see where the goblin hunter rises in the marsh, and to hear about the *fairishes*, as you call them—but make haste! What's the matter? Get my horse, I say."

"I'll see thee damned, before I be *thy* servant!" growled the lad.

"You'll see me *what?*" asked Catherine in surprise.

"Damned—thou saucy witch!" he replied.

"There, Miss Cathy! you see you have got into pretty company," I interposed. "Nice words to be used to a young lady! Pray don't begin to dispute with him. Come, let us seek for Minny ourselves, and begone."

"But, Ellen," cried she, staring, fixed in astonishment. "How dare he speak so to me? Mustn't he be made to do as I ask him? You wicked creature, I shall tell papa what you said—Now then!"

Hareton did not appear to feel this threat; so the tears sprung into her eyes with indignation. "You bring the pony," she exclaimed, turning to the woman, "and let my dog free this moment!"

"Softly, Miss," answered the addressed. "You'll lose nothing by being civil. Though Mr. Hareton, there, be not the master's son, he's your cousin; and I was never hired to serve you."

"*He* my cousin!" cried Cathy with a scornful laugh.

"Yes, indeed," responded her reprover.

"Oh, Ellen! don't let them say such things," she pursued in great trouble. "Papa is gone to fetch my cousin from London—my cousin is a gentleman's son. That my—" she stopped, and wept outright; upset at the bare notion of relationship with such a clown.

"Hush, hush!" I whispered, "people can have many cousins and of all sorts, Miss Cathy, without being any the worse for it; only they needn't keep their company, if they be disagreeable and bad."

"He's not, he's not my cousin, Ellen!" she went on, gathering fresh grief from reflection, and flinging herself into my arms for refuge from the idea.

I was much vexed at her and the servant for their mutual revelations; having no doubt of Linton's approaching arrival, communicated by the former, being reported to Mr. Heathcliff; and feeling as confident that Catherine's first thought on her father's return would be to seek an explanation of the latter's assertion concerning her rude-bred kindred.

Hareton, recovering from his disgust at being taken for a servant, seemed moved by her distress; and, having fetched the pony round to the door, he took, to propitiate her, a fine crooked-legged terrier whelp from the kennel, and putting it into her hand, bid her wisht[2] for he meant naught.

Pausing in her lamentations, she surveyed him with a glance of awe and horror, then burst forth anew.

I could scarcely refrain from smiling at this antipathy to the poor fellow, who was a well-made, athletic youth, good-looking in features, and stout and healthy, but attired in garments befitting his daily occupations of working on the farm, and lounging among the moors after rabbits and game. Still, I thought I could detect in his physiognomy a mind owning better qualities than his father ever possessed. Good things lost amid a wilderness of weeds, to be sure, whose rankness far over-topped their neglected growth; yet, notwithstanding, evidence of a wealthy soil that might yield luxuriant crops under other and favourable circumstances. Mr. Heathcliff, I believe, had not treated him physically ill; thanks to his fearless nature, which offered no temptation to that course of oppression; it had none of the timid susceptibility that would have given zest to ill-treatment, in Heathcliff's judgment. He appeared to have bent his malevolence on making him a brute: he was never taught to read or write; never rebuked for any bad habit which did not annoy his keeper; never led a single step towards virtue, or guarded by a single precept against vice. And from what I heard, Joseph contributed much to his deterioration by a narrow-minded partiality which prompted him to flatter and pet him, as a boy, because he was the head of the old family. And as he had been in the habit of accusing Catherine Earnshaw and Heathcliff, when children, of putting the master past his patience, and compelling him to seek solace in drink, by what he termed their "offald ways,"[3] so at present he laid the whole burden of Hareton's faults on the shoulders of the usurper of his property.

If the lad swore, he wouldn't correct him; nor however culpably he behaved. It gave Joseph satisfaction, apparently, to watch him go the worst lengths. He allowed that he was ruined; that his soul was abandoned to perdition; but then, he reflected that Heathcliff

2. Hush.                                         3. Disreputable.

must answer for it. Hareton's blood would be required at his hands; and there lay immense consolation in that thought.

Joseph had instilled into him a pride of name, and of his lineage; he would, had he dared, have fostered hate between him and the present owner of the Heights, but his dread of that owner amounted to superstition; and he confined his feelings regarding him to muttered innuendoes and private comminations.

I don't pretend to be intimately acquainted with the mode of living customary in those days at Wuthering Heights. I only speak from hearsay; for I saw little. The villagers affirmed Mr. Heathcliff was *near*,[4] and a cruel hard landlord to his tenants; but the house, inside, had regained its ancient aspect of comfort under female management; and the scenes of riot common in Hindley's time were not now enacted within its walls. The master was too gloomy to seek companionship with any people, good or bad, and he is yet.

This, however, is not making progress with my story. Miss Cathy rejected the peace-offering of the terrier, and demanded her own dogs, Charlie and Phœnix. They came limping, and hanging their heads; and we set out for home, sadly out of sorts, every one of us.

I could not wring from my little lady how she had spent the day; except that, as I supposed, the goal of her pilgrimage was Penistone Crags; and she arrived without adventure to the gate of the farmhouse, when Hareton happened to issue forth, attended by some canine followers who attacked her train.

They had a smart battle, before their owners could separate them: that formed an introduction. Catherine told Hareton who she was, and where she was going; and asked him to show her the way, finally beguiling him to accompany her.

He opened the mysteries of the Fairy cave, and twenty other queer places; but, being in disgrace, I was not favoured with a description of the interesting objects she saw.

I could gather, however, that her guide had been a favourite till she hurt his feelings by addressing him as a servant; and Heathcliff's housekeeper hurt hers by calling him her cousin.

Then the language he had held to her rankled in her heart; she who was always "love," and "darling," and "queen," and "angel," with everybody at the Grange, to be insulted so shockingly by a stranger! She did not comprehend it; and hard work I had to obtain a promise that she would not lay the grievance before her father.

I explained how he objected to the whole household at the Heights, and how sorry he would be to find she had been there; but I insisted most on the fact, that if she revealed my negligence

4. Niggardly.

of his orders, he would perhaps be so angry that I should have to leave; and Cathy couldn't bear that prospect: she pledged her word, and kept it, for my sake—after all, she was a sweet little girl.

## Chapter XIX

A letter, edged with black, announced the day of my master's return. Isabella was dead; and he wrote to bid me get mourning for his daughter, and arrange a room and other accommodations for his youthful nephew.

Catherine ran wild with joy at the idea of welcoming her father back, and indulged most sanguine anticipations of the innumerable excellencies of her "real" cousin.

The evening of their expected arrival came. Since early morning, she had been busy, ordering her own small affairs; and now, attired in her new black frock—poor thing! her aunt's death impressed her with no definite sorrow—she obliged me, by constant worrying, to walk with her down through the grounds to meet them.

"Linton is just six months younger than I am," she chattered, as we strolled leisurely over the swells and hollows of mossy turf, under shadow of the trees. "How delightful it will be to have him for a playfellow! Aunt Isabella sent papa a beautiful lock of his hair; it was lighter than mine—more flaxen, and quite as fine. I have it carefully preserved in a little glass box; and I've often thought what pleasure it would be to see its owner. Oh! I am happy—and papa, dear, dear papa! Come, Ellen, let us run! come run!"

She ran, and returned and ran again, many times before my sober footsteps reached the gate, and then she seated herself on the grassy bank beside the path, and tried to wait patiently, but that was impossible; she couldn't be still a minute.

"How long they are!" she exclaimed. "Ah, I see some dust on the road—they are coming! No! When will they be here? May we not go a little way—half a mile, Ellen, only just half a mile? Do say yes, to that clump of birches at the turn!"

I refused staunchly; and, at length, her suspense was ended: the travelling carriage rolled in sight.

Miss Cathy shrieked, and stretched out her arms, as soon as she caught her father's face, looking from the window. He descended, nearly as eager as herself; and a considerable interval elapsed ere they had a thought to spare for any but themselves.

While they exchanged caresses, I took a peep in to see after Linton. He was asleep in a corner, wrapped in a warm, fur-lined cloak, as if it had been winter. A pale, delicate, effeminate boy, who might have been taken for my master's younger brother, so strong was the resemblance; but there was a sickly peevishness in his aspect that Edgar Linton never had.

The latter saw me looking; and having shaken hands, advised me to close the door, and leave him undisturbed; for the journey had fatigued him.

Cathy would fain have taken one glance; but her father told her to come on, and they walked together up the park, while I hastened before to prepare the servants.

"Now, darling," said Mr. Linton, addressing his daughter, as they halted at the bottom of the front steps, "your cousin is not so strong or so merry as you are, and he has lost his mother, remember, a very short time since; therefore, don't expect him to play and run about with you directly. And don't harass him much by talking—let him be quiet this evening, at least, will you?"

"Yes, yes, papa," answered Catherine; "but I do want to see him; and he hasn't once looked out."

The carriage stopped; and the sleeper, being roused, was lifted to the ground by his uncle.

"This is your cousin Cathy, Linton," he said, putting their little hands together. "She's fond of you already; and mind you don't grieve her by crying to-night. Try to be cheerful now; the travelling is at an end, and you have nothing to do but rest and amuse yourself as you please."

"Let me go to bed, then," answered the boy, shrinking from Catherine's salute; and he put his fingers to his eyes to remove incipient tears.

"Come, come, there's a good child," I whispered, leading him in. "You'll make her weep too—see how sorry she is for you!"

I do not know whether it were sorrow for him, but his cousin put on as sad a countenance as himself, and returned to her father. All three entered, and mounted to the library, where tea was laid ready.

I proceeded to remove Linton's cap and mantle, and placed him on a chair by the table; but he was no sooner seated than he began to cry afresh. My master inquired what was the matter.

"I can't sit on a chair," sobbed the boy.

"Go to the sofa, then, and Ellen shall bring you some tea," answered his uncle, patiently.

He had been greatly tried during the journey, I felt convinced, by his fretful, ailing charge.

Linton slowly trailed himself off, and lay down. Cathy carried a foot-stool and her cup to his side.

At first she sat silent; but that could not last; she had resolved to make a pet of her little cousin, as she would have him to be; and she commenced stroking his curls, and kissing his cheek, and offering him tea in her saucer, like a baby. This pleased him, for he was not much better; he dried his eyes, and lightened into a faint smile.

"Oh, he'll do very well," said the master to me, after watching them a minute. "Very well, if we can keep him, Ellen. The company of a child of his own age will instil new spirit into him soon, and by wishing for strength he'll gain it."

"Aye, if we can keep him!" I mused to myself; and sore misgivings came over me that there was slight hope of that. And then, I thought, however will that weakling live at Wuthering Heights, between his father and Hareton? What playmates and instructors they'll be.

Our doubts were presently decided—even earlier than I expected. I had just taken the children upstairs, after tea was finished, and seen Linton asleep—he would not suffer me to leave him till that was the case. I had come down, and was standing by the table in the hall, lighting a bed-room candle for Mr. Edgar, when a maid stepped out of the kitchen and informed me that Mr. Heathcliff's servant, Joseph, was at the door, and wished to speak with the master.

"I shall ask him what he wants first," I said, in considerable trepidation. "A very unlikely hour to be troubling people, and the instant they have returned from a long journey. I don't think the master can see him."

Joseph had advanced through the kitchen, as I uttered these words, and now presented himself in the hall. He was donned in his Sunday garments, with his most sanctimonious and sourest face; and holding his hat in one hand and his stick in the other, he proceeded to clean his shoes on the mat.

"Good evening, Joseph," I said, coldly. "What business brings you here to-night?"

"It's Maister Linton Aw mun spake tull,"[1] he answered, waving me disdainfully aside.

"Mr. Linton is going to bed; unless you have something particular to say, I'm sure he won't hear it now," I continued. "You had better sit down in there, and entrust your message to me."

"Which is his rahm?" pursued the fellow, surveying the range of closed doors.

I perceived he was bent on refusing my mediation; so very reluctantly I went up to the library, and announced the unseasonable visitor, advising that he should be dismissed till next day.

Mr. Linton had no time to empower me to do so, for he mounted close at my heels, and, pushing into the apartment, planted himself at the far side of the table, with his two fists clapped on the head of his stick, and began in an elevated tone, as

1. Speak to.

if anticipating opposition—

"Hathecliff has send me for his lad, un Aw 'munn't goa back 'baht him."[2]

Edgar Linton was silent a minute; an expression of exceeding sorrow overcast his features; he would have pitied the child on his own account; but, recalling Isabella's hopes and fears, and anxious wishes for her son, and her commendations of him to his care, he grieved bitterly at the prospect of yielding him up, and searched in his heart how it might be avoided. No plan offered itself: the very exhibition of any desire to keep him would have rendered the claimant more peremptory: there was nothing left but to resign him. However, he was not going to rouse him from his sleep.

"Tell Mr. Heathcliff," he answered, calmly, "that his son shall come to Wuthering Heights to-morrow. He is in bed, and too tired to go the distance now. You may also tell him that the mother of Linton desired him to remain under my guardianship; and, at present, his health is very precarious."

"Noa!" said Joseph, giving a thud with his prop on the floor, and assuming an authoritative air. "Noa! that manes nowt—Hathecliff maks noa 'cahnt uh t' mother, nur yah norther—bud he'll hev his lad; und Aw mun tak him—soa nah yah knaw!"[3]

"You shall not to-night!" answered Linton, decisively. "Walk down stairs at once, and repeat to your master what I have said. Ellen, show him down. Go—"

And, aiding the indignant elder with a lift by the arm, he rid the room of him, and closed the door.

"Varrah weel!" shouted Joseph, as he slowly drew off. "Tuh morn, he's come hisseln, un' thrust *him* aht, if yah darr!"

## Chapter XX

To obviate the danger of this threat being fulfilled, Mr. Linton commissioned me to take the boy home early, on Catherine's pony, and, said he—

"As we shall now have no influence over his destiny, good or bad, you must say nothing of where he is gone to my daughter; she cannot associate with him hereafter, and it is better for her to remain in ignorance of his proximity, lest she should be restless, and anxious to visit the Heights. Merely tell her, his father sent for him suddenly, and he has been obliged to leave us."

Linton was very reluctant to be roused from his bed at five o'clock, and astonished to be informed that he must prepare for further travelling; but I softened off the matter by stating that he

2. Without him.
3. *Manes nowt:* means nothing; *maks noa* *'cahnt:* takes no account; *norther:* neither.

was going to spend some time with his father, Mr. Heathcliff, who wished to see him so much, he did not like to defer the pleasure till he should recover from his late journey.

"My father?" he cried, in strange perplexity. "Mamma never told me I had a father. Where does he live? I'd rather stay with uncle."

"He lives a little distance from the Grange," I replied, "just beyond those hills—not so far but you may walk over here, when you get hearty. And you should be glad to go home, and to see him. You must try to love him, as you did your mother, and then he will love you."

"But why have I not heard of him before?" asked Linton; "why didn't mamma and he live together, as other people do?"

"He had business to keep him in the north," I answered; "and your mother's health required her to reside in the south."

"And why didn't mamma speak to me about him?" persevered the child. "She often talked of uncle, and I learnt to love him long ago. How am I to love papa? I don't know him."

"Oh, all children love their parents," I said. "Your mother, perhaps, thought you would want to be with him, if she mentioned him often to you. Let us make haste. An early ride on such a beautiful morning is much preferable to an hour's more sleep."

"Is *she* to go with us?" he demanded. "The little girl I saw yesterday?"

"Not now," replied I.

"Is uncle?" he continued.

"No, I shall be your companion there," I said.

Linton sank back on his pillow, and fell into a brown study.

"I won't go without uncle," he cried at length; "I can't tell where you mean to take me."

I attempted to persuade him of the naughtiness of showing reluctance to meet his father; still he obstinately resisted any progress towards dressing, and I had to call for my master's assistance in coaxing him out of bed.

The poor thing was finally got off with several delusive assurances that his absence should be short; that Mr. Edgar and Cathy would visit him; and other promises, equally ill-founded, which I invented and reiterated at intervals throughout the way.

The pure heather-scented air, and the bright sunshine, and. the gentle canter of Minny relieved his despondency, after a while. He began to put questions concerning his new home, and its inhabitants, with greater interest and liveliness.

"Is Wuthering Heights as pleasant a place as Thrushcross Grange?" he inquired, turning to take a last glance into the valley, whence a light mist mounted and formed a fleecy cloud on the skirts of the blue.

"It is not so buried in trees," I replied, "and it is not quite so large, but you can see the country beautifully, all round; and the air is healthier for you—fresher and dryer. You will, perhaps, think the building old and dark at first—though it is a respectable house, the next best in the neighbourhood. And you will have such nice rambles on the moors! Hareton Earnshaw—that is Miss Cathy's other cousin, and so yours in a manner—will show you all the sweetest spots; and you can bring a book in fine weather, and make a green hollow your study; and, now and then, your uncle may join you in a walk: he does, frequently, walk out on the hills."

"And what is my father like?" he asked. "Is he as young and handsome as uncle?"

"He's as young," said I, "but he has black hair and eyes, and looks sterner, and he is taller and bigger altogether. He'll not seem to you so gentle and kind at first, perhaps, because it is not his way —still, mind you be frank and cordial with him; and naturally he'll be fonder of you than any uncle, for you are his own."

"Black hair and eyes!" mused Linton. "I can't fancy him. Then I am not like him, am I?"

"Not much," I answered. Not a morsel, I thought, surveying with regret the white complexion and slim frame of my companion, and his large languid eyes—his mother's eyes, save that, unless a morbid touchiness kindled them a moment, they had not a vestige of her sparkling spirit.

"How strange that he should never come to see mamma and me," he murmured. "Has he ever seen me? If he have, I must have been a baby—I remember not a single thing about him!"

"Why, Master Linton," said I, "three hundred miles is a great distance; and ten years seem very different in length to a grown up person, compared with what they do to you. It is probable Mr. Heathcliff proposed going, from summer to summer, but never found a convenient opportunity; and now it is too late. Don't trouble him with questions on the subject: it will disturb him for no good."

The boy was fully occupied with his own cogitations for the remainder of the ride, till we halted before the farm-house garden gate. I watched to catch his impressions in his countenance. He surveyed the carved front and low-browed lattices, the straggling gooseberry bushes and crooked firs, with solemn intentness, and then shook his head: his private feelings entirely disapproved of the exterior of his new abode; but he had sense to postpone complaining—there might be compensation within.

Before he dismounted, I went and opened the door. It was half-past six; the family had just finished breakfast; the servant was clearing and wiping down the table. Joseph stood by his master's chair telling some tale concerning a lame horse; and Hareton was preparing for the hay-field.

"Hallo, Nelly!" cried Mr. Heathcliff, when he saw me. "I feared I should have to come down and fetch my property myself. You've brought it, have you? Let us see what we can make of it."

He got up and strode to the door: Hareton and Joseph followed in gaping curiosity. Poor Linton ran a frightened eye over the faces of the three.

"Sure-ly," said Joseph after a grave inspection, "he's swopped wi' ye, maister, an' yon's his lass!"

Heathcliff, having stared his son into an ague of confusion, uttered a scornful laugh.

"God! what a beauty! what a lovely, charming thing!" he exclaimed. "Haven't they reared it on snails and sour milk, Nelly? Oh, damn my soul! but that's worse than I expected—and the devil knows I was not sanguine!"

I bid the trembling and bewildered child get down, and enter. He did not thoroughly comprehend the meaning of his father's speech, or whether it were intended for him: indeed, he was not yet certain that the grim, sneering stranger was his father; but he clung to me with growing trepidation, and on Mr. Heathcliff's taking a seat, and bidding him "come hither," he hid his face on my shoulder, and wept.

"Tut, tut!" said Heathcliff, stretching out a hand and dragging him roughly between his knees, and then holding up his head by the chin. "None of that nonsense! We're not going to hurt thee, Linton—isn't that thy name? Thou art thy mother's child, entirely! Where is *my* share in thee, puling chicken?"

He took off the boy's cap and pushed back his thick flaxen curls, felt his slender arms, and his small fingers; during which examination, Linton ceased crying, and lifted his great blue eyes to inspect the inspector.

"Do you know me?" asked Heathcliff, having satisfied himself that the limbs were all equally frail and feeble.

"No!" said Linton, with a gaze of vacant fear.

"You've heard of me, I dare say?"

"No," he replied again.

"No? What a shame of your mother, never to waken your filial regard for me! You are my son, then, I'll tell you; and your mother was a wicked slut to leave you in ignorance of the sort of father you possessed. Now, don't wince, and colour up! Though it *is* something to see you have not white blood. Be a good lad; and I'll do for you. Nelly, if you be tired you may sit down; if not get home again. I guess you'll report what you hear and see, to the cipher at the Grange; and this thing won't be settled while you linger about it."

"Well," replied I, "I hope you'll be kind to the boy, Mr. Heathcliff, or you'll not keep him long, and he's all you have akin in the wide world that you will ever know—remember."

"I'll be *very* kind to him, you needn't fear!" he said, laughing. "Only nobody else must be kind to him—I'm jealous of monopolizing his affection. And, to begin my kindness, Joseph! bring the lad some breakfast. Hareton, you infernal calf, begone to your work. Yes, Nell," he added when they were departed, "my son is prospective owner of your place, and I should not wish him to die till I was certain of being his successor. Besides, he's *mine*, and I want the triumph of seeing *my* descendent fairly lord of their estates; my child hiring their children to till their fathers' lands for wages. That is the sole consideration which can make me endure the whelp—I despise him for himself, and hate him for the memories he revives! But that consideration is sufficient; he's as safe with me, and shall be tended as carefully as your master tends his own. I have a room upstairs, furnished for him in handsome style; I've engaged a tutor, also, to come three times a week, from twenty miles distance, to teach him what he pleases to learn. I've ordered Hareton to obey him; and in fact I've arranged everything with a view to preserve the superior and the gentleman in him, above his associates. I do regret, however, that he so little deserves the trouble. If I wished any blessing in the world, it was to find him a worthy object of pride, and I'm bitterly disappointed with the whey-faced whining wretch!"

While he was speaking, Joseph returned, bearing a basin of milk-porridge, and placed it before Linton. He stirred round the homely mess with a look of aversion, and affirmed he could not eat it.

I saw the old man-servant shared largely in his master's scorn of the child, though he was compelled to retain the sentiment in his heart, because Heathcliff plainly meant his underlings to hold him in honour.

"Cannot ate it?" repeated he, peering in Linton's face, and subduing his voice to a whisper, for fear of being overheard. "But Maister Hareton nivir ate nowt else, when he wer a little un: und what wer gooid eneugh fur him's gooid eneugh fur yah, Aw's rayther think!"

"I *shan't* eat it!" answered Linton, snappishly. "Take it away."

Joseph snatched up the food indignantly, and brought it to us.

"Is there owt ails th' victuals?" he asked, thrusting the tray under Heathcliff's nose.

"What should ail them?" he said.

"Wah!" answered Joseph, "yon dainty chap says he cannut ate

'em. Bud Aw guess it's raight! His mother wer just soa—we wer a'most too mucky[1] tuh sow t' corn fur makking her breead."

"Don't mention his mother to me," said the master, angrily. "Get him something that he can eat, that's all. What is his usual food, Nelly?"

I suggested boiled milk or tea; and the housekeeper received instructions to prepare some.

Come, I reflected, his father's selfishness may contribute to his comfort. He perceives his delicate constitution, and the necessity of treating him tolerably. I'll console Mr. Edgar by acquainting him with the turn Heathcliff's humour has taken.

Having no excuse for lingering longer, I slipped out, while Linton was engaged in timidly rebuffing the advances of a friendly sheep-dog. But he was too much on the alert to be cheated: as I closed the door, I heard a cry, and a frantic repetition of the words—

"Don't leave me! I'll not stay here! I'll not stay here!"

Then the latch was raised and fell: they did not suffer him to come forth. I mounted Minny, and urged her to a trot; and so my brief guardianship ended.

## Chapter XXI

We had sad work with little Cathy that day: she rose in high glee, eager to join her cousin; and such passionate tears and lamentations followed the news of his departure, that Edgar himself was obliged to sooth her, by affirming he should come back soon; he added, however, "if I can get him"; and there were no hopes of that.

This promise poorly pacified her, but time was more potent; and though still, at intervals, she inquired of her father when Linton would return, before she did see him again, his features had waxed so dim in her memory that she did not recognise him.

When I chanced to encounter the housekeeper of Wuthering Heights, in paying business-visits to Gimmerton, I used to ask how the young master got on; for he lived almost as secluded as Catherine herself, and was never to be seen. I could gather from her that he continued in weak health, and was a tiresome inmate. She said Mr. Heathcliff seemed to dislike him ever longer and worse, though he took some trouble to conceal it. He had an antipathy to the sound of his voice, and could not do at all with his sitting in the same room with him many minutes together.

There seldom passed much talk between them; Linton learnt his lessons, and spent his evenings in a small apartment they called

1. Dirty.

the parlour; or else lay in bed all day, for he was constantly getting coughs, and colds, and aches, and pains of some sort.

"And I never knew such a faint-hearted creature," added the woman; "nor one so careful of hisseln. He *will* go on, if I leave the window open, a bit late in the evening. Oh! it's killing, a breath of night air! And he must have a fire in the middle of summer; and Joseph's 'bacca pipe is poison; and he must always have sweets and dainties, and always milk, milk for ever—heeding naught how the rest of us are pinched in winter; and there he'll sit, wrapped in his furred cloak in his chair by the fire, and some toast and water, or other slop on the hob to sip at; and if Hareton, for pity, comes to amuse him—Hareton is not bad-natured, though he's rough— they're sure to part, one swearing and the other crying. I believe the master would relish Earnshaw's thrashing him to a mummy, if he were not his son; and I'm certain he would be fit to turn him out of doors, if he knew half the nursing he gives hisseln. But then, he won't go into danger of temptation; he never enters the parlour, and should Linton show those ways in the house where he is, he sends him upstairs directly."

I divined, from this account, that utter lack of sympathy had rendered young Heathcliff selfish and disagreeable, if he were not so originally; and my interest in him, consequently, decayed, though still I was moved with a sense of grief at his lot, and a wish that he had been left with us.

Mr. Edgar encouraged me to gain information; he thought a great deal about him, I fancy, and would have run some risk to see him; and he told me once to ask the housekeeper whether he ever came into the village?

She said he had only been twice, on horseback, accompanying his father; and both times he pretended to be quite knocked up for three or four days afterwards.

That housekeeper left, if I recollect rightly, two years after he came; and another, whom I did not know, was her successor: she lives there still.

Time wore on at the Grange in its former pleasant way, till Miss Cathy reached sixteen. On the anniversary of her birth we never manifested any signs of rejoicing, because it was also the anniversary of my late mistress's death. Her father invariably spent that day alone in the library; and walked, at dusk, as far as Gimmerton kirkyard, where he would frequently prolong his stay beyond midnight. Therefore Catherine was thrown on her own resources for amusement.

This twentieth of March was a beautiful spring day, and when her father had retired, my young lady came down dressed for going out, and said she had asked to have a ramble on the edge of the moors with me; and Mr. Linton had given her leave, if we went only a short distance and were back within the hour.

"So make haste, Ellen!" she cried. "I know where I wish to go; where a colony of moor game are settled. I want to see whether they have made their nests yet."

"That must be a good distance up," I answered; "they don't breed on the edge of the moor."

"No, it's not," she said. "I've gone very near with papa."

I put on my bonnet and sallied out, thinking nothing more of the matter. She bounded before me, and returned to my side, and was off again like a young greyhound; and, at first, I found plenty of entertainment in listening to the larks singing far and near, and enjoying the sweet, warm sunshine, and watching her, my pet and my delight, with her golden ringlets flying loose behind, and her bright cheek, as soft and pure in its bloom as a wild rose, and her eyes radiant with cloudless pleasure. She was a happy creature, and an angel, in those days. It's a pity she could not be content.

"Well," said I, "where are your moor game, Miss Cathy? We should be at them—the Grange park-fence is a great way off now."

"Oh, a little further—only a little further, Ellen," was her answer, continually. "Climb to that hillock, pass that bank, and by the time you reach the other side, I shall have raised the birds."

But there were so many hillocks and banks to climb and pass, that, at length, I began to be weary, and told her we must halt, and retrace our steps.

I shouted to her, as she had outstripped me, a long way; she either did not hear or did not regard, for she still sprang on, and I was compelled to follow. Finally, she dived into a hollow; and before I came in sight of her again, she was two miles nearer Wuthering Heights than her own home; and I beheld a couple of persons arrest her, one of whom I felt convinced was Mr. Heathcliff himself.

Cathy had been caught in the fact of plundering, or, at least, hunting out the nests of the grouse.

The Heights were Heathcliff's land, and he was reproving the poacher.

"I've neither taken any nor found any," she said, as I toiled to them, expanding her hands in corroboration of the statement. "I didn't mean to take them; but papa told me there were quantities up here, and I wished to see the eggs."

Heathcliff glanced at me with an ill-meaning smile, expressing his acquaintance with the party, and, consequently, his malevolence towards it, and demanded who "papa" was?

"Mr. Linton of Thrushcross Grange," she replied. "I thought you did not know me, or you wouldn't have spoken in that way."

"You suppose papa is highly esteemed and respected then?" he said, sarcastically.

"And what are you?" inquired Catherine, gazing curiously on the speaker. "That man I've seen before. Is he your son?"

She pointed to Hareton, the other individual, who had gained nothing but increased bulk and strength by the addition of two years to his age: he seemed as awkward and rough as ever.

"Miss Cathy," I interrupted, "it will be three hours instead of one that we are out, presently. We really must go back."

"No, that man is not my son," answered Heathcliff, pushing me aside. "But I have one, and you have seen him before, too; and, though your nurse is in a hurry, I think both you and she would be the better for a little rest. Will you just turn this nab of heath,[2] and walk into my house? You'll get home earlier for the ease; and you shall receive a kind welcome."

I whispered Catherine that she mustn't, on any account, accede to the proposal; it was entirely out of the question.

"Why?" she asked, aloud. "I'm tired of running, and the ground is dewy—I can't sit here. Let us go, Ellen! Besides, he says I have seen his son. He's mistaken, I think; but I guess where he lives— at the farm-house I visited in coming from Penistone Crags. Don't you?"

"I do. Come, Nelly, hold your tongue—it will be a treat for her to look in on us. Hareton, get forwards with the lass. You shall walk with me, Nelly."

"No, she's not going to any such place," I cried, struggling to release my arm which he had seized; but she was almost at the doorstones already, scampering round the brow at full speed. Her appointed companion did not pretend to escort her; he shyed off by the road-side, and vanished.

"Mr. Heathcliff, it's very wrong," I continued; "you know you mean no good. And there she'll see Linton, and all will be told, as soon as ever we return; and I shall have the blame."

"I want her to see Linton," he answered; "he's looking better these few days; it's not often he's fit to be seen. And we'll soon persuade her to keep the visit secret—where is the harm of it?"

"The harm of it is, that her father would hate me if he found I suffered her to enter your house; and I am convinced you have a bad design in encouraging her to do so," I replied.

"My design is as honest as possible. I'll inform you of its whole scope," he said. "That the two cousins may fall in love, and get married. I'm acting generously to your master; his young chit has

---

2. A *nab* is an abrupt termination of a range of uplands. Emily Brontë probably has in mind the bold escarpment of Millstone Grit from which one could see the whole of the Haworth moorlands. It was known as the "Nab."

no expectations, and should she second my wishes, she'll be provided for, at once, as joint successor with Linton."

"If Linton died," I answered, "and his life is quite uncertain, Catherine would be the heir."

"No, she would not," he said. "There is no clause in the will to secure it so; his property would go to me; but, to prevent disputes, I desire their union, and am resolved to bring it about."

"And I'm resolved she shall never approach your house with me again," I returned, as we reached the gate, where Miss Cathy waited our coming.

Heathcliff bid me be quiet; and, preceding us up the path, hastened to open the door. My young lady gave him several looks, as if she could not exactly make up her mind what to think of him; but now he smiled when he met her eye, and softened his voice in addressing her, and I was foolish enough to imagine the memory of her mother might disarm him from desiring her injury.

Linton stood on the hearth. He had been out walking in the fields, for his cap was on, and he was calling to Joseph to bring him dry shoes.

He had grown tall of his age, still wanting some months of sixteen. His features were pretty yet, and his eye and complexion brighter than I remembered them, though with merely temporary lustre borrowed from the salubrious air and genial sun.

"Now, who is that?" asked Mr. Heathcliff, turning to Cathy. "Can you tell?"

"Your son?" she said, having doubtfully surveyed first one and then the other.

"Yes, yes," answered he; "but is this the only time you have beheld him? Think! Ah! you have a short memory. Linton, don't you recall your cousin, that you used to tease us so with wishing to see?"

"What, Linton!" cried Cathy, kindling into joyful surprise at the name. "Is that little Linton? He's taller than I am! Are you Linton?"

The youth stepped forward, and acknowledged himself: she kissed him fervently, and they gazed with wonder at the change time had wrought in the appearance of each.

Catherine had reached her full height; her figure was both plump and slender, elastic as steel, and her whole aspect sparkling with health and spirits. Linton's looks and movements were very languid, and his form extremely slight; but there was a grace in his manner that mitigated these defects, and rendered him not unpleasing.

After exchanging numerous marks of fondness with him, his cousin went to Mr. Heathcliff, who lingered by the door, dividing his attention between the objects inside and those that lay without, pretending, that is, to observe the latter, and really noting the former alone.

"And you are my uncle, then!" she cried, reaching up to salute him. "I thought I liked you, though you were cross, at first. Why don't you visit at the Grange with Linton? To live all these years such close neighbours, and never see us, is odd; what have you done so for?"

"I visited it once or twice too often before you were born," he answered. "There—damn it! If you have any kisses to spare, give them to Linton—they are thrown away on me."

"Naughty Ellen!" exclaimed Catherine, flying to attack me next with her lavish caresses. "Wicked Ellen! to try to hinder me from entering. But I'll take this walk every morning in future. May I, uncle—and sometimes bring papa? Won't you be glad to see us?"

"Of course!" replied the uncle, with a hardly surpressed grimace, resulting from his deep aversion to both the proposed visitors. "But stay," he continued, turning towards the young lady. "Now I think of it, I'd better tell you. Mr. Linton has a prejudice against me; we quarrelled at one time of our lives, with unchristian ferocity; and, if you mention coming here to him, he'll put a veto on your visits altogether. Therefore, you must not mention it, unless you be careless of seeing your cousin hereafter. You may come, if you will, but you must not mention it."

"Why did you quarrel?" asked Catherine, considerably crestfallen.

"He thought me too poor to wed his sister," answered Heathcliff," and was grieved that I got her. His pride was hurt, and he'll never forgive it."

"That's wrong!" said the young lady: "some time, I'll tell him so. But Linton and I have no share in your quarrel. I'll not come here, then; he shall come to the Grange."

"It will be too far for me," murmured her cousin; "to walk four miles would kill me. No, come here, Miss Catherine, now and then, not every morning, but once or twice a week."

The father launched towards his son a glance of bitter contempt.

"I am afraid, Nelly, I shall lose my labour," he muttered to me. "Miss Catherine, as the ninny calls her, will discover his value, and send him to the devil. Now, if it had been Hareton—do you know that, twenty times a day, I covet Hareton, with all his degradation? I'd have loved the lad had he been some one else. But I think he's safe from *her* love. I'll pit him against that paltry creature, unless it bestir itself briskly. We calculate it will scarcely last till it is eighteen. Oh, confound the vapid thing. He's absorbed in drying his feet, and never looks at her—Linton!"

"Yes, father," answered the boy.

"Have you nothing to show your cousin, anywhere about; not even a rabbit, or a weasel's nest? Take her into the garden, before you change your shoes; and into the stable to see your horse."

"Wouldn't you rather sit here?" asked Linton, addressing Cathy in a tone which expressed reluctance to move again.

"I don't know," she replied, casting a longing look to the door, and evidently eager to be active.

He kept his seat, and shrank closer to the fire.

Heathcliff rose, and went into the kitchen, and from thence to the yard, calling out for Hareton.

Hareton responded, and presently the two re-entered. The young man had been washing himself, as was visible by the glow on his cheeks, and his wetted hair.

"Oh, I'll ask *you*, uncle," cried Miss Cathy, recollecting the housekeeper's assertion. "That's not my cousin, is he?"

"Yes," he replied, "Your mother's nephew. Don't you like him?"

Catherine looked queer.

"Is he not a handsome lad?" he continued.

The uncivil little thing stood on tiptoe, and whispered a sentence in Heathcliff's ear.

He laughed; Hareton darkened; I perceived he was very sensitive to suspected slights, and had obviously a dim notion of his inferiority. But his master or guardian chased the frown by exclaiming—

"You'll be the favourite among us, Hareton! She says you are a—what was it? Well, something very flattering. Here! you go with her round the farm. And behave like a gentleman, mind! Don't use any bad words; and don't stare, when the young lady is not looking at you, and be ready to hide your face when she is; and, when you speak, say your words slowly, and keep your hands out of your pockets. Be off, and entertain her as nicely as you can."

He watched the couple walking past the window. Earnshaw had his countenance completely averted from his companion. He seemed studying the familiar landscape with a stranger's and an artist's interest.

Catherine took a sly look at him, expressing small admiration. She then turned her attention to seeking out objects of amusement for herself, and tripped merrily on, lilting a tune to supply the lack of conversation.

"I've tied his tongue," observed Heathcliff. "He'll not venture a single syllable, all the time! Nelly, you recollect me at his age—nay, some years younger. Did I ever look so stupid, so 'gaumless,'[3] as Joseph calls it?"

---

3. Witless, lacking in understanding.

"Worse," I replied, "because more sullen with it."

"I've a pleasure in him," he continued reflecting aloud. "He has satisfied my expectations. If he were a born fool I should not enjoy it half so much. But he's no fool; and I can sympathise with all his feelings, having felt them myself. I know what he suffers now, for instance, exactly—it is merely a beginning of what he shall suffer, though. And he'll never be able to emerge from his bathos of coarseness and ignorance. I've got him faster than his scoundrel of a father secured me, and lower; for he takes a pride in his brutishness. I've taught him to scorn everything extra-animal as silly and weak. Don't you think Hindley would be proud of his son, if he could see him? almost as proud as I am of mine. But there's this difference; one is gold put to the use of paving stones, and the other is tin polished to ape a service of silver. *Mine* has nothing valuable about it; yet I shall have the merit of making it go as far as such poor stuff can go. *His* had first-rate qualities, and they are lost—rendered worse than unavailing. I have nothing to regret; he would have more than any but I are aware of. And the best of it is, Hareton is damnably fond of me! You'll own that I've out-matched Hindley there. If the dead villain could rise from his grave to abuse me for his offspring's wrongs, I should have the fun of seeing the said offspring fight him back again, indignant that he should dare to rail at the one friend he has in the world!"

Heathcliff chuckled a fiendish laugh at the idea; I made no reply, because I saw that he expected none.

Meantime, our young companion, who sat too removed from us to hear what was said, began to evince symptoms of uneasiness, probably repenting that he had denied himself the treat of Catherine's society for fear of a little fatigue.

His father remarked the restless glances wandering to the window, and the hand irresolutely extended towards his cap.

"Get up, you idle boy!" he exclaimed with assumed heartiness. "Away after them! they are just at the corner, by the stand of hives."

Linton gathered his energies, and left the hearth. The lattice was open, and, as he stepped out, I heard Cathy inquiring of her unsociable attendant, what was that inscription over the door?

Hareton stared up, and scratched his head like a true clown.

"It's some damnable writing," he answered. "I cannot read it."

"Can't read it?" cried Catherine; "I can read it: it's English. But I want to know why it is there."

Linton giggled—the first appearance of mirth he had exhibited.

"He does not know his letters," he said to his cousin. "Could you believe in the existence of such a colossal dunce?"

"Is he all as he should be?" asked Miss Cathy seriously, "or is he simple—not right? I've questioned him twice now, and each time he looked so stupid I think he does not understand me; I can hardly understand *him*, I'm sure!"

Linton repeated his laugh, and glanced at Hareton tauntingly, who certainly did not seem quite clear of comprehension at that moment.

"There's nothing the matter but laziness, is there, Earnshaw?" he said. "My cousin fancies you are an idiot. There you experience the consequence of scorning 'book-larning,' as you would say. Have you noticed, Catherine, his frightful Yorkshire pronunciation?"

"Why, where the devil is the use on't?" growled Hareton, more ready in answering his daily companion. He was about to enlarge further, but the two youngsters broke into a noisy fit of merriment; my giddy Miss being delighted to discover that she might turn his strange talk to matter of amusement.

"Where is the use of the devil in that sentence?" tittered Linton. "Papa told you not to say any bad words, and you can't open your mouth without one. Do try to behave like a gentleman, now do!"

"If thou weren't more a lass than a lad, I'd fell thee this minute, I would; pitiful lath of a crater!" retorted the angry boor, retreating, while his face burnt with mingled rage and mortification; for he was conscious of being insulted, and embarrassed how to resent it.

Mr. Heathcliff, having overheard the conversation as well as I, smiled when he saw him go, but immediately afterwards cast a look of singular aversion on the flippant pair, who remained chattering in the door-way: the boy finding animation enough while discussing Hareton's faults and deficiencies, and relating anecdotes of his goings on; and the girl relishing his pert and spiteful sayings, without considering the ill-nature they evinced. But I began to dislike, more than to compassionate, Linton, and to excuse his father, in some measure, for holding him cheap.

We stayed till afternoon: I could not tear Miss Cathy away, before: but happily my master had not quitted his apartment, and remained ignorant of our prolonged absence.

As we walked home, I would fain have enlightened my charge on the characters of the people we had quitted; but she got it into her head that I was prejudiced against them.

"Aha!" she cried, "you take papa's side, Ellen—you are partial, I know, or else you wouldn't have cheated me so many years into the notion that Linton lived a long way from here. I'm really extremely angry, only I'm so pleased, I can't show it! But you must hold your tongue about my uncle: he's *my* uncle, remember, and I'll scold papa for quarrelling with him."

And so she ran on, till I dropped endeavouring to convince her of her mistake.

She did not mention the visit that night, because she did not

see Mr. Linton. Next day it all came out, sadly to my chagrin; and
still I was not altogether sorry: I thought the burden of directing
and warning would be more efficiently borne by him than me, but
he was too timid in giving satisfactory reasons for his wish that
she would shun connection with the household of the Heights, and
Catherine liked good reasons for every restraint that harassed her
petted will.

"Papa!" she exclaimed, after the morning's salutations, "guess
whom I saw yesterday, in my walk on the moors. Ah, papa, you
started! you've not done right, have you, now? I saw—But listen,
and you shall hear how I found you out, and Ellen, who is in
league with you, and yet pretended to pity me so, when I kept
hoping, and was always disappointed about Linton's coming back!"

She gave a faithful account of her excursion and its consequences;
and my master, though he cast more than one reproachful look
at me, said nothing till she had concluded. Then he drew her to
him, and asked if she knew why he had concealed Linton's near
neighbourhood from her? Could she think it was to deny her
a pleasure that she might harmlessly enjoy?

"It was because you disliked Mr. Heathcliff," she answered.

"Then you believe I care more for my own feelings than yours,
Cathy?" he said. "No, it was not because I disliked Mr. Heathcliff,
but because Mr. Heathcliff dislikes me; and is a most diabolical
man, delighting to wrong and ruin those he hates, if they give him
the slightest opportunity. I knew that you could not keep up an
acquaintance with your cousin, without being brought into contact with him; and I knew he would detest you, on my account; so,
for your own good, and nothing else, I took precautions that you
should not see Linton again. I meant to explain this some time as
you grew older, and I'm sorry I delayed it!"

"But Mr. Heathcliff was quite cordial, papa," observed Catherine,
not at all convinced; "and *he* didn't object to our seeing each other:
he said I might come to his house when I pleased, only I must not
tell you, because you had quarrelled with him, and would not forgive him for marrying Aunt Isabella. And you won't—*you* are the
one to be blamed. He is willing to let *us* be friends—at least Linton
and I—and you are not."

My master, perceiving that she would not take his word for
her uncle-in-law's evil disposition, gave a hasty sketch of his conduct to Isabella, and the manner in which Wuthering Heights became his property. He could not bear to discourse long upon the
topic, for though he spoke little of it, he still felt the same horror
and detestation of his ancient enemy that had occupied his heart
ever since Mrs. Linton's death. "She might have been living yet, if
it had not been for him!" was his constant bitter reflection; and,

in his eyes, Heathcliff seemed a murderer.

Miss Cathy, conversant with no bad deeds except her own slight acts of disobedience, in justice and passion, rising from hot temper and thoughtlessness, and repented of on the day they were committed, was amazed at the blackness of spirit that could brood on and cover revenge for years, and deliberately prosecute its plans, without a visitation of remorse. She appeared so deeply impressed and shocked at this new view of human nature—excluded from all her studies and all her ideas till now—that Mr. Edgar deemed it unnecessary to pursue the subject. He merely added—

"You will know hereafter, darling, why I wish you to avoid his house and family; now, return to your old employments and amusements, and think no more about them!"

Catherine kissed her father, and sat down quietly to her lessons for a couple of hours, according to custom; then she accompanied him into the grounds, and the whole day passed as usual: but in the evening, when she had retired to her room, and I went to help her to undress, I found her crying, on her knees by the bedside.

"Oh, fie, silly child!" I exclaimed. "If you had any real griefs, you'd be ashamed to waste a tear on this little contrariety. You never had one shadow of substantial sorrow, Miss Catherine. Suppose, for a minute, that master and I were dead, and you were by yourself in the world—how would you feel, then? Compare the present occasion with such an affliction as that, and be thankful for the friend you have, instead of coveting more."

"I'm not crying for myself, Ellen," she answered, "it's for him. He expected to see me again to-morrow, and there, he'll be so disappointed—and he'll wait for me, and I shan't come!"

"Nonsense!" said I, "do you imagine he has thought as much of you as you have of him? Hasn't he Hareton for a companion? Not one in a hundred would weep at losing a relation they had just seen twice, for two afternoons. Linton will conjecture how it is, and trouble himself no further about you."

"But may I not write a note to tell him why I cannot come?" she asked, rising to her feet. "And just send those books I promised to lend him? His books are not as nice as mine, and he wanted to have them extremely, when I told him how interesting they were. May I not, Ellen?"

"No, indeed, no, indeed!" replied I with decision. "Then he would write to you, and there'd never be an end of it. No, Miss Catherine, the acquaintance must be dropped entirely—so papa expects, and I shall see that it is done!"

"But how can one little note—" she recommenced, putting on an imploring countenance.

"Silence!" I interrupted. "We'll not begin with your little notes.

Get into bed!"

She threw at me a very naughty look, so naughty that I would not kiss her good-night at first: I covered her up, and shut her door, in great displeasure; but, repenting half-way, I returned softly, and lo! there was Miss, standing at the table with a bit of blank paper before her and a pencil in her hand, which she guiltily slipped out of sight, on my re-entrance.

"You'll get nobody to take that, Catherine," I said, "if you write it; and at present I shall put out your candle."

I set the extinguisher on the flame, receiving as I did so a slap on my hand, and a petulant "cross thing!" I then quitted her again, and she drew the bolt in one of her worst, most peevish humours.

The letter was finished and forwarded to its destination by a milk-fetcher who came from the village, but that I didn't learn till some time afterwards. Weeks passed on, and Cathy recovered her temper, though she grew wondrous fond of stealing off to corners by herself, and often, if I came near her suddenly while reading, she would start, and bend over the book, evidently desirous to hide it; and I detected edges of loose paper sticking out beyond the leaves.

She also got a trick of coming down early in the morning, and lingering about the kitchen, as if she were expecting the arrival of something; and she had a small drawer in a cabinet in the library, which she would trifle over for hours, and whose key she took special care to remove when she left it.

One day, as she inspected this drawer, I observed that the playthings and trinkets, which recently formed its contents, were transmuted into bits of folded paper.

My curiosity and suspicions were roused; I determined to take a peep at her mysterious treasures; so, at night, as soon as she and my master were safe upstairs, I searched and readily found among my house keys, one that would fit the lock. Having opened, I emptied the whole contents into my apron, and took them with me to examine at leisure in my own chamber.

Though I could not but suspect, I was still surprised to discover that they were a mass of correspondence—daily almost, it must have been—from Linton Heathcliff, answers to documents forwarded by her. The earlier dated were embarrassed and short; gradually, however, they expanded into copious love letters, foolish as the age of the writer rendered natural, yet with touches, here and there, which I thought were borrowed from a more experienced source.

Some of them struck me as singularly odd compounds of ardour and flatness; commencing in strong feeling, and concluding in the affected, wordy way that a schoolboy might use to a fancied, incorporeal sweetheart.

Whether they satisfied Cathy, I don't know, but they appeared very worthless trash to me.

After turning over as many as I thought proper, I tied them in a handkerchief and set them aside, re-locking the vacant drawer.

Following her habit, my young lady descended early, and visited the kitchen: I watched her go to the door, on the arrival of a certain little boy; and, while the dairy maid filled his can, she tucked something into his jacket pocket, and plucked something out.

I went round by the garden, and laid wait for the messenger, who fought valorously to defend his trust, and we spilt the milk between us; but I succeeded in abstracting the epistle, and, threatening serious consequences if he did not look sharp home, I remained under the wall, and perused Miss Cathy's affectionate composition. It was more simple and more eloquent than her cousin's—very pretty and very silly. I shook my head, and went meditating into the house.

The day being wet, she could not divert herself with rambling about the park; so, at the conclusion of her morning studies, she resorted to the solace of the drawer. Her father sat reading at the table; and I, on purpose, had sought a bit of work in some unripped fringes of the window curtain, keeping my eye steadily fixed on her proceedings.

Never did any bird flying back to a plundered nest which it had left brim-ful of chirping young ones, express more complete despair in its anguished cries and flutterings, than she by her single "Oh!" and the change that transfigured her late happy countenance. Mr. Linton looked up.

"What is the matter, love? Have you hurt yourself?" he said.

His tone and look assured her *he* had not been the discoverer of the hoard.

"No, papa—" she gasped. "Ellen! Ellen! come upstairs—I'm sick!"

I obeyed her summons, and accompanied her out.

"Oh, Ellen! you have got them," she commenced immediately, dropping on her knees, when we were enclosed alone. "O, give them to me, and I'll never never do so again! Don't tell papa. You have not told papa, Ellen, say you have not! I've been exceedingly naughty, but I won't do it any more!"

With a grave severity in my manner, I bid her stand up.

"So," I exclaimed, "Miss Catherine, you are tolerably far on, it seems—you may well be ashamed of them! A fine bundle of trash you study in your leisure hours, to be sure: why, it's good enough to be printed! And what do you suppose the master will think, when I display it before him? I haven't shown it yet, but you needn't imagine I shall keep your ridiculous secrets. For shame! And you must have led the way in writing such absurdities; he would not have thought of beginning, I'm certain."

"I didn't! I didn't!" sobbed Cathy, fit to break her heart. "I didn't once think of loving him till—"

"*Loving!*" cried I, as scornfully as I could utter the word. "*Loving!* Did anybody ever hear the like! I might just as well talk of loving the miller who comes once a year to buy our corn. Pretty loving, indeed, and both times together you have seen Linton hardly four hours in your life! Now here is the babyish trash. I'm going with it to the library; and we'll see what your father says to such *loving.*"

She sprang at her precious epistles, but I held them above my head; and then she poured out further frantic entreaties that I would burn them—do anything rather than show them. And being really fully as inclined to laugh as scold, for I esteemed it all girlish vanity, I at length relented in a measure, and asked—

"If I consent to burn them, will you promise faithfully, neither to send nor receive a letter again, nor a book—for I perceive you have sent him books—nor locks of hair, nor rings, nor playthings?"

"We don't send playthings!" cried Catherine, her pride overcoming her shame.

"Nor anything at all, then, my lady!" I said. "Unless you will, here I go."

"I promise, Ellen!" she cried, catching my dress. "Oh, put them in the fire, do, do!"

But when I proceeded to open a place with the poker, the sacrifice was too painful to be borne. She earnestly supplicated that I would spare her one or two.

"One or two, Ellen, to keep for Linton's sake!"

I unknotted the handkerchief, and commenced dropping them in from an angle, and the flame curled up the chimney.

"I will have one, you cruel wretch!" she screamed, darting her hand into the fire, and drawing forth some half consumed fragments, at the expense of her fingers.

"Very well—and I will have some to exhibit to papa!" I answered, shaking back the rest into the bundle, and turning anew to the door.

She emptied her blackened pieces into the flames, and motioned me to finish the immolation. It was done; I stirred up the ashes, and interred them under a shovel-full of coals; and she mutely, and with a sense of intense injury, retired to her private apartment. I descended to tell my master that the young lady's qualm of sickness was almost gone, but I judged it best for her to lie down a while.

She wouldn't dine; but she re-appeared at tea, pale and red about the eyes, and marvellously subdued in outward aspect.

Next morning, I answered the letter by a slip of paper inscribed, "Master Heathcliff is requested to send no more notes to Miss Linton, as she will not receive them." And, thenceforth, the little boy came with vacant pockets.

## Chapter XXII

Summer drew to an end, and early Autumn: it was past Michaelmas, but the harvest was late that year, and a few of our fields were still uncleared.

Mr. Linton and his daughter would frequently walk out among the reapers; at the carrying of the last sheaves, they stayed till dusk, and the evening happening to be chill and damp, my master caught a bad cold, that, settling obstinately on his lungs, confined him indoors throughout the whole of the winter, nearly without intermission.

Poor Cathy, frightened from her little romance, had been considerably sadder and duller since its abandonment; and her father insisted on her reading less, and taking more exercise. She had his companionship no longer; I esteemed it a duty to supply its lack, as much as possible, with mine: an inefficient substitute, for I could only spare two or three hours, from my numerous diurnal occupations, to follow her footsteps, and then my society was obviously less desirable than his.

On an afternoon in October, or the beginning of November— a fresh watery afternoon, when the turf and paths were rustling with moist, withered leaves, and the cold, blue sky was half hidden by clouds, dark grey streamers, rapidly mounting from the west, and boding abundant rain—I requested my young lady to forego her ramble because I was certain of showers. She refused; and I unwillingly donned a cloak, and took my umbrella to accompany her on a stroll to the bottom of the park: a formal walk which she generally affected if low-spirited—and that she invariably was when Mr. Edgar had been worse than ordinary; a thing never known from his confession, but guessed both by her and me from his increased silence, and the melancholy of his countenance.

She went sadly on: there was no running or bounding now, though the chill wind might well have tempted her to a race. And often, from the side of my eye, I could detect her raising a hand, and brushing something off her cheek.

I gazed round for a means of diverting her thoughts. On one side of the road rose a high, rough bank, where hazels and stunted oaks, with their roots half exposed, held uncertain tenure: the soil was too loose for the latter; and strong winds had blown some nearly horizontal. In summer, Miss Catherine delighted to climb along these trunks, and sit in the branches, swinging twenty feet above the ground; and I, pleased with her agility, and her light, childish heart, still considered it proper to scold every time I caught her at such an elevation, but so that she knew there was no necessity for descending. From dinner to tea she would lie in her breeze-rocked cradle, doing nothing except singing old songs—my nursery lore—to herself, or watching the birds, joint tenants, feed and entice their young ones to fly, or nestling with closed lids, half thinking, half dreaming, happier than words can express.

"Look, Miss!" I exclaimed, pointing to a nook under the roots of one twisted tree. "Winter is not here yet. There's a little flower, up yonder, the last bud from the multitude of blue-bells that clouded those turf steps in July with a lilac mist. Will you clamber up, and pluck it to show to papa?"

Cathy stared a long time at the lonely blossom trembling in its earthy shelter, and replied, at length—

"No, I'll not touch it—but it looks melancholy, does it not, Ellen?"

"Yes," I observed, "about as starved and sackless[1] as you—your cheeks are bloodless; let us take hold of hands and run. You're so low, I dare say I shall keep up with you."

"No," she repeated, and continued sauntering on, pausing, at intervals, to muse over a bit of moss, or a tuft of blanched grass, or a fungus spreading its bright orange among the heaps of brown foliage; and, ever and anon, her hand was lifted to her averted face.

"Catherine, why are you crying, love?" I asked, approaching and putting my arm over her shoulder. "You mustn't cry because papa has a cold; be thankful it is nothing worse."

She now put no further restraint on her tears; her breath was stifled by sobs.

"Oh, it *will* be something worse," she said. "And what shall I do when papa and you leave me, and I am by myself? I can't forget your words, Ellen, they are always in my ear. How life will be changed, how dreary the world will be, when papa and you are dead."

"None can tell, whether you won't die before us," I replied. "It's wrong to anticipate evil. We'll hope there are years and years to come before any of us go: master is young, and I am strong, and hardly forty-five. My mother lived till eighty, a canty[2] dame to the last. And suppose Mr. Linton were spared till he saw sixty, that would be more years than you have counted, Miss. And would

1. Feeble. 2. Brisk, lively.

it not be foolish to mourn a calamity above twenty years before-hand?"

"But Aunt Isabella was younger than papa," she remarked, gaz-ing up with timid hope to seek further consolation.

"Aunt Isabella had not you and me to nurse her," I replied. "She wasn't as happy as master; she hadn't as much to live for. All you need do, is to wait well on your father, and cheer him by letting him see you cheerful; and avoid giving him anxiety on any sub-ject—mind that, Cathy! I'll not disguise but you might kill him, if you were wild and reckless, and cherished a foolish, fanciful af-fection for the son of a person who would be glad to have him in his grave; and allowed him to discover that you fretted over the separation he has judged it expedient to make."

"I fret about nothing on earth except papa's illness," answered my companion. "I care for nothing in comparison with papa. And I'll never—never—oh, never, while I have my senses, do an act, or say a word to vex him. I love him better than myself, Ellen; and I know it by this: I pray every night that I may live after him, because I would rather be miserable than that he should be —that proves I love him better than myself."

"Good words," I replied. "But deeds must prove it also; and after he is well, remember you don't forget resolutions formed in the hour of fear."

As we talked, we neared a door that opened on the road; and my young lady, lightening into sunshine again, climbed up, and seated herself on the top of the wall, reaching over to gather some hips that bloomed scarlet on the summit branches of the wild rose trees, shadowing the highway side; the lower fruit had disappeared, but only birds could touch the upper, except from Cathy's present station.

In stretching to pull them, her hat fell off; and as the door was locked, she proposed scrambling down to recover it. I bid her be cautious lest she got a fall, and she nimbly disappeared.

But the return was no such easy matter; the stones were smooth and neatly cemented, and the rosebushes and blackberry stragglers could yield no assistance in re-ascending. I, like a fool, didn't rec-ollect that till I heard her laughing, and exclaiming—

"Ellen! you'll have to fetch the key, or else I must run round to the porter's lodge. I can't scale the ramparts on this side!"

"Stay where you are," I answered, "I have my bundle of keys in my pocket; perhaps I may manage to open it; if not, I'll go."

Catherine amused herself with dancing to and fro before the door, while I tried all the large keys in succession. I had applied the last, and found that none would do; so, repeating my desire that she would remain there, I was about to hurry home as fast as

I could, when an approaching sound arrested me. It was the trot of a horse; Cathy's dance stopped, and in a minute the horse stopped also.

"Who is that?" I whispered.

"Ellen, I wish you could open the door," whispered back my companion, anxiously.

"Ho, Miss Linton!" cried a deep voice (the rider's). "I'm glad to meet you. Don't be in haste to enter, for I have an explanation to ask and obtain."

"I shan't speak to you, Mr. Heathcliff!" answered Catherine. "Papa says you are a wicked man, and you hate both him and me; and Ellen says the same."

"That is nothing to the purpose," said Heathcliff. (He it was.) "I don't hate my son, I suppose, and it is concerning him that I demand your attention. Yes! you have cause to blush. Two or three months since, were you not in the habit of writing to Linton? making love in play, eh? You deserved, both of you, flogging for that! You especially, the elder, and less sensitive, as it turns out. I've got your letters, and if you give me any pertness, I'll send them to your father. I presume you grew weary of the amusement, and dropped it, didn't you? Well, you dropped Linton with it, into a Slough of Despond. He was in earnest—in love—really. As true as I live, he's dying for you—breaking his heart at your fickleness, not figuratively, but actually. Though Hareton has made him a standing jest for six weeks, and I have used more serious measures, and attempted to frighten him out of his idiocy, he gets worse daily, and he'll be under the sod before summer, unless you restore him!"

"How can you lie so glaringly to the poor child!" I called from the inside. "Pray ride on! How can you deliberately get up such paltry falsehoods? Miss Cathy, I'll knock the lock off with a stone. You won't believe that vile nonsense. You can feel in yourself, it is impossible that a person should die for love of a stranger."

"I was not aware there were eaves-droppers," muttered the detected villain. "Worthy Mrs. Dean, I like you, but I don't like your double dealing," he added, aloud. "How could *you* lie so glaringly, as to affirm I hated the 'poor child'? And invent bugbear stories to terrify her from my door-stones? Catherine Linton (the very name warms me), my bonny lass, I shall be from home all this week; go and see if I have not spoken truth; do, there's a darling! Just imagine your father in my place, and Linton in yours; then think how you would value your careless lover, if he refused to stir a step to comfort you, when your father, himself, entreated him; and don't, from pure stupidity, fall into the same error. I swear, on my salvation, he's going to his grave, and none but you can save him!"

The lock gave way, and I issued out.

"I swear Linton is dying," repeated Heathcliff, looking hard at me. "And grief and disappointment are hastening his death. Nelly, if you won't let her go, you can walk over yourself. But I shall not return till this time next week; and I think your master himself would scarcely object to her visiting her cousin!"

"Come in," said I, taking Cathy by the arm and half forcing her to re-enter, for she lingered, viewing with troubled eyes, the features of the speaker, too stern to express his inward deceit.

He pushed his horse close, and, bending down, observed—

"Miss Catherine, I'll own to you that I have little patience with Linton—and Hareton and Joseph have less. I'll own that he's with a harsh set. He pines for kindness, as well as love; and a kind word from you would be his best medicine. Don't mind Mrs. Dean's cruel cautions, but be generous, and contrive to see him. He dreams of you day and night, and cannot be persuaded that you don't hate him, since you neither write nor call."

I closed the door, and rolled a stone to assist the loosened lock in holding it; and spreading my umbrella, I drew my charge underneath, for the rain began to drive through the moaning branches of the trees, and warned us to avoid delay.

Our hurry prevented any comment on the encounter with Heathcliff, as we stretched towards home; but I divined instinctively that Catherine's heart was clouded now in double darkness. Her features were so sad, they did not seem hers: she evidently regarded what she had heard as every syllable true.

The master had retired to rest before we came in. Cathy stole to his room to inquire how he was; he had fallen asleep. She returned, and asked me to sit with her in the library. We took our tea together; and afterwards she lay down on the rug, and told me not to talk, for she was weary.

I got a book, and pretended to read. As soon as she supposed me absorbed in my occupation, she recommenced her silent weeping: it appeared, at present, her favourite diversion. I suffered her to enjoy it a while; then I expostulated, deriding and ridiculing all Mr. Heathcliff's assertions about his son, as if I were certain she would coincide. Alas! I hadn't the skill to counteract the effect his account had produced; it was just what he intended.

"You may be right, Ellen," she answered; "but I shall never feel at ease till I know. And I must tell Linton it is not my fault that I don't write; and convince him that I shall not change."

What use were anger and protestations against her silly credulity? We parted that night hostile; but next day beheld me on the road to Wuthering Heights, by the side of my wilful young mistress's pony. I couldn't bear to witness her sorrow, to see her pale, dejected countenance, and heavy eyes; and I yielded in the faint hope that Linton himself might prove, by his reception of us, how little of the tale was founded on fact.

## Chapter XXIII

The rainy night had ushered in a misty morning—half frost, half drizzle—and temporary brooks crossed our path, gurgling from the uplands. My feet were thoroughly wetted; I was cross and low, exactly the humour suited for making the most of these disagreeable things.

We entered the farm-house by the kitchen way to ascertain whether Mr. Heathcliff were really absent, because I put slight faith in his own affirmation.

Joseph seemed sitting in a sort of elysium alone, beside a roaring fire; a quart of ale on the table near him, bristling with large pieces of toasted oat cake, and his black, short pipe in his mouth.

Catherine ran to the hearth to warm herself. I asked if the master were in?

My question remained so long unanswered, that I thought the old man had grown deaf, and repeated it louder.

"Na—ay!" he snarled, or rather screamed through his nose. "Na—ay! yah muh goa back whear yah coom frough."

"Joseph!" cried a peevish voice, simultaneously with me, from the inner room. "How often am I to call you? There are only a few red ashes now. Joseph! come this moment."

Vigorous puffs, and a resolute stare into the grate, declared he had no ear for this appeal. The housekeeper and Hareton were invisible; one gone on an errand, and the other at his work, probably. We knew Linton's tones and entered.

"Oh, I hope you'll die in a garret! starved to death," said the boy, mistaking our approach for that of his negligent attendant.

He stopped, on observing his error; his cousin flew to him.

"Is that you, Miss Linton?" he said, raising his head from the arm of the great chair in which he reclined. "No—don't kiss me. It takes my breath—dear me! Papa said you would call," continued he, after recovering a little from Catherine's embrace, while she stood by looking very contrite. "Will you shut the door, if you please? you left it open, and those—those *detestable* creatures won't bring coals to the fire. It's so cold!"

I stirred up the cinders, and fetched a scuttle-full myself. The invalid complained of being covered with ashes; but he had a tiresome cough, and looked feverish and ill, so I did not rebuke his temper.

"Well, Linton," murmured Catherine, when his corrugated brow relaxed. "Are you glad to see me? Can I do you any good?"

"Why didn't you come before?" he said. "You should have come, instead of writing. It tired me dreadfully, writing those long letters. I'd far rather have talked to you. Now, I can neither bear to talk, nor anything else. I wonder where Zillah is! Will you (looking at me) step into the kitchen and see?"

I had received no thanks for my other service; and being unwilling to run to and fro at his behest, I replied—

"Nobody is out there but Joseph."

"I want to drink," he exclaimed, fretfully, turning away. "Zillah is constantly gadding off to Gimmerton since papa went. It's miserable! And I'm obliged to come down here—they resolved never to hear me upstairs."

"Is your father attentive to you, Master Heathcliff?" I asked, perceiving Catherine to be checked in her friendly advances.

"Attentive? He makes *them* a little more attentive, at least," he cried. "The wretches! Do you know, Miss Linton, that brute Hareton laughs at me. I hate him—indeed, I hate them all—they are odious beings."

Cathy began searching for some water; she lighted on a pitcher in the dresser, filled a tumbler, and brought it. He bid her add a spoonful of wine from a bottle on the table; and, having swallowed a small portion, appeared more tranquil, and said she was very kind.

"And are you glad to see me?" asked she, reiterating her former question, and pleased to detect the faint dawn of a smile.

"Yes, I am. It's something new to hear a voice like yours!" he replied, "but I *have* been vexed, because you wouldn't come. And papa swore it was owing to me; he called me a pitiful, shuffling, worthless thing; and said you despised me; and if he had been in my place, he would be more the master of the Grange than your father, by this time. But you don't despise me, do you, Miss—"

"I wish you would say Catherine, or Cathy!" interrupted my young lady. "Despise you? No! Next to papa, and Ellen, I love you better than anybody living. I don't love Mr. Heathcliff, though; and I dare not come when he returns; will he stay away many days?"

"Not many," answered Linton, "but he goes onto the moors frequently, since the shooting season commenced, and you might spend an hour or two with me, in his absence. Do! say you will! I think I should not be peevish with you; you'd not provoke me, and you'd always be ready to help me, wouldn't you?"

"Yes," said Catherine, stroking his long soft hair; "if I could only get papa's consent, I'd spend half my time with you. Pretty Linton! I wish you were my brother!"

"And then you would like me as well as your father?" observed he, more cheerfully. "But papa says you would love me better than him and all the world, if you were my wife—so I'd rather you were that!"

"No! I should never love anybody better than papa," she returned gravely. "And people hate their wives, sometimes; but not their sisters and brothers, and if you were the latter, you would live with us, and papa would be as fond of you as he is of me."

Linton denied that people ever hated their wives; but Cathy affirmed they did, and in her wisdom, instanced his own father's aversion to her aunt.

I endeavoured to stop her thoughtless tongue. I couldn't succeed till everything she knew was out Master Heathcliff, much irritated, asserted her relation was false.

"Papa told me; and papa does not tell falsehoods!" she answered pertly.

"*My* papa scorns yours!" cried Linton. "He calls him a sneaking fool!"

"Yours is a wicked man," retorted Catherine, "and you are very naughty to dare to repeat what he says. He must be wicked, to have made Aunt Isabella leave him as she did!"

"She didn't leave him," said the boy; "you shan't contradict me!"

"She did!" cried my young lady.

"Well, I'll tell *you* something!" said Linton. "Your mother hated your father, now then."

"Oh!" exclaimed Catherine, too enraged to continue.

"And she loved mine!" added he.

"You little liar! I hate you now," she panted, and her face grew red with passion.

"She did! she did!" sang Linton, sinking into the recess of his chair, and leaning back his head to enjoy the agitation of the other disputant, who stood behind.

"Hush, Master Heathcliff!" I said; "that's your father's tale too, I suppose."

"It isn't—you hold your tongue!" he answered. "She did, she did, Catherine, she did, she did!"

Cathy, beside herself, gave the chair a violent push, and caused him to fall against one arm. He was immediately seized by a suffocating cough that soon ended his triumph.

It lasted so long that it frightened even me. As to his cousin, she wept with all her might, aghast at the mischief she had done, though she said nothing.

I held him till the fit exhausted itself. Then he thrust me away, and leant his head down, silently. Catherine quelled her lamentations also, took a seat opposite, and looked solemnly into the fire.

"How do you feel now, Master Heathcliff?" I inquired, after

waiting ten minutes.

"I wish *she* felt as I do," he replied, "spiteful, cruel thing! Hareton never touches me, he never struck me in his life. And I was better to-day—and there—" his voice died in a whimper.

"*I* didn't strike you!" muttered Cathy, chewing her lip to prevent another burst of emotion.

He sighed and moaned like one under great suffering, and kept it up for a quarter of an hour, on purpose to distress his cousin, apparently, for whenever he caught a stifled sob from her, he put renewed pain and pathos into the inflexions of his voice.

"I'm sorry I hurt you, Linton!" she said at length, racked beyond endurance. "But *I* couldn't have been hurt by that little push; and I had no idea that you could, either—you're not much, are you, Linton? Don't let me go home thinking I've done you harm! Answer, speak to me."

"I can't speak to you," he murmured, "you've hurt me so, that I shall lie awake all night, choking with this cough! If you had it you'd know what it was; but *you'll* be comfortably asleep, while I'm in agony—and nobody near me! I wonder how you would like to pass those fearful nights!" And he began to wail aloud for very pity of himself.

"Since you are in the habit of passing dreadful nights," I said, "it won't be Miss who spoils your ease; you'd be the same, had she never come. However, she shall not disturb you again—and perhaps you'll get quieter when we leave you."

"Must I go?" asked Catherine dolefully, bending over him. "Do you want me to go, Linton?"

"You can't alter what you're done," he replied pettishly, shrinking from her, "unless you alter it for the worse, by teasing me into a fever."

"Well, then I must go?" she repeated.

"Let me alone, at least," said he; "I can't bear your talking!"

She lingered, and resisted my persuasions to departure, a tiresome while, but as he neither looked up nor spoke, she finally made a movement to the door and I followed.

We were recalled by a scream. Linton had slid from his seat on to the hearthstone, and lay writhing in the mere perverseness of an indulged plague of a child, determined to be as grievous and harassing as it can.

I thoroughly gauged his disposition from his behaviour, and saw at once it would be folly to attempt humouring him. Not so my companion: she ran back in terror, knelt down, and cried, and soothed, and entreated, till he grew quiet from lack of breath, by no means from compunction at distressing her.

"I shall lift him on to the settle," I said, "and he may roll about as he pleases; we can't stop to watch him. I hope you are satisfied, Miss Cathy, that *you* are not the person to benefit him, and that his condition of health is not occasioned by attachment to you. Now then, there he is! Come away; as soon as he knows there is nobody by to care for his nonsense, he'll be glad to lie still!"

She placed a cushion under his head, and offered him some water; he rejected the latter, and tossed uneasily on the former, as if it were a stone, or a block of wood.

She tried to put it more comfortably.

"I can't do with that," he said, "it's not high enough!"

Catherine brought another to lay above it.

"That's *too* high!" murmured the provoking thing.

"How must I arrange it, then?" she asked despairingly.

He twined himself up to her, as she half knelt by the settle, and converted her shoulder into a support.

"No, that won't do!" I said. "You'll be content with the cushion, Master Heathcliff! Miss has wasted too much time on you already; we cannot remain five minutes longer."

"Yes, yes, we can!" replied Cathy. "He's good and patient, now. He's beginning to think I shall have far greater misery than he will to-night, if I believe he is the worse for my visit; and then, I dare not come again. Tell the truth about it, Linton, for I mustn't come, if I have hurt you."

"You must come, to cure me," he answered. "You ought to come because you have hurt me. You know you have, extremely! I was not as ill when you entered, as I am at present—was I?"

"But you've made yourself ill by crying, and being in a passion."

"I didn't do it all," said his cousin. "However, we'll be friends now. And you want me—you would wish to see me sometimes, really?"

"I told you I did!" he replied impatiently. "Sit on the settle and let me lean on your knee. That's as mamma used to do, whole afternoons together. Sit quite still, and don't talk, but you may sing a song if you can sing, or you may say a nice, long interesting ballad —one of those you promised to teach me—or a story. I'd rather have a ballad, though: begin."

Catherine repeated the longest she could remember. The employment pleased both mightily. Linton would have another, and after that another, notwithstanding my strenuous objections; and so they went on until the clock struck twelve, and we heard Hareton in the court, returning for his dinner.

"And to-morrow, Catherine, will you be here to-morrow?" asked young Heathcliff, holding her frock, as she rose reluctantly.

"No!" I answered, "nor next day neither." She, however, gave a different response, evidently, for his forehead cleared as she stooped and whispered in his ear.

"You won't go to-morrow, recollect, Miss!" I commenced, when we were out of the house. "You are not dreaming of it, are you?"

She smiled.

"Oh, I'll take good care!" I continued; "I'll have that lock mended, and you can escape by no way else."

"I can get over the wall," she said, laughing. "The Grange is not a prison, Ellen, and you are not my jailer. And besides, I'm almost seventeen. I'm a woman—and I'm certain Linton would recover quickly if he had me to look after him. I'm older than he is, you know, and wiser, less childish, am I not? And he'll soon do as I direct him with some slight coaxing. He's a pretty little darling when he's good. I'd make such a pet of him, if he were mine. We should never quarrel, should we, after we were used to each other? Don't you like him, Ellen?"

"Like him?" I exclaimed. "The worst-tempered bit of a sickly slip that ever struggled into its teens! Happily, as Mr. Heathcliff conjectured, he'll not win twenty! I doubt whether he'll see spring, indeed—and small loss to his family, whenever he drops off; and lucky it is for us that his father took him. The kinder he was treated, the more tedious and selfish he'd be! I'm glad you have no chance of having him for a husband, Miss Catherine!"

My companion waxed serious at hearing this speech. To speak of his death so regardlessly wounded her feelings.

"He's younger than I," she answered, after a protracted pause of meditation, "and he ought to live the longest; he will—he must live as long as I do. He's as strong now as when he first came into the North, I'm positive of that! It's only a cold that ails him, the same as papa has. You say papa will get better, and why shouldn't he?"

"Well, well," I cried, "after all, we needn't trouble ourselves; for listen, Miss—and mind, I'll keep my word—if you attempt going to Wuthering Heights again, with or without me, I shall inform Mr. Linton, and, unless he allow it, the intimacy with your cousin must not be revived."

"It has been revived!" muttered Cathy sulkily.

"Must not be continued, then!" I said.

"We'll see!" was her reply, and she set off at a gallop, leaving me to toil in the rear.

We both reached home before our dinnertime; my master supposed we had been wandering through the park, and therefore he demanded no explanation of our absence. As soon as I entered, I hastened to change my soaked shoes and stockings; but sitting such a while at the Heights had done the mischief. On the succeeding morning, I was laid up; and during three weeks I remained incapacitated for attending to my duties—a calamity never experienced prior to that period, and never, I am thankful to say, since.

My little mistress behaved like an angel in coming to wait on me, and cheer my solitude: the confinement brought me exceedingly low. It is wearisome, to a stirring active body, but few have slighter reasons for complaint than I had. The moment Catherine left Mr. Linton's room, she appeared at my bed-side. Her day was divided between us; no amusement usurped a minute: she neglected her meals, her studies, and her play; and she was the fondest nurse that ever watched. She must have had a warm heart, when she loved her father so, to give so much to me!

I said her days were divided between us; but the master retired early, and I generally needed nothing after six o'clock, thus the evening was her own.

Poor thing, I never considered what she did with herself after tea. And though frequently, when she looked in to bid me good-night, I remarked a fresh colour in her cheeks, and a pinkness over her slender fingers; instead of fancying the hue borrowed from a cold ride across the moors, I laid it to the charge of a hot fire in the library.

## Chapter XXIV

At the close of three weeks, I was able to quit my chamber, and move about the house. And on the first occasion of my sitting up in the evening, I asked Catherine to read to me, because my eyes were weak. We were in the library, the master having gone to bed: she consented, rather unwillingly, I fancied; and imagining my sort of books did not suit her, I bid her please herself in the choice of what she perused.

She selected one of her own favourites, and got forward steadily about an hour; then came frequent questions.

"Ellen, are not you tired? Hadn't you better lie down now? You'll be sick, keeping up so long, Ellen."

"No, no, dear, I'm not tired," I returned, continually.

Perceiving me immovable, she essayed another method of showing her dis-relish for her occupation. It changed to yawning, and stretching, and—

"Ellen, I'm tired."

"Give over then and talk," I answered.

That was worse: she fretted and sighed, and looked at her watch till eight; and finally went to her room, completely overdone with sleep, judging by her peevish, heavy look, and the constant rubbing she inflicted on her eyes.

The following night she seemed more impatient still; and on the third from recovering my company, she complained of a head-ache, and left me.

I thought her conduct odd; and having remained alone a long while, I resolved on going, and inquiring whether she were better, and asking her to come and lie on the sofa, instead of upstairs, in the dark.

No Catherine could I discover upstairs, and none below. The servants affirmed they had not seen her. I listened at Mr. Edgar's door—all was silence. I returned to her apartment, extinguished my candle, and seated myself in the window.

The moon shone bright; a sprinkling of snow covered the ground, and I reflected that she might, possibly, have taken it into her head to walk about the garden, for refreshment. I did detect a figure creeping along the inner fence of the park, but it was not my young mistress; on its emerging into the light, I recognised one of the grooms.

He stood a considerable period, viewing the carriage-road through the grounds; then started off at a brisk pace, as if he had detected something, and reappeared presently, leading Miss's pony; and there she was, just dismounted, and walking by its side.

The man took his charge stealthily across the grass towards the stable. Cathy entered by the casement-window of the drawing-room, and glided noiselessly up to where I awaited her.

She put the door gently to, slipped off her snowy shoes, untied her hat, and was proceeding, unconscious of my espionage, to lay aside her mantle, when I suddenly rose and revealed myself. The surprise petrified her an instant: she uttered an inarticulate exclamation, and stood fixed.

"My dear Miss Catherine," I began, too vividly impressed by her recent kindness to break into a scold, "where have you been riding out at this hour? And why should you try to deceive me, by telling a tale? Where have you been? Speak!"

"To the bottom of the park," she stammered. "I didn't tell a tale."

"And nowhere else?" I demanded.

"No," was the muttered reply.

"Oh, Catherine," I cried, sorrowfully. "You know you have been doing wrong, or you wouldn't be driven to uttering an untruth to me. That does grieve me. I'd rather be three months ill, than hear you frame a deliberate lie."

She sprang forward, and bursting into tears, threw her arms round my neck.

"Well, Ellen, I'm so afraid of you being angry," she said. "Promise not to be angry, and you shall know the very truth. I hate to hide it."

We sat down in the window-seat; I assured her I would not scold, whatever her secret might be, and I guessed it, of course; so she commenced—

"I've been to Wuthering Heights, Ellen, and I've never missed going a day since you fell ill; except thrice before, and twice after you left your room. I gave Michael books and pictures to prepare Minny every evening, and to put her back in the stable; you mustn't scold *him* either, mind. I was at the Heights by half-past six, and generally stayed till half-past eight, and then galloped home. It was not to amuse myself that I went; I was often wretched all the time. Now and then, I was happy, once in a week perhaps. At first, I expected there would be sad work persuading you to let me keep my word to Linton, for I had engaged to call again next day, when we quitted him; but, as you stayed upstairs on the morrow, I escaped that trouble; and while Michael was refastening the lock of the park door in the afternoon, I got possession of the key, and told him how my cousin wished me to visit him, because he was sick, and couldn't come to the Grange; and how papa would object to my going. And then I negotiated with him about the pony. He is fond of reading, and he thinks of leaving soon to get married, so he offered, if I would lend him books out of the library, to do what I wished; but I preferred giving him my own, and that satisfied him better.

"On my second visit, Linton seemed in lively spirits; and Zillah—that is their housekeeper—made us a clean room and a good fire, and told us that, as Joseph was out at a prayer-meeting and Hareton Earnshaw was off with his dogs—robbing our woods of pheasants, as I heard afterwards—we might do what we liked.

"She brought me some warm wine and gingerbread, and appeared exceedingly good-natured; and Linton sat in the arm-chair, and I in the little rocking chair on the hearthstone, and we laughed and talked so merrily, and found so much to say; we planned where we would go, and what we would do in summer. I needn't repeat that, because you would call it silly.

"One time, however, we were near quarrelling. He said the pleasantest manner of spending a hot July day was lying from morning till evening on a bank of heath in the middle of the moors, with the bees humming dreamily about among the bloom, and the larks singing high up over head, and the blue sky and bright sun shining steadily and cloudlessly. That was his most perfect idea of heaven's happiness. Mine was rocking in a rustling green tree, with a west wind blowing, and bright, white clouds flitting rapidly above; and not only larks, but throstles, and blackbirds, and linnets, and cuckoos pouring out music on every side, and the moors seen at a distance, broken into cool dusky dells; but close by, great swells of long grass undulating in waves to the breeze; and woods and sounding water, and the whole world awake and wild with joy. He wanted all to lie in an ecstacy of peace; I wanted all to sparkle, and dance in a glorious jubilee.

"I said his heaven would be only half alive, and he said mine would be drunk; I said I should fall asleep in his, and he said he could not breathe in mine, and began to grow very snappish. At last, we agreed to try both as soon as the right weather came; and then we kissed each other and were friends. After sitting still an hour, I looked at the great room with its smooth, uncarpeted floor, and thought how nice it would be to play in, if we removed the table; and I asked Linton to call Zillah in to help us, and we'd have a game at blind-man's buff—she should try to catch us; you used to, you know, Ellen. He wouldn't; there was no pleasure in it, he said, but he consented to play at ball with me. We found two in a cupboard, among a heap of old toys: tops, and hoops, and battledores, and shuttlecocks. One was marked C., and the other H.; I wished to have the C., because that stood for Catherine, and the H. might be for Heathcliff, his name; but the bran came out of H., and Linton didn't like it.

"I beat him constantly; and he got cross again, and coughed, and returned to his chair. That night, though, he easily recovered his good humour; he was charmed with two or three pretty songs—*your* songs, Ellen; and when I was obliged to go, he begged and entreated me to come the following evening, and I promised.

"Minny and I went flying home as light as air: and I dreamt of Wuthering Heights, and my sweet, darling cousin, till morning.

"On the morrow, I was sad; partly because you were poorly, and partly that I wished my father knew, and approved of my excursions: but it was beautiful moonlight after tea; and, as I rode on, the gloom cleared.

"I shall have another happy evening, I thought to myself, and what delights me more, my pretty Linton will.

"I trotted up their garden, and was turning round to the back, when that fellow Earnshaw met me, took my bridle, and bid me go in by the front entrance. He patted Minny's neck, and said she was a bonny beast, and appeared as if he wanted me to speak to him. I only told him to leave my horse alone, or else it would kick him.

"He answered in his vulgar accent.

" 'It wouldn't do mitch hurt if it did'; and surveyed its legs with a smile.

"I was half inclined to make it try; however, he moved off to open the door, and, as he raised the latch, he looked up to the inscription above, and said, with a stupid mixture of awkwardness and elation—

" 'Miss Catherine! I can read yon, nah.'

" 'Wonderful,' I exclaimed. 'Pray let us hear you—you *are* grown clever!'

"He spelt, and drawled over by syllables, the name—

" 'Hareton Earnshaw.'

" 'And the figures?' I cried, encouragingly, perceiving that he came to a dead halt.

" 'I cannot tell them yet,' he answered.

" 'Oh, you dunce!' I said, laughing heartily at his failure.

"The fool stared, with a grin hovering about his lips, and a scowl gathering over his eyes, as if uncertain whether he might not join in my mirth; whether it were not pleasant familiarity, or what it really was, contempt.

"I settled his doubts by suddenly retrieving my gravity, and desiring him to walk away, for I came to see Linton, not him.

"He reddened—I saw that by the moonlight—dropped his hand from the latch, and skulked off, a picture of mortified vanity. He imagined himself to be as accomplished as Linton, I suppose, because he could spell his own name; and was marvellously discomfited that I didn't think the same."

"Stop, Miss Catherine, dear!" I interrupted. "I shall not scold, but I don't like your conduct there. If you had remembered that Hareton was your cousin as much as Master Heathcliff, you would have felt how improper it was to behave in that way. At least, it was praiseworthy ambition for him to desire to be as accomplished as Linton; and probably he did not learn merely to show off; you had made him ashamed of his ignorance before, I have no doubt; and he wished to remedy it and please you. To sneer at his imperfect attempt was very bad breeding. Had *you* been brought up in his circumstances, would you be less rude? He was as quick and as intelligent a child as ever you were, and I'm hurt that he should be despised now, because that base Heathcliff has treated him so unjustly."

"Well, Ellen, you won't cry about it, will you?" she exclaimed, surprised at my earnestness. "But wait, and you shall hear if he conned his A B C to please me; and if it were worth while being civil to the brute. I entered; Linton was lying on the settle, and half got up to welcome me.

" 'I'm ill to-night, Catherine, love,' he said, 'and you must have all the talk, and let me listen. Come, and sit by me. I was sure you wouldn't break your word, and I'll make you promise again, before you go.'

"I knew now that I mustn't tease him, as he was ill; and I spoke softly and put no questions, and avoided irritating him in any way.

I had brought some of my nicest books for him; he asked me to read a little of one, and I was about to comply, when Earnshaw burst the door open, having gathered venom with reflection. He advanced direct to us, seized Linton by the arm, and swung him off the seat.

" 'Get to thy own room!' he said in a voice almost inarticulate with passion, and his face looked swelled and furious. 'Take her there if she comes to see thee—thou shalln't keep me out of this. Begone, wi' ye both!'

"He swore at us, and left Linton no time to answer, nearly throwing him into the kitchen; and he clenched his fist, as I followed, seemingly longing to knock me down. I was afraid, for a moment, and I let one volume fall; he kicked it after me, and shut us out.

"I heard a malignant, crackly laugh by the fire, and turning, beheld that odious Joseph, standing rubbing his bony hands, and quivering.

" 'Aw wer sure he'd sarve ye eht! He's a grand lad! He's getten t'raight sperrit in him! *He* knaws—Aye, he knaws, as weel as Aw do, who sud be t'maister yonder. Ech, ech, ech! He mad ye skift properly! Ech, ech, ech!'[1]

" 'Where must we go?' I said to my cousin, disregarding the old wretch's mockery.

"Linton was white and trembling. He was not pretty then, Ellen. Oh, no! he looked frightful! for his thin face and large eyes were wrought into an expression of frantic, powerless fury. He grasped the handle of the door, and shook it—it was fastened inside.

" 'If you don't let me in, I'll kill you! If you don't let me in, I'll kill you!' he rather shrieked than said. 'Devil! devil! I'll kill you, I'll kill you!'

"Joseph uttered his croaking laugh again.

" 'Thear, that's t'father!' he cried. 'That's father! We've allas summut uh orther side[2] in us. Niver heed Hareton, lad—dunnut be 'feard—he cannot get at thee!'

"I took hold of Linton's hands, and tried to pull him away; but he shrieked so shockingly that I dared not proceed. At last, his cries were choked by a dreadful fit of coughing; blood gushed from his mouth, and he fell on the ground.

"I ran into the yard, sick with terror; and called for Zillah, as loud as I could. She soon heard me; she was milking the cows in a shed behind the barn, and hurrying from her work, she inquired what there was to do?

"I hadn't breath to explain; dragging her in, I looked about for Linton. Earnshaw had come out to examine the mischief he had

---

1. *Sarve ye eht*: punish you, give you what's coming; *skift*: move.

2. Something of (the) other side (i.e., something inherited from Heathcliff).

caused, and he was then conveying the poor thing upstairs. Zillah and I ascended after him; but he stopped me at the top of the steps, and said I shouldn't go in, I must go home.

"I exclaimed that he had killed Linton and I *would* enter.

"Joseph locked the door, and declared I should do 'no sich stuff,' and asked me whether I were 'bahn[3] to' be as mad as him.'

"I stood crying, till the housekeeper re-appeared; she affirmed he would be better in a bit, but he couldn't do with that shrieking and din, and she took me, and nearly carried me into the house.

"Ellen, I was ready to tear my hair off my head! I sobbed and wept so that my eyes were almost blind; and the ruffian you have such sympathy with stood opposite, presuming every now and then to bid me 'wisht,' and denying that it was his fault; and finally, frightened by my assertions that I would tell papa, and that he should be put in prison and hanged, he commenced blubbering himself, and hurried out to hide his cowardly agitation.

"Still, I was not rid of him: when at length they compelled me to depart, and I had got some hundred yards off the premises, he suddenly issued from the shadow of the road-side, and checked Minny and took hold of me.

" 'Miss Catherine, I'm ill grieved,' he began, 'but it's rayther too bad—'

"I gave him a cut with my whip, thinking perhaps he would murder me. He let go, thundering one of his horrid curses, and I galloped home more than half out of my senses.

"I didn't bid you good-night, that evening; and I didn't go to Wuthering Heights, the next. I wished to, exceedingly; but I was strangely excited, and dreaded to hear that Linton was dead, sometimes; and sometimes shuddered at the thoughts of encountering Hareton.

"On the third day I took courage; at least, I couldn't bear longer suspense and stole off once more. I went at five o'clock, and walked, fancying I might manage to creep into the house, and up to Linton's room, unobserved. However, the dogs gave notice of my approach: Zillah received me, and saying 'the lad was mending nicely,' showed me into a small, tidy, carpeted apartment, where, to my inexpressible joy, I beheld Linton laid on a little sofa, reading one of my books. But he would neither speak to me nor look at me, through a whole hour, Ellen. He has such an unhappy temper— and what quite confounded me, when he did open his mouth it was to utter the falsehood that I had occasioned the uproar, and Hareton was not to blame!

"Unable to reply, except passionately, I got up and walked from the room. He sent after me a faint 'Catherine!' He did not reckon

3. Born.

on being answered so, but I wouldn't turn back; and the morrow was the second day on which I stayed at home, nearly determined to visit him no more.

"But it was so miserable going to bed, and getting up, and never hearing anything about him, that my resolution melted into air before it was properly formed. It *had* appeared wrong to take the journey once; now it seemed wrong to refrain. Michael came to ask if he must saddle Minny; I said 'Yes,' and considered myself doing a duty as she bore me over the hills.

"I was forced to pass the front windows to get to the court; it was no use trying to conceal my presence.

"'Young master is in the house,' said Zillah, as she saw me making for the parlour.

"I went in; Earnshaw was there also, but he quitted the room directly. Linton sat in the great arm chair half asleep; walking up to the fire, I began in a serious tone, partly meaning it to be true—

"'As you don't like me, Linton, and as you think I come on purpose to hurt you, and pretend that I do so every time, this is our last meeting—let us say good-bye; and tell Mr. Heathcliff that you have no wish to see me, and that he mustn't invent any more falsehoods on the subject.'

"'Sit down and take your hat off, Catherine,' he answered. 'You are so much happier than I am, you ought to be better. Papa talks enough of my defects, and shows enough scorn of me, to make it natural I should doubt myself. I doubt whether I am not altogether as worthless as he calls me, frequently; and then I feel so cross and bitter, I hate everybody! I *am* worthless, and bad in temper, and bad in spirit, almost always—and if you choose, you *may* say good-bye. You'll get rid of an annoyance. Only, Catherine, do me this justice; believe that if I might be as sweet, and as kind, and as good as you are, I would be, as willingly and more so, than as happy and as healthy. And believe that your kindness has made me love you deeper than if I deserved your love, and though I couldn't, and cannot help showing my nature to you, I regret it and repent it, and shall regret and repent it, till I die!'

"I felt he spoke the truth; and I felt I must forgive him; and, though he should quarrel the next moment, I must forgive him again. We were reconciled, but we cried, both of us, the whole time I stayed. Not entirely for sorrow, yet I *was* sorry Linton had that distorted nature. He'll never let his friends be at ease, and he'll never be at ease himself!

"I have always gone to his little parlour, since that night; because his father returned the day after. About three times, I think, we have been merry and hopeful, as we were the first evening; the rest of my visits were dreary and troubled—now, with his selfishness and spite; and now, with his sufferings: but I've learnt to endure the former with nearly as little resentment as the latter.

"Mr. Heathcliff purposely avoids me. I have hardly seen him at all. Last Sunday, indeed, coming earlier than usual, I heard him abusing poor Linton, cruelly, for his conduct of the night before. I can't tell how he knew of it, unless he listened. Linton had certainly behaved provokingly; however, it was the business of nobody but me; and I interrupted Mr. Heathcliff's lecture by entering and telling him so. He burst into a laugh, and went away, saying he was glad I took that view of the matter. Since then, I've told Linton he must whisper his bitter things.

"Now, Ellen, you have heard all; and I can't be prevented from going to Wuthering Heights, except by inflicting misery on two people; whereas, if you'll only not tell papa, my going need disturb the tranquillity of none. You'll not tell, will you? It will be very heartless if you do."

"I'll make up my mind on that point by to-morrow, Miss Catherine," I replied. "It requires some study; and so I'll leave you to your rest, and go think it over."

I thought it over aloud, in my master's presence; walking straight from her room to his, and relating the whole story, with the exception of her conversations with her cousin, and any mention of Hareton.

Mr. Linton was alarmed and distressed more than he would acknowledge to me. In the morning, Catherine learnt my betrayal of her confidence, and she learnt also that her secret visits were to end.

In vain she wept and writhed against the interdict, and implored her father to have pity on Linton: all she got to comfort her was a promise that he would write, and give him leave to come to the Grange when he pleased; but explaining that he must no longer expect to see Catherine at Wuthering Heights. Perhaps, had he been aware of his nephew's disposition and state of health, he would have seen fit to withhold even that slight consolation.

## Chapter XXV

"These things happened last winter, sir," said Mrs. Dean; "hardly more than a year ago. Last winter, I did not think, at another twelve months' end, I should be amusing a stranger to the family with relating them! Yet, who knows how long you'll be a stranger? You're too young to rest always contented, living by yourself; and I some way fancy no one could see Catherine Linton, and not love her. You smile; but why do you look so lively and interested, when

I talk about her? and why have you asked me to hang her picture over your fireplace? and why—"

"Stop, my good friend!" I cried. "It may be very possible that I should love her; but would she love me? I doubt it too much to venture my tranquillity by running into temptation; and then my home is not here. I'm of the busy world, and to its arms I must return. Go on. Was Catherine obedient to her father's commands?"

"She was," continued the housekeeper. "Her affection for him was still the chief sentiment in her heart; and he spoke without anger. He spoke in the deep tenderness of one about to leave his treasures amid perils and foes, where his remembered words would be the only aid that he could bequeath to guide her.

He said to me, a few days afterwards—

"I wish my nephew would write, Ellen, or call. Tell me, sincerely, what you think of him—is he changed for the better, or is there a prospect of improvement, as he grows a man?"

"He's very delicate, sir," I replied; "and scarcely likely to reach manhood; but this I can say, he does not resemble his father; and if Miss Catherine had the misfortune to marry him, he would not be beyond her control, unless she were extremely and foolishly indulgent. However, master, you'll have plenty of time to get acquainted with him, and see whether he would suit her: it wants four years and more to his being of age."

Edgar sighed; and, walking to the window, looked out towards Gimmerton Kirk. It was a misty afternoon, but the February sun shone dimly, and we could just distinguish the two fir trees in the yard, and the sparely scattered gravestones.

"I've prayed often," he half soliloquized, "for the approach of what is coming; and now I begin to shrink, and fear it. I thought the memory of the hour I came down that glen a bridegroom would be less sweet than the anticipation that I was soon, in a few months, or, possibly, weeks, to be carried up, and laid in its lonely hollow! Ellen, I've been very happy with my little Cathy. Through winter nights and summer days she was a living hope at my side. But I've been as happy musing by myself among those stones, under that old church—lying, through the long June evenings, on the green mound of her mother's grave, and wishing, yearning for the time when I might lie beneath it. What can I do for Cathy? How must I quit her? I'd not care one moment for Linton being Heathcliff's son; nor for his taking her from me, if he could console her for my loss. I'd not care that Heathcliff gained his ends, and triumphed in robbing me of my last blessing! But should Linton be unworthy —only a feeble tool to his father—I cannot abandon her to him! And, hard though it be to crush her buoyant spirit, I must persevere in making her sad while I live, and leaving her solitary when I die. Darling! I'd rather resign her to God, and lay her in the earth before me."

"Resign her to God, as it is, sir," I answered, "and if we should lose you—which may He forbid—under His providence, I'll stand her friend and counsellor to the last. Miss Catherine is a good girl; I don't fear that she will go wilfully wrong; and people who do their duty are always finally rewarded."

Spring advanced; yet my master gathered no real strength, though he resumed his walks in the grounds with his daughter. To her inexperienced notions, this itself was a sign of convalescence; and then his cheek was often flushed, and his eyes were bright: she felt sure of his recovering.

On her seventeenth birthday, he did not visit the churchyard; it was raining, and I observed—

"You'll surely not go out to-night, sir?"

He answered—

"No, I'll defer it this year, a little longer."

He wrote again to Linton, expressing his great desire to see him; and, had the invalid been presentable, I've no doubt his father would have permitted him to come. As it was, being instructed, he returned an answer, intimating that Mr. Heathcliff objected to his calling at the Grange; but his uncle's kind remembrance delighted him, and he hoped to meet him, sometimes, in his rambles, and personally to petition that his cousin and he might not remain long so utterly divided.

That part of his letter was simple, and probably his own. Heathcliff knew he could plead eloquently enough for Catherine's company, then—

"I do not ask," he said, "that she may visit here; but am I never to see her, because my father forbids me to go to her home, and you forbid her to come to mine? Do, now and then, ride with her towards the Heights; and let us exchange a few words, in your presence! We have done nothing to deserve this separation; and you are not angry with me—you have no reason to dislike me, you allow, yourself. Dear uncle! send me a kind note to-morrow; and leave to join you anywhere you please, except at Thrushcross Grange. I believe an interview would convince you that my father's character is not mine; he affirms I am more your nephew than his son; and though I have faults which render me unworthy of Catherine, she has excused them, and, for her sake, you should also. You inquire after my health—it is better; but while I remain cut off from all hope, and doomed to solitude, or the society of those who never did, and never will like me, how can I be cheerful and well?"

Edgar, though he felt for the boy, could not consent to grant his request; because he could not accompany Catherine.

He said, in summer, perhaps, they might meet: meantime, he wished him to continue writing at intervals, and engaged to give him what advice and comfort he was able by letter; being well aware of his hard position in his family.

Linton complied; and had he been unrestrained, would probably have spoiled all by filling his epistles with complaints and lamentations; but his father kept a sharp watch over him; and, of course, insisted on every line that my master sent being shown; so, instead of penning his peculiar personal sufferings and distresses, the themes constantly uppermost in his thoughts, he harped on the cruel obligation of being held asunder from his friend and love; and gently intimated that Mr. Linton must allow an interview soon, or he should fear he was purposely deceiving him with empty promises.

Cathy was a powerful ally at home; and, between them, they at length persuaded my master to acquiesce in their having a ride or a walk together, about once a week, under my guardianship, and on the moors nearest the Grange, for June found him still declining; and, though he had set aside, yearly, a portion of his income for my young lady's fortune, he had a natural desire that she might retain—or, at least, return in a short time to—the house of her ancestors; and he considered her only prospect of doing that was by a union with his heir; he had no idea that the latter was failing almost as fast as himself; nor had any one, I believe: no doctor visited the Heights, and no one saw Master Heathcliff to make report of his condition, among us.

I, for my part, began to fancy my forebodings were false, and that he must be actually rallying, when he mentioned riding and walking on the moors, and seemed so earnest in pursuing his object.

I could not picture a father treating a dying child as tyrannically and wickedly as I afterwards learnt Heathcliff had treated him, to compel this apparent eagerness; his efforts redoubling the more imminently his avaricious and unfeeling plans were threatened with defeat by death.

## Chapter XXVI

Summer was already past its prime, when Edgar reluctantly yielded his assent to their entreaties, and Catherine and I set out on our first ride to join her cousin.

It was a close, sultry day, devoid of sunshine, but with a sky too dappled and hazy to threaten rain; and our place of meeting had been fixed at the guide-stone, by the crossroads. On arriving there, however, a little herd-boy, despatched as a messenger, told us that—

"Maister Linton wer just ut this side th' Heights: and he'd be mitch obleeged to us to gang on a bit further."

"Then Master Linton has forgot the first injunction of his uncle," I observed: "he bid us keep on the Grange land, and here we are, off at once."

"Well, we'll turn our horses' heads round, when we reach him," answered my companion; "our excursion shall lie towards home."

But when we reached him, and that was scarcely a quarter of a mile from his own door, we found he had no horse, and we were forced to dismount, and leave ours to graze.

He lay on the heath, awaiting our approach, and did not rise till we came within a few yards. Then he walked so feebly, and looked so pale, that I immediately exclaimed—

"Why, Master Heathcliff, you are not fit for enjoying a ramble this morning. How ill you do look!"

Catherine surveyed him with grief and astonishment; she changed the ejaculation of joy on her lips, to one of alarm, and the congratulation on their long postponed meeting, to an anxious inquiry, whether he were worse than usual?

"No—better—better!" he panted, trembling, and retaining her hand as if he needed its support, while his large blue eyes wandered timidly over her; the hollowness round them, transforming to haggard wildness the languid expression they once possessed.

"But you have been worse," persisted his cousin, "worse than when I saw you last—you are thinner, and—"

"I'm tired," he interrupted, hurriedly. "It is too hot for walking, let us rest here. And, in the morning, I often feel sick—papa says I grow so fast."

Badly satisfied, Cathy sat down, and he reclined beside her.

"This is something like your paradise," said she, making an effort at cheerfulness. "You recollect the two days we agreed to spend in the place and way each thought pleasantest? This is nearly yours, only there are clouds; but then, they are so soft and mellow, it is nicer than sunshine. Next week, if you can, we'll ride down to the Grange Park, and try mine."

Linton did not appear to remember what she talked of; and he had evidently great difficulty in sustaining any kind of conversation. His lack of interest in the subjects she started, and his equal incapacity to contribute to her entertainment, were so obvious that she could not conceal her disappointment. An indefinite alteration had come over his whole person and manner. The pettishness that might be caressed into fondness, had yielded to a listless apathy; there was less of the peevish temper of a child which frets and teases on purpose to be soothed, and more of the self-absorbed moroseness of a confirmed invalid, repelling consolation, and ready to regard the good-humoured mirth of others as an insult.

Catherine perceived, as well as I did, that he held it rather a punishment, than a gratification, to endure our company; and she made no scruple of proposing, presently, to depart.

That proposal, unexpectedly, roused Linton from his lethargy, and threw him into a strange state of agitation. He glanced fearfully towards the Heights, begging she would remain another half-hour, at least.

"But, I think," said Cathy, "you'd be more comfortable at home than sitting here; and I cannot amuse you to-day, I see, by my tales, and songs, and chatter; you have grown wiser than I, in these six months; you have little taste for my diversions now; or else, if I could amuse you, I'd willingly stay."

"Stay to rest yourself," he replied. "And, Catherine, don't think, or say that I'm *very* unwell—it is the heavy weather and heat that make me dull; and I walked about, before you came, a great deal, for me. Tell uncle, I'm in tolerable health, will you?"

"I'll tell him that *you* say so, Linton. I couldn't affirm that you are," observed my young lady, wondering at his pertinacious assertion of what was evidently an untruth.

"And be here again next Thursday," continued he, shunning her puzzled gaze. "And give him my thanks for permitting you to come —my best thanks, Catherine. And—and if you *did* meet my father, and he asked you about me, don't lead him to suppose that I've been extremely silent and stupid; don't look sad and downcast, as you *are* doing—he'll be angry."

"I care nothing for his anger," exclaimed Cathy, imagining she would be its object.

"But I do," said her cousin, shuddering. "*Don't* provoke him against me, Catherine, for he is very hard."

"Is he severe to you, Master Heathcliff?" I inquired. "Has he grown weary of indulgence, and passed from passive, to active hatred?"

Linton looked at me, but did not answer; and, after keeping her seat by his side another ten minutes, during which his head fell drowsily on his breast, and he uttered nothing except suppressed moans of exhaustion or pain, Cathy began to seek solace in looking for bilberries, and sharing the produce of her researches with me: she did not offer them to him, for she saw further notice would only weary and annoy.

"Is it half an hour now, Ellen?" she whispered in my ear, at last. "I can't tell why we should stay. He's asleep, and papa will be wanting us back."

"Well, we must not leave him asleep," I answered; "wait till he wakes and be patient. You were mighty eager to set off, but your longing to see poor Linton has soon evaporated!"

"Why did *he* wish to see me?" returned Catherine. "In his crossest humours, formerly, I liked him better than I do in his present curious mood. It's just as if it were a task he was compelled to perform—this interview—for fear his father should scold him. But I'm hardly going to come to give Mr. Heathcliff pleasure, whatever reason he may have for ordering Linton to undergo this penance. And, though I'm glad he's better in health, I'm sorry he's so much less pleasant, and so much less affectionate to me."

"You think *he is* better in health, then?" I said.

"Yes," she answered; "because he always made such a great deal of his sufferings, you know. He is not tolerably well, as he told me to tell papa, but he's better, very likely."

"Then you differ with me, Miss Cathy," I remarked; "I should conjecture him to be far worse."

Linton here started from his slumber in bewildered terror, and asked if any one had called his name.

"No," said Catherine; "unless in dreams. I cannot conceive how you manage to doze, out of doors, in the morning."

"I thought I heard my father," he gasped, glancing up to the frowning nab above us. "You are sure nobody spoke?"

"Quite sure," replied his cousin. "Only Ellen and I were disputing concerning your health. Are you truly stronger, Linton, than when we separated in winter? If you be, I'm certain one thing is not stronger—your regard for me—speak, are you?"

The tears gushed from Linton's eyes as he answered—

"Yes, yes, I am!"

And, still under the spell of the imaginary voice, his gaze wandered up and down to detect its owner.

Cathy rose.

"For to-day we must part," she said. "And I won't conceal that I have been sadly disappointed with our meeting, though I'll mention it to nobody but you—not that I stand in awe of Mr. Heathcliff!"

"Hush," murmured Linton; "for God's sake, hush! He's coming." And he clung to Catherine's arm, striving to detain her; but, at that announcement, she hastily disengaged herself, and whistled to Minny, who obeyed her like a dog.

"I'll be here next Thursday," she cried, springing to the saddle. "Good-bye. Quick, Ellen!"

And so we left him, scarcely conscious of our departure, so absorbed was he in anticipating his father's approach.

Before we reached home, Catherine's displeasure softened into a perplexed sensation of pity and regret largely blended with vague, uneasy doubts about Linton's actual circumstances, physical and social; in which I partook, though I counselled her not to say much, for a second journey would make us better judges.

My master requested an account of our ongoings: his nephew's offering of thanks was duly delivered, Miss Cathy gently touching on the rest: I also threw little light on his inquiries, for I hardly knew what to hide, and what to reveal.

## Chapter XXVII

Seven days glided away, every one marking its course by the henceforth rapid alteration of Edgar Linton's state. The havoc that months had previously wrought was now emulated by the inroads of hours.

Catherine, we would fain have deluded yet, but her own quick spirit refused to delude her. It divined, in secret, and brooded on the dreadful probability, gradually ripening into certainty.

She had not the heart to mention her ride, when Thursday came round; I mentioned it for her, and obtained permission to order her out of doors; for the library, where her father stopped a short time daily—the brief period he could bear to sit up—and his chamber had become her whole world. She grudged each moment that did not find her bending over his pillow, or seated by his side. Her countenance grew wan with watching and sorrow, and my master gladly dismissed her to what he flattered himself would be a happy change of scene and society, drawing comfort from the hope that she would not now be left entirely alone after his death.

He had a fixed idea, I guessed by several observations he let fall, that as his nephew resembled him in person, he would resemble him in mind; for Linton's letters bore few or no indications of his defective character. And I, through pardonable weakness, refrained from correcting the error; asking myself what good there would be in disturbing his last moments with information that he had neither power nor opportunity to turn to account.

We deferred our excursion till the afternoon; a golden afternoon of August—every breath from the hills so full of life, that it seemed whoever respired it, though dying, might revive.

Catherine's face was just like the landscape—shadows and sunshine flitting over it, in rapid succession; but the shadows rested longer and the sunshine was more transient, and her poor little heart reproached itself for even that passing forgetfulness of its cares.

We discerned Linton watching at the same spot he had selected before. My young mistress alighted, and told me that as she was resolved to stay a very little while, I had better hold the pony and remain on horseback; but I dissented; I wouldn't risk losing sight of the charge committed to me a minute; so we climbed the slope of heath together.

Master Heathcliff received us with greater animation on this occasion; not the animation of high spirits though, nor yet of joy; it looked more like fear.

"It is late!" he said, speaking short, and with difficulty. "Is not your father very ill? I thought you wouldn't come."

"*Why* won't you be candid?" cried Catherine, swallowing her greeting. "Why cannot you say at once, you don't want me? It is strange, Linton, that for the second time, you have brought me here on purpose, apparently, to distress us both, and for no reason besides!"

Linton shivered, and glanced at her, half supplicating, half ashamed, but his cousin's patience was not sufficient to endure this enigmatical behaviour.

"My father *is* very ill," she said, "and why am I called from his bedside—why didn't you send to absolve me from my promise, when you wished I wouldn't keep it? Come! I desire an explanation; playing and trifling are completely banished out of my mind, and I can't dance attendance on your affectations, now!"

"My affectations!" he murmured; "what are they? For heaven's sake, Catherine, don't look so angry! Despise me as much as you please; I am a worthless, cowardly wretch—I can't be scorned enough! but I'm too mean for your anger—hate my father, and spare me, for contempt!"

"Nonsense!" cried Catherine in a passion. "Foolish, silly boy! And there! he trembles, as if I were really going to touch him! You needn't bespeak contempt, Linton; anybody will have it spontaneously, at your service. Get off! I shall return home; it is folly dragging you from the hearth-stone, and pretending—what do we pretend? Let go my frock! If I pitied you for crying and looking so very frightened, you should spurn such pity. Ellen, tell him how disgraceful this conduct is. Rise, and don't degrade yourself into an abject reptile—*don't.*"

With streaming face and an expression of agony, Linton had thrown his nerveless frame along the ground; he seemed convulsed with exquisite terror.

"Oh!" he sobbed, "I cannot bear it! Catherine, Catherine, I'm a traitor too, and I dare not tell you! But leave me and I shall be killed! *Dear* Catherine, my life is in your hands; and you have said you loved me—and if you did, it wouldn't harm you. You'll not go, then? kind, sweet, good Catherine! And perhaps you *will* consent—and he'll let me die with you!"

My young lady, on witnessing his intense anguish, stooped to raise him. The old feeling of indulgent tenderness overcame her vexation, and she grew thoroughly moved and alarmed.

"Consent to what?" she asked. "To stay? Tell me the meaning of this strange talk, and I will. You contradict your own words, and distract me! Be calm and frank, and confess at once all that weighs on your heart. You wouldn't injure me, Linton, would you? You wouldn't let any enemy hurt me, if you could prevent it? I'll believe you are a coward, for yourself, but not a cowardly betrayer of your best friend."

"But my father threatened me," gasped the boy, clasping his attenuated fingers, "and I dread him—I dread him! I *dare* not tell!"

"Oh well!" said Catherine, with scornful compassion, "keep your secret, *I'm* no coward—save yourself, I'm not afraid!"

Her magnanimity provoked his tears; he wept wildly, kissing her supporting hands, and yet could not summon courage to speak out.

I was cogitating what the mystery might be, and determined Catherine should never suffer to benefit him or any one else, by my good will; when hearing a rustle among the ling,[1] I looked up, and saw Mr. Heathcliff almost close upon us, descending the Heights. He didn't cast a glance towards my companions, though they were sufficiently near for Linton's sobs to be audible; but hailing me in the almost hearty tone he assumed to none besides, and the sincerity of which I couldn't avoid doubting, he said—

"It is something to see you so near to my house, Nelly! How are you at the Grange? Let us hear! The rumour goes," he added in a lower tone, "that Edgar Linton is on his death-bed—perhaps they exaggerate his illness?"

"No; my master is dying," I replied; "it is true enough. A sad thing it will be for us all, but a blessing for him!"

"How long will he last, do you think?" he asked.

"I don't know," I said.

"Because," he continued, looking at the two young people, who were fixed under his eye—Linton appeared as if he could not venture to stir, or raise his head, and Catherine could not move, on his account—"Because that lad yonder seems determined to beat me—and I'd thank his uncle to be quick, and go before him. Hallo! Has the whelp been playing that game long? I *did* give him some lessons about snivelling. Is he pretty lively with Miss Linton generally?"

"Lively? no—he has shown the greatest distress," I answered. "To see him, I should say, that instead of rambling with his sweetheart on the hills, he ought to be in bed, under the hands of a doctor."

"He shall be, in a day or two," muttered Heathcliff. "But first

1. Heather.

—get up, Linton! Get up!" he shouted. "Don't grovel on the ground, there—up this moment!"

Linton had sunk prostrate again in another paroxysm of helpless fear, caused by his father's glance towards him, I suppose: there was nothing else to produce such humiliation. He made several efforts to obey, but his little strength was annihilated for the time, and he fell back again with a moan.

Mr. Heathcliff advanced, and lifted him to lean against a ridge of turf.

"Now," said he with curbed ferocity, "I'm getting angry—and if you don't command that paltry spirit of yours—*Damn* you! Get up, directly!"

"I will, father!" he panted. "Only, let me alone, or I shall faint! I've done as you wished, I'm sure. Catherine will tell you that—that I—have been cheerful. Ah! keep by me, Catherine; give me your hand."

"Take mine," said his father; "stand on your feet! There now—she'll lend you her arm. That's right, look at *her*. You would imagine I was the devil himself, Miss Linton, to excite such horror. Be so kind as to walk home with him, will you? He shudders, if I touch him."

"Linton, dear!" whispered Catherine, "I can't go to Wuthering Heights—papa has forbidden me. He'll not harm you, why are you so afraid?"

"I can never re-enter that house," he answered. "I am *not* to re-enter it without you!"

"Stop!" cried his father. "We'll respect Catherine's filial scruples. Nelly, take him in, and I'll follow your advice concerning the doctor, without delay."

"You'll do well," replied I, "but I must remain with my mistress. To mind your son is not my business."

"You are very stiff!" said Heathcliff; "I know that—but you'll force me to pinch the baby, and make it scream, before it moves your charity. Come then, my hero. Are you willing to return, escorted by me?"

He approached once more, and made as if he would seize the fragile being; but shrinking back, Linton clung to his cousin, and implored her to accompany him, with a frantic importunity that admitted no denial.

However I disapproved, I couldn't hinder her; indeed, how could she have refused him herself? What was filling him with dread, we had no means of discerning, but there he was, powerless under its gripe, and any addition seemed capable of shocking him into idiocy.

We reached the threshold; Catherine walked in; and I stood waiting till she had conducted the invalid to a chair, expecting her out immediately; when Mr. Heathcliff, pushing me forward, exclaimed—

"My house is not stricken with the plague, Nelly; and I have a mind to be hospitable to-day; sit down, and allow me to shut the door."

He shut and locked it also. I started.

"You shall have tea, before you go home," he added. "I am by myself. Hareton is gone with some cattle to the Lees—and Zillah and Joseph are off on a journey of pleasure. And, though I'm used to being alone, I'd rather have some interesting company, if I can get it. Miss Linton, take your seat by *him*. I give you what I have; the present is hardly worth accepting; but I have nothing else to offer. It is Linton, I mean. How she does stare! It's odd what a savage feeling I have to anything that seems afraid of me! Had I been born where laws are less strict, and tastes less dainty, I should treat myself to a slow vivisection of those two, as an evening's amusement."

He drew in his breath, struck the table, and swore to himself—

"By hell! I hate them."

"I'm not afraid of you!" exclaimed Catherine, who could not hear the latter part of his speech.

She stepped close up, her black eyes flashing with passion and resolution.

"Give me that key—I will have it!" she said. "I wouldn't eat or drink here, if I were starving."

Heathcliff had the key in his hand that remained on the table. He looked up, seized with a sort of surprise at her boldness, or, possibly, reminded by her voice and glance, of the person from whom she inherited it.

She snatched at the instrument, and half succeeded in getting it out of his loosened fingers; but her action recalled him to the present; he recovered it speedily.

"Now, Catherine Linton," he said, "stand off, or I shall knock you down; and that will make Mrs. Dean mad."

Regardless of this warning, she captured his closed hand and its contents again.

"We *will* go!" she repeated, exerting her utmost efforts to cause the iron muscles to relax; and finding that her nails made no impression, she applied her teeth pretty sharply.

Heathcliff glanced at me a glance that kept me from interfering a moment. Catherine was too intent on his fingers to notice his face. He opened them suddenly, and resigned the object of dispute; but, ere she had well secured it, he seized her with the liberated hand, and, pulling her on his knee, administered with the other a shower of terrific slaps on both sides of the head, each sufficient to have fulfilled his threat, had she been able to fall.

At this diabolical violence, I rushed on him furiously.

"You villain!" I began to cry, "you villain!"

A touch on the chest silenced me; I am stout, and soon put out of breath; and, what with that and the rage, I staggered dizzily back, and felt ready to suffocate, or to burst a blood-vessel.

The scene was over in two minutes; Catherine, released, put her two hands to her temples, and looked just as if she were not sure whether her ears were off or on. She trembled like a reed, poor thing, and leant against the table perfectly bewildered.

"I know how to chastise children, you see," said the scoundrel, grimly, as he stooped to repossess himself of the key, which had dropped to the floor. "Go to Linton now, as I told you; and cry at your ease! I shall be your father to-morrow—all the father you'll have in a few days—and you shall have plenty of that—you can bear plenty—you're no weakling—you shall have a daily taste, if I catch such a devil of a temper in your eyes again!"

Cathy ran to me instead of Linton, and knelt down, and put her burning cheek on my lap, weeping aloud. Her cousin had shrunk into a corner of the settle, as quiet as a mouse, congratulating himself, I dare say, that the correction had lighted on another than him.

Mr. Heathcliff, perceiving us all confounded, rose, and expeditiously made the tea himself. The cups and saucers were laid ready. He poured it out, and handed me a cup.

"Wash away your spleen," he said. "And help your own naughty pet and mine. It is not poisoned, though I prepared it. I'm going out to seek your horses."

Our first thought, on his departure, was to force an exit somewhere. We tried the kitchen door, but that was fastened outside; we looked at the windows—they were too narrow for even Cathy's little figure.

"Master Linton," I cried, seeing we were regularly imprisoned, "you know what your diabolical father is after, and you shall tell us, or I'll box your ears, as he has done your cousin's."

"Yes, Linton; you must tell," said Catherine. "It was for your sake I came; and it will be wickedly ungrateful if you refuse."

"Give me some tea, I'm thirsty, and then I'll tell you," he answered. "Mrs. Dean, go away. I don't like you standing over me. Now, Catherine, you are letting your tears fall into my cup! I won't drink that. Give me another."

Catherine pushed another to him, and wiped her face. I felt disgusted at the little wretch's composure, since he was no longer in terror for himself. The anguish he had exhibited on the moor subsided as soon as ever he entered Wuthering Heights; so I guessed he had been menaced with an awful visitation of wrath if he failed in decoying us there; and, that accomplished, he had no further immediate fears.

"Papa wants us to be married," he continued, after sipping some of the liquid. "And he knows your papa wouldn't let us marry now; and he's afraid of my dying, if we wait; so we are to be married in the morning, and you are to stay here all night; and, if you do as he wishes, you shall return home next day, and take me with you."

"Take you with her, pitiful changeling?" I exclaimed. "*You* marry? Why, the man is mad, or he thinks us fools, every one. And do you imagine that beautiful young lady, that healthy, hearty girl, will tie herself to a little perishing monkey like you? Are you cherishing the notion that *anybody*, let alone Miss Catherine Linton, would have you for a husband? You want whipping for bringing us in here at all, with your dastardly, puling tricks; and—don't look so silly now! I've a very good mind to shake you severely, for your contemptible treachery, and your imbecile conceit."

I did give him a slight shaking, but it brought on the cough, and he took to his ordinary resource of moaning and weeping, and Catherine rebuked me.

"Stay all night? No!" she said, looking slowly round. "Ellen, I'll burn that door down, but I'll get out."

And she would have commenced the execution of her threat directly, but Linton was up in alarm, for his dear self, again. He clasped her in his two feeble arms, sobbing—

"Won't you have me, and save me? Not let me come to the Grange? Oh! darling Catherine! you mustn't go, and leave me, after all. You *must* obey my father, you *must!*"

"I must obey my own," she replied, "and relieve him from this cruel suspense. The whole night! What would he think? he'll be distressed already. I'll either break or burn a way out of the house. Be quiet! You're in no danger—but, if you hinder me—Linton, I love papa better than you!"

The mortal terror he felt of Mr. Heathcliff's anger restored to the boy his coward's eloquence. Catherine was near distraught; still, she persisted that she must go home, and tried entreaty, in her turn, persuading him to subdue his selfish agony.

While they were thus occupied, our jailer re-entered.

"Your beasts have trotted off," he said, "and—Now, Linton! snivelling again? What has she been doing to you? Come, come— have done, and get to bed. In a month or two, my lad, you'll be able to pay her back her present tyrannies, with a vigorous hand. You're pining for pure love, are you not? nothing else in the world —and she shall have you! There, to bed! Zillah won't be here to-night; you must undress yourself. Hush! hold your noise! Once in your own room, I'll not come near you, you needn't fear. By chance, you've managed tolerably. I'll look to the rest."

He spoke these words, holding the door open for his son to pass; and the latter achieved his exit exactly as a spaniel might, which suspected the person who attended on it of designing a spiteful squeeze.

The lock was re-secured. Heathcliff approached the fire, where my mistress and I stood silent. Catherine looked up, and instinctively raised her hand to her cheek: his neighbourhood revived a painful sensation. Anybody else would have been incapable of regarding the childish act with sternness, but he scowled on her, and muttered—

"Oh, you are not afraid of me? Your courage is well disguised— you *seem* damnably afraid!"

"I *am* afraid now," she replied; "because if I stay, papa will be miserable; and how can I endure making him miserable—when he —when he—Mr. Heathcliff, *let* me go home! I promise to marry Linton—papa would like me to, and I love him—and why should you wish to force me to do what I'll willingly do of myself?"

"Let him dare to force you!" I cried. "There's law in the land, thank God, there is! though we *be* in an out-of-the-way place. I'd inform, if he were my own son, and it's felony without benefit of clergy!"

"Silence!" said the ruffian. "To the devil with your clamour! I don't want *you* to speak. Miss Linton, I shall enjoy myself remarkably in thinking your father will be miserable; I shall not sleep for satisfaction. You could have hit on no surer way of fixing your residence under my roof, for the next twenty-four hours, than informing me that such an event would follow. As to your promise to marry Linton, I'll take care you shall keep it, for you shall not quit the place till it is fulfilled."

"Send Ellen then, to let papa know I'm safe!" exclaimed Catherine, weeping bitterly. "Or marry me now. Poor papa! Ellen, he'll think we're lost. What shall we do?"

"Not he! He'll think you are tired of waiting on him, and run off, for a little amusement," answered Heathcliff. "You cannot deny that you entered my house of your own accord, in contempt of his injunctions to the contrary. And it is quite natural that you should desire amusement at your age; and that you should weary of nursing a sick man, and that man *only* your father. Catherine, his happiest days were over when your days began. He cursed you, I dare say, for coming into the world (I did, at least). And it would just do if he cursed you as *he* went out of it. I'd join him. I don't love you! How should I? Weep away. As far as I can see, it will be your chief diversion hereafter, unless Linton make amends for other losses; and your provident parent appears to fancy he may. His letters of advice and consolation entertained me vastly. In his last, he recommended my jewel to be careful of his; and kind to her when he got her. Careful and kind—that's paternal! But Linton requires his whole stock of care and kindness for himself. Linton can play the little tyrant well. He'll undertake to torture any number of cats if their teeth be drawn, and their claws pared. You'll be able to tell his uncle fine tales of his *kindness*, when you get home again, I assure you."

"You're right there!" I said; "explain your son's character. Show his resemblance to yourself; and then, I hope, Miss Cathy will think twice before she takes the cockatrice!"

"I don't much mind speaking of his amiable qualities now," he answered, "because she must either accept him, or remain a prisoner, and you along with her, till your master dies. I can detain you both, quite concealed, here. If you doubt, encourage her to retract her word, and you'll have an opportunity of judging!"

"I'll not retract my word," said Catherine. "I'll marry him, within this hour, if I may go to Thrushcross Grange afterwards. Mr. Heathcliff, you're a cruel man, but you're not a fiend; and you won't, from *mere* malice, destroy, irrevocably, all my happiness. If papa thought I had left him on purpose, and if he died before I returned, could I bear to live? I've given over crying; but I'm going to kneel here, at your knee; and I'll not get up, and I'll not take my eyes from your face, till you look back at me! No, don't turn away! *do* look! You'll see nothing to provoke you. I don't hate you. I'm not angry that you struck me. Have you never loved *anybody*, in all your life, uncle? *never*? Ah! you must look once—I'm so wretched—you can't help being sorry and pitying me."

"Keep your eft's fingers off; and move, or I'll kick you!" cried Heathcliff, brutally repulsing her. "I'd rather be hugged by a snake. How the devil can you dream of fawning on me? I *detest* you!"

He shrugged his shoulders—shook himself, indeed, as if his flesh crept with aversion, and thrust back his chair, while I got up, and opened my mouth, to commence a downright torrent of abuse; but I was rendered dumb in the middle of the first sentence, by a threat that I should be shown into a room by myself, the very next syllable I uttered.

It was growing dark—we heard a sound of voices at the garden gate. Our host hurried out, instantly; *he* had his wits about him; *we* had not. There was a talk of two or three minutes, and he returned alone.

"I thought it had been your cousin Hareton," I observed to Catherine. "I wish he would arrive! Who knows but he might take our part?"

"It was three servants sent to seek you from the Grange," said Heathcliff, overhearing me. "You should have opened a lattice and called out; but I could swear that chit is glad you didn't. She's glad to be obliged to stay, I'm certain."

At learning the chance we had missed, we both gave vent to our grief without control, and he allowed us to wail on till nine o'clock; then he bid us go upstairs, through the kitchen, to Zillah's chamber, and I whispered my companion to obey; perhaps we might contrive to get through the window there, or into a garret, and out by its skylight.

The window, however, was narrow like those below, and the garret trap was safe from our attempts; for we were fastened in as before.

We neither of us lay down: Catherine took her station by the lattice, and watched anxiously for morning—a deep sigh being the only answer I could obtain to my frequent entreaties that she would try to rest.

I seated myself in a chair, and rocked, to and fro, passing harsh judgment on my many derelictions of duty; from which, it struck me then, all the misfortunes of all my employers sprang. It was not the case, in reality, I am aware; but it was, in my imagination, that dismal night, and I thought Heathcliff himself less guilty than I.

At seven o'clock he came, and inquired if Miss Linton had risen. She ran to the door immediately, and answered—

"Yes."

"Here, then," he said, opening it, and pulling her out.

I rose to follow, but he turned the lock again. I demanded my release.

"Be patient," he replied; "I'll send up your breakfast in a while."

I thumped on the panels, and rattled the latch angrily; and Catherine asked why I was still shut up? He answered, I must try to endure it another hour, and they went away.

I endured it two or three hours; at length, I heard a footstep, not Heathcliff's.

"I've brought you something to eat," said a voice; "oppen t' door!"

Complying eagerly, I beheld Hareton, laden with food enough to last me all day.

"Tak it," he added, thrusting the tray into my hand.

"Stay one minute," I began.

"Nay!" cried he, and retired, regardless of any prayers I could pour forth to detain him.

And there I remained enclosed, the whole day, and the whole of the next night; and another, and another. Five nights and four days I remained, altogether, seeing nobody but Hareton, once every morning, and he was a model of a jailer—surly, and dumb, and deaf to every attempt at moving his sense of justice or compassion.

## Chapter XXVIII

On the fifth morning, or rather afternoon, a different step approached—lighter and shorter—and, this time, the person entered the room. It was Zillah, donned in her scarlet shawl, with a black silk bonnet on her head, and a willow basket swung to her arm.

"Eh, dear! Mrs. Dean," she exclaimed. "Well! there is a talk about you at Gimmerton. I never thought but you were sunk in the Blackhorse marsh, and Missy with you, till master told me you'd been found, and he'd lodged you here! What, and you must have got on an island, sure? And how long were you in the hole? Did master save you, Mrs. Dean? But you're not so thin—you've not been so poorly, have you?"

"Your master is a true scoundrel!" I replied. "But he shall answer for it. He needn't have raised that tale—it shall all be laid bare!"

"What do you mean?" asked Zillah. "It's not his tale: they tell that in the village—about your being lost in the marsh; and I calls to Earnshaw, when I come in—"

" 'Eh, they's queer things, Mr. Hareton, happened since I went off. It's a sad pity of that likely young lass, and cant[1] Nelly Dean.'

"He stared. I thought he had not heard aught, so I told him the rumour.

"The master listened, and he just smiled to himself, and said—

" 'If they have been in the marsh, they are out now, Zillah. Nelly Dean is lodged, at this minute, in your room. You can tell her to flit, when you go up; here is the key. The bog-water got into her head, and she would have run home, quite flighty, but I fixed her, till she came round to her senses. You can bid her go to the Grange, at once, if she be able, and carry a message from me, that her young lady will follow in time to attend the Squire's funeral."

"Mr. Edgar is not dead?" I gasped. "Oh! Zillah, Zillah!"

"No, no—sit you down, my good mistress," she replied; "you're right sickly yet. He's not dead: Doctor Kenneth thinks he may last another day. I met him on the road and asked."

Instead of sitting down, I snatched my outdoor things, and hastened below, for the way was free.

On entering the house, I looked about for some one to give information of Catherine.

The place was filled with sunshine, and the door stood wide

1. Brisk.

open, but nobody seemed at hand.

As I hesitated whether to go off at once, or return and seek my mistress, a slight cough drew my attention to the hearth.

Linton lay on the settle, sole tenant, sucking a stick of sugar-candy, and pursuing my movements with apathetic eyes.

"Where is Miss Catherine?" I demanded, sternly, supposing I could frighten him into giving intelligence, by catching him thus, alone.

He sucked on like an innocent.

"Is she gone?" I said.

"No," he replied; "she's upstairs—she's not to go; we won't let her."

"You won't let her, little idiot!" I exclaimed. "Direct me to her room immediately, or I'll make you sing out sharply."

"Papa would make you sing out, if you attempted to get there," he answered. "He says I'm not to be soft with Catherine; she's my wife, and it's shameful that she should wish to leave me! He says, she hates me, and wants me to die, that she may have my money, but she shan't have it; and she shan't go home! She never shall! she may cry, and be sick as much as she pleases!"

He resumed his former occupation, closing his lids, as if he meant to drop asleep.

"Master Heathcliff," I resumed, "have you forgotten all Catherine's kindness to you, last winter, when you affirmed you loved her, and when she brought you books, and sung you songs, and came many a time through wind and snow to see you? She wept to miss one evening, because you would be disappointed; and you felt then, that she was a hundred times too good to you; and now you believe the lies your father tells, though you know he detests you both! And you join him against her. That's fine gratitude, is it not?"

The corner of Linton's mouth fell, and he took the sugar-candy from his lips.

"Did she come to Wuthering Heights, because she hated you?" I continued. "Think for yourself! As to your money, she does not even know that you will have any. And you say she's sick; and yet, you leave her alone, up there in a strange house! *You*, who have felt what it is to be so neglected! You could pity your own sufferings, and she pitied them, too, but you won't pity hers! I shed tears, Master Heathcliff, you see—an elderly woman, and a servant merely —and you, after pretending such affection, and having reason to worship her almost, store every tear you have for yourself, and lie there quite at ease. Ah! you're a heartless, selfish boy!"

"I can't stay with her," he answered crossly. "I'll not stay, by myself. She cries so I can't bear it. And she won't give over, though

I say I'll call my father. I did call him once; and he threatened to strangle her, if she was not quiet, but she began again, the instant he left the room; moaning and grieving, all night long, though I screamed for vexation that I couldn't sleep."

"Is Mr. Heathcliff out?" I inquired, perceiving that the wretched creature had no power to sympathise with his cousin's mental tortures.

"He's in the court," he replied, "talking to Doctor Kenneth, who says uncle is dying, truly, at last. I'm glad, for I shall be master of the Grange after him—and Catherine always spoke of it as *her* house. It isn't hers! It's mine—papa says everything she has is mine. All her nice books are mine; she offered to give me them, and her pretty birds, and her pony Minny, if I would get the key of our room, and let her out; but I told her she had nothing to give, they were all, all mine. And then she cried, and took a little picture from her neck, and said I should have that—two pictures in a gold case, on one side her mother, and on the other, uncle, when they were young. That was yesterday—I said *they* were mine, too; and tried to get them from her. The spiteful thing wouldn't let me; she pushed me off, and hurt me. I shrieked out—that frightens her —she heard papa coming, and she broke the hinges, and divided the case and gave me her mother's portrait; the other she attempted to hide; but papa asked what was the matter and I explained it. He took the one I had away; and ordered her to resign hers to me; she refused, and he—he struck her down, and wrenched it off the chain, and crushed it with his foot."

"And were you pleased to see her struck?" I asked, having my designs in encouraging his talk.

"I winked," he answered. "I wink to see my father strike a dog, or a horse, he does it so hard. Yet I was glad at first—she deserved punishing for pushing me: but when papa was gone, she made me come to the window and showed me her cheek cut on the inside, against her teeth, and her mouth filling with blood; and then she gathered up the bits of the picture, and went and sat down with her face to the wall, and she has never spoken to me since, and I sometimes think she can't speak for pain. I don't like to think so! but she's a naughty thing for crying continually; and she looks so pale and wild, I'm afraid of her!"

"And you can get the key if you choose?" I said.

"Yes, when I am upstairs," he answered; "but I can't walk upstairs now."

"In what apartment is it?" I asked.

"Oh," he cried, "I shan't tell *you* where it is! It is our secret. Nobody, neither Hareton, nor Zillah are to know. There! you've tired me—go away, go away!" And he turned his face onto his arm, and shut his eyes, again.

I considered it best to depart without seeing Mr. Heathcliff; and bring a rescue for my young lady, from the Grange.

On reaching it, the astonishment of my fellow servants to see me, and their joy also, was intense; and when they heard that their little mistress was safe, two or three were about to hurry up, and shout the news at Mr. Edgar's door: but I bespoke the announcement of it, myself.

How changed I found him, even in those few days! He lay an image of sadness, and resignation, waiting his death. Very young he looked: though his actual age was thirty-nine, one would have called him ten years younger, at least. He thought of Catherine, for he murmured her name. I touched his hand, and spoke.

"Catherine is coming, dear master!" I whispered; "she is alive, and well; and will be here I hope to-night."

I trembled at the first effects of this intelligence: he half rose up, looked eagerly round the apartment, and then sunk back in a swoon.

As soon as he recovered, I related our compulsory visit, and detention at the Heights. I said Heathcliff forced me to go in, which was not quite true; I uttered as little as possible against Linton; nor did I describe all his father's brutal conduct, my intentions being to add no bitterness, if I could help it, to his already overflowing cup.

He divined that one of his enemy's purposes was to secure the personal property, as well as the estate, to his son, or rather himself; yet why he did not wait till his decease, was a puzzle to my master, because ignorant how nearly he and his nephew would quit the world together.

However, he felt his will had better be altered. Instead of leaving Catherine's fortune at her own disposal, he determined to put it in the hands of trustees, for her use during life, and for her children, if she had any, after her. By that means, it could not fall to Mr. Heathcliff should Linton die.

Having received his orders, I despatched a man to fetch the attorney, and four more, provided with serviceable weapons, to demand my young lady of her jailer. Both parties were delayed very late. The single servant returned first.

He said Mr. Green, the lawyer, was out when he arrived at his house, and he had to wait two hours for his re-entrance: and then Mr. Green told him he had a little business in the village that must be done, but he would be at Thrushcross Grange before morning.

The four men came back unaccompanied, also. They brought word that Catherine was ill, too ill to quit her room, and Heathcliff would not suffer them to see her.

I scolded the stupid fellows well, for listening to that tale, which I would not carry to my master; resolving to take a whole bevy up to the Heights, at daylight, and storm it, literally, unless the prisoner were quietly surrendered to us.

Her father *shall* see her, I vowed, and vowed again, if that devil be killed on his own doorstones in trying to prevent it!

Happily, I was spared the journey, and the trouble.

I had gone downstairs at three o'clock to fetch a jug of water; and was passing through the hall with it in my hand, when a sharp knock at the front door made me jump.

"Oh! it is Green," I said, recollecting myself, "—only Green," and I went on, intending to send somebody else to open it; but the knock was repeated, not loud, and still importunately.

I put the jug on the banister, and hastened to admit him myself. The harvest moon shone clear outside. It was not the attorney. My own sweet little mistress sprung on my neck sobbing—

"Ellen! Ellen! Is papa alive?"

"Yes!" I cried, "yes, my angel, he is! God be thanked, you are safe with us again!"

She wanted to run, breathless as she was, upstairs to Mr. Linton's room; but I compelled her to sit down on a chair, and made her drink, and washed her pale face, chafing it into a faint colour with my apron. Then I said I must go first, and tell of her arrival; imploring her to say, she should be happy with young Heathcliff. She stared, but soon comprehending why I counselled her to utter the falsehood, she assured me she would not complain.

I couldn't abide to be present at their meeting. I stood outside the chamber-door a quarter of an hour, and hardly ventured near the bed, then.

All was composed, however; Catherine's despair was as silent as her father's joy. She supported him calmly, in appearance; and he fixed on her features his raised eyes, that seemed dilating with ecstasy.

He died blissfully, Mr. Lockwood; he died so. Kissing her cheek, he murmured—

"I am going to her, and you, darling child, shall come to us"; and never stirred or spoke again, but continued that rapt, radiant gaze, till his pulse imperceptibly stopped, and his soul departed. None could have noticed the exact minute of his death, it was so entirely without a struggle.

Whether Catherine had spent her tears, or whether the grief were too weighty to let them flow, she sat there dry-eyed till the sun rose; she sat till noon, and would still have remained, brooding over that death-bed, but I insisted on her coming away, and taking some repose.

It was well I succeeded in removing her, for at dinner-time appeared the lawyer, having called at Wuthering Heights to get his instructions how to behave. He had sold himself to Mr. Heathcliff, and that was the cause of his delay in obeying my master's summons. Fortunately, no thought of worldly affairs crossed the latter's mind, to disturb him, after his daughter's arrival.

Mr. Green took upon himself to order everything and everybody about the place. He gave all the servants but me, notice to quit. He would have carried his delegated authority to the point of insisting that Edgar Linton should not be buried beside his wife, but in the chapel, with his family. There was the will, however, to hinder that, and my loud protestations against any infringement of its directions.

The funeral was hurried over; Catherine, Mrs. Linton Heathcliff now, was suffered to stay at the Grange, till her father's corpse had quitted it.

She told me that her anguish had at last spurred Linton to incur the risk of liberating her. She heard the men I sent, disputing at the door, and she gathered the sense of Heathcliff's answer. It drove her desperate. Linton, who had been conveyed up to the little parlour soon after I left, was terrified into fetching the key before his father re-ascended.

He had the cunning to unlock, and re-lock the door, without shutting it; and when he should have gone to bed, he begged to sleep with Hareton, and his petition was granted, for once.

Catherine stole out before break of day. She dare not try the doors, lest the dogs should raise an alarm; she visited the empty chambers, and examined their windows; and, luckily, lighting on her mother's, she got easily out of its lattice, and onto the ground, by means of the fir tree, close by. Her accomplice suffered for his share in the escape, notwithstanding his timid contrivances.

## Chapter XXIX

The evening after the funeral, my young lady and I were seated in the library; now musing mournfully, one of us despairingly, on our loss, now venturing conjectures as to the gloomy future.

We had just agreed the best destiny which could await Catherine, would be a permission to continue resident at the Grange, at least during Linton's life: he being allowed to join her there, and I to remain as housekeeper. That seemed rather too favourable an arrangement to be hoped for, and yet I did hope, and began to cheer up under the prospect of retaining my home, and my employment, and, above all, my beloved young mistress, when a servant—one of the discarded ones, not yet departed—rushed hastily in, and said, "that devil Heathcliff" was coming through the court: should he fasten the door in his face?

If we had been mad enough to order that proceeding, we had not time. He made no ceremony of knocking, or announcing his name; he was master, and availed himself of the master's privilege to walk straight in, without saying a word.

The sound of our informant's voice directed him to the library; he entered, and motioning him out, shut the door.

It was the same room into which he had been ushered, as a guest, eighteen years before: the same moon shone through the window; and the same autumn landscape lay outside. We had not yet lighted a candle, but all the apartment was visible, even to the portraits on the wall—the splendid head of Mrs. Linton, and the graceful one of her husband.

Heathcliff advanced to the hearth. Time had little altered his person either. There was the same man, his dark face rather sallower, and more composed, his frame a stone or two heavier, perhaps, and no other difference.

Catherine had risen with an impulse to dash out, when she saw him.

"Stop!" he said, arresting her by the arm. "No more runnings away! Where would you go? I'm come to fetch you home; and I hope you'll be a dutiful daughter, and not encourage my son to further disobedience. I was embarrassed how to punish him, when I discovered his part in the business—he's such a cobweb, a pinch would annihilate him—but you'll see by his look that he has received his due! I brought him down one evening, the day before yesterday, and just set him in a chair, and never touched him afterwards. I sent Hareton out, and we had the room to ourselves. In two hours, I called Joseph to carry him up again; and, since then, my presence is as potent on his nerves as a ghost; and I fancy he sees me often, though I am not near. Hareton says he wakes and shrieks in the night by the hour together; and calls you to protect him from me; and, whether you like your precious mate or not, you must come—he's your concern now; I yield all my interest in him to you."

"Why not let Catherine continue here?" I pleaded, "and send Master Linton to her. As you hate them both, you'd not miss them; they *can* only be a daily plague to your unnatural heart."

"I'm seeking a tenant for the Grange," he answered; "and I want my children about me, to be sure—besides, that lass owes me her services for her bread; I'm not going to nurture her in luxury and idleness after Linton is gone. Make haste and get ready now. And don't oblige me to compel you."

"I shall," said Catherine. "Linton is all I have to love in the world, and, though you have done what you could to make him hateful to me, and me to him, you *cannot* make us hate each other! and I defy you to hurt him when I am by, and I defy you to frighten me."

"You are a boastful champion!" replied Heathcliff; "but I don't like you well enough to hurt him: you shall get the full benefit of the torment, as long as it lasts. It is not I who will make him hateful to you—it is his own sweet spirit. He's as bitter as gall at your desertion, and its consequences; don't expect thanks for this noble devotion. I heard him draw a pleasant picture to Zillah of what he would do, if he were as strong as I. The inclination is there, and his very weakness will sharpen his wits to find a substitute for strength."

"I know he has a bad nature," said Catherine; "he's your son. But I'm glad I've a better, to forgive it; and I know he loves me and for that reason I love him. Mr. Heathcliff, *you* have *nobody* to love you; and, however miserable you make us, we shall still have the revenge of thinking that your cruelty rises from your greater misery! You *are* miserable, are you not? Lonely, like the devil, and envious like him? *Nobody* loves you—*nobody* will cry for you, when you die! I wouldn't be you!"

Catherine spoke with a kind of dreary triumph: she seemed to have made up her mind to enter into the spirit of her future family, and draw pleasure from the griefs of her enemies.

"You shall be sorry to be yourself presently," said her father-in-law, "if you stand there another minute. Begone, witch, and get your things."

She scornfully withdrew.

In her absence, I began to beg for Zillah's place at the Heights, offering to resign her mine; but he would suffer it on no account. He bid me be silent, and then, for the first time, allowed himself a glance round the room, and a look at the pictures. Having studied Mrs. Linton, he said—

"I shall have that at home. Not because I need it, but—"

He turned abruptly to the fire, and continued, with what, for lack of a better word, I must call a smile—

"I'll tell you what I did yesterday! I got the sexton, who was digging Linton's grave, to remove the earth off her coffin lid, and I opened it. I thought, once, I would have stayed there, when I saw her face again—it is hers yet—he had hard work to stir me; but he said it would change, if the air blew on it, and so I struck one side of the coffin loose, and covered it up—not Linton's side, damn him! I wish he'd been soldered in lead—and I bribed the sexton to pull it away, when I'm laid there, and slide mine out too. I'll have it made so, and then, by the time Linton gets to us, he'll not know which is which!"

"You were very wicked, Mr. Heathcliff!" I exclaimed; "were you not ashamed to disturb the dead?"

"I disturbed nobody, Nelly," he replied; "and I gave some ease to myself. I shall be a great deal more comfortable now; and you'll have a better chance of keeping me underground, when I get there. Disturbed her? No! she has disturbed me, night and day, through eighteen years—incessantly—remorselessly—till yesternight; and yesternight, I was tranquil. I dreamt I was sleeping the last sleep, by that sleeper, with my heart stopped, and my cheek frozen against hers."

"And if she had been dissolved into earth, or worse, what would you have dreamt of then?" I said.

"Of dissolving with her, and being more happy still!" he answered. "Do you suppose I dread any change of that sort? I expected such a transformation on raising the lid, but I'm better pleased that it should not commence till I share it. Besides, unless I had received a distinct impression of her passionless features, that strange feeling would hardly have been removed. It began oddly. You know, I was wild after she died, and eternally, from dawn to dawn, praying her to return to me—her spirit. I have a strong faith in ghosts; I have a conviction that they can, and do exist, among us!

"The day she was buried there came a fall of snow. In the evening I went to the churchyard. It blew bleak as winter—all round was solitary: I didn't fear that her fool of a husband would wander up the den so late; and no one else had business to bring them there.

"Being alone, and conscious two yards of loose earth was the sole barrier between us, I said to myself—

" 'I'll have her in my arms again! If she be cold, I'll think it is this north wind that chills *me*; and if she be motionless, it is sleep.'

"I got a spade from the toolhouse, and began to delve with all my might—it scraped the coffin; I fell to work with my hands; the wood commenced cracking about the screws, I was on the point of attaining my object, when it seemed that I heard a sigh from some one above, close at the edge of the grave, and bending down. 'If I can only get this off,' I muttered, 'I wish they may shovel in the earth over us both!' and I wrenched at it more desperately still. There was another sigh, close at my ear. I appeared to feel the warm breath of it displacing the sleet-laden wind. I knew no living thing in flesh and blood was by; but as certainly as you perceive the approach to some substantial body in the dark, though it cannot be discerned, so certainly I felt that Cathy was there, not under me, but on the earth.

"A sudden sense of relief flowed from my heart through every limb. I relinquished my labour of agony, and turned consoled at once, unspeakably consoled. Her presence was with me; it remained while I re-filled the grave, and led me home. You may laugh, if you will, but I was sure I should see her there. I was sure she was with me, and I could not help talking to her.

"Having reached the Heights, I rushed eagerly to the door. It was fastened; and, I remember, that accursed Earnshaw and my wife opposed my entrance. I remember stopping to kick the breath out of him, and then hurrying upstairs, to my room, and hers. I looked round impatiently—I felt her by me—I could *almost* see her, and yet I *could not!* I ought to have sweat blood then, from the anguish of my yearning, from the fervour of my supplications to have but one glimpse! I had not one. She showed herself, as she often was in life, a devil to me! And, since then, sometimes more, and sometimes less, I've been the sport of that intolerable torture! Infernal—keeping my nerves at such a stretch, that, if they had not resembled catgut, they would, long ago, have relaxed to the feebleness of Linton's.

"When I sat in the house with Hareton, it seemed that on going out, I should meet her; when I walked on the moors I should meet her coming in. When I went from home, I hastened to return; she *must* be somewhere at the Heights, I was certain! And when I slept in her chamber—I was beaten out of that—I couldn't lie there; for the moment I closed my eyes, she was either outside the window, or sliding back the panels, or entering the room, or even resting her darling head on the same pillow as she did when a child. And I must open my lids to see. And so I opened and closed them a hundred times a night—to be always disappointed! It racked me! I've often groaned aloud, till that old rascal Joseph no doubt believed that my conscience was playing the fiend inside of me.

"Now since I've seen her, I'm pacified—a little. It was a strange way of killing, not by inches, but by fractions of hair-breadths, to beguile me with the spectre of a hope, through eighteen years!"

Mr. Heathcliff paused and wiped his forehead. His hair clung to it, wet with perspiration; his eyes were fixed on the red embers of the fire; the brows not contracted, but raised next the temples, diminishing the grim aspect of his countenance, but imparting a peculiar look of trouble, and a painful appearance of mental tension towards one absorbing subject. He only half addressed me, and I maintained silence—I didn't like to hear him talk!

After a short period, he resumed his meditation on the picture, took it down, and leant it against the sofa to contemplate it at better advantage; and while so occupied Catherine entered, announcing that she was ready, when her pony should be saddled.

"Send that over to-morrow," said Heathcliff to me, then turning to her he added, "You may do without your pony; it is a fine evening, and you'll need no ponies at Wuthering Heights, for what journeys you take, your own feet will serve you—Come along."

"Good-bye, Ellen!" whispered my dear little mistress. As she kissed me, her lips felt like ice. "Come and see me, Ellen, don't forget."

"Take care you do no such thing, Mrs. Dean!" said her new father. "When I wish to speak to you I'll come here. I want none of your prying at my house!"

He signed her to precede him; and casting back a look that cut my heart, she obeyed.

I watched them from the window walk down the garden. Heathcliff fixed Catherine's arm under his, though she disputed the act, at first, evidently, and with rapid strides, he hurried her into the alley, whose trees concealed them.

## Chapter XXX

I have paid a visit to the Heights, but I have not seen her since she left; Joseph held the door in his hand, when I called to ask after her, and wouldn't let me pass. He said Mrs. Linton was "thrang,"[1] and the master was not in. Zillah has told me something of the way they go on, otherwise I should hardly know who was dead, and who living.

She thinks Catherine haughty, and does not like her, I can guess by her talk. My young lady asked some aid of her, when she first came, but Mr. Heathcliff told her to follow her own business, and let his daughter-in-law look after herself, and Zillah willingly acquiesced, being a narrow-minded, selfish woman. Catherine evinced a child's annoyance at this neglect; repaid it with contempt, and thus enlisted my informant among her enemies, as securely as if she had done her some great wrong.

I had a long talk with Zillah, about six weeks ago, a little before you came, one day when we foregathered on the moor; and this is what she told me.

"The first thing Mrs. Linton did," she said, "on her arrival at the Heights, was to run upstairs without even wishing good-evening to me and Joseph; she shut herself into Linton's room, and remained till morning. Then, while the master and Earnshaw were at breakfast, she entered the house and asked all in a quiver if the doctor might be sent for? her cousin was very ill."

" 'We know that!' answered Heathcliff, 'but his life is not worth

1. Busy.

a farthing, and I won't spend a farthing on him.'

" 'But I cannot tell how to do,' she said, 'and if nobody will help me, he'll die!'

" 'Walk out of the room!' cried the master, 'and let me never hear a word more about him! None here care what becomes of him; if you do, act the nurse; if you do not, lock him up and leave him.'

"Then she began to bother me, and I said I'd had enough plague with the tiresome thing; we each had our tasks, and hers was to wait on Linton; Mr. Heathcliff bid me leave that labour to her.

"How they managed together, I can't tell. I fancy he fretted a great deal, and moaned hisseln,[2] night and day; and she had precious little rest, one could guess by her white face, and heavy eyes. She sometimes came into the kitchen all wildered like, and looked as if she would fain beg assistance: but I was not going to disobey the master. I never dare disobey him, Mrs. Dean, and though I thought it wrong that Kenneth should not be sent for, it was no concern of mine, either to advise or complain; and I always refused to meddle.

"Once or twice, after we had gone to bed, I've happened to open my door again, and seen her sitting crying, on the stairs' top; and then I've shut myself in, quick, for fear of being moved to interfere. I did pity her then, I'm sure; still, I didn't wish to lose my place, you know!

"At last, one night she came boldly into my chamber, and frightened me out of my wits, by saying—

" 'Tell Mr. Heathcliff that his son is dying—I'm sure he is, this time. Get up, instantly, and tell him!'

"Having uttered this speech, she vanished again. I lay a quarter of an hour listening and trembling. Nothing stirred—the house was quiet.

" 'She's mistaken,' I said to myself. 'He's got over it. I needn't disturb them.' And I began to doze. But my sleep was marred a second time, by a sharp ringing of the bell—the only bell we have, put up on purpose for Linton; and the master called to me, to see what was the matter, and inform them that he wouldn't have that noise repeated.

"I delivered Catherine's message. He cursed to himself, and in a few minutes, came out with a lighted candle, and proceeded to their room. I followed. Mrs. Heathcliff was seated by the bedside, with her hands folded on her knees. Her father-in-law went up, held the light to Linton's face, looked at him, and touched him; afterwards he turned to her.

" 'Now—Catherine,' he said, 'how do you feel?'

2. Himself.

"She was dumb.

" 'How do you feel, Catherine?' he repeated.

" 'He's safe, and I'm free,' she answered, 'I should feel well—but,' she continued with a bitterness she couldn't conceal, 'you have left me so long to struggle against death, alone, that I feel and see only death! I feel like death!'

"And she looked like it, too! I gave her a little wine. Hareton and Joseph, who had been wakened by the ringing and the sound of feet, and heard our talk from outside, now entered. Joseph was fain, I believe, of the lad's removal: Hareton seemed a thought bothered, though he was more taken up with staring at Catherine than thinking of Linton. But the master bid him get off to bed again—we didn't want his help. He afterwards made Joseph remove the body to his chamber, and told me to return to mine, and Mrs. Heathcliff remained by herself.

"In the morning, he sent me to tell her she must come down to breakfast. She had undressed, and appeared going to sleep, and said she was ill; at which I hardly wondered. I informed Mr. Heathcliff, and he replied—

" 'Well, let her be till after the funeral; and go up now and then to get her what is needful; and as soon as she seems better, tell me.'

Cathy stayed upstairs a fortnight, according to Zillah, who visited her twice a day, and would have been rather more friendly, but her attempts at increasing kindness were proudly and promptly repelled.

Heathcliff went up once, to show her Linton's will. He had bequeathed the whole of his, and what had been her, moveable property to his father. The poor creature was threatened, or coaxed, into that act during her week's absence, when his uncle died. The lands, being a minor, he could not meddle with. However, Mr. Heathcliff has claimed and kept them in his wife's right, and his also, I suppose legally. At any rate Catherine, destitute of cash and friends, cannot disturb his possession.

"Nobody," said Zillah, "ever approached her door, except that once, but I; and nobody asked anything about her. The first occasion of her coming down into the house, was on a Sunday afternoon.

"She had cried out, when I carried up her dinner, that she couldn't bear any longer being in the cold; and I told her the master was going to Thrushcross Grange; and Earnshaw and I needn't hinder her from descending; so, as soon as she heard Heathcliff's horse trot off, she made her appearance, donned in black, and her yellow curls combed back behind her ears, as plain as a Quaker; she couldn't comb them out.

"Joseph and I generally go to chapel on Sundays," (the Kirk, you know, has no minister now, explained Mrs. Dean, and they call the Methodists' or Baptists' place, I can't say which it is, at Gimmerton, a chapel). "Joseph had gone," she continued, "but I thought proper to bide at home. Young folks are always the better for an elder's over-looking, and Hareton, with all his bashfulness, isn't a model of nice behaviour. I let him know that his cousin would very likely sit with us, and she had been always used to see the Sabbath respected, so he had as good leave his guns and bits of in-door work alone, while she stayed.

"He coloured up at the news, and cast his eyes over his hands and clothes. The train-oil[3] and gunpowder were shoved out of sight in a minute. I saw he meant to give her his company; and I guessed, by his way, he wanted to be presentable; so, laughing, as I durst not laugh when the master is by, I offered to help him, if he would, and joked at his confusion. He grew sullen, and began to swear.

"Now, Mrs. Dean," she went on, seeing me not pleased by her manner, "you happen think your young lady too fine for Mr. Hareton, and happen you're right; but, I own, I should love well to bring her pride a peg lower. And what will all her learning and her daintiness do for her, now? She's as poor as you or I—poorer, I'll be bound; you're saving, and I'm doing my little all, that road."[4]

Hareton allowed Zillah to give him her aid; and she flattered him into a good humour; so, when Catherine came, half forgetting her former insults, he tried to make himself agreeable, by the house-keeper's account.

"Missis walked in," she said, "as chill as an icicle, and as high as a princess. I got up and offered her my seat in the arm-chair. No, she turned up her nose at my civility. Earnshaw rose too, and bid her come to the settle, and sit close by the fire; he was sure she was starved.

" 'I've been starved a month and more,' she answered, resting on the word, as scornful as she could.

"And she got a chair for herself, and placed it at a distance from both of us.

"Having sat till she was warm, she began to look round, and discovered a number of books in the dresser; she was instantly upon her feet again, stretching to reach them, but they were too high up.

"Her cousin, after watching her endeavours a while, at last summoned courage to help her; she held her frock, and he filled it with the first that came to hand.

"That was a great advance for the lad. She didn't thank him; still, he felt gratified that she had accepted his assistance, and ventured to stand behind as she examined them, and even to stoop and point out what struck his fancy in certain old pictures which they contained; nor was he daunted by the saucy style in which she jerked

3. Oil from whales or seals.          4. That way.

the page from his finger; he contented himself with going a bit farther back, and looking at her instead of the book.

"She continued reading, or seeking for something to read. His attention became, by degrees, quite centred in the study of her thick, silky curls; her face he couldn't see, and she couldn't see him. And, perhaps, not quite awake to what he did, but attracted like a child to a candle, at last he proceeded from staring to touching; he put out his hand and stroked one curl, as gently as if it were a bird. He might have stuck a knife into her neck, she started round in such a taking.

" 'Get away, this moment! How dare you touch me? Why are you stopping there?' she cried, in a tone of disgust. 'I can't endure you! I'll go up stairs again, if you come near me.'

"Mr. Hareton recoiled, looking as foolish as he could do; he sat down in the settle, very quiet, and she continued turning over her volumes, another half hour; finally, Earnshaw crossed over, and whispered to me—

" 'Will you ask her to read to us, Zillah? I'm stalled of doing naught; and I do like—I could like to hear her! Dunnot say I wanted it, but ask of yourseln.'

" 'Mr. Hareton wishes you would read to us, ma'am,' I said, immediately. 'He'd take it very kind—he'd be much obliged.'

"She frowned; and, looking up, answered—

" 'Mr. Hareton, and the whole set of you, will be good enough to understand that I reject any pretence at kindness you have the hypocrisy to offer! I despise you, and will have nothing to say to any of you! When I would have given my life for one kind word, even to see one of your faces, you all kept off. But I won't complain to you! I'm driven down here by the cold, not either to amuse you, or enjoy your society.'

" 'What could I ha' done?' began Earnshaw. 'How was I to blame?'

" 'Oh! you are an exception,' answered Mrs. Heathcliff. 'I never missed such a concern as you.'

" 'But I offered more than once, and asked,' he said, kindling up at her pertness, 'I asked Mr. Heathcliff to let me wake for[5] you—'

" 'Be silent! I'll go out of doors, or anywhere, rather than have your disagreeable voice in my ear!' said my lady.

"Hareton muttered, she might go to hell, for him! and unslinging his gun, restrained himself from his Sunday occupations no longer.

"He talked now, freely enough; and she presently saw fit to retreat to her solitude: but the frost had set in, and, in spite of her pride, she was forced to condescend to our company, more and

5. Watch, guard.

more. However, I took care there should be no further scorning at my good nature. Ever since, I've been as stiff as herself; and she has no lover, or liker among us—and she does not deserve one—for, let them say the least word to her, and she'll curl back without respect of any one! She'll snap at the master himself, and as good as dares him to thrash her; and the more hurt she gets, the more venomous she grows."

At first, on hearing this account from Zillah, I determined to leave my situation, take a cottage, and get Catherine to come and live with me; but Mr. Heathcliff would as soon permit that, as he would set up Hareton in an independent house; and I can see no remedy, at present, unless she could marry again; and that scheme, it does not come within my province to arrange.

Thus ended Mrs. Dean's story. Notwithstanding the doctor's prophecy, I am rapidly recovering strength, and, though it be only the second week in January, I propose getting out on horseback, in a day or two, and riding over to Wuthering Heights, to inform my landlord that I shall spend the next six months in London; and, if he likes, he may look out for another tenant to take the place, after October—I would not pass another winter here, for much.

## Chapter XXXI

Yesterday was bright, calm, and frosty. I went to the Heights as I proposed; my housekeeper entreated me to bear a little note from her to her young lady, and I did not refuse, for the worthy woman was not conscious of anything odd in her request.

The front door stood open, but the jealous gate was fastened, as at my last visit; I knocked and invoked Earnshaw from among the garden beds; he unchained it, and I entered. The fellow is as handsome a rustic as need be seen. I took particular notice of him this time; but then he does his best, apparently, to make the least of his advantages.

I asked if Mr. Heathcliff were at home? He answered, no; but he would be in at dinner-time. It was eleven o'clock, and I announced my intention of going in, and waiting for him, at which he immediately flung down his tools and accompanied me, in the office of watchdog, not as a substitute for the host.

We entered together; Catherine was there, making herself useful in preparing some vegetables for the approaching meal; she looked more sulky, and less spirited than when I had seen her first. She hardly raised her eyes to notice me, and continued her employment with the same disregard to common forms of politeness, as before; never returning my bow and good morning by the slightest acknowledgment.

"She does not seem so amiable," I thought, "as Mrs. Dean would persuade me to believe. She's a beauty, it is true; but not an angel."

Earnshaw surlily bid her remove her things to the kitchen.

"Remove them yourself," she said, pushing them from her, as soon as she had done, and retiring to a stool by the window, where she began to carve figures of birds and beasts, out of the turnip parings in her lap.

I approached her, pretending to desire a view of the garden; and, as I fancied, adroitly dropped Mrs. Dean's note onto her knee, unnoticed by Hareton—but she asked aloud—

"What is that?" And chucked it off.

"A letter from your old acquaintance, the housekeeper at the Grange," I answered, annoyed at her exposing my kind deed, and fearful lest it should be imagined a missive of my own.

She would gladly have gathered it up at this information, but Hareton beat her; he seized, and put it in his waistcoat, saying Mr. Heathcliff should look at it first.

Thereat, Catherine silently turned her face from us, and, very stealthily, drew out her pocket-handkerchief and applied it to her eyes; and her cousin, after struggling a while to keep down his softer feelings, pulled out the letter and flung it on the floor beside her as ungraciously as he could.

Catherine caught and perused it eagerly; then she put a few questions to me concerning the inmates, rational and irrational, of her former home; and gazing towards the hills, murmured in soliloquy—

"I should like to be riding Minny down there! I should like to be climbing up there—Oh! I'm tired—I'm *stalled*, Hareton!"

And she leant her pretty head back against the sill, with half a yawn and half a sigh, and lapsed into an aspect of abstracted sadness, neither caring nor knowing whether we remarked her.

"Mrs. Heathcliff," I said, after sitting some time mute, "you are not aware that I am an acquaintance of yours? so intimate, that I think it strange you won't come and speak to me. My housekeeper never wearies of talking about and praising you; and she'll be greatly disappointed if I return with no news of, or from you, except that you received her letter, and said nothing!"

She appeared to wonder at this speech and asked—

"Does Ellen like you?"

"Yes, very well," I replied unhesitatingly.

"You must tell her," she continued, "that I would answer her letter, but I have no materials for writing, not even a book from which I might tear a leaf."

"No books!" I exclaimed. "How do you contrive to live here

without them, if I may take the liberty to inquire? Though provided with a large library, I'm frequently very dull at the Grange; take my books away, and I should be desperate!"

"I was always reading, when I had them," said Catherine, "and Mr. Heathcliff never reads; so he took it into his head to destroy my books. I have not had a glimpse of one, for weeks. Only once, I searched through Joseph's store of theology, to his great irritation; and once, Hareton, I came upon a secret stock in your room— some Latin and Greek, and some tales and poetry; all old friends. I brought the last here—and you gathered them, as a magpie gathers silver spoons, for the mere love of stealing! They are of no use to you; or else you concealed them in the bad spirit, that as you cannot enjoy them, nobody else shall. Perhaps *your* envy counselled Mr. Heathcliff to rob me of my treasures? But I've most of them written on my brain and printed in my heart, and you cannot deprive me of those!"

Earnshaw blushed crimson, when his cousin made this revelation of his private literary accumulations, and stammered an indignant denial of her accusations.

"Mr. Hareton is desirous of increasing his amount of knowledge," I said, coming to his rescue. "He is not *envious* but *emulous* of your attainments. He'll be a clever scholar in a few years!"

"And he wants *me* to sink into a dunce, meantime," answered Catherine. "Yes, I hear him trying to spell and read to himself, and pretty blunders he makes! I wish you would repeat Chevy Chase, as you did yesterday; it was extremely funny! I heard you—and I heard you turning over the dictionary, to seek out the hard words, and then cursing, because you couldn't read their explanations!"

The young man evidently thought it too bad that he should be laughed at for his ignorance, and then laughed at for trying to remove it. I had a similar notion, and, remembering Mrs. Dean's anecdote of his first attempt at enlightening the darkness in which he had been reared, I observed—

"But, Mrs. Heathcliff, we have each had a commencement, and each stumbled and tottered on the threshold, and had our teachers scorned, instead of aiding us, we should stumble and totter yet."

"Oh!" she replied, "I don't wish to limit his acquirements. Still, he has no right to appropriate what is mine, and make it ridiculous to me with his vile mistakes and mis-pronunciations! Those books, both prose and verse, were consecrated to me by other associations, and I hate to have them debased and profaned in his mouth! Besides, of all, he has selected my favourite pieces that I love the most to repeat, as if out of deliberate malice!"

Hareton's chest heaved in silence a minute; he laboured under a severe sense of mortification and wrath, which it was no easy task to suppress.

I rose, and, from a gentlemanly idea of relieving his embarrassment, took up my station in the door-way, surveying the external prospect, as I stood.

He followed my example, and left the room, but presently reappeared, bearing half-a-dozen volumes in his hands, which he threw into Catherine's lap, exclaiming—

"Take them! I never want to hear, or read, or think of them again!"

"I won't have them, now!" she answered. "I shall connect them with you, and hate them."

She opened one that had obviously been often turned over, and read a portion in the drawling tone of a beginner; then laughed, and threw it from her.

"And listen!" she continued provokingly, commencing a verse of an old ballad in the same fashion.

But his self-love would endure no further torment. I heard, and not altogether disapprovingly, a manual check given to her saucy tongue. The little wretch had done her utmost to hurt her cousin's sensitive though uncultivated feelings, and a physical argument was the only mode he had of balancing the account and repaying its effects on the inflicter.

He afterwards gathered the books and hurled them on the fire. I read in his countenance what anguish it was to offer that sacrifice to spleen. I fancied that as they consumed, he recalled the pleasure they had already imparted, and the triumph and ever increasing pleasure he had anticipated from them; and, I fancied, I guessed the incitement to his secret studies, also. He had been content with daily labour and rough animal enjoyments, till Catherine crossed his path. Shame at her scorn, and hope of her approval were his first prompters to higher pursuits; and instead of guarding him from one, and winning him the other, his endeavours to raise himself had produced just the contrary result.

"Yes, that's all the good that such a brute as you can get from them!" cried Catherine, sucking her damaged lip, and watching the conflagration with indignant eyes.

"You'd *better* hold your tongue, now!" he answered fiercely.

And his agitation precluding further speech, he advanced hastily to the entrance, where I made way for him to pass. But, ere he had crossed the door-stones, Mr. Heathcliff, coming up the causeway, encountered him and laying hold of his shoulder, asked—

"What's to do now, my lad?"

"Naught, naught!" he said, and broke away, to enjoy his grief and anger in solitude.

Heathcliff gazed after him, and sighed.

"It will be odd, if I thwart myself!" he muttered, unconscious that I was behind him. "But, when I look for his father in his face, I find *her* every day more! How the devil is he so like? I can hardly bear to see him."

He bent his eyes to the ground, and walked moodily in. There was a restless, anxious expression in his countenance I had never remarked there before, and he looked sparer in person.

His daughter-in-law, on perceiving him through the window, immediately escaped to the kitchen, so that I remained alone.

"I'm glad to see you out of doors again, Mr. Lockwood," he said in reply to my greeting, "from selfish motives partly; I don't think I could readily supply your loss in this desolation. I've wondered, more than once, what brought you here."

"An idle whim, I fear, sir," was my answer, "or else an idle whim is going to spirit me away. I shall set out for London next week, and I must give you warning, that I feel no disposition to retain Thrushcross Grange, beyond the twelvemonths I agreed to rent it. I believe I shall not live there any more."

"Oh, indeed! you're tired of being banished from the world, are you?" he said. "But, if you be coming to plead off paying for a place you won't occupy, your journey is useless. I never relent in exacting my due, from any one."

"I'm coming to plead off nothing about it!" I exclaimed, considerably irritated. "Should you wish it, I'll settle with you now," and I drew my notebook from my pocket.

"No, no," he replied coolly; "you'll leave sufficient behind, to cover your debts, if you fail to return. I'm not in such a hurry—sit down and take your dinner with us; a guest that is safe from repeating his visit, can generally be made welcome. Catherine! bring the things in—where are you?"

Catherine re-appeared, bearing a tray of knives and forks.

"You may get your dinner with Joseph," muttered Heathcliff aside, "and remain in the kitchen till he is gone."

She obeyed his directions very punctually; perhaps she had no temptation to transgress. Living among clowns and misanthropists, she probably cannot appreciate a better class of people, when she meets them.

With Mr. Heathcliff, grim and saturnine, on one hand, and Hareton, absolutely dumb, on the other, I made a somewhat cheerless meal, and bid adieu early. I would have departed by the back way to get a last glimpse of Catherine, and annoy old Joseph; but Hareton received orders to lead up my horse, and my host himself escorted me to the door, so I could not fulfil my wish.

"How dreary life gets over in that house!" I reflected, while riding down the road. "What a realization of something more romantic than a fairy tale it would have been for Mrs. Linton Heathcliff, had she and I struck up an attachment, as her good nurse desired, and migrated together into the stirring atmosphere of the town!"

## *Chapter XXXII*

1802.—This September, I was invited to devastate the moors of a friend, in the North; and, on my journey to his abode, I unexpectedly came within fifteen miles of Gimmerton. The hostler at a roadside public-house was holding a pail of water to refresh my horses, when a cart of very green oats, newly reaped, passed by, and he remarked—

"Yon's frough Gimmerton, nah! They're allas three wick' after other folk wi' ther harvest."

"Gimmerton?" I repeated—my residence in that locality had already grown dim and dreamy. "Ah! I know! How far is it from this?"

"Happen fourteen mile' o'er th' hills, and a rough road," he answered.

A sudden impulse seized me to visit Thrushcross Grange. It was scarcely noon, and I conceived that I might as well pass the night under my own roof, as in an inn. Besides, I could spare a day easily, to arrange matters with my landlord, and thus save myself the trouble of invading the neighbourhood again.

Having rested a while, I directed my servant to inquire the way to the village; and, with great fatigue to our beasts, we managed the distance in some three hours.

I left him there, and proceeded down the valley alone. The grey church looked greyer, and the lonely churchyard lonelier. I distinguished a moor sheep cropping the short turf on the graves. It was sweet, warm weather—too warm for travelling; but the heat did not hinder me from enjoying the delightful scenery above and below; had I seen it nearer August, I'm sure it would have tempted me to waste a month among its solitudes. In winter, nothing more dreary, in summer, nothing more divine, than those glens shut in by hills, and those bluff, bold swells of heath.

I reached the Grange before sunset, and knocked for admittance; but the family had retreated into the back premises, I judged by one thin, blue wreath curling from the kitchen chimney, and they did not hear.

I rode into the court. Under the porch, a girl of nine or ten sat knitting, and an old woman reclined on the horse-steps, smoking a meditative pipe.

"Is Mrs. Dean within?" I demanded of the dame.

"Mistress Dean? Nay!" she answered, "shoo doesn't bide here;

shoo's up at th' Heights."

"Are you the housekeeper, then?" I continued.

"Eea, Aw keep th' hause," she replied.

"Well, I'm Mr. Lockwood, the master. Are there any rooms to lodge me in, I wonder? I wish to stay here all night."

"'T' maister!" she cried in astonishment. "Whet, whoiver knew yah wur coming? Yah sud ha' send word! They's nowt norther dry, nor mensful[1] abaht t' place—nowt there isn't!"

She threw down her pipe and bustled in, the girl followed, and I entered too; soon perceiving that her report was true, and, moreover, that I had almost upset her wits by my unwelcome apparition.

I bid her be composed—I would go out for a walk; and, meantime, she must try to prepare a corner of a sitting-room for me to sup in, and a bed-room to sleep in. No sweeping and dusting, only good fires and dry sheets were necessary.

She seemed willing to do her best; though she thrust the hearth-brush into the grates in mistake for the poker, and mal-appropriated several other articles of her craft; but I retired, confiding in her energy for a resting-place against my return.

Wuthering Heights was the goal of my proposed excursion. An after-thought brought me back, when I had quitted the court.

"All well at the Heights?" I enquired of the woman.

"Eea, f'r owt Ee knaw!" she answered, skurrying away with a pan of hot cinders.

I would have asked why Mrs. Dean had deserted the Grange; but it was impossible to delay her at such a crisis, so I turned away and made my exit, rambling leisurely along with the glow of a sinking sun behind, and the mild glory of a rising moon in front—one fading, and the other brightening, as I quitted the park, and climbed the stony by-road branching off to Mr. Heathcliff's dwelling.

Before I arrived in sight of it, all that remained of day was a beamless, amber light along the west; but I could see every pebble on the path, and every blade of grass by that splendid moon.

I had neither to climb the gate, nor to knock—it yielded to my hand.

That is an improvement! I thought. And I noticed another, by the aid of my nostrils; a fragrance of stocks and wall flowers, wafted on the air, from amongst the homely fruit trees.

Both doors and lattices were open; and yet, as is usually the case in a coal district, a fine, red fire illumined the chimney; the comfort which the eye derives from it, renders the extra heat endurable. But the house of Wuthering Heights is so large, that the inmates have plenty of space for withdrawing out of its influence; and, accordingly, what inmates there were had stationed themselves not

1. Neither dry nor proper.

far from one of the windows. I could both see them and hear them talk before I entered, and looked and listened in consequence, being moved thereto by a mingled sense of curiosity and envy that grew as I lingered.

"Con-*trary!*" said a voice, as sweet as a silver bell—"That for the third time, you dunce! I'm not going to tell you, again—Recollect, or I pull your hair!"

"Contrary, then," answered another, in deep, but softened tones. "And now, kiss me, for minding so well."

"No, read it over first correctly, without a single mistake."

The male speaker began to read. He was a young man, respectably dressed, and seated at a table, having a book before him. His handsome features glowed with pleasure, and his eyes kept impatiently wandering from the page to a small white hand over his shoulder, which recalled him by a smart slap on the cheek, whenever its owner detected such signs of inattention.

Its owner stood behind; her light shining ringlets blending, at intervals, with his brown locks, as she bent to superintend his studies; and her face—it was lucky he could not see her face, or he would never have been so steady. I could, and I bit my lip, in spite, at having thrown away the chance I might have had of doing something besides staring at its smiting beauty.

The task was done, not free from further blunders, but the pupil claimed a reward, and received at least five kisses, which, however, he generously returned. Then, they came to the door, and from their conversation, I judged they were about to issue out and have a walk on the moors. I supposed I should be condemned in Hareton Earnshaw's heart, if not by his mouth, to the lowest pit in the infernal regions if I showed my unfortunate person in his neighbourhood then, and feeling very mean and malignant, I skulked round to seek refuge in the kitchen.

There was unobstructed admittance on that side also; and, at the door, sat my old friend, Nelly Dean, sewing and singing a song, which was often interrupted from within, by harsh words of scorn and intolerance, uttered in far from musical accents.

"Aw'd rayther, by th' haulf, hev 'em swearing i' my lugs frough morn tuh neeght, nur hearken yah, hahsiver!" said the tenant of the kitchen, in answer to an unheard speech of Nelly's. "It's a blazing shaime, ut Aw cannut oppen t' Blessed Book, bud yah set up them glories tuh Sattan, un' all t' flaysome wickednesses ut iver wer born intuh t' warld! Oh! yah're a raight nowt, un' shoo's another; un' that poor lad 'ull be lost, atween ye. Poor lad!" he added, with a groan; "he's witched, Aw'm sartin on't! O, Lord, judge 'em, for they's norther law nur justice amang wer rullers!"[2]

2. *lugs:* ears; *Sattan:* Satan; *amang wer rullers:* among our rulers.

"No! or we should be sitting in flaming fagots, I suppose," retorted the singer. "But wisht, old man, and read your Bible, like a Christian, and never mind me. This is 'Fairy Annie's Wedding'— a bonny tune—it goes to a dance."

Mrs. Dean was about to recommence, when I advanced, and recognising me directly, she jumped to her feet, crying—

"Why, bless you, Mr. Lockwood! How could you think of returning in this way? All's shut up at Thrushcross Grange. You should have given us notice!"

"I've arranged to be accommodated there, for as long as I shall stay," I answered. "I depart again to-morrow. And how are you transplanted here, Mrs. Dean? tell me that."

"Zillah left, and Mr. Heathcliff wished me to come, soon after you went to London, and stay till you returned. But, step in, pray! Have you walked from Gimmerton this evening?"

"From the Grange," I replied; "and, while they make me lodging room there, I want to finish my business with your master, because I don't think of having another opportunity in a hurry."

"What business, sir?" said Nelly, conducting me into the house. "He's gone out, at present, and won't return soon."

"About the rent," I answered.

"Oh! then it is with Mrs. Heathcliff you must settle," she observed, "or rather with me. She has not learnt to manage her affairs yet, and I act for her; there's nobody else."

I looked surprised.

"Ah! you have not heard of Heathcliff's death, I see!" she continued.

"Heathcliff dead?" I exclaimed, astonished. "How long ago?"

"Three months since—but, sit down, and let me take your hat, and I'll tell you all about it. Stop, you have had nothing to eat, have you?"

"I want nothing. I have ordered supper at home. You sit down too. I never dreamt of his dying! Let me hear how it came to pass. You say you don't expect them back for some time—the young people?"

"No—I have to scold them every evening, for their late rambles, but they don't care for me. At least, have a drink of our old ale; it will do you good—you seem weary."

She hastened to fetch it, before I could refuse, and I heard Joseph asking whether "it warn't a crying scandal that she should have fellies at her time of life? And then, to get them jocks out uh t' Maister's cellar! He fair shaamed to 'bide still and see it."[3]

She did not stay to retaliate, but re-entered, in a minute, bearing a reaming, silver pint, whose contents I lauded with becoming ear-

---

3. *Fellies*: fellows; *jocks*: jugs.

nestness. And afterwards she furnished me with the sequel of Heathcliff's history. He had a "queer" end, as she expressed it.

I was summoned to Wuthering Heights, within a fortnight of
your leaving us, she said; and I obeyed joyfully, for Catherine's sake.

My first interview with her grieved and shocked me! she had
altered so much since our separation. Mr. Heathcliff did not explain
his reasons for taking a new mind about my coming here; he only
told me he wanted me, and he was tired of seeing Catherine; I must
make the little parlour my sitting room, and keep her with me. It
was enough if he were obliged to see her once or twice a day.

She seemed pleased at this arrangement; and, by degrees, I smug-
gled over a great number of books and other articles, that had
formed her amusement at the Grange; and flattered myself we
should get on in tolerable comfort.

The delusion did not last long. Catherine, contented at first, in
a brief space grew irritable and restless. For one thing, she was forbidden to move out of the garden, and it fretted her sadly to be
confined to its narrow bounds, as Spring drew on; for another, in
following the house, I was forced to quit her frequently, and she
complained of loneliness; she preferred quarrelling with Joseph in
the kitchen, to sitting at peace in her solitude.

I did not mind their skirmishes; but Hareton was often obliged
to seek the kitchen also, when the master wanted to have the house
to himself; and, though, in the beginning, she either left it at his
approach, or quietly joined in my occupations, and shunned remarking, or addressing him—and though he was always as sullen
and silent as possible—after a while, she changed her behaviour, and
became incapable of letting him alone: talking at him; comment-
ing on his stupidity and idleness; expressing her wonder how he
could endure the life he lived—how he could sit a whole evening
staring into the fire, and dozing.

"He's just like a dog, is he not, Ellen?" she once observed, "or
a cart-horse? He does his work, eats his food, and sleeps, eternally!
What a blank, dreary mind he must have! Do you ever dream,
Hareton? And, if you do, what is it about? But you can't speak to
me!"

Then she looked at him; but he would neither open his mouth,
nor look again.

"He's perhaps dreaming now," she continued. "He twitched his
shoulder as Juno twitches hers.. Ask him, Ellen."

"Mr. Hareton will ask the master to send you upstairs, if you
don't behave!" I said. He had not only twitched his shoulder, but
clenched his fist, as if tempted to use it.

"I know why Hareton never speaks, when I am in the kitchen," she exclaimed, on another occasion. "He is afraid I shall laugh at him. Ellen, what do you think? He began to teach himself to read once; and, because I laughed, he burned his books, and dropped it—was he not a fool?"

"Were not you naughty?" I said; "answer me that."

"Perhaps I was," she went on, "but I did not expect him to be so silly. Hareton, if I gave you a book, would you take it now? I'll try!"

She placed one she had been perusing on his hand; he flung it off, and muttered, if she did not give over, he would break her neck.

"Well, I shall put it here," she said, "in the table drawer, and I'm going to bed."

Then she whispered me to watch whether he touched it, and departed. But he would not come near it, and so I informed her in the morning, to her great disappointment. I saw she was sorry for his persevering sulkiness and indolence. Her conscience reproved her for frightening him off improving himself; she had done it effectually.

But her ingenuity was at work to remedy the injury; while I ironed, or pursued other stationary employments I could not well do in the parlour, she would bring some pleasant volume, and read it aloud to me. When Hareton was there, she generally paused in an interesting part, and left the book lying about—that she did repeatedly; but he was as obstinate as a mule, and, instead of snatching at her bait, in wet weather he took to smoking with Joseph, and they sat like automatons, one on each side of the fire, the elder happily too deaf to understand her wicked nonsense, as he would have called it, the younger doing his best to seem to disregard it. On fine evenings the latter followed his shooting expeditions, and Catherine yawned and sighed, and teased me to talk to her, and ran off into the court or garden, the moment I began; and, as a last resource, cried and said she was tired of living, her life was useless.

Mr. Heathcliff, who grew more and more disinclined to society, had almost banished Earnshaw out of his apartment. Owing to an accident, at the commencement of March, he became for some days a fixture in the kitchen. His gun burst while out on the hills by himself; a splinter cut his arm, and he lost a good deal of blood before he could reach home. The consequence was, that, perforce, he was condemned to the fire-side and tranquillity, till he made it up again.

It suited Catherine to have him there: at any rate, it made her hate her room upstairs more than ever; and she would compel me to find out business below, that she might accompany me.

On Easter Monday, Joseph went to Gimmerton fair with some cattle; and, in the afternoon, I was busy getting up linen in the kitchen. Earnshaw sat, morose as usual, at the chimney corner, and my little mistress was beguiling an idle hour with drawing pictures on the window panes, varying her amusement by smothered bursts of songs, and whispered ejaculations, and quick glances of annoyance and impatience in the direction of her cousin, who steadfastly smoked, and looked into the grate.

At a notice that I could do with her no longer intercepting my light, she removed to the hearthstone. I bestowed little attention on her proceedings, but, presently, I heard her begin—

"I've found out, Hareton, that I want—that I'm glad—that I should like you to be my cousin, now, if you had not grown so cross to me, and so rough."

Hareton returned no answer.

"Hareton, Hareton, Hareton! do you hear?" she continued.

"Get off wi' ye!" he growled, with uncompromising gruffness.

"Let me take that pipe," she said, cautiously advancing her hand, and abstracting it from his mouth.

Before he could attempt to recover it, it was broken, and behind the fire. He swore at her and seized another.

"Stop," she cried, "you must listen to me, first; and I can't speak while those clouds are floating in my face."

"Will you go to the devil!" he exclaimed, ferociously, "and let me be!"

"No," she persisted, "I won't—I can't tell what to do to make you talk to me, and you are determined not to understand. When I call you stupid, I don't mean anything—I don't mean that I despise you. Come, you shall take notice of me, Hareton—you are my cousin, and you shall own me."

"I shall have naught to do wi' you, and your mucky pride, and your damned, mocking tricks!" he answered. "I'll go to hell, body and soul, before I look sideways after you again! Side out of t' gait,[4] now; this minute!"

Catherine frowned, and retreated to the window-seat, chewing her lip, and endeavouring, by humming an eccentric tune, to conceal a growing tendency to sob.

"You should be friends with your cousin, Mr. Hareton," I interrupted, "since she repents of her sauciness! It would do you a great deal of good—it would make you another man, to have her for a companion."

"A companion!" he cried; "when she hates me, and does not think me fit to wipe her shoon! Nay, if it made me a king, I'd not be scorned for seeking her good will any more."

"It is not I who hate you, it is you who hate me!" wept Cathy, no longer disguising her trouble. "You hate me as much as Mr.

4. Get out of the way.

Heathcliff does, and more."

"You're a damned liar," began Earnshaw; "why have I made him angry, by taking your part then, a hundred times? and that, when you sneered at, and despised me, and—Go on plaguing me, and I'll step in yonder, and say you worried me out of the kitchen!"

"I didn't know you took my part," she answered, drying her eyes; "and I was miserable and bitter at everybody; but, now I thank you and beg you to forgive me, what can I do besides?"

She returned to the hearth, and frankly extended her hand.

He blackened, and scowled like a thunder cloud, and kept his fists resolutely clenched, and his gaze fixed on the ground.

Catherine, by instinct, must have divined it was obdurate perversity, and not dislike, that prompted this dogged conduct; for, after remaining an instant undecided, she stooped, and impressed on his cheek a gentle kiss.

The little rogue thought I had not seen her, and, drawing back, she took her former station by the window, quite demurely.

I shook my head reprovingly; and then she blushed, and whispered—

"Well! what should I have done, Ellen? He wouldn't shake hands, and he wouldn't look. I must show him some way that I like him, that I want to be friends."

Whether the kiss convinced Hareton, I cannot tell; he was very careful, for some minutes, that his face should not be seen; and when he did raise it, he was sadly puzzled where to turn his eyes.

Catherine employed herself in wrapping a handsome book neatly in white paper; and having tied it with a bit of riband, and addressed it to "Mr. Hareton Earnshaw," she desired me to be her ambassadress, and convey the present to its destined recipient.

"And tell him, if he'll take it, I'll come and teach him to read it right," she said, "and, if he refuse it, I'll go upstairs, and never tease him again."

I carried it, and repeated the message, anxiously watched by my employer. Hareton would not open his fingers, so I laid it on his knee. He did not strike it off either. I returned to my work. Catherine leaned her head and arms on the table, till she heard the slight rustle of the covering being removed; then she stole away, and quietly seated herself beside her cousin. He trembled, and his face glowed. All his rudeness and all his surly harshness had deserted him—he could not summon courage, at first, to utter a syllable, in reply to her questioning look, and her murmured petition.

"Say you forgive me, Hareton, do! You can make me so happy, by speaking that little word."

He muttered something inaudible.

"And you'll be my friend?" added Catherine, interrogatively.

"Nay! you'll be ashamed of me every day of your life," he answered. "And the more, the more you know me, and I cannot bide it."

"So, you won't be my friend?" she said, smiling as sweet as honey, and creeping close up.

I overheard no further distinguishable talk; but, on looking round again, I perceived two such radiant countenances bent over the page of the accepted book, that I did not doubt the treaty had been ratified on both sides, and the enemies were, thenceforth, sworn allies.

The work they studied was full of costly pictures; and those, and their position, had charm enough to keep them unmoved, till Joseph came home. He, poor man, was perfectly aghast at the spectacle of Catherine seated on the same bench with Hareton Earnshaw, leaning her hand on his shoulder; and confounded at his favourite's endurance of her proximity. It affected him too deeply to allow an observation on the subject that night. His emotion was only revealed by the immense sighs he drew, as he solemnly spread his large Bible on the table, and overlaid it with dirty bank-notes from his pocket-book, the produce of the day's transactions. At length, he summoned Hareton from his seat.

"Tak' these in tuh t' maister, lad," he said, "un' bide theare; Aw's gang up tuh my awn rahm. This hoile's norther mensful, nor seemly fur us—we mun side aht, and search another!"[5]

"Come, Catherine," I said, "we must 'side out,' too—I've done my ironing, are you ready to go?"

"It is not eight o'clock!" she answered, rising unwillingly, "Hareton, I'll leave this book upon the chimney-piece, and I'll bring some more to-morrow."

"Ony books ut yah leave, Aw suall tak' intuh th' hahse," said Joseph, "un' it 'ull be mitch[6] if yah find 'em agean; soa, yah muh plase yourseln!"

Cathy threatened that his library should pay for hers; and, smiling as she passed Hareton, went singing upstairs, lighter of heart, I venture to say, than ever she had been under that roof before, except, perhaps, during her earliest visits to Linton.

The intimacy, thus commenced, grew rapidly, though it encountered temporary interruptions. Earnshaw was not to be civilized with a wish; and my young lady was no philosopher, and no paragon of patience; but both their minds tending to the same point—one loving and desiring to esteem, and the other loving and desiring to be esteemed—they contrived in the end to reach it.

You see, Mr. Lockwood, it was easy enough to win Mrs. Heath-

5. *Hoile:* room or house (probably house in this context); *mensful:* proper; *side aht:* get out.
6. A strange thing, a marvel.

cliff's heart; but now, I'm glad you did not try. The crown of all my wishes will be the union of those two; I shall envy no one on their wedding-day—there won't be a happier woman than myself in England!

### Chapter XXXIiI

On the morrow of that Monday, Earnshaw being still unable to follow his ordinary employments, and, therefore, remaining about the house, I speedily found it would be impracticable to retain my charge beside me, as heretofore.

She got downstairs before me, and out into the garden, where she had seen her cousin performing some easy work; and when I went to bid them come to breakfast, I saw she had persuaded him to clear a large space of ground from currant and gooseberry bushes, and they were busy planning together an importation of plants from the Grange.

I was terrified at the devastation which had been accomplished in a brief half hour; the black currant trees were the apple of Joseph's eye, and she had just fixed her choice of a flower bed in the midst of them!

"There! That will be all shewn to the master," I exclaimed, "the minute it is discovered. And what excuse have you to offer for taking such liberties with the garden? We shall have a fine explosion on the head of it: see if we don't! Mr. Hareton, I wonder you should have no more wit, than to go and make that mess at her bidding!"

"I'd forgotten they were Joseph's," answered Earnshaw, rather puzzled, "but I'll tell him I did it."

We always ate our meals with Mr. Heathcliff. I held the mistress's post in making tea and carving; so I was indispensable at table. Catherine usually sat by me; but to-day, she stole nearer to Hareton, and I presently saw she would have no more discretion in her friendship, than she had in her hostility.

"Now, mind you don't talk with and notice your cousin too much," were my whispered instructions as we entered the room. "It will certainly annoy Mr. Heathcliff, and he'll be mad at you both."

"I'm not going to," she answered.

The minute after, she had sidled to him, and was sticking primroses in his plate of porridge.

He dared not speak to her, there; he dared hardly look, and yet she went on teasing, till he was twice on the point of being provoked to laugh; and I frowned, and then she glanced towards the master, whose mind was occupied on other subjects than his company, as his countenance evinced, and she grew serious for an instant, scrutinizing him with deep gravity. Afterwards she turned, and re-commenced her nonsense; at last, Hareton uttered a smothered laugh.

Mr. Heathcliff started; his eye rapidly surveyed our faces. Catherine met it with her accustomed look of nervousness, and yet defiance, which he abhorred.

"It is well you are out of my reach"; he exclaimed. "What fiend possesses you to stare back at me, continually, with those infernal eyes? Down with them! and don't remind me of your existence again. I thought I had cured you of laughing!"

"It was me," muttered Hareton.

"What do you say?" demanded the master.

Hareton looked at his plate, and did not repeat the confession.

Mr. Heathcliff looked at him a bit, and then silently resumed his breakfast, and his interrupted musing.

We had nearly finished, and the two young people prudently shifted wider asunder, so I anticipated no further disturbance during that sitting, when Joseph appeared at the door, revealing by his quivering lip and furious eyes, that the outrage committed on his precious shrubs was detected.

He must have seen Cathy and her cousin about the spot before he examined it, for while his jaws worked like those of a cow chewing its cud, and rendered his speech difficult to understand, he began—

"Aw mun hev my wage, and Aw mun goa! Aw *hed* aimed tuh dee,[1] wheare Aw'd sarved fur sixty year; un' Aw thowt Aw'd lug my books up intuh t' garret, un' all my bits uh stuff, un' they sud hev t' kitchen tuh theirseln; fur t' sake uh quietness. It wur hard tuh gie up my awn hearthstun, bud Aw thowt Aw *could* do that! Bud nah, shoo's taan my garden frough me, un' by th' heart, Maister, Aw cannot stand it! Yah muh bend[2] tuh th' yoak, an ye will— Aw' noan used to't and an ow'd man doesn't sooin get used tuh new barthens.[3] Aw'd rayther arn my bite an' my sup, wi' a hammer in th' road!"

"Now, now, idiot!" interrupted Heathcliff, "cut it short! What's your grievance? I'll interfere in no quarrels between you and Nelly. She may thrust you into the coal-hole for anything I care."

"It's noan Nelly!" answered Joseph. "Aw sudn't shift fur Nelly— nasty, ill nowt as shoo is. Thank God! *shoo* cannot stale t'sowl uh nob'dy! Shoo wer niver soa handsome, bud whet a body mud look at her 'baht winking. It's yon flaysome, graceless quean, ut's witched ahr lad, wi' her bold een, un' her forrard ways till—Nay! It fair

---

1. Die.
2. May bend.

3. *Barthens* (*barth*): literally, a warm place for cattle.

brusts my heart! He's forgetten all E done for him, un made on him, un' goan un' riven up a whole row ut t' grandest currant trees i' t' garden!"[4] And here he lamented outright, unmanned by a sense of his bitter injuries, and Earnshaw's ingratitude and dangerous condition.

"Is the fool drunk?" asked Mr. Heathcliff. "Hareton, is it you he's finding fault with?"

"I've pulled up two or three bushes," replied the young man, "but I'm going to set 'em again."

"And why have you pulled them up?" said the master.

Catherine wisely put in her tongue.

"We wanted to plant some flowers there," she cried. "I'm the only person to blame, for I wished him to do it."

"And who the devil gave *you* leave to touch a stick about the place?" demanded her father-in-law, much surprised. "And who ordered *you* to obey her?" he added, turning to Hareton.

The latter was speechless; his cousin replied—

"You shouldn't grudge a few yards of earth for me to ornament, when you have taken all my land!"

"Your land, insolent slut? you never had any!" said Heathcliff.

"And my money," she continued, returning his angry glare, and, meantime, biting a piece of crust, the remnant of her breakfast.

"Silence!" he exclaimed. "Get done, and begone!"

"And Hareton's land, and his money," pursued the reckless thing. "Hareton and I are friends now; and I shall tell him all about you!"

The master seemed confounded a moment; he grew pale, and rose up, eyeing her all the while, with an expression of mortal hate.

"If you strike me, Hareton will strike you!" she said; "so you may as well sit down."

"If Hareton does not turn you out of the room, I'll strike him to hell," thundered Heathcliff. "Damnable witch! dare you pretend to rouse him against me? Off with her! Do you hear? Fling her into the kitchen! I'll kill her, Ellen Dean, if you let her come into my sight again!"

Hareton tried under his breath to persuade her to go.

"Drag her away!" he cried savagely. "Are you staying to talk?" And he approached to execute his own command.

"He'll not obey you, wicked man, any more!" said Catherine, "and he'll soon detest you, as much as I do!"

"Wisht! wisht!" muttered the young man reproachfully. "I will not hear you speak so to him. Have done!"

"But you won't let him strike me?" she cried.

"Come then!" he whispered earnestly.

4. *Sudn't shift fur Nelly:* shouldn't leave on Nelly's account; *nasty, ill nowt as shoo is:* nasty, evil nothing as she is; *t'sowl:* the soul; *'baht:* without; *brusts:* breaks; *E:* I; *riven up:* torn up.

It was too late—Heathcliff had caught hold of her.

"Now *you* go!" he said to Earnshaw. "Accursed witch! this time she has provoked me, when I could not bear it; and I'll make her repent it for ever!"

He had his hand in her hair; Hareton attempted to release the locks, entreating him not to hurt her that once. His black eyes flashed; he seemed ready to tear Catherine in pieces, and I was just worked up to risk coming to the rescue, when of a sudden, his fingers relaxed, he shifted his grasp from her head to her arm, and gazed intently in her face. Then, he drew his hand over his eyes, stood a moment to collect himself apparently, and turning anew to Catherine, said with assumed calmness—

"You must learn to avoid putting me in a passion, or I shall really murder you, some time! Go with Mrs. Dean, and keep with her, and confine your insolence to her ears. As to Hareton Earnshaw, if I see him listen to you, I'll send him seeking his bread where he can get it! Your love will make him an outcast, and a beggar. Nelly, take her, and leave me, all of you! Leave me!"

I led my young lady out; she was too glad of her escape, to resist; the other followed, and Mr. Heathcliff had the room to himself, till dinner.

I had counselled Catherine to get her upstairs; but, as soon as he perceived her vacant seat, he sent me to call her. He spoke to none of us, ate very little, and went out directly afterwards, intimating that he should not return before evening.

The two new friends established themselves in the house, during his absence, where I heard Hareton sternly check his cousin, on her offering a revelation of her father-in-law's conduct to his father.

He said he wouldn't suffer a word to be uttered to him, in his disparagement; if he were the devil, it didn't signify; he would stand by him; and he'd rather she would abuse himself, as she used to, than begin on Mr. Heathcliff.

Catherine was waxing cross at this; but he found means to make her hold her tongue, by asking, how she would like *him* to speak ill of her father? and then she comprehended that Earnshaw took the master's reputation home to himself, and was attached by ties stronger than reason could break—chains, forged by habit, which it would be cruel to attempt to loosen.

She showed a good heart, thenceforth, in avoiding both complaints and expressions of antipathy concerning Heathcliff, and confessed to me her sorrow that she had endeavoured to raise a bad spirit between him and Hareton; indeed, I don't believe she has ever breathed a syllable, in the latter's hearing, against her oppressor, since.

When this slight disagreement was over, they were thick again, and as busy as possible, in their several occupations, of pupil and teacher. I came in to sit with them, after I had done my work, and I felt so soothed and comforted to watch them, that I did not notice how time got on. You know, they both appeared, in a measure, my children: I had long been proud of one, and now, I was sure, the other would be a source of equal satisfaction. His honest, warm, and intelligent nature shook off rapidly the clouds of ignorance and degradation in which it had been bred; and Catherine's sincere commendations acted as a spur to his industry. His brightening mind brightened his features, and added spirit and nobility to their aspect. I could hardly fancy it the same individual I had beheld on the day I discovered my little lady at Wuthering Heights, after her expedition to the Crags.

While I admired, and they laboured, dusk drew on, and with it returned the master. He came upon us quite unexpectedly, entering by the front way, and had a full view of the whole three, ere we could raise our heads to glance at him.

Well, I reflected, there was never a pleasanter, or more harmless sight; and it will be a burning shame to scold them. The red fire-light glowed on their two bonny heads, and revealed their faces, animated with the eager interest of children; for, though he was twenty-three, and she eighteen, each had so much of novelty to feel and learn, that neither experienced nor evinced the sentiments of sober disenchanted maturity.

They lifted their eyes together, to encounter Mr. Heathcliff. Perhaps you have never remarked that their eyes are precisely similar, and they are those of Catherine Earnshaw. The present Catherine has no other likeness to her, except a breadth of forehead, and a certain arch of the nostril that makes her appear rather haughty, whether she will or not. With Hareton the resemblance is carried farther; it is singular, at all times—then, it was particularly striking, because his senses were alert, and his mental faculties wakened to unwonted activity.

I suppose this resemblance disarmed Mr. Heathcliff: he walked to the hearth in evident agitation, but it quickly subsided, as he looked at the young man; or, I should say, altered its character, for it was there yet.

He took the book from his hand, and glanced at the open page, then returned it without any observation, merely signing Catherine away. Her companion lingered very little behind her, and I was about to depart also, but he bid me sit still.

"It is a poor conclusion, is it not," he observed, having brooded a while on the scene he had just witnessed. "An absurd termination to my violent exertions? I get levers and mattocks to demolish the two houses, and train myself to be capable of working like Hercules, and when everything is ready, and in my power, I find the will to lift a slate off either roof has vanished! My old enemies have not beaten me; now would be the precise time to revenge myself on their representatives: I could do it; and none could hinder me. But where is the use? I don't care for striking, I can't take the trouble to raise my hand! That sounds as if I had been labouring the whole time, only to exhibit a fine trait of magnanimity. It is far from being the case—I have lost the faculty of enjoying their destruction, and I am too idle to destroy for nothing.

"Nelly, there is a strange change approaching—I'm in its shadow at present. I take so little interest in my daily life, that I hardly remember to eat, and drink. Those two, who have left the room, are the only objects which retain a distinct material appearance to me; and that appearance causes me pain, amounting to agony. About *her* I won't speak; and I don't desire to think; but I earnestly wish she were invisible—her presence invokes only maddening sensations. *He* moves me differently; and yet if I could do it without seeming insane, I'd never see him again! You'll perhaps think me rather inclined to become so," he added, making an effort to smile, "if I try to describe the thousand forms of past associations and ideas he awakens, or embodies—But you'll not talk of what I tell you, and my mind is so eternally secluded in itself, it is tempting, at last, to turn it out to another.

"Five minutes ago, Hareton seemed a personification of my youth, not a human being. I felt to him in such a variety of ways, that it would have been impossible to have accosted him rationally.

"In the first place, his startling likeness to Catherine connected him fearfully with her. That, however, which you may suppose the most potent to arrest my imagination, is actually the least, for what is not connected with her to me? and what does not recall her? I cannot look down to this floor, but her features are shaped on the flags! In every cloud, in every tree—filling the air at night, and caught by glimpses in every object by day, I am surrounded with her image! The most ordinary faces of men and women—my own features—mock me with a resemblance. The entire world is a dreadful collection of memoranda that she did exist, and that I have lost her!

"Well, Hareton's aspect was the ghost of my immortal love, of my wild endeavours to hold my right, my degradation, my pride, my happiness, and my anguish—

"But it is frenzy to repeat these thoughts to you; only it will let you know why, with a reluctance to be always alone, his society is no benefit, rather an aggravation of the constant torment I suffer; and it partly contributes to render me regardless how he and his cousin go on together. I can give them no attention, any more."

"But what do you mean by a *change*, Mr. Heathcliff?" I said, alarmed at his manner, though he was neither in danger of losing his senses, nor dying; according to my judgment he was quite strong and healthy; and, as to his reason, from childhood he had a delight in dwelling on dark things, and entertaining odd fancies. He might have had a monomania on the subject of his departed idol; but on every other point his wits were as sound as mine.

"I shall not know that, till it comes," he said, "I'm only half conscious of it now."

"You have no feeling of illness, have you?" I asked.

"No, Nelly, I have not," he answered.

"Then, you are not afraid of death?" I pursued.

"Afraid? No!" he replied. "I have neither a fear, nor a presentiment, nor a hope of death. Why should I? With my hard constitution, and temperate mode of living, and unperilous occupations, I ought to, and probably *shall* remain above ground, till there is scarcely a black hair on my head. And yet I cannot continue in this condition! I have to remind myself to breathe—almost to remind my heart to beat! And it is like bending back a stiff spring; it is by compulsion that I do the slightest act not prompted by one thought, and by compulsion, that I notice anything alive, or dead, which is not associated with one universal idea. I have a single wish, and my whole being and faculties are yearning to attain it. They have yearned towards it so long, and so unwaveringly, that I'm convinced it *will* be reached—and *soon*—because it has devoured my existence. I am swallowed in the anticipation of its fulfilment.

"My confessions have not relieved me, but they may account for some otherwise unaccountable phases of humour, which I show. O, God! It is a long fight, I wish it were over!"

He began to pace the room, muttering terrible things to himself, till I was inclined to believe, as he said Joseph did, that conscience had turned his heart to an earthly hell. I wondered greatly how it would end.

Though he seldom before had revealed this state of mind, even by looks, it was his habitual mood, I had no doubt: he asserted it himself; but not a soul, from his general bearing, would have conjectured the fact. You did not, when you saw him, Mr. Lockwood; and at the period of which I speak, he was just the same as then, only fonder of continued solitude, and perhaps still more laconic in company.

## Chapter XXXIV

For some days after that evening, Mr. Heathcliff shunned meeting us at meals; yet he would not consent, formally, to exclude

Hareton and Cathy. He had an aversion to yielding so completely to his feelings, choosing rather to absent himself; and eating once in twenty-four hours seemed sufficient sustenance for him.

One night, after the family were in bed, I heard him go down-stairs, and out at the front door: I did not hear him re-enter and, in the morning, I found he was still away.

We were in April then: the weather was sweet and warm, the grass as green as showers and sun could make it, and the two dwarf apple trees, near the southern wall, in full bloom.

After breakfast, Catherine insisted on my bringing a chair, and sitting with my work under the fir trees at the end of the house; and she beguiled Hareton, who had perfectly recovered from his accident, to dig and arrange her little garden, which was shifted to that corner by the influence of Joseph's complaints.

I was comfortably revelling in the spring fragrance around, and the beautiful soft blue overhead, when my young lady, who had run down near the gate to procure some primrose roots for a border, returned only half laden, and informed us that Mr. Heathcliff was coming in.

"And he spoke to me," she added with a perplexed countenance.

"What did he say?" asked Hareton.

"He told me to begone as fast as I could," she answered. "But he looked so different from his usual look that I stopped a moment to stare at him."

"How?" he enquired.

"Why, almost bright and cheerful—No, almost nothing—*very much* excited, and wild and glad!" she replied.

"Night-walking amuses him, then," I remarked, affecting a care-less manner. In reality, as surprised as she was, and, anxious to ascertain the truth of her statement, for to see the master looking glad would not be an every day spectacle, I framed an excuse to go in.

Heathcliff stood at the open door; he was pale, and he trembled; yet, certainly, he had a strange joyful glitter in his eyes that altered the aspect of his whole face.

"Will you have some breakfast?" I said, "You must be hungry rambling about all night!"

I wanted to discover where he had been; but I did not like to ask directly.

"No, I'm not hungry," he answered, averting his head, and speaking rather contemptuously, as if he guessed I was trying to divine the occasion of his good humour.

I felt perplexed: I didn't know whether it were not a proper opportunity to offer a bit of admonition.

"I don't think it right to wander out of doors," I observed, "instead of being in bed: it is not wise, at any rate, this moist season. I dare say you'll catch a bad cold, or a fever—you have something the matter with you now!"

"Nothing but what I can bear," he replied, "and with the greatest pleasure, provided you'll leave me alone. Get in, and don't annoy me."

I obeyed; and, in passing, I noticed he breathed as fast as a cat.

"Yes!" I reflected to myself, "we shall have a fit of illness. I cannot conceive what he has been doing!"

That noon, he sat down to dinner with us, and received a heaped-up plate from my hands, as if he intended to make amends for previous fasting.

"I've neither cold, nor fever, Nelly," he remarked, in allusion to my morning's speech. "And I'm ready to do justice to the food you give me."

He took his knife and fork, and was going to commence eating, when the inclination appeared to become suddenly extinct. He laid them on the table, looked eagerly towards the window, then rose and went out.

We saw him walking, to and fro, in the garden, while we concluded our meal; and Earnshaw said he'd go and ask why he would not dine; he thought we had grieved him some way.

"Well, is he coming?" cried Catherine, when her cousin returned.

"Nay," he answered, "but he's not angry; he seemed rare and pleased[1] indeed; only, I made him impatient by speaking to him twice; and then he bid me be off to you; he wondered how I could want the company of any body else."

I set his plate, to keep warm, on the fender: and after an hour or two, he re-entered, when the room was clear, in no degree calmer: the same unnatural—it was unnatural—appearance of joy under his black brows; the same bloodless hue, and his teeth visible, now and then, in a kind of smile; his frame shivering, not as one shivers with chill or weakness, but as a tight-stretched cord vibrates—a strong thrilling, rather than trembling.

I will ask what is the matter, I thought, or who should? And I exclaimed—

"Have you heard any good news, Mr. Heathcliff? You look uncommonly animated."

"Where should good news come from, to me?" he said. "I'm animated with hunger; and, seemingly, I must not eat."

"Your dinner is here," I returned; "why won't you get it?"

"I don't want it now," he muttered, hastily. "I'll wait till supper. And, Nelly, once for all, let me beg you to warn Hareton and the

---

1. Very pleased.

other away from me. I wish to be troubled by nobody—I wish to have this place to myself."

"Is there some new reason for this banishment?" I inquired. "Tell me why you are so queer, Mr. Heathcliff? Where were you last night? I'm not putting the question through idle curiosity, but—"

"You are putting the question through very idle curiosity," he interrupted, with a laugh. "Yet, I'll answer it. Last night, I was on the threshold of hell. To-day, I am within sight of my heaven. I have my eyes on it—hardly three feet to sever me! And now you'd better go. You'll neither see nor hear anything to frighten you, if you refrain from prying."

Having swept the hearth and wiped the table, I departed more perplexed than ever.

He did not quit the house again that afternoon, and no one intruded on his solitude, till, at eight o'clock, I deemed it proper, though unsummoned, to carry a candle and his supper to him.

He was leaning against the ledge of an open lattice, but not looking out; his face was turned to the interior gloom. The fire had smouldered to ashes; the room was filled with the damp, mild air of the cloudy evening, and so still, that not only the murmur of the beck down Gimmerton was distinguishable, but its ripples and its gurgling over the pebbles, or through the large stones which it could not cover.

I uttered an ejaculation of discontent at seeing the dismal grate, and commenced shutting the casements, one after another, till I came to his.

"Must I close this?" I asked, in order to rouse him, for he would not stir.

The light flashed on his features, as I spoke. Oh, Mr. Lockwood, I cannot express what a terrible start I got, by the momentary view! Those deep black eyes! That smile, and ghastly paleness! It appeared to me, not Mr. Heathcliff, but a goblin; and, in my terror, I let the candle bend towards the wall, and it left me in darkness.

"Yes, close it," he replied, in his familiar voice. "There, that is pure awkwardness! Why did you hold the candle horizontally? Be quick, and bring another."

I hurried out in a foolish state of dread, and said to Joseph—

"The master wishes you to take him a light, and rekindle the fire." For I dared not go in myself again just then.

Joseph rattled some fire into the shovel, and went; but he brought it back, immediately, with the supper tray in his other hand, explaining that Mr. Heathcliff was going to bed, and he wanted nothing to eat till morning.

We heard him mount the stairs directly; he did not proceed to his ordinary chamber, but turned into that with the panelled bed. Its window, as I mentioned before, is wide enough for anybody to get through, and it struck me that he plotted another midnight excursion, which he had rather we had no suspicion of.

"Is he a ghoul, or a vampire?" I mused. I had read of such hideous, incarnate demons. And then I set myself to reflect how I had tended him in infancy; and watched him grow to youth; and followed him almost through his whole course; and what absurd nonsense it was to yield to that sense of horror.

"But where did he come from, the little dark thing, harboured by a good man to his bane?" muttered superstition, as I dozed into unconsciousness. And I began, half dreaming, to weary myself with imaging some fit parentage for him; and repeating my waking meditations, I tracked his existence over again, with grim variations; at last, picturing his death and funeral; of which, all I can remember is, being exceedingly vexed at having the task of dictating an inscription for his monument, and consulting the sexton about it; and, as he had no surname, and we could not tell his age, we were obliged to content ourselves with the single word, "Heathcliff." That came true; we were. If you enter the kirkyard, you'll read on his headstone only that, and the date of his death.

Dawn restored me to common sense. I rose, and went into the garden, as soon as I could see, to ascertain if there were any footmarks under his window. There were none.

"He has stayed at home," I thought, "and he'll be all right, to-day!"

I prepared breakfast for the household, as was my usual custom, but told Hareton and Catherine to get theirs ere the master came down, for he lay late. They preferred taking it out of doors, under the trees, and I set a little table to accommodate them.

On my re-entrance, I found Mr. Heathcliff below. He and Joseph were conversing about some farming business; he gave clear, minute directions concerning the matter discussed, but he spoke rapidly, and turned his head continually aside, and had the same excited expression, even more exaggerated.

When Joseph quitted the room, he took his seat in the place he generally chose, and I put a basin of coffee before him. He drew it nearer, and then rested in his arms on the table, and looked at the opposite wall, as I supposed, surveying one particular portion, up and down, with glittering, restless eyes, and with such eager interest, that he stopped breathing, during half a minute together.

"Come now," I exclaimed, pushing some bread against his hand. "Eat and drink that, while it is hot. It has been waiting near an hour."

He didn't notice me, and yet he smiled. I'd rather have seen him gnash his teeth than smile so.

"Mr. Heathcliff! master!" I cried. "Don't, for God's sake, stare as if you saw an unearthly vision."

"Don't, for God's sake, shout so loud," he replied. "Turn round, and tell me, are we by ourselves?"

"Of course," was my answer, "of course, we are!"

Still, I involuntarily obeyed him, as if I were not quite sure.

With a sweep of his hand, he cleared a vacant space in front among the breakfast things, and leant forward to gaze more at his ease.

Now, I perceived he was not looking at the wall, for when I regarded him alone, it seemed exactly that he gazed at something within two yards' distance. And, whatever it was, it communicated, apparently, both pleasure and pain, in exquisite extremes; at least, the anguished, yet raptured expression of his countenance suggested that idea.

The fancied object was not fixed, either; his eyes pursued it with unwearied vigilance, and, even in speaking to me, were never weaned away.

I vainly reminded him of his protracted abstinence from food; if he stirred to touch anything in compliance with my entreaties, if he stretched his hand out to get a piece of bread, his fingers clenched, before they reached it, and remained on the table, forgetful of their aim.

I sat, a model of patience, trying to attract his absorbed attention from its engrossing speculation, till he grew irritable, and got up, asking why I would not allow him to have his own time in taking his meals? and saying that, on the next occasion, I needn't wait; I might set the things down, and go.

Having uttered these words, he left the house, slowly sauntered down the garden path, and disappeared through the gate.

The hours crept anxiously by: another evening came. I did not retire to rest till late, and when I did, I could not sleep. He returned after midnight, and, instead of going to bed, shut himself into the room beneath. I listened, and tossed about; and, finally, dressed and descended. It was too irksome to lie up there, harassing my brain with a hundred idle misgivings.

I distinguished Mr. Heathcliff's step, restlessly measuring the floor; and he frequently broke the silence by a deep inspiration, resembling a groan. He muttered detached words also; the only one I could catch was the name of Catherine, coupled with some wild term of endearment or suffering, and spoken as one would speak to a person present—low and earnest, and wrung from the depth of his soul.

I had not courage to walk straight into the apartment; but I desired to divert him from his reverie, and, therefore fell foul of the kitchen fire, stirred it, and began to scrape the cinders. It drew him forth sooner than I expected. He opened the door immediately, and said—

"Nelly, come here—is it morning? Come in with your light."

"It is striking four," I answered; "you want a candle to take upstairs—you might have lit one at this fire."

"No, I don't wish to go upstairs," he said. "Come in, and kindle *me* a fire, and do anything there is to do about the room."

"I must blow the coals red first, before I can carry any," I replied, getting a chair and the bellows.

He roamed to and fro, meantime, in a state approaching distraction; his heavy sighs succeeding each other so thick as to leave no space for common breathing between.

"When day breaks, I'll send for Green," he said; "I wish to make some legal inquiries of him while I can bestow a thought on those matters, and while I can act calmly. I have not written my will yet, and how to leave my property, I cannot determine! I wish I could annihilate it from the face of the earth."

"I would not talk so, Mr. Heathcliff," I interposed. "Let your will be, a while—you'll be spared to repent of your many injustices, yet! I never expected that your nerves would be disordered: they are, at present, marvellously so, however; and, almost entirely, through your own fault. The way you've passed these three last days might knock up a Titan. Do take some food, and some repose. You need only look at yourself in a glass to see how you require both. Your cheeks are hollow, and your eyes blood-shot, like a person starving with hunger, and going blind with loss of sleep."

"It is not my fault, that I cannot eat or rest," he replied. "I assure you it is through no settled designs. I'll do both, as soon as I possibly can. But you might as well bid a man struggling in the water, rest within arms-length of the shore! I must reach it first, and then I'll rest. Well, never mind Mr. Green; as to repenting of my injustices, I've done no injustice, and I repent of nothing— I'm too happy, and yet I'm not happy enough. My soul's bliss kills my body, but does not satisfy itself."

"Happy, master?" I cried. "Strange happiness! If you would hear me without being angry, I might offer some advice that would make you happier."

"What is that?" he asked. "Give it."

"You are aware, Mr. Heathcliff," I said, "that from the time you were thirteen years old, you have lived a selfish, unchristian life; and probably hardly had a Bible in your hands during all that period. You must have forgotten the contents of the book, and you may not have space to search it now. Could it be hurtful to send for some one—some minister of any denomination, it does not matter which, to explain it, and show you how very far you have erred from its precepts, and how unfit you will be for its heaven, unless a change takes place before you die?"

"I'm rather obliged than angry, Nelly," he said, "for you remind me of the manner that I desire to be buried in. It is to be carried to the churchyard, in the evening. You and Hareton may, if you please accompany me—and mind, particularly, to notice that the sexton obeys my directions concerning the two coffins! No minister need come; nor need anything be said over me. I tell you, I have nearly attained *my* heaven; and that of others is altogether un-valued and uncoveted by me!"

"And supposing you persevered in your obstinate fast, and died by that means, and they refused to bury you in the precincts of the Kirk?" I said, shocked at his godless indifference. "How would you like it?"

"They won't do that," he replied; "if they did, you must have me removed secretly; and if you neglect it, you shall prove, prac-tically, that the dead are not annihilated!"

As soon as he heard the other members of the family stirring he retired to his den, and I breathed freer. But in the afternoon, while Joseph and Hareton were at their work, he came into the kitchen again, and with a wild look, bid me come, and sit in the house—he wanted somebody with him.

I declined, telling him plainly that his strange talk and manner frightened me, and I had neither the nerve nor the will to be his companion, alone.

"I believe you think me a fiend!" he said, with his dismal laugh, "something too horrible to live under a decent roof!"

Then turning to Catherine, who was there, and who drew behind me at his approach, he added, half sneeringly—

"Will *you* come, chuck? I'll not hurt you. No! to you, I've made myself worse than the devil. Well, there is *one* who won't shrink from my company! By God! she's relentless. Oh, damn it! It's unutterably too much for flesh and blood to bear, even mine."

He solicited the society of no one more. At dusk, he went into his chamber. Through the whole night, and far into the morning, we heard him groaning, and murmuring to himself. Hareton was anxious to enter, but I bid him fetch Mr. Kenneth, and he should go in and see him.

When he came, and I requested admittance and tried to open the door, I found it locked; and Heathcliff bid us be damned. He was better, and would be left alone; so the doctor went away.

The following evening was very wet; indeed it poured down, till day-dawn; and, as I took my morning walk round the house, I observed the master's window swinging open, and the rain driving straight in.

He cannot be in bed, I thought; those showers would drench him through! He must either be up, or out. But I'll make no more ado, I'll go boldly and look!

Having succeeded in obtaining entrance with another key, I ran to unclose the panels, for the chamber was vacant; quickly pushing them aside, I peeped in. Mr. Heathcliff was there—laid on his back. His eyes met mine so keen and fierce, I started; and then he seemed to smile.

I could not think him dead, but his face and throat were washed with rain; the bedclothes dripped, and he was perfectly still. The lattice, flapping to and fro, had grazed one hand that rested on the sill; no blood trickled from the broken skin, and when I put my fingers to it, I could doubt no more—he was dead and stark!

I hasped the window; I combed his black long hair from his forehead; I tried to close his eyes—to extinguish, if possible, that frightful, life-like gaze of exultation, before any one else beheld it. They would not shut; they seemed to sneer at my attempts, and his parted lips and sharp, white teeth sneered too! Taken with another fit of cowardice, I cried out for Joseph. Joseph shuffled up and made a noise, but resolutely refused to meddle with him.

"Th' divil's harried off his soul," he cried, "and he muh hev his carcass intuh t' bargin, for ow't Aw care! Ech! what a wicked un he looks girnning[2] at death!" and the old sinner grinned in mockery.

I thought he intended to cut a caper round the bed; but suddenly composing himself, he fell on his knees, and raised his hands, and returned thanks that the lawful master and the ancient stock were restored to their rights.

I felt stunned by the awful event; and my memory unavoidably recurred to former times with a sort of oppressive sadness. But poor Hareton, the most wronged, was the only one that really suffered much. He sat by the corpse all night, weeping in bitter earnest. He pressed its hand, and kissed the sarcastic, savage face that every one else shrank from contemplating; and bemoaned him with that strong grief which springs naturally from a generous heart, though it be tough as tempered steel.

Kenneth was perplexed to pronounce of what disorder the master died. I concealed the fact of his having swallowed nothing for four days, fearing it might lead to trouble, and then, I am persuaded he did not abstain on purpose; it was the consequence of his strange illness, not the cause.

2. Grinning.

We buried him, to the scandal of the whole neighbourhood, as he had wished. Earnshaw, and I, the sexton and six men to carry the coffin, comprehended the whole attendance.

The six men departed when they had let it down into the grave: we stayed to see it covered. Hareton, with a streaming face, dug green sods, and laid them over the brown mould himself. At present it is as smooth and verdant as its companion mounds—and I hope its tenant sleeps as soundly. But the country folks, if you asked them, would swear on their Bible that he *walks*. There are those who speak to having met him near the church, and on the moor, and even within this house. Idle tales, you'll say, and so say I. Yet that old man by the kitchen fire affirms he has seen two on 'em looking out of his chamber window, on every rainy night, since his death—and an odd thing happened to me about a month ago.

I was going to the Grange one evening—a dark evening threatening thunder—and, just at the turn of the Heights, I encountered a little boy with a sheep and two lambs before him; he was crying terribly, and I supposed the lambs were skittish, and would not be guided.

"What is the matter, my little man?" I asked.

"They's Heathcliff and a woman, yonder, under t' Nab," he blubbered, "un' Aw darnut pass 'em."

I saw nothing; but neither the sheep nor he would go on, so I bid him take the road lower down.

He probably raised the phantoms from thinking, as he traversed the moors alone, on the nonsense he had heard his parents and companions repeat—yet still, I don't like being out in the dark, now; and I don't like being left by myself in this grim house. I cannot help it, I shall be glad when they leave it, and shift to the Grange!

"They are going to the Grange, then?" I said.

"Yes," answered Mrs. Dean, "as soon as they are married; and that will be on New Year's day."

"And who will live here then?"

"Why, Joseph will take care of the house, and, perhaps, a lad to keep him company. They will live in the kitchen, and the rest will be shut up."

"For the use of such ghosts as choose to inhabit it," I observed.

"No, Mr. Lockwood," said Nelly, shaking her head. "I believe the dead are at peace, but it is not right to speak of them with levity."

At that moment the garden gate swung to; the ramblers were returning.

"*They* are afraid of nothing," I grumbled, watching their approach through the window. "Together they would brave Satan and all his legions."

As they stepped onto the door-stones, and halted to take a last look at the moon, or, more correctly, at each other, by her light, I felt irresistibly impelled to escape them again; and, pressing a remembrance into the hand of Mrs. Dean, and disregarding her expostulations at my rudeness, I vanished through the kitchen, as they opened the house-door, and so should have confirmed Joseph in his opinion of his fellow-servant's gay indiscretions, had he not, fortunately, recognised me for a respectable character by the sweet ring of a sovereign at his feet.

My walk home was lengthened by a diversion in the direction of the Kirk. When beneath its walls, I perceived decay had made progress, even in seven months: many a window showed black gaps deprived of glass; and slates jutted off, here and there, beyond the right line of the roof, to be gradually worked off in coming autumn storms.

I sought, and soon discovered, the three head-stones on the slope next the moor—the middle one, grey, and half buried in heath—Edgar Linton's only harmonized by the turf, and moss creeping up its foot—Heathcliff's still bare.

I lingered round them, under that benign sky; watched the moths fluttering among the heath and hare-bells; listened to the soft wind breathing through the grass; and wondered how any one could ever imagine unquiet slumbers for the sleepers in that quiet earth.

THE END.

# Textual Commentary

## By William M. Sale, Jr.

An account of the printing and publishing of *Wuthering Heights* helps to make clear the problems that an editor must face. We know that each of the three Brontë sisters had written first novels and had had a discouraging experience in finding a publisher. After a prolonged search, Emily and her sister Anne finally had to come to terms with Thomas C. Newby, who seems to have been primarily a printer, but sometimes undertook to publish the books he printed.[1] Newby agreed to print their novels only if they shared the risk, and demanded £50 as advance payment.[2] *Wuthering Heights* finally appeared as Volumes I and II of a three-volume set (the third volume contained Anne Brontë's *Agnes Grey*), but in dealing with Newby the two sisters had had their troubles. He was to print 350 copies but printed only 250; he was dilatory in supplying proof-sheets; and he was indifferent to corrections in proof made by the author.[3]

Charlotte Brontë, whose *Jane Eyre* had been published by Smith, Elder, and Company shortly before *Wuthering Heights*, wrote to her publisher that "the orthography and punctuation of the books [*Wuthering Heights* and *Agnes Grey*] are mortifying to a degree: almost all the errors that were corrected in the proof-sheets appear intact in what should have been the fair copies. If Mr. Newby always does business in this way, few authors would like to have him for their publisher a second time."[4] Charlotte's judgment that the novels "abound in errors of the press" is clearly corroborated by even a casual examination of the text of the first edition, but it seems impossible to deny that some of the errors and inconsistencies in matters of form were the responsibility of Emily herself. Charlotte is thought to have been more meticulous about such matters than her sister, but she wrote to her far more responsible publisher to thank him for "punctuating the sheets" of *Jane Eyre*, "as I found the task very puzzling, and, besides, I consider your mode of punctuation a great deal more correct and rational than my own."[5] Thus we can see that even Charlotte was uncertain about formal matters and gave evidence of continued uncertainty in the large number of changes she made between the first edition of *Jane Eyre* (1847) and the second and third (1848).[6] When she came to revise *Wuthering Heights* for the second edition two years after Emily's death (1850), she made changes of the same sort in Emily's text. But if Charlotte had much to learn about these matters, Emily surely had as much or more.

Newby, however, is certainly responsible for many of the errors in Emily's text. Typographical errors abound (*modlled* for *modelled*, *had'nt* for *hadn't*, *wick* for *wicked*); letters are transposed and out of alignment; ellipsis dots are sometimes used in place of dashes; hyphens are occasionally omitted at the ends of lines when words are divided. Some of the mispunctuation is hard to account for except as a consequence of Newby's ignorance or carelessness. But the degree to which printer and author should share in the responsibility for the state of the text can never be exactly determined. The manuscript of the novel has never been discovered and probably was destroyed before or shortly after Emily's death. A copy of the first volume of the first edition, said to have been her own copy and to contain a few revisions in her handwriting, provides little help, for the emendations are too few to make clear the nature and degree of her dissatisfaction with the text.[7] Consequently the responsibility of an editor of this novel is serious if he wants to respect at the same time the text of the author and the needs of the modern reader.

Faced with this responsibility, most of those who have undertaken to make the book available solved their problem by simply reprinting, more or less accurately, the second edition, elaborately revised by Charlotte Brontë and apparently so paragraphed that *Wuthering Heights* and *Agnes Grey*, originally containing 1,127 pages, might be issued in one volume of 504 pages.[8] In this century, however, beginning with Clement Shorter's edition in 1911, there has been a growing tendency to reject Charlotte Brontë's version of the text—a version perhaps justly stigmatized by H. W. Garrod in 1930 as frequently indicating "misunderstanding or defective appreciation of the original."[9] But no editor or publisher who has decided to return to the text of the first edition has contemplated reprinting that edition with all its errors. Among modern reprints the nature and the number of retained errors varies radically, however, and, with one exception, the editing has been done silently. It is particularly unfortunate that the handsomely printed Shakespeare Head Edition of *Wuthering Heights* (Vol. III of the nineteen-volume works of all the Brontës, edited by Thomas J. Wise and John Alexander Symington) should have laid itself open to the charge of having retained "variant spellings of proper names" and a host of "unnecessary and misleading commas."[10] It is true that in a note of this edition of the novel the editors promised that the "chief variations [between the first and second editions] will be noted in the bibliography to be printed in a later volume." The failure to provide this information was perhaps due to Wise's death, which occurred shortly before the publication of the last volume of this work, but in any case, it would be more interesting to have had a note indicating why certain changes were *not* made.

If, however, Charlotte's Brontë's edition should not be used as the basis for the text, and Emily Brontë's first edition must be edited, how ought an editor proceed? I do not believe that Charlotte's painstaking efforts should be rejected in toto, especially when we know that she was aware of the printer's failure to make corrections proposed by the author in her proof-sheets, nor do I believe that an editor need be scrupulous to retain the erratic punctuations of the first edition under the impression that Emily's prose rhythms might be lost if her pointing is not preserved. On the other hand, having said this much for the need of revising the punctuation, we must recognize that this punctuation, inconsistent as it is and corrupted by a shoddy printer, often seems representative of the author's intent and is characteristic of her country and of her century. Certain intentions can be discerned, despite the author's inconsistencies and the printer's indifference. These intentions I have tried to recognize.[11] I have also retained Emily's paragraphing, for there is no reason to believe that Charlotte's drastic reduction in the number of paragraphs represented anything more than the publisher's desire to print three volumes as one.

1. See an exchange of letters between Newby and the editors of the *Examiner*, July 29, August 5, 12, 1848. See also *The Brontës: Their Lives, Friendships and Correspondence*, ed. Wise and Symington, Oxford, Shakespeare Head Press, 4 vols., 1932, II, 241–45.
2. *The Brontës*, II, 145; III, 160.
3. *Ibid.*, III, 156; II, 154–56; 165.
4. *Ibid.*, II, 165.
5. *Ibid.*, II, 142.
6. M. L. Parrish, *Victorian Lady Novelists*, Constable and Co., London, 1933, pp. 99–155.
7. See below, p. 263.
8. The text of the novels concludes on p. 468, followed by literary remains of Emily and Anne.
9. *Wuthering Heights* (World's Classics edition), Oxford University Press, London, 1961, p. vii. (Editor's Introduction dated 1930.)
10. *Brontë Society Publications*, Part XLII (No. 1 of Vol. VIII), 1932, p. 34.
11. For instance, the almost unrestrained use of the exclamation point; the frequent use of the colon when the sentence that follows is explanatory of the one that precedes; the use of the semicolon preceding a final participial phrase; and the use of the question mark in indirect questions which usually retain the word order of the direct from (e.g., *I asked, how was the baby?*).

# NOTES TO THE TEXT

In each entry below, the numbers refer to the page and line of the present text where the word or phrase under discussion is located. The following abbreviations are used in these notes:

A: *Wuthering Heights*, 1847 (the first edition)

B: *Wuthering Heights*, 1850 (the second edition, revised by Charlotte Brontë)

B *et al*: The second edition and most of the later editions

C: *Wuthering Heights*, Vol. 1, 1847 (said to have corrections in Emily Brontë's handwriting. See p. 263.)

C.B.: Charlotte Brontë

E.B.: Emily Brontë

S.H.: *Wuthering Heights*, 1931. (Vol. III of the Shakespeare Head Edition)

Shorter: *Wuthering Heights*, 1911 (Vol. II of *The Complete Works of Emily Brontë*, ed. Clement Shorter)

**3.30 court—**
In A, dialogue is introduced by a concluding semicolon, period, comma, or dash at the close of the preceding paragraph. Since *E.B.* most frequently used the dash, I have used this mark throughout.

**7.12 chipping off**
A: *chipping of*, surely a misprint.

**7.24–28 On coming \* \* \*—on mounting**
A: "On coming up from dinner. \* \* \* On mounting the stairs. \* \* \*" I have punctuated this sentence so that the opening phrase may not stand as an awkward fragment.

**8.11 Nor-ne me**
In A, *nor-ne me* becomes *nor nuh me* on p. 107. At that point *C.B.* substitutes *none o' me.*

**8.28 door**
A: *floor*, when the sense requires *door.*

**11.13 bordering on repulsive**
C: "bordering on *the* repulsive."

**14.44 Wisht**
In A, *wisht* is used with comparative frequency and by several characters. It is a less common variant of *whisht* or *whish*, meaning *hush, be silent, hold your tongue.*

**20.28 gripe**
A variant spelling of *grip.*

**22.27 access**
*B et al: excess*; perhaps advisedly, but *E.B.* uses *access* in similar contexts on pp. 89 and 102, and may mean to do so.

**22.34–35 his shadow's arm**
*B et al:* "by the motion of his arm's shadow." The reading of A is more interesting.

**32.11–13 our curate \* \* \* he**
*B et al:* omits the colloquial *he* in this construction.

**32.36 last**
B: *latter.*

**34.12 done so longer**
A: *done longer.*

**36.8 Heathcliff bore**
A: "He bore"; B: "*Heathcliff* bore."

**41.7–8 I removed \* \* \* shoes**
A: "I removed the habit, and there shone forth, beneath a grand plaid silk frock, white trousers, and burnisheds shoes"; I have supplied the punctuation of B, for surely *E.B.* meant that three items—frock, trousers, and shoes—shone forth when the habit was removed.

**41.28 counterpart**
A and B: counterpart *to*

**47.5–6 the place was so full**
A: "it was so full"; C: "*the place* was so full."

**48.28 surface change**
B: *surface, change*, but this punctuation changes the meaning and seems unwarranted.

**49.38 when**
A: *then*; B: *when*, advisedly.

**50.11 I asked, how was the baby?**
I have followed E.B.'s practice of using question marks in such indirect questions as *I asked, what was the matter?* But A at this point reads: *I asked, how was the baby?"* with a closing but no opening quotation mark. Modern editors frequently attempt to remedy matters by supplying an opening quotation mark: *I asked, "how was the baby?"* E.B. never resorts to this curious punctuation for indirect questions.

**51.11 there was**
A: "he had plenty of wickedness"; C: "*there was* plenty of wickedness," an improvement, perhaps, but the sentence is still an awkward one.

**53.37 Pennistow**
Probably not a misprint for *Penistone*, but a spelling to suggest a dialect sound.

**59.5 Maker**
A: *maker*; B: *Maker*, presumably to make the blasphemy more apparent.

**65.40 Hathecliff's**
B: *Heathcliff's*, but surely unwarranted.

**67.33 the room filled**
C: "the room *was* filled," an acceptable change, but of no real importance.

**68.8 und bolt intuh th' hahs**
A: "nud bolt intuh th' haks"; C: "and bolt intuh th' house." I have merely corrected the apparent misprints, *nud* and *haks.*

**70.40 sizer's**
An alternative spelling of *sizar*, retained in B.

**72.1 It had got dusk**
C: "It *was* dusk."

**81.6 lugs**
A: *higs*, a misprint; C: *ears.*

**83.6 pining**
B: *dining*, a misprint, changed by some modern editors to *dying!*

**84.35 trembled**
*Shorter:* "trembled *in* every limb," but the verb can take a direct object. Keats uses it as a transitive verb.

**85.20 barn**
B and *S.H.: bairn*, but *barn* is an alternative dialect spelling.

**86.36 the art**
*Shorter:* the *heart*, but why?

**87.13 jealous of \* \* \* jealous for**
A: "I'm not jealous of you" \* \* \* "I'm jealous for you." B: italicizes *of* and *for*, and I have adopted this emendation.

**92.9 rung**
B: *rang*, but *C.B.* used *rung* as the past tense of *ring* in the first edition of *Jane Eyre* (1847), changing it (but not always) to *rang* in the second edition (1848). See M. L. Parrish, *Victorian Lady Novelists* (London, 1933), pp. 99–155. *E.B.* uses *sprung* instead of *sprang*, *sunk* instead of *sank.*

**93.8 and while**
A: "and she fasted pertinaciously"; C: "and *while* she fasted pertinaciously." By this change a firmer parallelism is established between this clause and the one that opens the sentence.

**93.27 ate**
A: *eat*, but A has *ate* for the past tense on p. 243. *C.B.* uses *eat* for the past tense in the first edition of *Jane Eyre* changing later to *ate.* See Parrish, *op. cit.*, in note to 92.9.

**95.29 Penistone**
A: *Peniston*, a misprint. This natural phenomenon is usually referred to as Penistone Crags, but *E.B.* thinks of it sometimes as *it*, sometimes as *them*, and hence uses both Penistone *Crag* and Penistone *Crags.* I have followed her text with respect to the number of the noun, but have used the spelling *Crags* throughout, though she occasionally uses the alternative

spelling *Craggs*. See note to 146.9. Ponden Kirk, a black gloomy rock, towering above the head of Ponden Valley, has been identified as "Penistone Crags."

**100.29–30 suspended by a handkerchief**
A: "suspended *to* a handkerchief"; B: "suspended *by* a handkerchief."

**101.23 thick**
C: *friendly*; B: *intimate. Shorter*, alone among modern editors, follows C.

**102.7–8 if pursued instantly**
In some modern editions (e.g., the Oxford World's Classics edition, p. 162, and the Rinehart edition, p. 139), this passage is revised to read "if *I* pursued instantly." But *E.B.* may have intended "if pursued instantly," that is, in effect, "if they were pursued instantly." *B* retains the reading of A.

**103.16 mistake him, besides—**
*Shorter* alone omits *besides*, perhaps on the authority of C. See p. 274.

**117.18 one bit**
A: "a bit"; B: "*one* bit."

**118.45–129.1 and watch * * * mischief**
A: "and watch till I departed—your conscience quite calm, you would be hindering mischief." I think the meaning requires the punctuation I have adopted.

**120.14 mother!**
A: Vol. I ends here.

**122.43 if *you***
A: "if you"; B: "if *you*."

**125.25 westering**
B: *western*, but *C.B.* uses *westering* in the first edition of *Jane Eyre*. See Parrish, *op. cit.*, in note to 92.9.

**128.3–4 inhabitant**
A and B: *inhabitants*, but surely the singular form is required.

**129.33–34 The murdered * * * on earth**
A: "The murdered *do* haunt their murderers. I believe—I know that ghosts *have* wandered on earth." The punctuation I have adopted seems to secure E.B.'s meaning, to contrast what is believed with what is known.

**130.26 grave; he**
A: "grave; *and* he sent no excuse, but he never came." B deletes the *and* as I have done.

**133.30 proceeded**
A and B: "He was worked up * * * and *proceeding* to murderous violence"; I have followed later editions in changing *proceeding* to *proceeded*.

**135.12 for a sympathy**
A: "searching in my eyes, a sympathy"; B: "searching in my eyes *for* a sympathy."

**138.7 Heathcliff was not**
A: "he was not"; B: "*Heathcliff* was not."

**138.12 his opponent was ignorant**
A: "he was ignorant"; B: "*his opponent* was ignorant."

**142.28 there were**
A: there *was*.

**146.9 Penistone Crags**
A: Penistone Crags, but *E.B.* immediately refers to the Crags as "it." Later, in the same conversation, she writes: "*they* are not worth the trouble."

**149.23 Hareton offered**
A: "*But* Hareton offered"; B: "Hareton offered."

**154.28 were sorrow**
B et al: "*was* sorrow."

**158.27 If he have**
B et al: "If he *has*."

**165.33–34 Are you Linton?**
A: *Are you, Linton?*; B et al: *Are you Linton?*. This change in punctuation seems to secure the intended meaning.

**176.1 tenure**
A: *tenour*; B: *tenor*.

**179.38 hadn't the skill to**
A: *hadn't skill to*, retained by B.

**180.16–17 if the master were in?**
B et al: "if the master *was* in?"

**198.15 she changed**
A: "and changed"; B: "*she* changed."

**205.16 vivisection**
A: *vivifisection*, possibly a misprint.

**212.42 store every tear**
B follows A with "store every tear." Some later editions read "store *up* every tear."

**232.23 Ee**
*E.B.* usually employs *Aw* for *I* in rendering dialect, but here she uses *Ee* and on p. 242 she uses E. *Ee* is the usual dialect form for *eye*, and *E* the usual form for *he*.

**242.10 wisely**
*Unwisely* might be expected.

**243.23 ate**
See note to 93.27.

**243.44 thick again**
B: "*friends* again." See p. 101 and note to 101.23.

**246.1–3 he was * * * healthy**
A: "he was neither in danger of losing his senses, nor dying, according to my judgment he was quite strong and healthy." The punctuation here leaves the meaning in doubt. Mine secures what seems the likeliest meaning.

**248.25–26 rare and pleased**
B: *rarely pleased*, which distorts the meaning.

**250.14 imaging**
B: *imagining*, but *C.B.* uses *imaging* in the first edition of *Jane Eyre*, revising for the second edition. See Parrish, *op. cit.*, in note to 92.9.

**255.21 Nab**
*E.B.* spells *Nab* with a small *n* on earlier pages. See p. 164, for example.

APPENDIX I. A NOTE ON EMILY BRONTË'S SPELLING AND CAPITALIZATION

Since Emily Brontë's corrections in proof were ignored by her printer, we cannot be sure which misspellings were printer's errors and which were Emily's. I have silently corrected such errors as *to* for *two*, *moddled* for *modelled*, *dam'n* for *damn*, *staunchily* for *staunchly*, *whose* for *who's*, Lin-

*ton's* for *Lintons*, and *her's* for *hers*. Beyond this, I have adopted the accepted spelling or capitalization for the following words which appear in two forms in the text. Those words marked with an asterisk appeared in the less conventional form in the first edition of *Jane Eyre* and were changed by Charlotte Brontë either in the second or third edition of her novel (M. L. Parrish, *Victorian Lady Novelists*, London, 1933, pp. 99–155). Perhaps neither sister was very sure of herself.

| | |
|---|---|
| awhile, a while: *a while* | methodist, Methodist: *Methodist* |
| *bible, Bible: *Bible* | miss, Miss: *Miss* |
| *christian, Christian: *Christian* | mistress, Mistress: *mistress* |
| christmas, Christmas: *Christmas* | parlor, parlour: *parlour* |
| dose, doze: *doze* | *ribband, riband: *riband* |
| *eat, ate (past tense): *ate* | satan, Satan: *Satan* |
| *good bye, good-bye: *good-bye* | soliloquise, soliloquize: *soliloquize* |
| *heaven, Heaven: *heaven* | staid, stayed: *stayed* |
| hell, Hell: *hell* | teazing, teasing: *teasing* |
| him, Him (God): *Him* | up stairs, up-stairs: *upstairs* |
| lighted, alighted: *alighted* | wont, won't: *won't* |
| mama, mamma: *mamma* | |

The following words I have changed as indicated. When used more than once, they are used in the same form. Some may be misprints.

| | |
|---|---|
| affected: *effected* | in doors: *indoors* |
| bannister: *banister* | journies: *journeys* |
| changling: *changeling* | no where: *nowhere* |
| confidant: *confident* | quaker: *Quaker* |
| down stairs: *downstairs* | sometime: *some time* |
| every body: *everybody* | tormenter: *tormentor* |
| every thing: *everything* | transcient: *transient* |
| gallopped: *galloped* | visiter: *visitor* |

Charlotte Brontë changed *bannister* to *banister* for the second edition of *Jane Eyre*, and she never quite made up her mind about *upstairs*.

### APPENDIX II. THE YORKSHIRE DIALECT

When Charlotte Brontë was preparing the second and revised edition of *Wuthering Heights*, she wrote to her publisher: "It seems to me advisable to modify the orthography of the old servant Joseph's speeches; for though as it stands it exactly renders the Yorkshire dialect to a Yorkshire ear, yet I am sure Southerns must find it unintelligible; and thus one of the most graphic characters in the book is lost on them" (*The Brontës: Their Lives, Friendships and Correspondence*, ed. Wise and Symington, 4 vols., Oxford, 1932, III, 165). Charlotte's method of modifying the orthography I have commented on in my preface. She is probably right in saying that to a

Yorkshire ear the dialect would be intelligible though few of the words are specifically Yorkshire. Christopher Dean, who is well informed about these matters, says that the "dialect used is northern in which there are no elements foreign to the West Riding" of Yorkshire ("Joseph's Speech in 'Wuthering Heights,' " *Notes and Queries*, N.S. VII, February, 1960, 73–76), though he qualifies the statement in one respect, which I shall point out below. Most of the words are marked in the *New English Dictionary* and in Joseph Wright's *English Dialect Dictionary* as Scottish and north of England.

It has been generally assumed that Emily Brontë became familiar with the dialect largely through a servant of the Brontës, Tabitha (Tabby) Akyroyd, who, according to a fragment of Emily's diary written when she was sixteen, said, "Ya pitter pottering there instead of pilling a potate"—Emily's early attempt at rendering dialect (*The Brontës*, I, 124). Tabby is reported to have sung "the children ballads and told them tales of the 'fairish' (fairies) which lived in the Bottom before machinery drove them away, stories of 'the graves under the rectory back-kitchen,' of witches running red-hot needles into human flesh" (Romer Wilson, *All Alone: The Life and Private History of Emily Jane Brontë*, London, 1928, p. 65).

Emily Brontë seems to have been surprisingly successful in rendering the sounds of the northern dialect, though her method is not always consistently employed, and occasionally her words are directed to the eye and not the ear as when, for example, she uses *wer* for *were*, *ses* for *says*, and *holld* for *hold*. Christopher Dean points out that sometimes her spelling suggests a sound not common to the north of England but sugestive of Irish, as when she uses *spake* for *speak*, *clane* for *clean*, *stale* for *steal*, *dacent* for *decent*.

The reader will soon become familiar with the use of such forms as *t'* for *the*, *'t* for *it*, *i* for *in*, *nut* for *not*, *tuh* for *to*, *on* for *of*, *soa* for *so* or *therefore*.

APPENDIX III. EMILY BRONTË'S COPY OF WUTHERING HEIGHTS

When Clement Shorter edited *Wuthering Heights* in 1911 (Vol. II of a two-volume edition of *The Works of Emily Brontë*), he said in his preface (p. xi) that his text was "set up in type from Emily Brontë's own copy of *Wuthering Heights*, which was carried by Mr. Arthur Bell Nicholls [Charlotte's husband] from Haworth to his later home in Banagher in Ireland, where it rested on his shelves for more than forty years." His declared intention "to present the book here as it left its author's hands" was not fully realized, as has been pointed out in Frederick Page's textual notes to the World's Classics edition (Oxford University Press, 1930). But Page did not record all the changes made by Shorter and failed to note some interesting instances in which Shorter provided readings that differ from the first edition and from all other reprintings of the text. Shorter himself gave no authority for these variant readings, but Thomas J. Wise in his *Bibliography of the Writings and Prose and Verse of the Members of the Brontë Family* (1917) says that Clement Shorter's copy of *Wuthering Heights*, "formerly the property of Emily Brontë herself," has fifteen corrections in Vol. I "marked in pencil in her own handwriting" (p. 101). Wise lists nine of these fifteen corrections, and Shorter silently introduces these nine (and perhaps the six others) into his edition. After Shorter's death in 1926, this copy was sold at Sotheby's to Walter Spencer, a London bookseller, for £26 (*Book Auction Records*, XXV, 359, Sale of June 18, 1928) and in 1952 was acquired by J. E. Kite, then of Hove, Sussex. My efforts to locate Mr. Kite have finally proved successful, and he would have graciously permitted me to examine Emily's copy had it still been in his library. He had, however, sold it at Sotheby's in 1964, where it was purchased by Horace G. Commin, a bookseller at Bournemouth, presumably for a private collector (Sale of July 28, 1964, and *Book Auction Records*, Vol. 61, where the price was given as £420). I have not been able to secure from Mr. Commin any information about the present location of the copy.

Conflicting evidence abounds as to the number of corrections in Vol. I. Wise, as I have said, counted fifteen but listed only nine. In 1954 Mr. Kite reported that there were twelve corrections "in her own unmistakable writing" (*The Sunday Times*, September 26). When the copy was sold at Sotheby's, it was described as having "twenty-three corrections written in pencil, in her hand," those on the nine pages listed by Wise and on twelve other pages. Since nine and twelve add up to only twenty-one, there must have been more than one correction on one or two of these pages to make up the sum of twenty-three noted by Sotheby's. To make matters worse, Sotheby's reports that pp. 163–168 of Vol. I are missing, as are the title-pages in both volumes.

Shorter, as I have said, failed to identify any of the variants that he introduced. Even more inexplicably, Wise, when he edited the novel for the Shakespeare Head Edition (1931), failed to introduce the variants which he himself had listed in 1917. I have indicated in my textual notes the nine revisions listed by Wise and silently introduced by Shorter (see notes to 11.13, 47.5–6, 51.11, 67.33, 68.8, 72.1, 81.6, 93.8, and 101.23). For my text, however, I have adopted only three of these nine changes, since only these three make for greater clarity. A laborious collation of Shorter's text with the other modern editions might serve to locate other corrections found by Wise and by Sotheby's for their catalogue of 1964. But I suspect that if found they would prove of little significance. A casual collation of Shorter revealed only such variants as the following: Shorter (173.9) omits the *besides* in my edition on 103.16; he substitutes a *these* (174.2) for the *those* on 103.38, and a *here* (190.34) for the *there* on 114.11.

# BACKGROUNDS

# Poems from the 1850
# *Wuthering Heights* †

As Charlotte Brontë explained in the biographical notice she wrote for the 1850 *Wuthering Heights*, her accidental discovery of a manuscript volume of Emily's poems five years earlier caused her to urge their publication. She recalled thinking they "were not common effusions, nor at all like the poetry women generally write. I thought them condensed and terse, vigorous and genuine. To my ear, they had also a peculiar music—wild, melancholy, and elevating." Choosing pseudonyms that would leave their gender ambiguous, Charlotte and her sisters in 1846 published their volume, *Poems* by Currer, Ellis and Acton Bell. As Charlotte later remarked, the book was scarcely known, but she remained convinced of the quality of Emily's poetry, and to the 1850 *Wuthering Heights* and *Agnes Grey* appended a selection of Emily's and Anne's poems along with an introductory memoir of Emily. Charlotte thus brought Emily's poems to the attention of many readers, including Emily Dickinson, who owned the 1850 edition and admired especially "No Coward Soul," which was read at Dickinson's funeral. Charlotte's choice of poems and of titles for some of them, as well as her few annotative comments and numerous editorial changes, documents her role as intermediary between her late sister and the many readers who were perplexed by if not hostile to *Wuthering Heights*. Through inclusion of the poems as well as through biographical and critical commentary in the 1850 edition, Charlotte furthered interest in Emily's originality, poetic prose, and mysticism. By not distinguishing which of the poems were parts of Emily's Gondal saga and which may have been independent efforts, Charlotte inadvertently initiated misunderstandings about which poems speak dramatically or narratively and which are more personal and lyrical.

For twelve of the Emily Brontë poems that Charlotte included in the 1850 edition, Juliet R. V. Barker in *The Brontës: Selected Poems* (1985) has provided annotation that describes what is known of the compositional history and of Charlotte's editorial changes. The text for the other six poems that Charlotte published is from C. W. Hatfield, *The Complete Poems of Emily Jane Brontë* (1941). In order to understand the nature and extent of Charlotte's editing, this edition presents the poems as Emily left them, and the annotations indicate Charlotte's changes.

# [CHARLOTTE BRONTË]

## Selections

It would not have been difficult to compile a volume out of the papers left by my sisters, had I, in making the selection, dismissed from my consideration the scruples and the wishes of those whose written thoughts these

---

† The poems on pp. 269–88 are reprinted from *The Brontës: Selected Poems*, edited by Juliet R. V. Barker, by permission of J. M. Dent and Sons Ltd.

papers held. But this was impossible: an influence, stronger than could be exercised by any motive of expediency, necessarily regulated the selection. I have, then, culled from the mass only a little poem here and there. The whole makes but a tiny nosegay, and the colour and perfume of the flowers are not such as fit them for festal uses.

It has been already said that my sisters wrote much in childhood and girlhood. Usually, it seems a sort of injustice to expose in print the crude thoughts of the unripe mind, the rude efforts of the unpractised hand; yet I venture to give three little poems of my sister Emily's, written in her sixteenth year, because they illustrate a point in her character.

At that period she was sent to school. Her previous life, with the exception of a single half-year, had been passed in the absolute retirement of a village parsonage, amongst the hills bordering Yorkshire and Lancashire. The scenery of these hills is not grand—it is not romantic; it is scarcely striking. Long low moors, dark with heath, shut in little valleys, where a stream waters, here and there, a fringe of stunted copse. Mills and scattered cottages chase romance from these valleys; it is only higher up, deep in amongst the ridges of the moors, that Imagination can find rest for the sole of her foot: and even if she finds it there, she must be a solitude-loving raven—no gentle dove. If she demand beauty to inspire her, she must bring it inborn: these moors are too stern to yield any product so delicate. The eye of the gazer must *itself* brim with a 'purple light,' intense enough to perpetuate the brief flower-flush of August on the heather, or the rare sunset-smile of June; out of his heart must well the freshness, that in latter spring and early summer brightens the bracken, nurtures the moss, and cherishes the starry flowers that spangle for a few weeks the pasture of the moor-sheep. Unless that light and freshness are innate and self-sustained, the drear prospect of a Yorkshire moor will be found as barren of poetic as of agricultural interest: where the love of wild nature is strong, the locality will perhaps be clung to with the more passionate constancy, because from the hill-lover's self comes half its charm.

My sister Emily loved the moors. Flowers brighter than the rose bloomed in the blackest of the heath for her; out of a sullen hollow in a livid hillside her mind could make an Eden. She found in the bleak solitude many and dear delights; and not the least and best loved was—liberty.

Liberty was the breath of Emily's nostrils; without it, she perished. The change from her own home to a school, and from her own very noiseless, very secluded, but unrestricted and inartificial mode of life, to one of disciplined routine (though under the kindliest auspices) was what she failed in enduring. Her nature proved here too strong for her fortitude. Every morning when she woke, the vision of home and the moors rushed on her, and darkened and saddened the day that lay before her. Nobody knew what ailed her but me—I knew only too well. In this struggle her health was quickly broken: her white face, attenuated form, and failing strength threatened rapid decline. I felt in my heart she would die, if she did not go home, and with this conviction obtained her recall. She had only been three months at school; and it was some years before the experiment of sending her from home was again ventured on. After the age of twenty, having meantime studied alone with diligence and perseverance, she went with me to an establishment on the Continent: the same suffering and conflict ensued, heightened by the strong recoil of her upright, heretic and English spirit from the gentle Jesuitry of the foreign and Romish system. Once more she seemed sinking, but this time she rallied through the mere force of resolution: with inward remorse and shame she looked back on her former failure, and resolved to conquer in this second ordeal. She did conquer: but the victory cost her dear. She was never happy till she carried her hard-won knowledge back to the remote English village, the old parsonage-house, and desolate Yorkshire hills. A very few years more, and she looked her last on those hills, and breathed her last in that house, and under the aisle of that obscure village church found her last lowly resting-place. Merciful was the decree that spared her when she was a stranger in a strange land, and guarded her dying bed with kindred love and congenial constancy.

The following pieces[1] were composed at twilight, in the schoolroom, when the leisure of the evening play-hour brought back in full tide the thoughts of home.

## Stanzas†

A little while, a little while,
The noisy crowd are barred away;[1]
And I can sing and I can smile
A little while I've holyday![2]

Where wilt thou go, my harassed heart?
Full many a land invites thee now;[3]
And places near and far apart
Have rest for thee, my weary brow.[4]

---

1. Charlotte refers to the first three reprinted poems.
† (4 December 1838). This poem is one of the few which can, with some confidence, be placed in a personal rather than a Gondal setting. Again, the poem was a result of Emily's employment at Law Hill: freed from the daily grind of teaching for a few hours, she is at liberty to indulge in dreams. Two ways are open to her: one is to linger on thoughts of her dearly loved home, the other is to take the more adventurous path to Gondal, and this is the one she finally chooses. The moorland scenery of Gondal is so similar to that of Haworth that the two have often been confused. There are distinct differences, however, including the more dramatic mountains and glens of the imaginary kingdom. Charlotte's substitution of the word 'sheep' for the more exotic 'deer' when she published the poem seems to be a deliberate attempt to obscure a Gondal allusion. The result of Charlotte's alterations is to make the second alternative open to the dreamer of the poem a more mundane one which, taken at face value by the uninitiated reader, could be misconstrued as simply meaning a moorland landscape in the real world.

1. The weary task is put away (1850).
2. A *little*: Alike (1850). A misreading by Charlotte.
3. What spot, or near or far apart (1850).
4. *Have*: Has (1850).

There is a spot mid barren hills
Where winter howls and driving rain,
But if the dreary tempest chills
There is a light that warms again.

The house is old, the trees are bare
And moonless bends the misty dome[5]
But what on earth is half so dear,
So longed for as the hearth of home?

The mute bird sitting on the stone,
The dank moss dripping from the wall,
The garden-walk with weeds o'er-grown,[6]
I love them—how I love them all!

Shall I go there? or shall I seek
Another clime, another sky,
Where tongues familiar music speak
In accents dear to memory?

Yes, as I mused, the naked room,[7]
The flickering firelight died away[8]
And from the midst of cheerless gloom
I passed to bright, unclouded day—

A little and a lone green lane,
That opened on a common wide;
A distant, dreamy, dim blue chain
Of mountains circling every side;

A heaven so clear, an earth so calm,
So sweet, so soft, so hushed an air
And, deepening still the dream-like charm,
Wild moor-sheep feeding everywhere—

That was the scene; I knew it well,
I knew the path-ways far and near[9]
That winding o'er each billowy swell
Marked out the tracks of the wandering deer.[1]

Could I have lingered but an hour
It well had paid a week of toil,
But truth has banished fancy's power;
I hear my dungeon bars recoil—[2]

---

5. Moonless above bends twilight's dome (1850).
6. The thorn trees gaunt, the walks o'er grown (1850).
7. *Yes*: Still (1850).
8. *flickering*: alien (1850).
9. I knew the turfy pathway's sweep (1850).
1. *deer*: sheep (1850).
2. Restraint of heavy task recoil (1850).

Even as I stood with raptured eye
Absorbed in bliss so deep and dear
My hour of rest had fleeted by
And given me back to weary care.[3]

## The Bluebell†

The blue bell is the sweetest flower
That waves in summer air;
Its blossoms have the mightiest power
To soothe my spirit's care.

There is a spell in purple heath
Too wildly, sadly dear;
The violet has a fragrant breath,
But fragrance will not cheer.

The trees are bare, the sun is cold,
And seldom, seldom seen;
The heavens have lost their zone of gold
The earth its robe of green;[1]

And ice upon the glancing stream
Has cast its sombre shade
And distant hills and valleys seem
In frozen mist arrayed.

The blue bell cannot charm me now,
The heath has lost its bloom,
The violets in the glen below
They yield no sweet perfume.

But though I mourn the heather-bell[2]
'Tis better far, away;
I know how fast my tears would swell
To see it smile to-day;

3. And back came labour, bondage, care (1850).
† (18 December 1838). This poem, severely truncated by Charlotte, was published in 1850. Though the date suggests it was written during the holiday period, on internal evidence it seems to have been at least begun during Emily's brief foray into the world of the governess at Law Hill. * * * A winter landscape, consonant with the December date of the manuscript, is evocatively described in lines 9–16, but it is the memory of summer flowers which causes the poet to mourn the fields of home. The thought of heather, with its associations with Emily's beloved moors, is too painful to dwell on, but bluebells have a softer and more soothing spell. The description of the bluebell in lines 29–32 suggests, however, that the flower Emily had in mind was the harebell which, with its delicate stem, silvery blue flowers and slender buds, better fits her picture than the bluebell with its coarse stem and spray of dark blue flowers. * * *

1. *its*: her (1850).
2. *heather-bell*: sweet Bluebell (1850). This change was necessitated by Charlotte's omission of the next four verses elaborating on the three flowers which had most powerful associations for Emily.

And that wood flower that hides so shy[3]
Beneath its mossy stone
Its balmy scent and dewy eye:
'Tis not for them I moan.

It is the slight and stately stem,
The blossoms silvery blue,
The buds hid like a sapphire gem
In sheaths of emerald hue.

'Tis these that breathe upon my heart
A calm and softening spell
That if it makes the tear-drop start
Has power to soothe as well.

For these I weep, so long divided
Through winter's dreary day,
In longing weep—but most when guided
On withered banks to stray.

If chilly then the light should fall
Adown the dreary sky[4]
And gild the dank and darkened wall[5]
With transient brilliancy,

How do I yearn, how do I pine[6]
For the time of flowers to come,
And turn me from that fading shine
To mourn the fields of home.

## Stanzas[†]

Loud without the wind was roaring
Through the waned autumnal sky;[1]

3. 25–40 omitted (1850). The woodflower in line 25 is the violet.
4. *the*: that (1850).
5. *the*: yon (1850).
6. *yearn*: weep (1850).
† (11 November 1838). This poem probably had a Gondal setting though it was inspired by the circumstances of Emily's own life. For the first time since her brief and unhappy few months as a pupil at Roe Head school, she had left the family home, this time as a teacher at Law Hill school near Halifax. (Charlotte mistakenly attributed the composition of this, and the two following poems, to Emily's school days at Roe Head when she published them in 1850.) Understandably, given her reserved temperament and imaginative nature, she stood only six months of what Charlotte described as 'hard labour from six in the morning until near eleven at night, with only one half hour of exercise between' before her health gave way and she returned home. This poem, beginning gloomily with a description of an unpromising November evening, is suddenly sprung to life by the hearing of a song in the distance which sends the poet into a lyrical outpouring of longing for the moorlands of home. The sight of a few 'half blighted heather bells' similarly rouses her passionate longing for the carefree liberty of former years, just as the sight of bluebells growing near Scarborough revived Anne's homesickness. This poem ends on the hopeful note that the poet will see her beloved mountains again. Charlotte made a large number of changes when she published this poem in 1850.
1. Through th'autumnal sky (1850).

Drenching wet, the cold rain pouring
  Spoke of stormy winters nigh.[2]

All too like that dreary eve
Sighed within repining grief;[3]
Sighed at first, but sighed not long—
Sweet—How softly sweet it came!
Wild words of an ancient song,
Undefined, without a name.

'It was spring, for the skylark was singing.'[4]
  Those words, they awakened a spell—
They unlocked a deep fountain whose springing
Nor Absence nor Distance can quell.

In the gloom of a cloudy November,
They uttered the music of May;
They kindled the perishing ember
Into fervour that could not decay.

Awaken on all my dear moorlands[5]
The wind in its glory and pride!
O call me from valleys and highlands
To walk by the hill-river's side!

It is swelled with the first snowy weather;
The rocks they are icy and hoar,
And darker waves round the long heather,[6]
And the fern-leaves are sunny no more.

There are no yellow-stars on the mountain,
The blue-bells have long died away
From the brink of the moss-bedded fountain,
From the side of the wintery brae—

But lovelier than cornfields all waving
In emerald and scarlet and gold[7]
Are the slopes where the north-wind is raving,[8]
And the glens where I wandered of old.[9]

'It was morning, the bright sun was beaming.'
How sweetly that brought back to me[1]
The time when nor labour nor dreaming
Broke the sleep of the happy and free.

2. Spoke of winter nigh (1850).
3. Did my exiled spirit grieve
  Grieved at first, but grieved not long (1850).
4. 'It was spring, and the skylark was singing'
  (1850).
5. Awaken o'er all my dear moorland
  West wind, in thy glory and pride

  Oh! call me from valley and lowland
  To walk by the hill torrent's side. (1850).
6. And sullenly waves the long heather (1850).
7. In emerald and vermeil, and gold (1850).
8. *Slopes*: heights (1850).
9. *glens*: crags (1850).
1. *that*: it (1850).

But blithely we rose as the dusk heaven[2]
Was melting to amber and blue;
And swift were the wings to our feet given
While we traversed the meadows of dew,[3]

For the moors, for the moors where the short grass
Like velvet beneath us should lie!
For the moors, for the moors where each high pass
Rose sunny against the clear sky!

For the moors where the linnet was trilling
Its song on the old granite stone;
Where the lark—the wild sky-lark was filling
Every breast with delight like its own.

What language can utter the feeling
That rose when, in exile afar,[4]
On the brow of a lonely hill kneeling
I saw the brown heath growing there.

It was scattered and stunted, and told me
That soon even that would be gone;
It whispered, 'The grim walls enfold me;
I have bloomed in my last summer's sun.'

But not the loved music whose waking
Makes the soul of the Swiss die away
Has a spell more adored and heart-breaking
Than in its half-blighted bells lay.[5]

The spirit that bent 'neath its power,[6]
How it longed, how it burned to be free!
If I could have wept in that hour
Those tears had been heaven to me.

Well, well, the sad minutes are moving
Though loaded with trouble and pain;
And sometime the loved and the loving
Shall meet on the mountains again.

2. *dusk*: dawn (1850).
3. *While*: As (1850).
4. *That*: Which (1850).

5. Than, for me, in that blighted heath lay (1850).
6. *that*: which (1850).

## "Shall Earth no more inspire thee"†

Shall Earth no more inspire thee,
Thou lonely dreamer now?
Since passion may not fire thee
Shall Nature cease to bow?

Thy mind is ever moving
In regions dark to thee;
Recall its useless roving—
Come back, and dwell with me.

I know my mountain breezes
Enchant and soothe thee still—
I know my sunshine pleases
Despite thy wayward will.

When day with evening blending
Sinks from the summer sky,
I've seen thy spirit bending
In fond idolatry.

I've watched thee every hour;
I know my mighty sway:
I know my magic power
To drive thy griefs away.

Few hearts to mortals given
On earth so wildly pine;
Yet few would ask a Heaven
More like this Earth than thine.

Then let my winds caress thee;
Thy comrade let me be—
Since nought beside can bless thee,
Return and dwell with me.

---

† (16 May 1841). When Charlotte published this poem in 1850 (one of the few she did not heavily edit) she added a helpful note: 'The following little piece has no title, but in it the genius of a solitary region seems to address his wandering and wayward votary, and to recall within his influences the proud mind which rebelled at times against what it most loved.' * * * Though a Gondal context is again intimated, the sentiments coincide so exactly with Emily's own, as Charlotte and indeed Emily herself bore witness, that there is little point in trying to separate the two. The ideas introduced in lines 21–4 were further explored in *Wuthering Heights* where Catherine Earnshaw dreams that she is in heaven: 'heaven did not seem to be my home; and I broke my heart with weeping to come back to earth; and the angels were so angry that they flung me out into the middle of the heath on the top of Wuthering Heights; where I woke sobbing for joy' (chapter 9). Later, in chapter 15, the dying Catherine tells Heathcliff: 'The thing that irks me most is this shattered prison, after all. I'm tired, tired of being enclosed here. I'm wearying to escape into that glorious world, and to be always there: not seeing it dimly through tears, and yearning for it through the walls of an aching heart; but really with it, and in it.'

# The Night Wind†

In summer's mellow midnight,
A cloudless moon shone through
Our open parlour window
And rosetrees wet with dew.

I sat in silent musing,
The soft wind waved my hair:
It told me Heaven was glorious,
And sleeping Earth was fair.

I needed not its breathing
To bring such thoughts to me;
But still it whispered lowly;
'How dark the woods will be!

'The thick leaves in my murmur
Are rustling like a dream,
And all their myriad voices
Instinct with spirit seem.'

I said, 'Go, gentle singer,
Thy wooing voice is kind,
But do not think its music
Has power to reach my mind.

'Play with the scented flower,
The young tree's supple bough,
And leave my human feelings
In their own course to flow.'

The wanderer would not leave me;[1]
Its kiss grew warmer still—
'O come,' it sighed so sweetly,
'I'll win thee 'gainst thy will.[2]

'Have we not been from childhood friends?
Have I not loved thee long?

† (11 September 1840). Unlike many of Emily's poems which plunge straight into their theme with little or no introduction, this poem has an evocative opening which gives it a graphic and immediate setting. The poet, and in this instance she clearly is speaking in her own character, is sitting in the Parsonage parlour late at night while the wind blows through an open window. The wind is here personified and given direct speech so that a conversation between wind and poet is possible. Surprisingly, Emily at first rejects the seductive words of the wind which seeks to draw her back to nature, preferring to leave 'my human feelings in their own course to flow'. As the wind gets the last word it is to be presumed that Emily was won over and abandoned the solitude necessary for her thoughts to accompany the wind in mind at least, if not in physical form. The changes which Charlotte made to the last two verses when she published the poem in 1850 were intended to correct the metre which had suddenly gained an extra syllable in the first and third lines.

1. *leave*: heed (1850).
2. Were we not friends from childhood? (1850).

As long as thou hast loved the night[3]
Whose silence wakes my song.

'And when thy heart is laid at rest[4]
Beneath the church-yard stone[5]
I shall have time enough to mourn[6]
And thou to be alone.'[7]

## "Aye, there it is!"†

Aye, there it is! It wakes to-night
Sweet thoughts that will not die[1]
And feeling's fires flash all as bright[2]
As in the years gone by![3]

And I can tell by thine altered cheek[4]
And by thy kindled gaze[5]
And by the words thou scarce dost speak,
How wildly fancy plays.

Yes, I could swear that glorious wind
Has swept the world aside,
Has dashed its memory from thy mind
Like foam-bells from the tide—

And thou art now a spirit pouring
Thy presence into all—
The essence of the Tempest's roaring[6]
And of the Tempest's fall—[7]

A universal influence
From Thine own influence free;[8]
A principle of life, intense,
Lost to mortality.

Thus truly when that breast is cold
Thy prisoned soul shall rise,

3. As long as thou, the solemn night (1850).
4. *laid at rest*: resting (1850).
5. *church-yard*: church aisle (1850). A deliberate change on Charlotte's part, for Emily was buried in the family vault beneath Haworth church and not in the churchyard itself.
6. *I* shall have time for mourning (1850).
7. And *thou* for being alone (1850).
† In these stanzas a louder gale has roused the sleeper on her pillow: the wakened soul struggles to blend with the storm by which it is

swayed. (*Note by Charlotte Brontë*)
1. Deep feelings I thought dead (1850).
2. Strong in the blast—quick gathering light— (1850).
3. The heart's flame kindles red (1850).
4. "Now I can tell by thine altered cheek (1850).
5. And by thine eyes' full gaze (1850).
6. The thunder of the tempest's roaring (1850).
7. The whisper of its fall (1850).
8. An universal influence (1850).

The dungeon mingle with the mould—
The captive with the skies.[9]

## Love and Friendship†

Love is like the wild rose-briar,
Friendship like the holly-tree—
The holly is dark when the rose-briar blooms
But which will bloom most constantly?

The wild rose-briar is sweet in spring,
Its summer blossoms scent the air;
Yet wait till winter comes again,
And who will call the wild-briar fair?

Then, scorn the silly rose-wreath now
And deck thee with the holly's sheen,
That when December blights thy brow
He still may leave thy garland green.

## The Elder's Rebuke††

"Listen! when your hair, like mine,
Takes a tint of silver grey;
When your eyes, with dimmer shine,
Watch life's bubbles float away;

"When you, young man, have borne like me,
The weary weight of sixty-three,
Then shall penance sore be paid
For these hours so wildly squandered;[1]
And the words that now fall dead

9. At the end of the poem Charlotte Brontë added 5 lines:

Nature's deep being, thine shall hold,
Her spirit all thy spirit fold,
     Her breath absorb thy sighs.
Mortal! though soon life's tale is told,
Who once lives, never dies!

† (undated). This short poem, undated but transcribed into a manuscript book of poetry in February 1844, is on a familiar poetic theme. The rose-briar, with its beautiful flowers and sweet fragrance, is an analogy for love which is exquisite but ephemeral. Contrasted with this is the holly tree which has no showy blossóms but which remains unchanged throughout the year; the holly tree is an analogy for friendship which is not seasonal but constant throughout periods of joy and sorrow alike. There is no indication whether this is a personal or a Gondal poem, though the rejection of love is typical of the embittered heroes of Gondal. Charlotte published the poem in 1850 without alterations, perhaps feeling that it was conventional enough to stand on its own since there was no specific Gondal reference.

†† Under the heading in the manuscript, Charlotte Brontë has written "T[he] Old Man's lecture"; but she gave the title "The Elder's Rebuke" to that part of the poem (lines 1 to 28) which she selected for printing in 1850, and added 6 lines which are not in the manuscript.
1. For those hours so wildly squandered (1850).

On your ears, be deeply pondered;[2]
Pondered and approved at last,
But their virtue will be past!

"Glorious is the prize of Duty,
Though she be a serious power;[3]
Treacherous all the lures of Beauty,
Thorny bud and poisonous flower!

"Mirth is but a mad beguiling
Of the golden-gifted Time;
Love, a demon-meteor, wiling
Heedless feet to gulfs of crime.

"Those who follow earthly pleasure,
Heavenly knowledge will not lead;
Wisdom hides from them her treasure,
Virtue bids them evil-speed!

"Vainly may their hearts, repenting,
Seek for aid in future years;
Wisdom scorned knows no relenting;
Virtue is not won by tears.[4]

# The Wanderer from the Fold†

How few, of all the hearts that loved,
Are grieving for thee now!
And why should mine, to-night, be moved
With such a sense of woe?

2. On your ear, be deeply pondered (1850).
3. Though she be a "serious power" (1850).
4. Virtue is not won by fears (1850). After line 28, the poem ends with 6 lines added by Charlotte Brontë:

Thus spake the ice-blooded elder gray:
The young man scoffed as he turned away,
Turned to the call of a sweet lute's measure,
Waked by the lightsome touch of pleasure:
Had he ne'er met a gentler teacher,
Woe had been wrought by that pitiless
    preacher.

† (11 March 1844). Clement Shorter suggested that this poem, lamenting the way that the subject went astray in life, was 'probably the last poem composed by Emily Brontë and refers, doubtless, to her brother, Patrick Branwell Brontë . . .' Neither of these surmises was correct, though Charlotte's pencilled heading in the manuscript, 'On a life perverted', and the title she gave it when she published it in 1850, 'The Wanderer from the Fold', suggest that she may have seen a parallel between the lives of the subject and her brother. However, the manuscript is dated 11 March 1844—a period when Branwell was apparently doing well as a tutor at Thorp Green—and is headed 'E.W. to A.G.A.'. These are clearly Gondal characters; A.G.A. is Augusta Geraldine Almeda, Queen of Gondal, and E.W. is Lord Eldred W., Captain of the Queen's Guard, who was her lifelong friend and faithful retainer. Lord Eldred frequently appears as the narrator or bystander who observes the chaotic events of the kingdoms with both objectivity and sensitivity. Here he appears in his usual role, mourning the death of Augusta who has been murdered at her stepdaughter's instigation and who is forgotten by everyone but himself, despite her passionate friendships and loves. Here he laments the quirk of fortune which turned the beautiful and brilliant child into a heartless, pleasure-loving and power-seeking Queen.

Too often, thus, when left alone
Where none my thoughts can see,
Comes back a word, a passing tone
From thy strange history.

Sometimes I seem to see thee rise,
A glorious child again—
All virtues beaming from thine eyes
That ever honoured men—

Courage and Truth, a generous breast
Where Love and Gladness lay;[1]
A being whose very Memory blest[2]
And made the mourner gay.[3]

O fairly spread thy early sail,
And fresh and pure and free
Was the first impulse of the gale
That urged life's wave for thee![4]

Why did the pilot, too confiding,
Dream o'er that Ocean's foam,
And trust in Pleasure's careless guiding
To bring his vessel home?

For well he knew what dangers frowned,
What mists would gather dim;
What rocks and shelves and sands lay round
Between his port and him.

The very brightness of the sun,
The splendour of the main,
The wind that bore him wildly on[5]
Should not have warned in vain.

An anxious gazer from the shore,
I marked the whitening wave,
And wept above thy fate the more
Because I could not save.

It recks not now, when all is over;
But yet my heart will be
A mourner still, though friend and lover
Have both forgotten thee!

1. *Love and Gladness*: sinless sunshine (1850).
2. *Memory*: presence (1850).
3. Like gladsome summer day (1850).
4. *That*: Which (1850).
5. *that*: which (1850).

## Warning and Reply†

In the earth, the earth, thou shalt be laid,
A grey stone standing over thee;
Black mould beneath thee spread
And black mould to cover thee.

'Well, there is rest there,
So fast come thy prophecy;
The time when my sunny hair
Shall with grass roots twinèd be.'[1]

But cold, cold is that resting place,
Shut out from Joy and Liberty,
And all who loved thy living face
Will shrink from its gloom and thee.[2]

'Not so: *here* the world is chill,
And sworn friends fall from me;
But *there*, they'll own me still[3]
And prize my memory.'

Farewell, then, all that love,
All that deep sympathy:
Sleep on; heaven laughs above,
Earth never misses thee.

Turf-sod and tombstone drear
Part human company;
One heart broke only there—[4]
*That* heart was worthy thee![5]

---

† (6 September 1843). A Gondal poem, published by Charlotte in 1850 under the title 'Warning and Reply'. The poem takes the form of a soliloquy, part of which is expressed in direct speech. The poet is reminded of her mortality; death will come one day and cut her off from everything and everyone she has loved and confine her to the tomb. To this the poet replies that she welcomes death for the rest it brings: she has nothing to fear from separation for none of her friends are true to her on earth. There is only one heart on earth that will lament her, though that heart is a worthy one.

The identity of the narrator, called 'E.' at the head of the manuscript, is not clear, though Ratchford identifies 'E.' as a relative of Gerald, a prince of Gondal deposed by Julius Brenzaida. The changes which Charlotte made to the poem when she published it in 1850 were dictated by her desire to correct Emily's lapses in metre.

1. *twinèd*: entwined (1850).
2. *its gloom and thee*: it shudderingly (1850).
3. *they'll*: they will (1850).
4. *broke only there*: breaks only—here (1850).
5. *That* [italic]: But that (1850).

# Last Words†

I knew not 'twas so dire a crime
To say the word, Adieu;
But this shall be the only time
My slighted heart shall sue.[1]

The wild moorside, the winter morn,[2]
The gnarled and ancient tree—
If in your breast they waken scorn,
Shall wake the same in me.

I can forget black eyes and brows,
And lips of rosy charm,[3]
If you forget the sacred vows
Those faithless lips could form.

If hard commands can tame your love,
Or prison walls can hold,[4]
I would not wish to grieve above
A thing so false and cold.

And there are bosoms bound to mine
With links both tried and strong;
And there are eyes whose lightning shine
Has warmed and blest me long:

Those eyes shall make my only day,
Shall set my spirit free,
And chase the foolish thoughts away
That mourn your memory.

# The Lady to Her Guitar

For him who struck thy foreign string,
I ween this heart hath ceased to care;[1]

---

† (17 October 1838). The manuscript of this poem is entitled 'Song by J. Brenzaida to G. S.'; beneath this title is written 'Love's Farewell', possibly in Charlotte's hand. Separation from a loved one through death, imprisonment, exile or, as here, through the faithlessness of one of the parties is a common theme in Gondal poetry. Julius Brenzaida, in whose character this poem is written, was Emperor of Gondal and Gaaldine. His adulterous love affair with Augusta Geraldine Almeda has been brought to a head by his demands that she leave her husband, Lord Alfred S., and marry him. When Augusta (or Geraldine as she appears here) demurred because she still loved Lord Alfred, Julius taunted her with having already betrayed him through her adultery and threatened to abandon her himself and seek solace among his former lovers. Since Julius was the great love of her life, Augusta gave in and parted from Lord Alfred, who later committed suicide.

Charlotte made several changes when she published the poem in 1850.
1. *slighted heart*: lips or heart (1850).
2. *moorside*: hillside (1850).
3. *rosy*: falsest (1850).
4. *prison*: strongest (1850).

1. I ween this heart has ceased to care (1850).

Then why doest thou such feelings bring
To my sad spirit, old guitar?

It is as if the warm sunlight
In some deep glen should lingering stay,
When clouds of tempest and of night[2]
Had wrapt the parent orb away.[3]

It is as if the glassy brook
Should image still its willows fair,
Though years ago the woodman's stroke
Laid low in dust their gleaming hair.[4]

Even so, guitar, thy magic tone
Has moved the tear and waked the sigh,[5]
Has bid the ancient torrent flow[6]
Although its very source is dry!

## The Two Children[†]

[1]

Heavy bangs the raindrop
From the burdened spray;
Heavy broods the damp mist
On uplands far away;

Heavy looms the dull sky,
Heavy rolls the sea—
And heavy beats the young heart[1]
Beneath that lonely tree.

Never has a blue streak
Cleft the clouds since morn—
Never has his grim Fate
Smiled since he was born.

Frowning on the infant,
Shadowing childhood's joy,
Guardian angel knows not
That melancholy boy.

---

2. When clouds of storm, or shades of night (1850).
3. Have wrapt the parent orb away (1850).
4. Laid low in dust their Dryad-hair (1850).
5. Hath moved the tear, and waked the sigh (1850).

6. Hath bid the ancient torrent moan (1850).
† Above the heading to the first of these two poems, Charlotte Brontë has written "The Two Children," the title which she gave to the poems when they were first printed in 1850.
1. And heavy throbs the young heart (1850).

Day is passing swiftly
Its sad and sombre prime;
Youth is fast invading[2]
Sterner manhood's time.[3]

All the flowers are praying
For sun before they close,
And he prays too, unknowing,[4]
That sunless human rose!

Blossoms, that the west wind[5]
Has never wooed to blow,
Scentless are your petals,[6]
Your dew as cold as snow.[7]

Soul, where kindred kindness
No early promise woke,
Barren is your beauty[8]
As weed upon the rock.[9]

Wither, Brothers, wither,[1]
You were vainly given—[2]
Earth reserves no blessing
For the unblessed of Heaven!

[2]

Child of Delight! with sunbright hair,
And seablue, seadeep eyes;
Spirit of Bliss, what brings thee here,
Beneath these sullen skies?

Thou shouldest live in eternal spring,
Where endless day is never dim;
Why, seraph, has thy erring wing[3]
Borne thee down to weep with him?[4]

"Ah, not from heaven am I descended,
And I do not come to mingle tears;[5]
But sweet is day, though with shadows blended;
And, though clouded, sweet are youthful years.

2. Boyhood sad is merging (1850).
3. In sadder manhood's time (1850).
4. And he prays too—unconscious (1850).
5. Blossom—that the west wind (1850).
6. Scentless are thy petals (1850).
7. Thy dew is cold as snow! (1850).
8. Barren is thy beauty (1850).
9. As weed upon a rock (1850).
1. Wither—soul and blossom! (1850).
2. You both were vainly given: (1850).
3. Why, Seraph, has thine erring wing (1850).
4. Wafted thee down to weep with him? (1850).
5. Nor do I come to mingle tears (1850).

"I, the image of light and gladness,
Saw and pitied that mournful boy,
And I swore to take his gloomy sadness,[6]
And give to him my beamy joy.[7]

"Heavy and dark the night is closing;
Heavy and dark may its biding be;
Better for all from grief reposing,
And better for all who watch like me.[8]

"Guardian angel, he lacks no longer;
Evil fortune he need not fear:
Fate is strong, but Love is stronger;
And more unsleeping than angel's care."[9]

# The Visionary†

Silent is the house: all are laid asleep;
One, alone, looks out o'er the snow-wreaths deep;
Watching every cloud, dreading every breeze
That whirls the wildering drift, and bends the groaning trees.[1]

Cheerful is the hearth, soft the matted floor;
Not one shivering gust creeps through pane or door;
The little lamp burns straight, its ray shoot strong and far;
I trim it well to be the Wanderer's guiding-star.

Frown, my haughty sire; chide, my angry dame;
Set your slaves to spy, threaten me with shame:
But neither sire nor dame, nor prying serf shall know
What angel nightly tracks that waste of frozen snow.[2]

6. And I vowed—if need were—to share his sadness (1850).
7. And give to him my sunny joy (1850).
8. After line 20 a stanza of four lines was added by Charlotte Brontë:

"Watch in love by a fevered pillow,
Cooling the fever with pity's balm;
Safe as the petrel on tossing billow,
Safe in mine own soul's golden calm!

9. And *my* love is truer than angel-care (1850).
† (9 October 1845). This is the opening of a much longer poem from the Gondal cycle entitled 'Julian M. and A.G. Rochelle'. The first twelve lines were published in 1850 by Charlotte who added a further eight lines of her own to make it stand as a complete poem in its own right. She did this because Emily had already published lines 13–44 in the 1846 volume of poems. The whole poem, without Charlotte's interpolations or Emily's omissions, is printed in Hatfield pp. 236–41. * * *

The poem as Emily wrote it, relates the earthly loves of two Gondal figures of noble rank, one of whom, Julian, is the defiant watcher in the house, waiting for A.G. Rochelle's secret visit. The reason for the secrecy is not fully explained though the lovers are in the Romeo and Juliet situation of coming from warring families and, as the full poem reveals, Julian had fallen in love with and released Rochelle from his kinsmen's prison. Charlotte's interpolations completely change the poem here, however, for instead of reverting to the memory of their first meeting in prison it ends with the watcher welcoming a spiritual visitation, a messenger of hope. The watcher has thus become Emily herself, and not her Gondal character, making nonsense of the guiding light in the window, but making it in keeping with many of Emily's own compositions where Imagination is personified as an external, physical presence.
1. *drift*: drifts (Hatfield MS).
2. *frozen*: winter (Hatfield MS).

What I love shall come like visitant of air,[3]
Safe in secret power from lurking human snare;
Who loves me, no word of mine shall e'er betray,
Thou for faith unstained my life must forfeit pay.

Burn then, little lamp; glimmer straight and clear—
Hush! a rustling wing stirs, methinks, the air:
He for whom I wait, thus ever comes to me;
Strange Power! I trust thy might; trust thou my constancy.


# Encouragement

I do not weep, I would not weep;
Our Mother needs no tears;
Dry thine eyes too, 'tis vain to keep
This causeless grief for years.

What though her brow be changed and cold,
Her sweet eyes closed for ever?
What though the stone—the darksome mould
Our mortal bodies sever?

What though her hand smoothe ne'er again
Those silken locks of thine—
Nor through long hours of future pain
Her kind face o'er thee shine?

Remember still she is not dead,
She sees us, Gerald, now,[1]
Laid where her angel spirit fled
'Mid heath and frozen snow.

And from that world of heavenly light
Will she not always bend,
To guide us in our lifetime's night
And guard us to the end?

Thou know'st she will, and well may'st mourn[2]
That we are left below,
But not that she can ne'er return
To share our earthly woe.

3. 13–20 These lines were written and inter-
polated by Charlotte.
1. She sees us, sister, now (1850).

2. Thou knowest she will; and thou may'st
mourn (1850).

*No Coward Soul* · 287

## Stanzas†

Often rebuked, yet always back returning
  To those first feelings that were born with me,
And leaving busy chase of wealth and learning
  For idle dreams of things which cannot be:

To-day, I will seek not the shadowy region:[1]
  Its unsustaining vastness waxes drear;
And visions rising, legion after legion,
  Bring the unreal world too strangely near.

I'll walk, but not in old heroic traces,
  And not in paths of high morality,
And not among the half-distinguished faces,
  The clouded forms of long-past history.

I'll walk where my own nature would be leading:
  It vexes me to choose another guide:
Where the gray flocks in ferny glens are feeding;
  Where the wild wind blows on the mountain side.

What have those lonely mountains worth revealing?
  More glory and more grief than I can tell:
The earth that wakes *one* human heart to feeling
  Can centre both the worlds of Heaven and Hell.

## No Coward Soul††

No coward soul is mine
No trembler in the world's storm-troubled sphere
I see Heaven's glories shine
And Faith shines equal arming me from Fear

† (manuscript lost). These twenty lines, which are among Emily's best, have aroused considerable controversy over their authorship since they seem to give an outsider's view of Emily rather than her own personal view. Hatfield (pp. 255–6) thought they were by Charlotte; Willett (BST: 18:92: 143–8) suggested Anne. As Chitham has pointed out, however (BST: 18:93:222–6), though Charlotte sometimes corrected metrical inconsistencies and obfuscated Gondal references when editing her sister's poetry, she did not stoop to fraud and would not have passed these lines off as Emily's if she had written them herself. Likewise, the last stanza is far too pantheistic for the deeply religious Anne to have written. There is therefore no reason to doubt Emily's authorship; indeed, the poem seems typical of her work,

exploring ideas which recur in other poems. As the one member of the family who did not repeatedly try to earn her own living she may well have felt 'Often rebuked' by her own conscience, particularly as this left her time to indulge in imagination. Having abandoned all hope of a career for the world of imagination, for once she also rejects Gondal since it threatens to engulf her, though the emphatic placing of 'Today' at the beginning of line 5 makes it clear this is only a temporary repudiation. The worlds of intellect and imagination, on this occasion, are to be subjugated to the sensual pleasure of feeling and it is the moors, which, being so akin to Emily's own nature, have the power to awaken her emotions.
1. *the shadowy region*: i.e. Gondal.
†† (2 January 1846). This magnificent poem

O God within my breast
Almighty ever present Deity
Life, that in me has rest
As I Undying Life, have power in Thee.

Vain are the thousand creeds
That move men's hearts, unutterably vain,
Worthless as withered weeds
Or idlest froth amid the boundless main

To waken doubt in one
Holding so fast by thy infinity[1]
So surely anchored on
The steadfast rock of Immortality

With wide-embracing love
Thy spirit animates eternal years
Pervades and broods above,
Changes, sustains, dissolves, creates, and rears.

Though Earth and moon were gone[2]
And suns and universes ceased to be
And thou wert left alone[3]
Every Existence would exist in thee

There is not room for Death
Nor atom that his might could render void
Since thou art Being and Breath[4]
And what thou art may never be destroyed.[5]

was first published after Emily's death by Charlotte, who noted that 'the following are the last
lines my sister Emily ever wrote'. This was not
strictly true, for in the three-year interval before
she died Emily wrote *Wuthering Heights*, probably began a second novel and revised much
of her earlier poetry. Though it may be the last
dated poem among her papers, it is possible
that Emily destroyed her later work. Given the
fact that these lines are unique among Emily's
poems because of their religious theme, it is
not surprising that Charlotte would have
wanted to believe that this great statement of
personal faith should be her sister's last poetic
effort. Typically, the God that Emily worships
is not the human Christ of Anne's poetry, but
rather the omnipotent, omni-present God, the
source of life. He is not bounded within the
different creeds but is spiritually and physically
both a part of and external to her own being—
much the same sort of dual existence that imagination had enjoyed in earlier poems. Emily's
contempt for sectarian religion is nowhere expressed more strongly than here, though the
caricature of Jabes Branderham in *Wuthering
Heights* also made her feelings plain. Characteristically, and contrasting with the ephemeral nature of most forms of worship, it is the
eternity of God that is the central theme of this
poem.
1. *thy*: thine (1850).
2. *moon*: man (1850). A misreading of the
manuscript by Charlotte.
3. *wert*: were (1850).
4. *Since thou*: Thou—THOU (1850).
5. *thou*: THOU (1850).

# WILLIAM M. SALE, JR.

## Emily Brontë's History of Gondal

Over a period of years Emily Brontë and her sister Anne wrote a kind of history in prose of the lives of imaginary characters on the imaginary islands of Gondal and Gaaldine. This history paralleled a story of events in Angria and Glasstown written by Charlotte and her brother Branwell. The prose history of Angria survived but that of Gondal has been lost or was destroyed. Miss Fanny Ratchford grew to believe, however, that an outline of the Gondal history could be found in the large number of poems that Emily wrote during the years 1836–1848, years in which she and Anne were writing Gondal's history in prose. Miss Ratchford finally concluded that the prose Gondal was a "compact and well-integrated whole," with the poems "highlighting such incidents and moods of the familiar Gondal world as stirred her imagination at the moment."[1] In consequence she presented the poems with her own narrative links in a volume which she called *Gondal's Queen, A Novel in Verse*, from which I have just quoted. She believed that Gondal's history was essentially the life story, from birth to death, of Gondal's queen, known variously as Augusta Geraldine Almeda (A.G.A.) and Rosina. The two principal male characters in Augusta's life were the Emperor Julius and Lord Alfred. Inevitably critics were to speculate on the possibility that these three characters were prototypes of Catherine Earnshaw, Heathcliff, and Edgar Linton.

Miss Ratchford, however, is not disposed to find in the Gondal poems close connections with characters and events in *Wuthering Heights*, though she is prepared to speculate that "a boy of dark and tragic aspect" in one of Emily's poems was a prototype of Heathcliff and that Angelica in another poem, who is found pitying a lonely boy, suggests the young Catherine Earnshaw.[2] Other critics have not been so cautious. Mary Visick, for example, feels that "the story they [the poems] can be shown to tell is the story of *Wuthering Heights*," and that "the central Gondal people themselves were reborn as Catherine, Heathcliff and Edgar. . . ."[3] In Miss Ratchford's *Gondal's Queen* Augusta first loves Julius, then abandons him for, among others, Lord Alfred, and finally leaves Alfred to return to Julius. It seems obvious to Miss Visick that we have here a sketch of the relations between Catherine, Heathcliff, and Edgar, though she recognizes that in the Gondal poems the narrative is revealed only in a series of lyric moments.

Either in *Gondal's Queen* or in C. W. Hatfield's edition of *The Complete Poems of Emily Jane Brontë* (New York, 1941), the poems are available for

1. Fanny Ratchford, *Gondal's Queen* (Austin: University of Texas Press, 1955). pp. 23, 28.
2. Ratchford, pp. 71, 74.

3. Mary Visick, *The Genesis of Wuthering Heights* (Hong Kong: University of Hong Kong Press, 1958), pp. 11, 38.

any reader who wants to judge for himself to what extent the poems fore-shadow Emily's novel. What some of these poems have meant to some critics may be seen in excerpts such as the following.

A dark boy and a fair girl as original projections of Catherine and Heath-cliff, or perhaps more persuasively, of Catherine Linton and Hareton Earnshaw:

> Heavy looms the dull sky,
> Heavy rolls the sea—
> And heavy beats the young heart
> Beneath that lonely tree.
>
> Never has a blue streak
> Cleft the clouds since morn—
> Never has his grim Fate
> Smiled since he was born.
>
> Frowning on the infant,
> Shadowing childhood's joy,
> Guardian angel knows not
> That melancholy boy.

And the girl:

> I, the image of light and gladness
> Saw and pitied that mournful boy,
> And I swore to take his gloomy sadness,
> And give to him my beamy joy.
>
> .   .   .   .   .   .   .   .   .   .   .   .
>
> Guardian angel, he lacks no longer;
> Evil fortune he need not fear:
> Fate is strong, but Love is stronger;
> And more unsleeping than angel's care.[4]

An anticipation of the passage in the novel which concludes with Cath-erine's "Nelly, I *am* Heathcliff" (p. oo):

> O God within my breast
> Almighty ever-present Deity
> Life, that in me hast rest
> As I Undying Life, have power in Thee.

4. Ratchford, pp. 74–76; *The Complete Poems of Emily Jane Brontë*, ed. C. W. Hatfield (New York: Columbia University Press, 1941), pp. 229, 230.

.   .   .   .   .   .   .   .   .   .   .

> Though Earth and moon were gone
> And suns and universes ceased to be
> And thou were left alone
> Every Existence would exist in thee.[5]

Augusta's love of Alfred as an earlier description of Catherine's mood in the first days of her marriage to Edgar:

> At such a time, in such a spot,
> The world seems made of light;
> Our blissful hearts remember not
> How surely follows night.
>
> I cannot, Alfred, dream of aught
> That casts a shade of woe;
> That heaven is reigning in my thought,
> Which wood and wave and earth have caught
> From skies that overflow.
>
> That heaven which my sweet lover's brow
> Has won me to adore,
> Which from his blue eyes beaming now
> Reflects a still intenser glow
> Than nature's heaven can pour.

.   .   .   .   .   .   .   .   .   .

> Then art thou not my golden June
> All mist and tempest free?
> As shines earth's sun in summer noon
> So heaven's sun shines in thee.[6]

Augusta's betrayal of Alfred as a foreshadowing of Catherine's betrayal of Edgar:

> I know that I have done thee wrong—
> Have wronged both thee and Heaven—
> And I may mourn my lifetime long
> Yet may not be forgiven.

.   .   .   .   .   .   .   .   .

5. Ratchford, pp. 173–174; Hatfield, p. 243.    6. Ratchford, pp. 69–70; Hatfield, pp. 143–144.

> Till far beyond earth's frenzied strife
> That makes destruction joy,
> Thy perished faith shall spring to life
> And my remorse shall die.[7]

Augusta's lament for the death of Julius as comparable to Heathcliff's mourning for the death of Catherine:

> Cold in the earth, and fifteen wild Decembers
> From those brown hills have melted into spring—
> Faithful indeed is the spirit that remembers
> After such years of change and suffering!
>
> Sweet Love of youth, forgive if I forget thee
> While the World's tide is bearing me along:
> Sterner desires and darker hopes beset me,
> Hopes which obscure but cannot do thee wrong.
>
> No other Sun has lightened up my heaven:
> No other Star has ever shone for me:
> All my life's bliss from thy dear life was given—
> All my life's bliss is in the grave with thee.[8]

An epitaph for Augusta as a suggestion of the peace of the graves at the end of *Wuthering Heights*:

> The linnet in the rocky dells,
> The moor-lark in the air,
> The bee among the heather-bells
> That hide my lady fair:
>
> The wild deer browse above her breast;
> The wild birds raise their brood;
> And they, her smiles of love caressed,
> Have left her solitude!
>
> .     .     .     .     .     .     .     .
>
> They thought the tide of grief would flow
> Unchecked through future years,
> But where is all their anguish now,
> And where are all their tears?
>
> .     .     .     .     .     .     .     .

7. Ratchford, p. 85; Hatfield, pp. 197–198.     8. Ratchford, p. 126; Hatfield, pp. 222–223.

Blow, west wind, by the lonely mound,
And murmur, summer streams,
There is no need of other sound
To soothe my Lady's dreams.[9]

9. Ratchford, pp. 159–160; Hatfield, pp. 204–205.

A page from Emily's diary, with her sketch of herself and Anne writing. Photocopy courtesy of the Brontë Society.

# Emily Brontë's Diary †

Apart from her novel and poems, few writings by Emily Brontë survive, but there are brief diary entries from 1834, 1837, 1841, and 1845. The last three are all birthday relections, one written on her brother Branwell's birthday, the other two on her twenty-third and twenty-seventh birthdays. The diaries give glimpses of life at the Haworth parsonage and describe Emily's ongoing involvement with the imaginary world of Gondal. The diary pages are on display at the Brontë Parsonage.

## November 24, 1834

November the 24 1834 Monday
Emily Jane Brontë
Anne Brontë

I fed Rainbow, Diamond Snowflake Jasper pheasant (alias) this morning Branwell went down to Mr. Driver's and brought news that Sir Robert Peel was going to be invited to stand for Leeds   Anne and I have been peeling apples for Charlotte to make us an apple pudding and for Aunt nuts and apples   Charlotte said she made puddings perfectly and she was of a quick but limited intellect. Tabby said just now Come Anne pilloputate (i.e. pill a potato) Aunt has come into the kitchen just now and said where are your feet Anne   Anne answered On the floor Aunt   papa opened the parlour door and gave Branwell a letter saying here Branwell read this and show it to your Aunt and Charlotte—the Gondals are discovering the interior of Gaaldine   Sally Mosley is washing in the back kitchen
It is past Twelve o'clock Anne and I have not tidied ourselves, done our bedwork or done our lessons and we want to go out to play   we are goin to have for Dinner Boiled Beef, Turnips, potatoes and applepudding.   The Kitchin is in a very unitdy state   Anne and I have not done our music exercise which consists of b major   Taby said on my putting a pen in her face Ya pitter pottering there instead of pilling a potate   I answered O Dear, O Dear, O dear I will directly with that I get up, take a knife and begin pilling (finished pilling the potatoes) papa going to walk   Mr. Sunderland expected
  Anne and I say I wonder what we shall be like and what we shall be and where we shall be if all goes well in the year 1874—in which year I shall be in my 54th year   Anne will be going in her 55th year Branwell will be going in his 58th year And Charlotte in her 57th year   hoping we shall all be well at that time we close our paper[1]

\* \* \*

† Diary entries are reprinted with the permission of the Brontë Society.
1. Emily miscalculates; Charlotte was born in 1816, Branwell in 1817, Emily in 1818, and Anne in 1820.

# June 26, 1837

Monday evening June 26th 1837
A bit past 4 o'clock Charlotte working in Aunt's room, Branwell reading *Eugene Aram* to her—Anne and I writing in the drawing-room—Anne a poem beginning "Fair was the evening and brightly the sun"—I Augusta Almeda's life 1st V. 1–4th page from the last—fine rather coolish thin grey cloudy but sunny day Aunt working in the little room the old nursery Papa gone out Tabby in the kitchen—the Emperors and Empresses of Gondal and Gaaldine preparing to depart from Gaaldine to Gondal to prepare for the coronation which will be on the 12th July Queen Vittoria ascended the throne this month. Northangerland in Monkey's Isle—Zamora at Eversham. All tight and right in which condition it is hoped we shall all be this day 4 years at which time Charlotte will be 25 and 2 months— Branwell just 24 it being his birthday—myself 22 and 10 months and a piece [*sic*] Anne 21 and nearly a half I wonder where we shall be and how we shall be and what kind of a day it will be then—let us hope for the best

Emily Jane Brontë—Anne Brontë
I guess that this day 4 years we shall all be in this drawing-room comfortable I hope it may be so. Anne guesses we shall all be gone somewhere comfortable We hope it may be so indeed.

Aunt: Come Emily it's past 4 o'clock
Emily: Yes, Aunt Exit Aunt
Ann: Well, do you intend to write in the evening
Emily: Well, what think you
(We agreed to go out 1st to make sure if we got into the humour. We may stay in—)

\* \* \*

# July 30, 1841

A PAPER to be opened
when Anne is
25 years old,
or my next birthday after
if
all be well.
Emily Jane Brontë. July the 30th, 1841
It is Friday evening, near 9 o'clock—wild rainy weather. I am seated in the dining-room alone, having just concluded tidying our desk boxes, writing this document. Papa is in the parlour—aunt upstairs in her room. She has been reading *Blackwood's Magazine* to papa. Victoria and Adelaide [the geese] are ensconced in the peat-house. Keeper [the dog] is in the kitchen—

Hero [a hawk] in his cage. We are all stout and hearty, as I hope is the case with Charlotte, Branwell, and Anne, of whom the first is at John White, Esq., Upperwood House, Rawdon; the second is at Luddended Foot; and the third is, I believe, at Scarborough, inditing perhaps a paper corresponding to this.

A scheme is at present in agitation for setting us up in a school of our own; as yet nothing is determined, but I hope and trust it may go on and prosper and answer our highest expectations. This day four years I wonder whether we shall still be dragging on in our present condition or established to our hearts' content. Time will show.

I guess that at the time appointed for the opening of this paper we i.e. Charlotte, Anne, and I, shall be all merrily seated in our own sitting-room in some pleasant and flourishing seminary, having just gathered in for the midsummer holyday. Our debts will be paid off, and we shall have cash in hand to a considerable amount. Papa, aunt, and Branwell will either have been or will be coming to visit us. It will be a fine warm summer evening, very different from this bleak look-out, and Anne and I will perchance slip out into the garden for a few minutes to peruse our papers. I hope either this or something better will be the case.

The Gondalians are at present in a threatening state, but there is no open rupture as yet. All the princes and princesses of the Royalty are at the Palace of Instruction. I have a good many books on hand, but I am sorry to say that as usual I make small progress with any. However, I have just made a new regularity paper! and I mean *verb sap* to do great things. And now I must close, sending from far an exhortation, "Courage, courage," to exiled and harassed Anne, wishing she was here.

*   *   *

## July 30, 1845

Haworth, Thursday, July 30th, 1845

My birthday—showery, breezy, cool. I am twenty-seven years old today. This morning Anne and I opened the papers we wrote four years since, on my twenty-third birthday. This paper we intend, if all be well, to open on my thirtieth—three years hence, in 1848. Since the 1841 paper the following events have taken place. Our school scheme has been abandoned, and instead Charlotte and I went to Brussels on the 8th February 1842.

Branwell left his place at Luddenden Foot. C. and I returned from Brussels, November 8th, 1842, in consequence of aunt's death.

Branwell went to Thorp Green as a tutor, where Anne still continued, January 1843.

Charlotte returned to Brussels the same month, and after staying a year, came back again on New Year's Day 1844.

Anne left her situation at Thorp Green of her own accord, June 1845.

Anne and I went our first long journey by ourselves together, leaving home on the 30th of June, Monday, sleeping at York, returning to Keighley Tuesday evening, sleeping there and walking home on Wednesday morning. Though the weather was broken we enjoyed ourselves very much, except during a few hours at Bradford. And during our excursion we were, Ronald Macalgin, Henry Angora, Juliet Augusteena, Rosabella Esmaldan, Ella and Julian Egremont, Catharine Navarre, and Cordelia Fitzaphnold, escaping from the palaces of instruction to join the Royalists who are hard driven at present by the victorious Republicans. The Gondals still flourish bright as ever. I am present writing a work on the First Wars. Anne has been writing some articles on this, and a book by Henry Sophona. We intend sticking firm by the rascals as long as they delight us, which I am glad to say they do at present. I should have mentioned that last summer the school scheme was revived in full vigour. We had prospectuses printed, despatched letters to all acquaintances imparting our plans, and did our little all; but it was found no go. Now I don't desire a school at all, and none of us have any great longing for it. We have cash enough for our present wants, with a prospect of accumulation. We are all in decent health, only that papa has a complaint in his eyes, and with the exception of B., who, I hope will be better and do better hereafter. I am quite contented for myself: not as idle as formerly, altogether as hearty, and having learnt to make the most of the present and long for the future with the figetiness that I cannot do all I wish; seldom or never troubled with nothing to do, and merely desiring that everybody could be as comfortable as myself and as undesponding, and then we should have a very tolerable world of it.

By mistake I find we have opened the paper on the 31st instead of the 30th. Yesterday was much such a day as this, but the morning was divine.

Tabby, who was gone in our last paper, is come back, and has lived with us two years and a half, and is in good health. Martha, who also departed, is here too. We have got Flossy; got and lost Tiger; lost the hawk Hero, which, with the geese, was given away, and is doubtless dead, for when I came back from Brussels, I inquired on all hands and could hear nothing of him. Tiger died early last year. Keeper and Flossy are well, also the canary acquired four years since. We are now all at home, and likely to be there some time. Branwell went to Liverpool on Tuesday to stay a week. Tabby has just been teasing me to turn as formerly to "Pilloputate." Anne and I should have picked the black currants if it had been fine and sunshiny. I must hurry off now to my turning and ironing. I have plenty of work on hands, and writing, and am altogether full of business. With best wishes for the whole house till 1848, July 30th, and as much longer as may be,— I conclude.

E.J. Brontë

# Contemporary Reception

## EMILY BRONTË'S FIRST EDITION REVIEWS†

Emily preserved five reviews of *Wuthering Heights*, which eventually found their way into the Brontë Parsonage Museum at Haworth as part of the contents of her writing desk. Four of the five have been identified as having appeared in the *Atlas*, in *Douglas Jerrold's Weekly Newspaper*, in the *Examiner* (only parts of this review seem to have been in Emily's possession), and in the *Britannia*. When Charlotte Brontë edited the second edition of her sister's novel in 1850, she or her publisher prefixed to that edition extracts from the reviews in the *Atlas* and the *Britannia*, and a somewhat longer portion of an essay by Sydney Dobell, which had appeared earlier in 1850 in the *Palladium*. From Charlotte's biographical notice it is evident that Dobell's essay had both impressed her as a rare recognition of Emily's "very real powers" and provided impetus for Charolotte's own biographical and critical comments. The justice of her sweeping attack on Emily's earlier critics can be best assayed after sampling the reviews and Dobell's essay. Early reviews of the 1850 edition show the impact of Charlotte's revelations and judgments but, nonetheless, continue to be interested in measuring *Wuthering Heights* against *Jane Eyre*.

## *Atlas*

### *January 1848*

About two years ago a small volume of poems by "Currer, Acton, and Ellis Bell" was given to the world. The poems were of varying excellence; those by Currer Bell, for the most part, exhibiting the highest order of merit; but, as a whole, the little work produced little or no sensation, and was speedily forgotten. Currer, Acton, and Ellis Bell have now all come before us as novelists, and all with so much success as to make their future career a matter of interesting speculation in the literary world.

Whether, as there is little reason to believe, the names which we have written are the genuine names of actual personages—whether they are, on the other hand, mere publishing names, as is our own private conviction—whether they represent three distinct individuals, or whether a single personage is the actual representative of the "three gentlemen at once" of the title-pages—whether the authorship of the poems and the novels is to be assigned to one gentleman or to one lady, to three gentlemen or three ladies,

---

† Reviews of the first edition of the novel are reprinted with the permission of the Brontë Society.

or to a mixed male and female triad of authors—are questions over which the curious may puzzle themselves, but are matters really of little account. One thing is certain; as in the poems, so in the novels, the signature of "Currer Bell" is attached to pre-eminently the best performance. We were the first to welcome the author of *Jane Eyre* as a new writer of no ordinary power. A new edition of that singular work had been called for, and we do not doubt that its success has done much to ensure a favourable reception for the volumes which are now before us.

*Wuthering Heights* is a strange, inartistic story. There are evidences in every chapter of a sort of rugged power—an unconscious strength—which the possessor seems never to think of turning to the best advantage. The general effect is inexpressibly painful. We know nothing in the whole range of our fictitious literature which presents such shocking pictures of the worst forms of humanity. *Jane Eyre* is a book which affects the reader to tears; it touches the most hidden sources of emotion. *Wuthering Heights* casts a gloom over the mind not easily to be dispelled. It does not soften; it harasses, it extenterates [sic]. There are passages in it which remind us of the *Nowlans* of the late John Banim; but of all pre-existent works the one which it most recalls to our memory is the *History of Mathew Wald*. It has not, however, the unity and concentration of that fiction; but is a *sprawling* story, carrying us, with no mitigation of anguish, through two generations of sufferers—though one presiding evil genius sheds a grim shadow over the whole and imparts a singleness of malignity to the somewhat disjointed tale. A more natural unnatural story we do not remember to have read. Inconceivable as are the combinations of human degradation which are here to be found moving within the circle of a few miles, the *vraisemblance* is so admirably preserved; there is so much truth in what we may call the *costumery* (not applying the word in its narrow acceptation)—the general mounting of the entire piece—that we readily identify the scenes and personages of the fiction; and when we lay aside the book it is some time before we can persuade ourselves that we have held nothing more than imaginary intercourse with the ideal creations of the brain. The reality of unreality has never been so aptly illustrated as in the scenes of almost savage life which Ellis Bell has brought so vividly before us.

The book wants relief. A few glimpses of sunshine would have increased the reality of the picture and given strength rather than weakness to the whole. There is not in the entire *dramatis personae* a single character which is not utterly hateful or thoroughly contemptible. If you do not detest the person, you despise him; and if you do not despise him, you detest him with your whole heart. Hindley, the brutal, degraded sot, strong in the desire to work all mischief, but impotent in his degradation; Linton Heathcliff, the miserable, drivelling coward, in whom we see selfishness in its most abject form; and Heathcliff himself, the presiding evil genius of the piece, the tyrant father of an imbecile son, a creature in whom every evil passion

seems to have reached a gigantic excess—form a group of deformities such
as we have rarely seen gathered together on the same canvas. The author
seems to have designed to throw some redeeming touches into the character
of the brutal Heathcliff by portraying him as one faithful to the "idol of his
boyhood"—loving to the very last—long, long after death had divided them,
the unhappy girl who had cheered and brightened up the early days of his
wretched life. Here is the touch of nature which makes the whole world
kin—but it fails of the intended effect. There is a selfishness—a ferocity in
the love of Heathcliff, which scarcely suffer it, in spite of its rugged constancy, to relieve the darker parts of his nature. Even the female characters
excite something of loathing and much of contempt. Beautiful and loveable
in their childhood, they all, to use a vulgar expression, "turn out badly."
Catherine the elder—wayward, impatient, impulsive—sacrifices herself and
her lover to the pitiful ambition of becoming the wife of a gentleman of
station. Hence her own misery—her early death—and something of a brutal
wickedness of Heathcliff's character and conduct; though we cannot persuade ourselves that even a happy love would have tamed down the natural
ferocity of the tiger. Catherine the younger is more sinned against than
sinning, and in spite of her moral defects, we have some hope of her at the
last.

\* \* \*

[The review reprints an extract from Catherine's last meeting with Heathcliff,
and after a brief comparison of *Agnes Grey* with *Jane Eyre* concludes with
the observation that Anne Brontë's novel,] though lacking the power and
originality of *Wuthering Heights*, is infinitely more agreeable. It leaves no
painful impression on the mind—some may think it leaves no impression
at all. We are not quite sure that the next new novel will not efface it; but
*Jane Eyre* and *Wuthering Heights* are not things to be forgotten. The work
of Currer Bell is a great performance; that of Ellis Bell is only a promise,
but it is a colossal one.

## *Douglas Jerrold's Weekly Newspaper*

### *January 1848*

Two of these volumes contain a tale by Mr. Ellis Bell, called *Wuthering
Heights*, and the third volume is devoted to another story told in an auto-
biographical form by Mr. Acton Bell, and is entitled *Agnes Grey*.

Dissimilar as they are in many respects, there is a distinct family likeness
between these two tales; and, if our organ of comparison be not out of order,
we are not far wrong is asserting that they are not so much like each other,
as they are both like a novelty recently published under the editorship of

Mr. Currer Bell, viz., *Jane Eyre*. We do not mean to say that either of the tales now before us is equal in merit to that novel, but they have somewhat of the same fresh, original, and unconventional spirit; while the style of composition is, undoubtedly, of the same north-country, Doric school; it is simple, energetic, and apparently disdainful of prettinesses and verbal display.

\* \* \*

*Wuthering Heights* is a strange sort of book—baffling all regular criticism; yet, it is impossible to begin and not finish it; and quite as impossible to lay it aside afterwards and say nothing about it. In the midst of the reader's perplexity the ideas predominant in his mind concerning this book are likely to be—brutal cruelty, and semi-savage love. What may be the moral which the author wishes the reader to deduce from his work, it is difficult to say; and we refrain from assigning any, because to speak honestly, we have discovered none but mere glimpses of hidden morals or secondary meanings. There seems to us great power in this book but a purposeless power, which we feel a great desire to see turned to better account. We are quite confident that the writer of *Wuthering Heights* wants but the practised skill to make a great artist; perhaps, a great dramatic artist. His qualities are, at present, excessive; a far more promising fault, let it be remembered, than if they were deficient. He may tone down, whereas the weak and inefficient writer, however carefully he may write by rule and line, will never work up his productions to the point of beauty in art. In *Wuthering Heights*, the reader is shocked, disgusted, almost sickened by details of cruelty, inhumanity, and the most diabolical hate and vengeance, and anon come passages of powerful testimony to the supreme power of love—even over demons in the human form. The women in the book are of a strange fiendish-angelic nature, tantalizing, and terrible, and the men are indescribable out of the book itself. Yet, towards the close of the story occurs the following pretty, soft picture, which comes like the rainbow after a storm. \* \* \* [The quoted passage is the one about Cathy teaching Hareton.]

We strongly recommend all our readers who love novelty to get this story, for we can promise them that they never have read anything like it before. It is very puzzling and very interesting; and if we had but space we would willingly devote a little more time to the analysis of this remarkable story, but we must leave it to our readers to decide what sort of a book it is.

## *Examiner*

### *January 1848*

This is a strange book. It is not without evidences of considerable power: but, as a whole, it is wild, confused; disjointed, and improbable; and the people who make up the drama, which is tragic enough in its consequences, are savages ruder than those who lived before the days of Homer. With the exception of Heathcliff, the story is confined to the family of Earnshaw, who intermarry with the Lintons; and the scene of their exploits is a rude old-fashioned house, at the top of one of the high moors or fells in the north of England. Whoever has traversed the bleak heights of Hartside or Cross Fell, on his road from Westmoreland to the dales of Yorkshire, and has been welcomed there by the winds and rain on a 'gusty day', will know how to estimate the comforts of Wuthering Heights in wintry weather. But it may be as well to give the author's own sketch of the spot, taken, it should be observed at a more genial season.

\* \* \*

This Heathcliff may be considered as the hero of the book, if a hero there be. He is an incarnation of evil qualities; implacable hate, ingratitude, cruelty, falsehood, selfishness, and revenge. He exhibits, moreover, a certain stoical endurance in early life, which enables him to 'bide his time', and nurse up his wrath till it becomes mature and terrible; and there is one portion of his nature, one only, wherein he appears to approximate to humanity. Like the Corsair, and other such melodramatic heroes, he is

Linked to one virtue and a thousand crimes;

and it is with difficulty that we can prevail upon ourselves to believe in the appearance of such a phenomenon, so near our own dwellings as the summit of a Lancashire or Yorkshire moor.

It is not easy to disentangle the incidents and set them forth in chronological order. The tale if confused, as we have said, nothwithstanding that the whole drama takes place in the house that we have described, and that the sole actors are the children of Earnshaw, by birth or adoption, and their servants.

\* \* \*

We are not disposed to ascribe any particular intention to the author in drawing the character of Heathcliff, nor can we perceive any very obvious moral in the story. There are certain good rough dashes at character; some of the incidents look like real events; and the book has the merit, which must not be undervalued, of avoiding common-place and affectation. The language, however, is not always appropriate and we entertain great doubts as to the truth, or rather the *vraisemblance* of the main character. The hardness, selfishness, and cruelty of Heathcliff are in our opinion inconsistent with the romantic love that he is stated to have felt for Catherine Earnshaw. As Nelly Dean says, "he is as hard as a whinstone." He has no gratitude, no affection, no liking for anything human except for one person, and that liking is thoroughly selfish and ferocious. He hates the son of Hindley, which is intelligible enough; but he also hates and tyrannizes over his own son and the daughter of his beloved Catherine, and this we cannot understand.

We have said that there are some good dashes at character. The first Catherine is sketched thus.

\* \* \*

From what we have said, the reader will imagine that the book is full of grim pictures. Here is one [Heathcliff's telling of his opening of Catherine's grave]. It should be premised that Heathcliff has manifested symptoms of restlessness and trouble for some time past.

\* \* \*

If this book be, as we apprehend it is, the first work of the author, we hope that he will produce a second,—giving himself more time in its composition than in the present case, developing his incidents more carefully, eschewing exaggeration and obscurity, and looking steadily at human life, under all its moods, for those pictures of the passions that he may desire to sketch for our public benefit. It may be well also to be sparing of certain oaths and phrases, which do not materially contribute to any character, and are by no means to be reckoned among the evidences of a writer's genius. We detest the affectation and effeminate frippery which is but too frequent in the modern novel, and willingly trust ourselves with an author who goes at once fearlessly into the moors and desolate places, for his heroes; but we must at the same time stipulate with him that he shall not drag into light all that he discovers, of coarse and loathsome, in his wanderings, but simply so much good and ill as he may find necessary to elucidate his history—so much only as my be interwoven inextricably with the persons whom he professes to paint. It is the province of an artist to modify and in some cases refine what he beholds in the ordinary world. There never was a man whose daily life (that is to say, *all* his deeds and sayings, entire and without exception) constituted fit materials for a book of fiction. Even the figures of the Greeks (which are

> In old marbles ever beautiful)

were without doubt selected from the vistors in the ancient games, and others, by Phidias and his scholars, and their forms and countenances made perfect before they were thought worthy to adorn the temple of the wise Athena.

The only book which occurs to us as resembling *Wuthering Heights* is a novel of the late Mr. Hooton's, a work of very great talent, in which the hero is a tramper or beggar, and the *dramatis personae* all derived from humble and middle life; but which, notwithstanding its defects, we remember thinking better in its peculiar kind than anything that had been produced since the days of Fielding.

# *Britannia*

## *January 1848*

There are scenes of savage wildness in nature which, though they inspire no pleasurable sensation, we are yet well satisfied to have seen. In the rugged rock, the gnarled roots which cling to it, the dark screen of overhanging vegetation, the dank, moist ground and tangled network of weeds and bushes,—even in the harsh cry of solitary birds, the cries of wild animals, and the startling motion of the snake as it springs away scared by the intruder's foot,—there is an image of primeval rudeness which has much to fascinate, though nothing to charm, the mind. The elements of beauty are round us in the midst of gloom and danger, and some forms are the more picturesque from their distorted growth amid so many obstacles. A tree clinging to the side of a precipice may more attract the eye than the pride of a plantation.

The principle may, to some extent, be applied to life. The uncultured freedom of native character presents more rugged aspects than we meet with in educated society. Its manners are not only more rough but its passions are more violent. It knows nothing of those breakwaters to the fury of tempest which civilized training establishes to subdue the harsher workings of the soul. Its wrath is unrestrained by reflection; the lips curse and the hand strikes with the first impulse of anger. It is more subject to brutal instinct than to divine reason.

It is humanity in this wild state that the author of *Wuthering Heights* essays to depict. His work is strangely original. It bears a resemblance to some of those irregular German tales in which the writers, giving the reins to their fancy, represent personages as swayed and impelled to evil by supernatural influences. But they give spiritual identity to evil impulses, while Mr. Bell more naturally shows them as the natural offspring of the unregulated heart. He displays considerable power in his creations. They have all the angularity of misshapen growth, and form in this respect a striking contrast to those regular forms we are accustomed to meet with in English fiction. They exhibit nothing of the composite character. There is in them no trace of ideal models. They are so new, so wildly grotesque, so entirely without art, that they strike us as proceeding from a mind of limited experience, but of original energy, and of a singular and distinctive cast.

In saying this we indicate both the merits and faults of the tale. It is in parts very unskilfully constructed: many passages in it display neither the grace of art nor the truth of nature, but only the vigour of one positive idea,—that of passionate ferocity. It blazes forth in the most unsuitable circumstances and from persons the least likely to be animated by it. The author is a Salvator Rosa with his pen. He delineates forms of savage grandeur when he wishes to represent sylvan beauty. His Griseldas are furies and his swains Polyphemi. For this reason his narrative leaves an unpleasant effect on the mind. There are no green spots in it on which the mind can linger with satisfaction. The story rushes onwards with impetuous force, but it is the force of a dark and sullen torrent, flowing between high and rugged rocks.

It is permitted to painting to seize one single aspect of nature, and, the pleasure arising from its contemplation proceeds partly from love of imitation, objects unattractive in themselves may be made interesting on canvas. But in fiction this kind of isolation is not allowed. The exhibition of one quality or passion is not sufficient for it. So far as the design extends it must present a true image of life, and if it takes in many characters it must show them animated by many motives. There may be a predominant influence of one strong emotion, perhaps that is necessary to unity of effect, but it should be relieved by contrasts, and set off by accessories. *Wuthering Heights* would have been a far better romance if Heathcliff alone had been a being of stormy passions, instead of all the other characters being nearly as violent and destructive as himself. In fiction, too, as the imitation of nature can never be so vivid and exact as in painting, that imitation is insufficient of itself to afford pleasure, and when it deals with brutal subjects it becomes positively disgusting. It is of course impossible to prescribe rules for either the admission or the rejection of what is shocking and dreadful. It is nothing to say that reality is faithfully followed. The aim of fiction is to afford some sensation of delight. We admit we cannot rejoice in the triumph of goodness—that triumph which consists in the superiority of spirit to body—without knowing its trials and sufferings. But the end of fictitious writings should always be kept in view; and that end is not merely mental excitement, for a very bad book may be very exciting. Generally we are satisfied there is some radical defect in those fictions which leave behind them an impression of pain and horror. It would not be difficult to show why this is, and must be, the case, but it would lead us into deeper considerations than are appropriate to this article.

Mr. Ellis Bell's romance is illuminated by some gleams of sunshine towards the end which serve to cast a grateful light on the dreary path we have travelled. Flowers rise over the grave of buried horrors. The violent passions of two generations are closed in death, yet in the vision of peace with which the tale closes we almost fear their revival in the warped nature of the young survivors.

*       *       *

It is difficult to pronounce any decisive judgment on a work in which there is so much rude ability displayed, yet in which there is so much matter for blame. The scenes of brutality are unnecessarily long and unnecessarily frequent; and as an imaginative writer the author has to learn the first principles of his art. But there is a singular power in his portraiture of strong passion. He exhibits it as convulsing the whole frame of nature, distracting the intellect to madness, and snapping the heart-strings. The anguish of Heathcliff on the death of Catherine approaches to sublimity.

We do not know whether the author writes with any purpose; but we can speak of one effect of his production. It strongly shows the brutalizing influence of unchecked passion. His characters are a commentary on the truth that there is no tyranny in the world like that which thoughts of evil exercise in the daring and reckless breast.

Another reflection springing from the narrative is, that temper is often spoiled in the years of childhood. "The child is the father of the man." The pains and crosses of its youthful years are engrafted in its blood, and form a sullen and a violent disposition. Grooms know how often the tempers of horses are irremediably spoiled in training. But some parents are less wise regarding their children. The intellect in its growth has the faculty of accommodating itself to adverse circumstances. To violence it sometimes opposes violence, sometimes dogged obstinacy. The consequence in either case is fatal to the tranquillity of life. Young Catherine Linton is represented as a naturally sensitive, high-spirited girl; subjected to the cruel usage of her brutal stepfather, she is roused to resistance, and answers his curses with taunts, and his stripes with threatenings. Released from his tyranny, a more gracious spirit comes over her, and she is gentle and peaceful.

There are some fine passages scattered through the pages. Here is a thought on the tranquillity of death:—

"I don't know if it be a pecularity in me, but I am seldom otherwise than happy while watching in the chamber of death, should no frenzied or despairing mourner share the duty with me. I see a repose that neither earth nor hell can break, and I feel an assurance of the endless and shadowless hereafter—the eternity they have entered—where life is boundless in its duration, and love in its sympathy, and joy in its fulness."

Of Joseph, the old sullen servant of Heathcliff, it is quaintly said that he was "the sourest-hearted pharisee that ever searched a Bible to rake all the blessings to himself and fling all the curses to his neighbours."

The third volume of the book is made up of a separate tale [*Agnes Grey*] relating to the fortunes of a governess. Some characters and scenes are nicely sketched in it, but it has nothing to call for special notice. The volumes abound in provincialisms. In many respects they remind us of the recent novel of *Jane Eyre*. We presume they proceed from one family, if not from one pen.

The tale to which we have more particularly alluded is but a fragment, yet of colossal proportion, and bearing evidence of some great design.

With all its power and originality, it is so rude, so unfinished, and so careless, that we are perplexed to pronounce an opinion on it, or to hazard a conjecture on the future career of the author. As yet it belongs to the future to decide whether he will remain a rough hewer of marble or become a great and noble sculptor.

## Unidentified Review

This is a work of great ability, and contains many chapters, to the production of which talent of no common order has contributed. At the same time, the materials which the author has placed at his own disposal have been but few. In the resources of his own mind, and in his own manifestly vivid perceptions of the peculiarities of character—in short, in his knowledge of human nature—has he found them all. An antiquated farm-house, and a neighbouring residence of a somewhat more pretending description, together with their respective inmates, amounting to some half a dozen souls in each, constitute the material and the personal components of one of the most interesting stories we have read for many a long day. The comfortable cheerfulness of the one abode, and the cheerless discomfort of the other—the latter being less the result of a cold and bleak situation, old and damp rooms, and (if we may use the term) of a sort of "haunted house" appearance, than of the strange and mysterious character of its inhabitants—the loves and marriages, separations and hatreds, hopes and disappointments, of two or three generations of the gentle occupants of the one establishment, and the ruder tenants of the other, are brought before us at one moment with a tenderness, at another with a fearfulness, which appeals to our sympathies with the truest tones of the voice of nature; and it is quite impossible to read the book—and this is no slight testimony to the merits of a work of the kind—without feeling that, if placed in the same position as any one of the characters in any page of it, the chances would be twenty to one in favour of our conduct in that position being precisely such as the author has assigned to the personages he has introduced into his domestic drama. But we must at once impose upon ourselves a task—and we confess it is a hard one—we must abstain (from a regard to the space at our disposal) from yielding to the temptation by which we are beset to enter into that minute description of the plot of this very dramatic production to which such a work has an undoubted claim. It is not every day that so good a novel makes its appearance; and to give its contents in detail would be depriving many a reader of half the delight he would experience from the perusal of the work itself. To its pages we must refer him, then; there will he have ample opportunity of sympathising—if he has one touch of nature that "makes the whole world kin"—with the feelings of childhood, youth, manhood, and age, and all the emotions and passions which agitate the restless bosom of humanity. May he derive from it the delight we have ourselves experienced, and be equally grateful to its author for the genuine pleasure he has afforded him.

# *Palladium*†

*September 1850*

[SYDNEY DOBELL]

\* \* \* Who is Currer Bell? is a question which has been variously answered, and has lately, we believe, received in well-informed quarters, a
satisfactory reply. A year or two ago, we mentally solved the problem thus:
Currer Bell is a woman. Every word she utters is female. Not feminine, but
female. There is a sex about it which cannot be mistaken, even in its manliest
attire. Though she translated the manuscript of angels—every thought neu-
tral and every feeling cryptogamous—her *voice* would betray her.

\* \* \* For her most perfect work the world is still waiting, and will be
content for some years to wait; and placing in an assumed order of production
(though not of publication) the novels called *Wuthering Heights*, *Wildfell
Hall*, *Jane Eyre* and *Shirley*, as the works of one author under sundry
disguises, we should have deemed, a few days since, that an analysis of the
first (and, by our theory, the earliest) of these was the amplest justice she
could at present receive. Opening, however, the third edition of *Jane Eyre*,
published before the appearance of *Shirley*, we find a preface in which all
other works are disclaimed. A *nom de guerrist* has many privileges, and we
are willing to put down to a *double entendre* all that is serious in this
disclaimer. That any hand but that which shaped *Jane Eyre* and *Shirley* cut
out the rougher earlier statues, we should require more than the evidence
of our senses to believe. That the author of *Jane Eyre* need fear nothing in
acknowledging these yet more immature creations of one of the most vigorous
of modern idiosyncrasies, we think we shall shortly demonstrate.

Laying aside *Wildfell Hall*, we open *Wuthering Heights*, as at once the
earlier in date and ruder in execution. We look upon it as the flight of an
impatient fancy fluttering in the very exultation of young wings; sometimes
beating against its solitary bars, but turning, rather to exhaust, in a circum-
scribed space, the energy and agility which it may not yet spend in the
heavens—a youthful story, written for oneself in solitude, and thrown aside
till other successes recall the eyes to it in hope. In this thought let the critic
take up the book; lay it down in what thought he will, there are some things
in it he can lay down no more.

That Catherine Earnshaw—at once so wonderfully fresh, so fearfully
natural—new, 'as if brought from other spheres,' and familiar as the recollection of some woeful experience—what can surpass the strange com-
patibility of her simultaneous loves; the involuntary art with which her two
natures are so made to co-exist, that in the very arms of her lover we dare

---

† An extract from an essay entitled "Currer Bell," reprinted from *The Life and Letters of Sydney Dobell*, ed. Jolly (London, 2 vols. 1878), I, 165–71. It originally appeared in the *Palladium* for September 1850.

not doubt her purity; the inevitable belief with which we watch the oscillations of the old and new elements in her mind, and the exquisite truth of the last victory of nature over education, when the past returns to her as a flood, sweeping every modern landmark from within her, and the soul of the child, expanding, fills the woman?

Found at last, by her husband, insensible on the breast of her lover, and dying of the agony of their parting, one looks back upon her, like that husband, without one thought of accusation or absolution; her memory is chaste as the loyalty of love, pure as the air of the Heights on which she dwelt.

Heathcliff *might* have been as unique a creation. The conception in his case was as wonderfully strong and original, but he is spoilt in detail. The authoress has too often disgusted, where she should have terrified, and has allowed us a familiarity with her fiend which had ended in unequivocal contempt. If *Wuthering Heights* had been written as lately as *Jane Eyre*, the figure of Heathcliff, symmetrised and elevated, might have been one of the most natural and most striking portraits in the gallery of fiction.

Not a subordinate place or person in this novel but bears more or less the stamp of high genius. Ellen Dean is the ideal of the peasant playmate and servant of 'the family.' The substratum in which her mind moves is finely preserved. Joseph, as a specimen of the sixty years' servitor of 'the house,' is worthy a museum case. We feel that if Catherine Earnshaw bore her husband a child, it must be that Cathy Linton, and no other. The very Jane Eyre, of quiet satire, peeps out in such a paragraph as this:—'He told me to put on my cloak, and run to Gimmerton for the doctor and the parson. I went through wind and rain, and brought one, the doctor, back with me: the other said, *he would come in the morning.*' What terrible truth, what nicety of touch, what 'uncanny' capacity for mental aberration in the first symptoms of Catherine's delirium. 'I'm not wandering; you're mistaken, or else I should believe you really *were* that withered hag, and I should think I *was* under Penistone Crags: and I'm conscious it's night, and there are two candles on the table making the black press shine like jet.' What an unobtrusive, unexpected sense of *keeping* in the hanging of Isabella's dog.

The book abounds in such things. But one looks back at the whole story as to a world of brilliant figures in an atmosphere of mist; shapes that come out upon the eye, and burn their colours into the brain, and depart into the enveloping fog. It is the unformed writing of a giant's hand: the 'large utterance' of a baby god. In the sprawling of the infant Hercules, however, there must have been attitudes from which the statuary might model. In the early efforts of unusual genius, there are not seldom unconscious felicities which maturer years may look back upon with envy. The child's hand wanders over the strings. It cannot combine them in the chords and melodies of manhood; but its separate notes are perfect in themselves, and perhaps sound all the sweeter for the Æolian discords from which they come.

We repeat, that there are passages in this book of *Wuthering Heights* of which any novelist, past or present, might be proud. Open the first volume at the fourteenth page, and read to the sixty-first. There are few things in modern prose to surpass these pages for native power. We cannot praise too warmly the brave simplicity, the unaffected air of intense belief, the admirable combination of extreme likelihood with the rarest originality, the nice provision of the possible even in the highest effects of the supernatural, the easy strength and instinct of keeping with which the accessory circumstances are grouped, the exquisite but unconscious art with which the chiaroscuro of the whole is managed, and the ungenial frigidity of place, time, weather, and persons, is made to heighten the unspeakable pathos of one ungovernable outburst.

The *thinking out* of some of these pages * * * is the masterpiece of a poet, rather than the hybrid creation of the novelist. The mass of readers will probably yawn over the whole; but, in the memory of those whose remembrance makes *fame*, the images in these pages will live—when every word that conveyed them is forgotten—as a recollection of *things heard and seen*. This is the highest triumph of description; and perhaps every creation of the fancy is more or less faulty, so long as, in a mind fitted to reproduce them, the images co-exist only with the words that called them up. The spiritual structure is not complete till the scaffolding can be safely struck away. That which thou sowest is not quickened except it die. This mortal must put on the immortality of the mind. Ideas should be permanent, words evanescent. Whoever has watched a trowel in the hands of a skilful mason, has seen an example of a very high excellence of authorship. The mortar is laid, but the trowel is already withdrawn. * * *

* * * We are at a loss to find anywhere in modern prose a less residuum from the fiery ordeal; or to discover, in the same space, such wealth and such economy, such apparent ease, such instinctive art. *Instinctive* art; for to the imaginative writer, all art that is not instinctive is dangerous. All art that is the application of principles, however astutely those principles be applied * * * smacks not of the artist, but the artisan. Let no man think to improve in his working by any knowledge that can be taken up or laid down at will, any means or appliances from without. All improvement in the creation must first exist in the creator. Say not to the artist, write, paint, play, by such and such a rule, but *grow* by it. Have you literary principles?— write them in your leisure hours on the fleshly tables of the heart. Have you theories of taste?—set your brain in idle time to their tune. Is there a virtue you would emulate, or a fault you would discard?—gaze on spare days upon the one till your soul has risen under it as the tide under the moon, or scourge the other in the sight of all your faculties till every internal sense recoils from its company. Then, when your error is no longer a trespass to be condemned by judgment, but an impiety at which feeling revolts— when your virtue is no more obedience to a formula, but the natural action of a reconstructed soul—strike off the clay mould from the bronze Apollo,

throw your critics to one wind and their sermons to the other, let Self be made absolute as you take up your pen and write, like a god, in a sublime egotism, to which your own likes and dislikes are unquestioned law. * * * What is true of the poet, the creator, the intellectual vicegerent of God, is true, in different degrees, of all who in any grade share the creative spirit— of every one of the apostlehood and priesthood through whom genius evangelises, sanctifies, and regenerates the world. And the higher in the scale, the more imperative is the duty of autocracy, and the more fatal any 'tempering of the iron with the clay.'

These truths supply us with the great secret of success and failure in the works of Currer Bell; and there is no admission we could make which could be a higher testimony to her powers as a creative artist. If this authoress had *published* any novel before *Jane Eyre*, *Jane Eyre* would not have been the moral wonder which it is, and will for many years remain. If *Jane Eyre* had met with a less triumphant *furore* of review, *Shirley* would have been a worthier successor.

To say that an artist is *spoilt* by criticism, is to disprove his right to the title; to say that he is, for the present, maimed and disabled by it, may be to bear the highest witness to his intrinsic genius—and this witness we bear to Currer Bell. When Currer Bell writes her next novel, let her remember, as far as possible, the frame of mind in which she sat down to her first. She cannot now commit the faults of that early effort; it will be well for her if she be still capable of the virtues. She will never sin so much against consistent keeping as to draw another Heathcliff; she is too much *au fait* of her profession to make again those sacrifices to machinery which deprive her early picture of any claim to be ranked as a work of art. Happy she, if her next book demonstrate the unimpaired possession of those powers of insight, that instinctive obedience to the nature within her, and those occurrences of infallible inspiration which astound the critic in the young author of *Wuthering Heights*. She will not let her next dark-haired hero babble away the respect of her reader and the awe of his antecedents; nor will she find another housekeeper who remembers two volumes *literatim*. Let her rejoice if she can again give us such an elaboration of a rare and fearful form of mental disease—so terribly strong, so exquisitely subtle— with such nicety in its transitions, such intimate symptomatic truth in its details, as to be at once a psychological and medical study. It has been said of Shakespeare, that he drew cases which the physician might study; Currer Bell has done no less. She will not, again, employ her wonderful pencil on a picture so destitute of moral beauty and human worth. Let her exult, if she can still invest such a picture with such interest. We stand painfully before her portraits; but our eyes are drawn towards them by the irresistible ties of blood relationship. Let her exult, if she can still make us weep with the simple pathos of that fading face, which looked from the golden crocuses on her pillow to the hills which concealed the old home and the churchyard of Gimmerton. 'These are the earliest flowers at the Heights,' she exclaimed.

'They remind me of thaw-winds, and warm sunshine, and nearly-melted snow. Edgar, is there not a south wind, and is not the snow almost gone?'— 'The snow is quite gone down here, darling,' replied her husband; 'and I only see two white spots on the whole range of moors. The sky is blue, and the larks are singing, and the becks and brooks are all brimful. Catherine, last spring, at this time, I was longing to have you under this roof; now, I wish you were a mile or two up those hills: the air blows so sweetly, I feel that it would cure you.'—'I shall never be there but once more,' said the invalid, 'and then you'll leave me, and I shall remain for ever. Next spring, you'll long again to have me under this roof, and you'll look back, and think you were happy to-day.'

Let Currer Bell prize the young intuition of character which dictated Cathy's speech to Ellen. There is a deep, unconscious philosophy in it. There are minds whose crimes and sorrows are not so much the result of intrinsic evil as of a false position in the scheme of things, which clashes their energies with the arrangements of surrounding life. It is difficult to cure such a soul from *within*. The point of view, not the eye or the landscape, is in fault. Move *that*, and as at the changing of a stop, the mental machine assumes its proper relative place, and the powers of discord become, in the same measure, the instruments of harmony. It was a fine instinct which saw this. Let Currer Bell be passing glad if it is as vigorous now as then; and let her thank God is she can now draw the apparition of the 'Wanderer of the Moor.'

# [CHARLOTTE BRONTË]

## Biographical Notice of Ellis and Acton Bell (1850)†

It has been thought that all the works published under the names of Currer, Ellis, and Acton Bell, were, in reality, the production of one person. This mistake I endeavoured to rectify by a few words of disclaimer prefixed to the third edition of *Jane Eyre*. These, too, it appears, failed to gain general credence, and now, on the occasion of a reprint of *Wuthering Heights* and *Agnes Grey*, I am advised distinctly to state how the case really stands.

Indeed, I feel myself that it is time the obscurity attending those two names—Ellis and Acton—was done away. The little mystery, which formerly yielded some harmless pleasure, has lost its interest; circumstances are changed. It becomes, then, my duty to explain briefly the origin and authorship of the books written by Currer, Ellis, and Acton Bell.

About five years ago, my two sisters and myself, after a somewhat pro-

† This notice and the preface that follows were written for the second edition of her sister's novel, 1850.

# WUTHERING HEIGHTS

### AND

# AGNES GREY.

### BY

## ELLIS AND ACTON BELL.

A NEW EDITION REVISED, WITH

### A BIOGRAPHICAL NOTICE OF THE AUTHORS,
### A SELECTION FROM THEIR LITERARY REMAINS,
### AND A PREFACE,

### BY CURRER BELL.

### LONDON:
SMITH, ELDER AND CO., 65, CORNHILL.

1850.

longed period of separation, found ourselves reunited, and at home. Resident in a remote district where education had made little progress, and where, consequently, there was no inducement to seek social intercourse beyond our own domestic circle, we were wholly dependent on ourselves and each other, on books and study, for the enjoyments and occupations of life. The highest stimulus, as well as the liveliest pleasure we had known from childhood upwards, lay in attempts at literary composition; formerly we used to show each other what we wrote, but of late years this habit of communication and consultation had been discontinued; hence it ensued, that we were mutually ignorant of the progress we might respectively have made.

One day, in the autumn of 1845, I accidentally lighted on a MS. volume of verse in my sister Emily's handwriting. Of course, I was not surprised, knowing that she could and did write verse: I looked it over, and something more than surprise seized me,—a deep conviction that these were not common effusions, nor at all like the poetry women generally write. I thought them condensed and terse, vigorous and genuine. To my ear, they had also a peculiar music—wild, melancholy, and elevating.

My sister Emily was not a person of demonstrative character, nor one, on the recesses of whose mind and feelings, even those nearest and dearest to her could, with impunity, intrude unlicensed; it took hours to reconcile her to the discovery I had made, and days to persuade her that such poems merited publication. I knew, however, that a mind like hers could not be without some latent spark of honourable ambition, and refused to be discouraged in my attempts to fan that spark to flame.

Meantime, my younger sister quietly produced some of her own compositions, intimating that since Emily's had given me pleasure, I might like to look at hers. I could not but be a partial judge, yet I thought that these verses too had a sweet sincere pathos of their own.

We had very early cherished the dream of one day becoming authors. This dream, never relinquished even when distance divided and absorbing tasks occupied us, now suddenly acquired strength and consistency: it took the character of a resolve. We agreed to arrange a small selection of our poems, and, if possible, get them printed. Averse to personal publicity, we veiled our own names under those of Currer, Ellis, and Acton Bell; the ambiguous choice being dictated by a sort of conscientious scruple at assuming Christian names, positively masculine, while we did not like to declare ourselves women, because—without at that time suspecting that our mode of writing and thinking was not what is called "feminine"—we had a vague impression that authoresses are liable to be looked on with prejudice; we had noticed how critics sometimes use for their chastisement the weapon of personality, and for their reward, a flattery, which is not true praise.

The bringing out of our little book was hard work. As was to be expected, neither we nor our poems were at all wanted; but for this we had been prepared at the outset; though inexperienced ourselves, we had read the experience of others. The great puzzle lay in the difficulty of getting answers of any kind from the publishers to whom we applied. Being greatly harassed by this obstacle, I ventured to apply to the Messrs. Chambers, of Edinburgh, for a word of advice; *they* may have forgotten the circumstance, but *I* have not, for from them I received a brief and business-like but civil and sensible reply, on which we acted, and at last made a way.

The book was printed: it is scarcely known, and all of it that merits to be known are the poems of Ellis Bell. The fixed conviction I held, and hold, of the worth of these poems has not indeed received the confirmation of much favourable criticism; but I must retain it notwithstanding.

Ill-success failed to crush us: the mere effort to succeed had given a wonderful zest to existence; it must be pursued. We each set to work on a prose tale: Ellis Bell produced *Wuthering Heights*, Acton Bell *Agnes Grey*, and Currer Bell also wrote a narrative in one volume. These MSS. were perseveringly obtruded upon various publishers for the space of a year and a half; usually, their fate was an ignominious and abrupt dismissal.

At last *Wuthering Heights* and *Agnes Grey* were accepted on terms somewhat impoverishing to the two authors; Currer Bell's book found acceptance nowhere, nor any acknowledgment of merit, so that something like the chill of despair began to invade his heart. As a forlorn hope, he tried one publishing house more—Messrs. Smith and Elder. Ere long, in a much shorter space than that on which experience had taught him to calculate—there came a letter, which he opened in the dreary expectation of finding two hard hopeless lines, intimating that Messrs. Smith and Elder "were not disposed to publish the MS." and, instead, he took out of the envelope a letter of two pages. He read it trembling. It declined, indeed, to publish that tale, for business reasons, but it discussed its merits and demerits so courteously, so considerately, in a spirit so rational, with a discrimination so enlightened, that this very refusal cheered the author better than a vulgarly-expressed acceptance would have done. It was added, that a work in three volumes would meet with careful attention.

I was then just completing *Jane Eyre*, at which I had been working while the one volume tale was plodding its weary round in London: in three weeks I sent it off; friendly and skilful hands took it in. This was in the commencement of September 1847; it came out before the close of October following, while *Wuthering Heights* and *Agnes Grey*, my sisters' works, which had already been in the press for months, still lingered under a different management.

They appeared at last. Critics failed to do them justice. The immature but very real powers revealed in *Wuthering Heights* were scarcely recognised; its import and nature were misunderstood; the identity of its author was misrepresented; it was said that this was an earlier and ruder attempt of the same pen which had produced *Jane Eyre*. Unjust and grievous error! We laughed at it at first, but I deeply lament it now. Hence, I fear, arose a prejudice against the book. That writer who could attempt to palm off an inferior and immature production under cover of one successful effort, must indeed be unduly eager after the secondary and sordid result of authorship, and pitiably indifferent to its true and honourable meed. If reviewers and the public truly believed this, no wonder that they looked darkly on the cheat.

Yet I must not be understood to make these things subject for reproach or complaint; I dare not do so; respect for my sister's memory forbids me. By her any such querulous manifestation would have been regarded as an unworthy, and offensive weakness.

It is my duty, as well as my pleasure, to acknowledge one exception to the general rule of criticism. One writer,[1] endowed with the keen vision and fine sympathies of genius, has discerned the real nature of *Wuthering Heights*, and has, with equal accuracy, noted its beauties and touched on its faults. Too often do reviewers remind us of the mob of Astrologers, Chaldeans, and Soothsayers gathered before the "writing on the wall," and unable to read the characters or make known the interpretation. We have a right to rejoice when a true seer comes at last, some man in whom is an excellent spirit, to whom have been given light, wisdom, and understanding; who can accurately read the "Mene, Mene, Tekel, Upharsin" of an original mind (however unripe, however inefficiently cultured and partially expanded that mind may be); and who can say with confidence, "This is the interpretation thereof."

Yet even the writer to whom I allude shares the mistake about the authorship, and does me the injustice to suppose that there was equivoque in my former rejection of this honour (as an honour, I regard it). May I assure him that I would scorn in this and in every other case to deal in equivoque; I believe language to have been given us to make our meaning clear, and not to wrap it in dishonest doubt.

*The Tenant of Wildfell Hall* by Acton Bell, had likewise an unfavourable reception. At this I cannot wonder. The choice of subject was an entire mistake. Nothing less congruous with the writer's nature could be conceived. The motives which dictated this choice were pure, but, I think, slightly morbid. She had, in the course of her life, been called on to contemplate, near at hand and for a long time, the terrible effects of talents misused and faculties abused; hers was naturally a sensitive, reserved, and dejected nature; what she saw sank very deeply into her mind; it did her harm. She brooded over it till she believed it to be a duty to reproduce every detail (of course with fictitious characters, incidents, and situations) as a warning to others. She hated her work, but would pursue it. When reasoned with on the subject, she regarded such reasonings as a temptation to self-indulgence. She must be honest; she must not varnish, soften, or conceal. This well-meant resolution brought on her misconstruction and some abuse, which she bore, as it was her custom to bear whatever was unpleasant, with mild, steady

---

1. See the *Palladium* for September 1850 [*Author's note*].

patience. She was a very sincere and practical Christian, but the tinge of religious melancholy communicated a sad shade to her brief, blameless life.

Neither Ellis nor Acton allowed herself for one moment to sink under want of encouragement; energy nerved the one, and endurance upheld the other. They were both prepared to try again; I would fain think that hope and the sense of power was yet strong within them. But a great change approached: affliction came in that shape which to anticipate is dread; to look back on, grief. In the very heat and burden of the day, the labourers failed over their work.

My sister Emily first declined. The details of her illness are deep-branded in my memory, but to dwell on them, either in thought or narrative, is not in my power. Never in all her life had she lingered over any task that lay before her, and she did not linger now. She sank rapidly. She made haste to leave us. Yet, while physically she perished, mentally, she grew stronger than we had yet known her. Day by day, when I saw with what a front she met suffering, I looked on her with an anguish of wonder and love. I have seen nothing like it; but, indeed, I have never seen her parallel in anything. Stronger than a man, simpler than a child, her nature stood alone. The awful point was, that, while full of ruth for others, on herself she had no pity; the spirit was inexorable to the flesh; from the trembling hand, the unnerved limbs, the faded eyes, the same service was exacted as they had rendered in health. To stand by and witness this, and not dare to remonstrate, was a pain no words can render.

Two cruel months of hope and fear passed painfully by, and the day came at last when the terrors and pains of death were to be undergone by this treasure, which had grown dearer and dearer to our hearts as it wasted before our eyes. Towards the decline of that day, we had nothing of Emily but her mortal remains as consumption left them. She died December 19, 1848.

We thought this enough; but we were utterly and presumptuously wrong. She was not buried ere Anne fell ill. She had not been committed to the grave a fortnight, before we received distinct intimation that it was necessary to prepare our minds to see the younger sister go after the elder. Accordingly, she followed in the same path with slower step, and with a patience that equalled the other's fortitude. I have said that she was religious, and it was by leaning on those Christian doctrines in which she firmly believed, that she found support through her most painful journey. I witnessed their efficacy in her latest hour and greatest trial, and must bear my testimony to the calm triumph with which they brought her through. She died May 28, 1849.

What more shall I say about them? I cannot and need not say much more. In externals, they were two unobtrusive women; a perfectly secluded life gave them retiring manners and habits. In Emily's nature the extremes of vigour and simplicity seemed to meet. Under an unsophisticated culture, inartificial tastes, and an unpretending outside, lay a secret power and fire that might have informed the brain and kindled the veins of a hero; but she had no worldly wisdom; her powers were unadapted to the practical business of life; she would fail to defend her most manifest rights, to consult her most legitimate advantage. An interpreter ought always to have stood between her and the world. Her will was not very flexible, and it generally opposed her interest. Her temper was magnanimous, but warm and sudden; her spirit altogether unbending.

Anne's character was milder and more subdued; she wanted the power, the fire, the originality of her sister, but was well-endowed with quiet virtues of her own. Long-suffering, self-denying, reflective, and intelligent, a constitutional reserve and taciturnity placed and kept her in the shade, and covered her mind, and especially her feelings, with a sort of nun-like veil, which was rarely lifted. Neither Emily nor Anne was learned; they had no thought of filling their pitchers at the well-spring of other minds; they always wrote from the impulse of nature, the dictates of intuition, and from such stores of observation as their limited experience had enabled them to amass. I may sum up all by saying, that for strangers they were nothing, for superficial observers less than nothing; but for those who had known them all their lives in the intimacy of close relationship, they were genuinely good and truly great.

This notice has been written, because I felt it a sacred duty to wipe the dust off their gravestones, and leave their dear names free from soil.

CURRER BELL.

*September* 19, 1850.

## [CHARLOTTE BRONTË]

### Editor's Preface
### to the New Edition of
### *Wuthering Heights* (1850)†

I have just read over "Wuthering Heights," and, for the first time, have obtained a clear glimpse of what are termed (and, perhaps, really are) its faults; have gained a definite notion of how it appears to other people—to strangers who knew nothing of the author; who are unacquainted with the locality where the scenes of the story are laid; to whom the inhabitants, the customs, the natural characteristics of the outlying hills and hamlets in the West-Riding of Yorkshire are things alien and unfamiliar.

† In a letter to W.S. Williams on September 29, 1850, Charlotte Brontë announced her "intention to write a few lines of remark on 'Wuthering Heights,' which, however, I propose to place apart as a brief preface before the tale. I am likewise compelling myself to read it over, for the first time of opening the book since my sister's death. Its power fills me with renewed admiration; but yet I am oppressed; the reader is scarcely ever permitted a taste of unalloyed pleasure; every beam of sunshine is poured downed through black bars of threatening cloud; every page is surcharged with a sort of moral electricity; and the writer was unconscious of all this—nothing could make her conscious of it" (*The Brontës: Their Lives, Friendships, and Correspondence* 3.165).

To all such "Wuthering Heights" must appear a rude and strange production. The wild moors of the north of England can for them have no interest; the language, the manners, the very dwellings and household customs of the scattered inhabitants of those districts, must be to such readers in a great measure unintelligible, and—where intelligible—repulsive. Men and women who, perhaps, naturally very calm, and with feelings moderate in degree, and little marked in kind, have been trained from their cradle to observe the utmost evenness of manner and guardedness of language, will hardly know what to make of the rough, strong utterance, the harshly manifested passions, the unbridled aversions, and headlong partialities of unlettered moorland hinds and rugged moorland squires, who have grown up untaught and unchecked, except by mentors as harsh as themselves. A large class of readers, likewise, will suffer greatly from the introduction into the pages of this work of words printed with all their letters, which it has become the custom to represent by the initial and final letter only—a blank line filling the interval. I may as well say at once that, for this circumstance, it is out of my power to apologize; deeming it, myself, a rational plan to write words at full length. The practice of hinting by single letters those expletives with which profane and violent persons are wont to garnish their discourse, strikes me as a proceeding which, however well meant, is weak and futile. I cannot tell what good it does—what feeling it spares—what horror it conceals.

With regard to the rusticity of "Wuthering Heights," I admit the charge, for I feel the quality. It is rustic all through. It is moorish, and wild, and knotty as a root of heath. Nor was it natural that it should be otherwise; the author being herself a native and nursling of the moors. Doubtless, had her lot been cast in a town, her writings, if she had written at all, would have possessed another character. Even had chance or taste led her to choose a similar subject, she would have treated it otherwise. Had Ellis Bell been a lady or a gentleman accustomed to what is called "the world," her view of a remote and unreclaimed region, as well as of the dwellers therein, would have differed greatly from that actually taken by the homebred country girl. Doubtless it would have been wider—more comprehensive: whether it would have been more original or more truthful is not so certain. As far as the scenery and locality are concerned, it could scarcely have been so sympathetic: Ellis Bell did not describe as one whose eye and taste alone found pleasure in the prospect; her native hills were far more to her than a spectacle; they were what she lived in, and by, as much as the wild birds, their tenants, or as the heather, their produce. Her descriptions, then, of natural scenery, are what they should be, and all they should be.

Where delineation of human character is concerned, the case is different. I am bound to avow that she had scarcely more practical knowledge of the peasantry amongst whom she lived, then a nun has of the country people who sometimes pass her convent gates. My sister's disposition was not naturally gregarious; circumstances favoured and fostered her tendency to seclusion; except to go to church or take a walk on the hills, she rarely crossed the threshold of home. Though her feeling for the people round was benevolent, intercourse with them she never sought; nor, with very few exceptions, ever experienced. And yet she knew them: knew their ways, their language, their family histories; she could hear of them with interest, and talk of them with detail, minute, graphic, and accurate; but *with* them, she rarely exchanged a word. Hence it ensued that what her mind had gathered of the real concerning them, was too exclusively confined to those tragic and terrible traits of which, in listening to the secret annals of every rude vicinage, the memory is sometimes compelled to receive the impress. Her imagination, which was a spirit more sombre than sunny, more powerful than sportive, found in such traits material whence it wrought creations like Heathcliff, like Earnshaw, like Catherine. Having formed these beings, she did not know what she had done. If the auditor of her work when read in manuscript, shuddered under the grinding influence of natures so relentless and implacable, of spirits so lost and fallen; if it was complained that the mere hearing of certain vivid and fearful scenes banished sleep by night, and disturbed mental peace by day, Ellis Bell would wonder what was meant, and suspect the complainant of affectation. Had she but lived, her mind would of itself have grown like a strong tree, loftier, straighter, wider-spreading, and its matured fruits would have attained a mellower ripeness and sunnier bloom; but on that mind time and experience alone could work: to the influence of other intellects, it was not amenable.

Having avowed that over much of "Wuthering Heights" there broods "a horror of great darkness;" that, in its storm-heated and electrical atmosphere, we seem at times to breathe lightning, let me point to those spots where clouded daylight and the eclipsed sun still attest their existence. For a specimen of true benevolence and homely fidelity, look at the character of Nelly Dean; for an example of constancy and tenderness, remark that of Edgar Linton. (Some people will think these qualities do not shine so well incarnate in a man as they would do in a woman, but Ellis Bell could never be brought to comprehend this notion: nothing moved her more than any insinuation that the faithfulness and clemency, the long-suffering and loving-kindness which are esteemed virtues in the daughers of Eve, become foibles in the sons of Adam. She held that mercy and forgiveness are the divinest attributes of the Great Being who made both man and woman, and that what clothes the Godhead in glory, can disgrace no form of feeble humanity.) There is a dry saturnine humour in the delineation of old Joseph, and some glimpses of grace and gaiety animate the younger Catherine. Nor is even the first heroine of the name destitute of a certain strange beauty in her fierceness, or of honesty in the midst of perverted passion and passionate perversity.

Heathcliff, indeed, stands unredeemed; never once swerving in his arrow-straight course to perdition, from the time when "the little black-haired, swarthy thing, as dark as if it came from the Devil," was first unrolled out of the bundle and set on its feet in the farm-house kitchen, to the hour when Nelly Dean found the grim, stalwart corpse laid on its back in the panel-enclosed bed, with wide-gazing eyes that seemed "to sneer at her attempt to close them, and parted lips and sharp white teeth that sneered too."

Heathcliff betrays one solitary human feeling, and that is *not* his love for Catherine; which is a sentiment fierce and inhuman: a passion such as might boil and glow in the bad essence of some evil genius; a fire that might form the tormented centre—the ever-suffering soul of a magnate of the infernal world: and by its quenchless and ceaseless ravage effect the execution of the decree which dooms him to carry Hell with him wherever he wanders. No; the single link that connects Heathcliff with humanity is his rudely confessed regard for Hareton Earnshaw—the young man whom he has ruined; and then his half-implied esteem for Nelly Dean. These solitary traits omitted, we should say he was child neither of Lascar nor gipsy, but a man's shape animated by demon life—a Ghoul—an Afreet.

Whether it is right or advisable to create beings like Heathcliff, I do not know: I scarcely think it is. But this I know; the writer who possesses the creative gift owns something of which he is not always master—something that at times strangely wills and works for itself. He may lay down rules and devise principles, and to rules and principles it will perhaps for years lie in subjection; and then, haply without any warning of revolt, there comes a time when it will not longer consent "to harrow the vallies, or be bound with a band in the furrow"—when it "laughs at the multitude of the city, and regards not the crying of the driver"—when, refusing absolutely to make ropes out of sea-sand any longer, it sets to work on statue-hewing, and you have a Pluto or a Jove, a Tisiphone or a Psyche, a Mermaid or a Madonna, as Fate or Inspiration direct. Be the work grim or glorious, dread or divine, you have little choice left but quiescent adoption. As for you—the nominal artist—your share in it has been to work passively under dictates you neither delivered nor could question—that would not be uttered at your prayer, nor suppressed nor changed at your caprice. If the result be attractive, the World will praise you, who little deserve praise; if it be repulsive, the same World will blame you, who almost as little deserve blame.

"Wuthering Heights" was hewn in a wild workshop, with simple tools, out of homely materials. The statuary found a granite block on a solitary moor: gazing thereon, he saw how from the crag might be elicited a head, savage, swart, sinister; a form moulded with at least one element of grandeur—power. He wrought with a rude chisel, and from no model but the vision of his meditations. With time and labour, the crag took human shape; and there it stands colossal, dark, and frowning, half statue, half rock: in the former sense, terrible and goblin-like; in the latter, almost beautiful, for its colouring is of mellow grey, and moorland moss clothes it; and heath, with its blooming bells and balmy fragrance, grows faithfully close to the giant's foot.

CURRER BELL

# REVIEWS OF THE 1850 EDITION OF *WUTHERING HEIGHTS*

Charlotte Brontë noted that by early 1851 the only notices she had "seen of the new edition of *Wuthering Heights* were those in the *Examiner*, the *Leader*, and the *Athenaeum*. That in the *Athenaeum* somehow gave me pleasure; it is quiet but respectful—so I thought, at least" (*The Brontës: Their Lives, Friendships, and Correspondence* 3.200).

## *Examiner*

### *December 21, 1850*

In a preface to this volume the author of *Jane Eyre* partially lifts the veil from a history and mystery of authorship which has occupied the Quidnuncs of literature for the past two years. * * *

* * * The reception of *Jane Eyre* is known to all. The other books also made appearance at last, but, according to Currer Bell, had a very different reception. "Critics," she says, "failed to do them justice. The immature but very real powers revealed in *Wuthering Heights* were scarcely recognized; its import and nature were misunderstood; the identity of its author was misrepresented; it was said that this was an earlier and ruder attempt of the same pen which produced *Jane Eyre*. Unjust and grievous error! We laughed at it at first, but I deeply lament it now. Hence, I fear, arose a prejudice against the book." This somewhat grave charge is advanced with but one exception to be shortly noticed; when we shall at the same time see what justice there is in the accusation.

The writer proceeds to describe the reception of Acton Bell's *Tenant of Wildfell Hall* as not more favourable, but more justly founded, than that of Ellis Bell's *Wuthering Heights*; but she adds that neither Ellis nor Acton suffered herself for one moment to sink under this want of encouragement. Energy nerved the one, endurance upheld the other, and both were prepared to try again; when there approached a more fell assailant than even unjust criticism. Both sisters were doomed to perish by rapid consumption. The illness of Emily is described in language steeped and interpenetrated with bleeding recollections. * * *

* * * So ends their brief, sad story. And if the sister who shared with them in these struggles and disappointments of genius, and excelled them in its instant manifestation and acceptance, may not thus lift their names to the level of her own success, she has at least fairly challenged for them dead, more honourable recognition than she believes to have fallen to them living. She has done her best to reverse what she holds to have been the unjust judgment of the critics who coldly disapproved or harshly misrepresented their productions. She has wiped off this dust, and freed them from this soil.

But let us not overstate Currer Bell's censure of the critical neglect by which her sisters suffered. She makes one exception.

> It is my duty, as well as my pleasure, to acknowledge one exception to the general rule of criticism. One writer, endowed with the keen vision and fine sympathies of genius, has discerned the real nature of *Wuthering Heights*, and has, with equal accuracy, noted its beauties and touched on its faults. Too often do reviewers remind us of the mob of Astrologers, Chaldeans, and Soothsayers gathered before the "writing on the wall," and unable to read the characters or make known the interpretation. We have a right to rejoice when a true seer comes at last, some man in whom is an excellent spirit, to whom have been given light, wisdom, and understanding; who can accurately read the "Mene, Mene, Tekel, Upharisin" of an original mind (however unripe, however inefficiently cultured and partially expanded that mind may be); and who can say with confidence, "This is the interpretation thereof."

The "general rule of criticism" is a phrase somewhat startling in connection with the wondrous unanimity of critical judgments on *Jane Eyre*; and there is another passage in the preface, where Currer Bell speaks of the assumed names of herself and her sisters, in which a yet stonger feeling of the same sort perhaps unconsciously escapes. "We had a vague impression that authoresses are liable to be looked on with prejudice; we had noticed how critics sometimes use for their chastisement the weapon of personality, *and for their reward, a flattery which is not true praise.*" Poor hapless critics! But nothing of this kind should surprise a writer who has had the most moderate experience of the thankless vocation. Whether it be censure contemptuously rejected as unworthy, or praise condescendingly received as not worthy enough, the reviewer's fate knows very little variation. Nor be it ours to say that he may not for the most part be worthy of it, and find himself justly in the position of the old lady in the fable whose ear was bitten off by her son at the gallows, for having refused to hear the truth of him, encouraged him in his extravagant courses, and (as Currer Bell expresses it) rewarded him with a flattery which was not true praise. But to the particular case recorded in this volume we have a word or two, on our own poor behalf, to plead in arrest of judgment.

The authors of *Wuthering Heights* and the *Tenant of Wildfell Hall* were not unjustly or contemptuously treated in the colums of the *Examiner*. We do not lay claim to the mene-tekel-upharsin powers assigned to the critic of "keen vision and fine sympathies" singled out by Currer Bell as having alone done justice to her sister, and who appears to have done his somewhat tardy justice so recently as last September in a journal called the *Palladium*. We dare say, judging from the tone of the extracted criticism prefixed to the volume, that our style of handling these things would seldom come up to the mark of Currer Bell's rejoicing. But it is right to mention notwithstanding, that reviews of the works in question by no means depreciatory appeared in this journal almost instantly on the appearance of the tales respectively named, and that we did not wait till

"deaf the closed ear and mute the tuneful tongue,"

before we gave expression to the praise which both Ellis and Acton Bell seemed fairly to challenge at our hands. Lengthy reviews with very copious extracts were given of both, at the opening of 1848 and in the summer of the same year.

*Wuthering Heights* we characterized as a strange but powerful book, containing good "rough dashes at character," the impress of "real events," and "no commonplace or affectation." We said that it had forcibly reminded us of a book which we remembered thinking "better in its peculiar kind than anything that had been produced since the days of Fielding." * * *

Was this scant or grudging praise? Did it refuse to recognize the "immature but very real powers" of these young and struggling authors? Did it "misunderstand" or "misrepresent" them?

If so, Currer Bell must herself share the reproach, for the language in which she speaks of her sister Emily's early habits and associations, as explaining what was faulty as well as was excellent in her writings, does not materially differ from this which has just been quoted. For ourselves we have nothing to add to it—neither praise to retract, nor censure to explain. We have only most unfeignedly to deplore the blight which fell prematurely on sure rich intellectual promise, and to regret that natures so rare and noble should so early have passed away.

## Leader

### December 28, 1850

There are various points of interest in this republication, some arising from the intrinsic excellence of the works themselves, other from the lustre reflected on them by *Jane Eyre*. The biographical notice of her two sisters is plainly and touchingly written by Currer Bell. * * *

Critics, we are told, failed to do them justice. But to judge from the extracts given of articles in the *Britannia* and *Atlas*, the critics were excessively indulgent, and we take it the great public was the most recalcitrant, and would *not* be amused with these strange wild pictures of incult humanity, painted as if by lurid torchlight, though painted with unmistakeable power—the very power only heightening their repulsiveness. The visions of madmen are not more savage, or more remote from ordinary life. The error committed is an error in art—the excessive predominance of shadows darkening the picture. One cannot dine off condiments, nor sup off horrors without an indigestion.

And yet, although there is a want of air and light in the picture we cannot deny its truth: sombre, rude, brutal, yet true. The fierce ungoverned instincts of powerful organizations, bred up amidst violence, revolt, and moral apathy, are here seen in operation; such brutes we should all be, or the most of us, were our lives as insubordinate to law; were our affections and sympathies as little cultivated, our imaginations as undirected. And herein lies the moral of the book, though most people will fail to draw the moral from very irritation at it.

Curious enough it is to read *Wuthering Heights* and *The Tenant of Wildfell Hall*, and remember that the writers were two retiring, solitary, consumptive girls! Books, coarse even for men, coarse in language and coarse in conception, the coarseness apparently of violent and uncultivated men—turn out to be the productions of two girls living almost alone, filling their loneliness with quiet studies, and writing these books from a sense of duty, hating the pictures they drew, yet drawing them with austere conscientiousness! There is matter here for the moralist or critic to speculate on.

That it was no caprice of a poor imagination wandering in search of an "exciting" subject we are most thoroughly convinced. The three sisters have been haunted by the same experience. Currer Bell throws more humanity into her picture; but Rochester belongs to the Earnshaw and Heathcliff family. Currer Bell's riper mind enables her to paint with a freer hand; nor can we doubt but that her two sisters, had they lived, would also have risen into greater strength and clearness, retaining the extraordinary power of vigorous delineation which makes their writings so remarkable.

The power, indeed, is wonderful. Heathcliff, devil though he may be, is drawn with a sort of dusky splendour which fascinates, and we feel the truth of his burning and impassioned love for Catherine, and of her inextinguishable love for him. It was a happy thought to make her love the kind, weak, elegant Edgar, and yet without lessening her passion for Heathcliff. Edgar appeals to her love of refinement, and goodness, and culture; Heathcliff clutches her soul in his passionate embrace. Edgar is the husband she has chosen, the man who alone is fit to call her wife; but although she is ashamed of her early playmate she loves him with a passionate abandonment which sets culture, education, the world, at defiance. It is in the treatment of this subject that Ellis Bell shows real mastery, and it shows more genius, in the highest sense of the word, than you will find in a thousand novels.

Creative power is so rare and so valuable that we should accept even its caprices with gratitude. Currer Bell, in a passage on this question, doubts whether the artist can control his power; she seems to think with Plato (see his argument in the *Ion*), that the artist does not possess, but is posed. * * *

This is so true that we suppose every writer will easily recall his sensations of being "carried away" by the thoughts which in moments of exaltation possessed his soul—will recall the headlong feeling of letting the reins slip —being himself as much astonished at the result as any reader can be. There is at such time a *momentum* which propels the mind into regions inaccessible to calculation, unsuspected in our calmer moods.

The present publication is decidedly an interesting one. Besides the two novels of *Wuthering Heights* and *Agnes Grey* it contains the biographical notices already spoken of, and a selection from the poems left by both sisters. We cannot share Currer Bell's partiality for them; in no one quality distinguishing poetry from prose are they remarkable; but although their poetic interest is next to nought they have a biographical interest which justifies their publication. The volume is compact, and may be slipped into a coat pocket for the railway, so that the traveller may wile away with it the long hours of his journey in grim pleasure.

# Athenaeum

## December 28, 1850

Female genius and female authorship may be said to present some peculiarities of aspect and circumstance in England, which we find associated with them in no other country. Among the most daring and original manifestations of invention by Englishwomen,—some of the most daring and original have owed their parentage, not to defying *Britomarts* at war with society, who choose to make their literature match with their lives,—not to brilliant women figuring in the world, in whom every gift and faculty has been enriched, and whetted sharp and encouraged into creative utterance, by perpetual communication with the most distinguished men of the time,—but to writers living retired lives in retired places, stimulated to activity by no outward influence, driven to confession by no history that demands apologetic parable or subtle plea. This, as a characteristic of English female genius, we have long noticed:—but it has rarely been more simply, more strongly, some will add more strangely, illustrated than in the volume before us.

The lifting of that veil which for a while concealed the authorship of *Jane Eyre* and its sister-novels, excites in us no surprise. It seemed evident from the first prose pages bearing the signatures of Currer, Ellis, and Acton Bell, that these were *Rosalinds*—or a *Rosalind*—in masquerade:—some doubt as to the plurality of persons being engendered by a certain uniformity of local colour and resemblance in choice of subject, which might have arisen either from identity, or from joint peculiarities of situation and of circumstance.— It seemed no less evident * * * that the writers described from personal experience the wild and rugged scenery of the northern parts of this kingdom; and no assertion or disproval, no hypothesis or rumour, which obtained circulation after the success of *Jane Eyre*, could shake convictions that had been gathered out of the books themselves. In similar cases, guessers are too apt to raise plausible arguments on some point of detail,—forgetting that this may have been thrown in *ex proposito* to mislead the bystander; and hence the most ingenious discoverers become so pertinaciously deluded as to lose eye and ear for those less obvious indications of general tone of style, colour of incident, and form of fable on which more phlegmatic persons base measurement and comparison. Whatever of truth there may or may not be generally in the above remarks,—certain it is, that in the novels now in question instinct or divination directed us aright. In the prefaces and notices before us, we find that the Bells were three sisters:— two of whom are no longer amongst the living.

\* \* \*

Though the above particulars be little more than the filling-up of an outline already clearly traced and constantly present whenever those characteristic tales recurred to us,—by those who have held other ideas with regard to the authorship of *Jane Eyre* they will be found at once curious and interesting from the plain and earnest sincerity of the writer. She subsequently enters on an analysis and discussion of *Wuthering Heights* as a work of Art:—in the closing paragraph of her preface to that novel, insinuating an argument, if not a defence, the urgency of which is not sufficiently admitted by the bulk of the world of readers. \* \* \*

It might have been added, that to those whose experience of men and manners is neither extensive nor various, the construction of a self-consistent monster is easier than the delineation of an imperfect or inconsistent reality— with all its fallings-short, its fitful aspirations, its mixed enterprises, and its interrupted dreams. But we must refrain from further speculation and illustration:—enough having been given to justify our characterizing this volume, with its preface, as a more than usually interesting contribution to the history of female authorship in England.

# CRITICISM

# CHARLES PERCY SANGER

## The Structure of *Wuthering Heights*†

By common consent *Wuthering Heights* is a remarkable book. I do not propose to discuss its literary merits, but to confine myself to the humbler task of investigating its structure, which presents certain peculiarities. Whether this is worth doing I do not know, but I found that it added to my interest in the book and made the tale much more vivid for me.

\* \* \*

How is a long story like this to be told? How is the reader's interest to be excited? How is the tale to be kept together? How are we to be made to feel the lapse of time without being pestered by dates? How far did the authoress accurately visualise the ages of the characters in the different incidents, the topography, and so on? And how did Heathcliff succeed in getting the property? These are the questions I attempt to answer.

The most obvious thing about the structure of the story which deals with three generations is the symmetry of the pedigree. Mr and Mrs Earnshaw at Wuthering Heights and Mr and Mrs Linton at Thrushcross Grange each have one son and one daughter. Mr Linton's son marries Mr Earnshaw's daughter, and their only child Catherine marries successively her two cousins—Mr Linton's grandson and Mr Earnshaw's grandson. See the following pedigree:—

| Mr Earnshaw | m. | Mrs Earnshaw | | | | | Mr Linton | m. | Mrs Linton |
|---|---|---|---|---|---|---|---|---|---|
| d. Oct. 1777. | | d. Spring 1773. | | | | | d. Autumn 1780. | | d. Autumn 1780. |

| Hindley | m. | *Frances* | Catherine | m. | Edgar | *Heathcliff* | m. | Isabella |
|---|---|---|---|---|---|---|---|---|
| b. Summer 1757. | 1777. | b. d. late 1778. | b. Summer 1765. | April 1783. | b. 1762. d. Sept. 1801 | b. 1764. d. April 1802. | Jan. 1784. | b. late 1765. d. June 1797. |
| d. Sept. 1784. | | | d. Mar. 20, 1784 | | | | | |

| | Hareton | m. Jan. 1, 1803. | Catherine | m. Aug. 1801. | Linton |
|---|---|---|---|---|---|
| | b. June 1778. | | b. Mar. 20, 1784. | | b. Sept. 1784. d. Oct. 1801. |

In actual life I have never come across a pedigree of such absolute symmetry. I shall have to refer to this pedigree again later. It is a remarkable piece of symmetry in a tempestuous book.

† This essay was published as by C.P.S., but the author was Charles Percy Sanger (1871–1930). The essay was a paper read to the Heretics, a society at Cambridge University. A version of the chronology of the novel, differing slightly from Sanger's, was written by Charles Travis Clay and published in the *Brontë Society Transactions*, Part LXII (No. 2 of Vol. 12), 1952, 100–05. Reprinted by permission of Daphne T. Sanger.

The method adopted to arouse the reader's interest and to give vividness and reality to the tale is one which has been used with great success by Joseph Conrad. But it requires great skill.

After Edgar Linton's death, Mr Lockwood, the narrator, takes Thrushcross Grange for a year. He goes to call on his landlord, Heathcliff, at Wuthering Heights, and is puzzled to find there a *farouche* young woman and an awkward boor. At first he supposes Catherine to be Heathcliff's wife; when told she is his daughter-in-law, he then supposes that Hareton is Heathcliff's son, and has again to be corrected. He, and the reader, are naturally puzzled at this strange trio. Lockwood calls again, and is forced to spend the night because of a heavy fall of snow. In his room he finds some books with the name Catherine Earnshaw and Catherine Linton, and a sort of diary of Catherine's in a childish hand which gives a vivid picture of the situation just after her father's death. Mr Lockwood has a nightmare in which Catherine's spirit comes to the window, and he also witnesses a strange scene of Heathcliff imploring Catherine's spirit. Our interest cannot fail now to be excited. What is this strange man and this strange menage? Who was this Catherine who died years before? What were her relations with Heathcliff? Naturally, Lockwood is much intrigued. On his way back next day he catches a chill and becomes ill. To pass the time he asks Ellen Dean, the housekeeper at Thrushcross Grange, what she knows about the family at Wuthering Heights. She, who was first Hareton's nurse and then the younger Catherine's, tells him the story of the past thirty years in considerable detail. So that during the major part of the book Mr Lockwood is telling us what Ellen Dean told him, but sometimes, also, what Ellen Dean told him that someone else—for instance, Isabella—had told her. Only a small part, perhaps one-tenth of the book, consists of direct narrative by Lockwood from his own knowledge. But such a scheme may be confusing, and it is easy to muddle the time. Did Emily Brontë realise and let us know the dates when each event happened? She did, but not by giving them directly. Look again at the pedigree. The dates there have all been derived from the book, yet only one is directly stated. What first brought me to study the book more closely was when I noticed that the first word in the book was a date—1801. I thought this must have some significance. Similarly, the first word of Chapter XXXII is 1802. Apart from this, only one other date is given directly. In the last sentence of Chapter VII, Ellen Dean says, "I will be content to pass on to the next summer—the summer of 1778, that is, nearly twenty-three years ago." This gives no further information, as 1801 is twenty-three years after 1778, but in the first sentence of the next chapter she tells us that Hareton was born in June. This is how I get June 1778 for Hareton's birth in the pedigree. But what about the rest of the dates, not only those in the pedigree but of all the incidents in the story? There are a considerable number (perhaps nearly a hundred) indications of various kinds to help us—intervals of time, ages of characters, the months, the harvest moon, the last grouse, and so forth, and we learn, incidentally, that the younger Catherine's birthday was on 20th March. Sometimes, too, we know the day of the week—thus Ellen Dean will remember something which happened on a Sunday, or on a Christmas Eve. Taking all these indications, it is, I think, possible to ascertain the year, and, in most cases, the month of the year in which every event takes place— also the ages of the various characters, exept, naturally, there is a slight doubt as to Heathcliff, because no one knows his exact age when he was found by Mr Earnshaw. But one has to go warily and consider all the indications together, for there is a curious subtlety that sometimes the characters are describd as *looking* some ages which are not exact. Thus Lockwood when he first describes them says that Heathcliff was about forty and Catherine did not look seventeen. In fact, Catherine was seventeen and three-quarters and Heathcliff cannot have been more than thirty-eight. * * *

* * *

* * * Heathcliff schemed to get all the property of both the Earnshaws and the Lintons. How did he do it? Emily Brontë clearly had a considerable knowledge of the law. We know the source of George Eliot's use of a base fee for the plot of *Felix Holt*. We do not know the source of Jane Austen's unerring grasp of the law of real property; but she lived among people who had settled estates and could easily have obtained it. But how Emily Brontë acquired her knowledge I cannot guess. There is also this difficulty. *Wuthering Heights* was written in the eighteen-forties. It was published in 1847. But the period of the tale is from 1771 to 1803. The Inheritance Act of 1834, the Wills Act of 1837, and, I think, the Game Act of 1831, had changed the law. Did Emily Brontë apply the law at the time she wrote or that at the period of the tale? In one case, as we shall see, she used the earlier law.

Novelists sometimes make their plots depend on the law and use legal terms. But they frequently make mistakes and sometimes are absurd as Trollope is in *Orley Farm*. What is remarkable about *Wuthering Heights* is that the ten or twelve legal references are, I think, sufficient to enable us to ascertain the various legal processes by which Heathcliff obtained the property. It is not a simple matter. There was a fundamental difference between the law of land (real property) and that of money and goods (personal property).

Let us begin with Wuthering Heights. The Earnshaws were farmers and not likely to have their estate settled. The property had been in their family since 1500. We may take it then that Mr Earnshaw was owner in fee-simple, that is in effect absolute owner, of Wuthering Heights, and was not likely to have possessed any investments. It is more likely that there was a mortgage on the house and farm. On Mr Earnshaw's death the land descended to Hindley as his heir-at-law. There is no mention of a will. The personal property, which, probably, was only the farming stock and the furniture, would go equally to his children, Hindley and Catherine, subject to the payment of his debts out of it. On Catherine's marriage Edgar would have become entitled to her personal property. Now Hindley drinks and gambles away all he has, and at his death the property is mortgaged up to the hilt. Heathcliff we find is the mortgagee. The personal property would also be liable to the debts. So that Heathcliff is mortgagee in possession and, for practical purposes, owner of all the Earnshaw property except any personalty that had gone to Catherine. This is all fairly simple; but it is more difficult when we come to the Linton property. They were landed gentry; they had a park, they had tenants. Mr Linton and Edgar after him, was a magistrate. Such people, generally, had a settlement of their land, and we find, in fact, that Mr Linton had settled it by his will. To understand what happens it is necessary to go into the intricacies of real property law and to look at the pedigree.

I must explain very shortly the law of entails. What is called an estate tail is an estate which descends according to the following rules: (1) Males are preferred to females; (2) males take in order according to seniority of birth, but females take equally; (3) descendants represent their ancestor. In case of a conflict between them, rule (3) prevails. A tenant in tail of full age in possession could by means of a fictitious action (for which a deed was substituted by the Fines and Recoveries Act, 1833) bar the entail and obtain the fee-simple, which practically amounts to absolute ownership. By his will a testator could settle his land on living persons for life, but could not give life estates to the children of such persons who were not alive at the testator's death. Consequently, if he wanted to tie up his estate as long as possible, he gave life estates to such of his descendants as were living at his death, followed by estates tail to their children.

Now the settlement made by Mr Linton's will must have been as follows: The estate was devised to Edgar, his only son, for life, then to Edgar's sons in tail; Edgar's daughters were passed over in favour of Mr Linton's daughter, Isabella, who, presumably, had a life interest with remainder to her sons in tail. This is the usual form. Thus on Edgar Linton's death, Linton Heathcliff became tenant in tail in possession during the few weeks he survived his uncle. As a minor he could not bar the entail. It is most improbable that he had an estate in fee-simple; that would have been too unusual. Isabella might have had an estate tail instead of a life interest. This is most improbable, but if she did, her son, Linton Heathcliff, would have become tenant in tail by descent, so the result is the same. Heathcliff claims the property—by what right? Ellen Dean says that he claimed and kept the Thrushcross Grange estate in his wife's right and in his son's also. She adds: "I suppose, legally at any rate, Catherine, destitute of cash and friends, cannot disturb his possession." She is quite right in her suspicions. Even if Isabella had had an estate tail, or even an estate in fee-simple, Heathcliff would not have had any right as husband to an estate for life—the estate known as an estate by courtesy—because Isabella was never in possession.

And even if, which to my mind is not possible, Linton Heathcliff had had an estate in fee-simple, his father would not have been his heir before the Inheritance Act, 1833, because it was considered unnatural that an inheritance should ascend directly; and, as Ellen Dean knows and states, Linton Heathcliff as a minor could not dispose of his land by will. There is no difficulty as to the personal property. Whatever Isabella had Heathcliff got by marrying her. There was no Married Women's Property Act in these days. They eloped, so there was no question of a marriage settlement. Edgar Linton had saved out of his rents to make a provision for his daughter, Catherine. When dying he decides, in order to prevent Heathcliff getting at them, to alter his will so as to settle them on Catherine for life and then for her children. The attorney for whom he sends is, however, kept from going by Heathcliff, and Edgar dies before his will is altered, so the money passes to Catherine and then to her husband, Linton. He, though a minor, could (before the year 1838) make a will of personalty. He is induced or forced to do so, and leaves it all to Heathcliff.

Thus, at Heathcliff's death, the position seems to be that he has acquired all the personal property of both families: he is mortgagee in possession of Wuthering Heights, and is, though wrongfully, in possession of Thrushcross Grange, which he has let to Lockwood. He thinks of making a will but does not do so. What then happens on his death? He has no relations, so that his real property will escheat, and his personal property will go to the Crown as *bona vacantia*. What then becomes of Hareton and Catherine who, when the tale ends, are to be happily married on New Year's Day, 1803? At one time I thought this was the climax of the tragedy. These young people, ill-educated and incompetent, were to be left destitute. But that would be going too far. Catherine, as you will see from the pedigree, is the sole living descendant of Mr Linton. In some way or other, I need not go through the various alternatives, she must have become entitled to Thrushcross Grange, which is plainly by far the most valuable property. Heathcliff had been mortgagee in possession of Wuthering Heights for eighteen years, but this was not long enough to obtain an absolute title by adverse possession. Hareton, as Hindley's heir, would be entitled to the equity of redemption. Now if Heathcliff, who managed well, properly accounted for his profits during the eighteen years as he could be made to do, it may well be that they were sufficient, if he was charged a proper occupation rent, to pay off the mortgage. So that Hareton would get the house and land unincumbered or, at any rate, only slightly burdened. The personal property was comparatively unimportant, and we can only hope that the Crown did not insist on its rights, if it knew of them, or that if it did insist, the happy couple could buy out the Crown's claim out of the rent which Lockwood, as we know, paid.

There is, so far as I know, no other novel in the world which it is possible to subject to an analysis of the kind I have tried to make. This in itself makes the book very unusual. Did the authoress carry all the dates in her head, or did she work with a calendar? Was 20th March 1784, for example, on a Monday? According to my calculations it was not, it was a Saturday, but I should like to have this confirmed by some competent chronologist; for if I am right, it shows that Emily Brontë did not use a calendar, and that nothing will be gained by finding out, for instance, the date of Easter in 1803.

However dull and technical the above details may be, they do, I believe, throw a light on the character of Emily Brontë and her book. German romances can hardly have been the source of her knowledge of English law. A great critic has spoken of the passionate chastity of the book; but the extreme care in realising the ages of the characters at the time of each incident which is described seems to me a more unusual characteristic of a novel. It demonstrates the vividness of the author's imagination.

# A. STUART DALEY

## The Moons and Almanacs of *Wuthering Heights*†

Among the distinctions of *Wuthering Heights* its painstaking chronology claims a prominent place. Occasionally the passage of time is abridged or summarized, but several quite long episodes are developed day by day or hour by hour; the narration of these may fill three, four, or more chapters. Just as precise in method as the sketching of locale and atmosphere is the timing of events, linking whole sequences of action to a stated or inferrable calendar. A witness of this emphasis on temporality is the fact that, of the novel's thirty-four chapters, the openings of twenty-two establish time. The first statement in *Wuthering Heights* sets a date.

These features suggest that Emily Brontë may have put together the time schemes with more calculation than is usual with novelists. On close examination, for example, one notices both the number and effectiveness of allusions as an appropriate means of dating and the organic incorporation of these in the narrative. In the natural rural setting of *Wuthering Heights*, reference to the phase of the moon seems a countryman's fitting and customary usage for reckoning time and noting visibility as well as marking major seasonal and religious periods of the year. This primary fact was neglected by Charles Percy Sanger in his classic demonstration of the careful time schemes of the novel, *The Structure of Wuthering Heights*, which appeared in 1926.[1] Its acceptance as definitive for almost fifty years unfor-

† First published in *Huntington Library Quarterly* 37 (1974): 337–53. Reprinted with the permission of the Henry E. Huntington Library.
1. *The Structure of Wuthering Heights* (Ann Arbor, Michigan: University Microfilms, 1969). Originally published as a "Hogarth Essay" by Leonard and Virginia Woolf (London, 1926). Sanger's "Chronology of *Wuthering Heights*" forms an Appendix to the essay, pp. 21–24.

tunately resulted in the closing off of a promising line of exploration into the art of Emily Brontë, including significant relationships between her novel and her poetry. Sanger was puzzled by the incongruity between the fictive dates and the actual dates of the years assigned to events in the novel. Overlooking the key to the solution, he jumped to a conclusion that his legal training should have precluded. He states the problem and conclusion as follows. "There is, so far as I know, no other novel in the world which it is possible to subject to an analysis of the kind I have tried to make. This in itself makes the book very unusual. Did the authoress carry all the dates in her head, or did she work with a calendar? Was 20th March 1784, for example, on a Monday? According to my calculations it was not, it was a Saturday, but I should like to have this confirmed by some competent chronologist; for if I am right, it shows that Emily Brontë did not use a calendar."[2]

Quite simply what it shows is that Emily Brontë did not use the calendar for 1784, just as she had not consulted the calendar for 1801, as this paper will show. (She was not, after all, composing a historical novel.) It does not prove that the authoress carried all the dates in her head. Indeed, that surmise can be dismissed at once because the issue will be settled in terms of practical probability by the results of matching the week-month dates and those of the monthly phases of the moon in the novel with those in real years. Where so many progressions and cycles must accord, synchronization by chance would strain both credulity and logic. The idea is repugnant to the concept of statistical probabilities. Therefore, if synchronization exists, conformance of dating to an actual, rather than an improvised and even unpremeditated, calendar may be supposed.

Because he overlooked essential evidence, Sanger's chronology leaves much to be explained or corrected. Thus, to cite a crucial case in method, Sanger leaves inconclusive the dates associated with the death of Edgar Linton despite numerous clues, one of which is all-important: the harvest moon. Only once in the novel does Emily Brontë mention an "almanack," a "framed sheet" hanging on the wall, yet she features the phase of the moon in major scenes to the extent that the moon becomes a structural factor and the principal key to time sequences in *Wuthering Heights*.

Consequently, this paper will attempt first to determine and explain the chronological basis of *Wuthering Heights* by an analysis of the moon's appearances. The analysis will reveal for the first time the concurrence of a harvest moon with each of three important episodes. The dates not only of these moons but also of other lunar data will then serve to establish control points in the chronology and thereby date more incidents and date them more closely than has hitherto been possible. Second, the paper will show how the correlation of the data with actual calendar years suggests that Emily Brontë founded the time schemes of the major narrative sequences of *Wuth-*

2. Sanger, p. 19.

*ering Heights* on the almanacs of two years of her own childhood, namely 1826 and 1827. It will be seen, I hope, that a number of puzzling inconsistencies in datings based upon the ostensible years of the novel are resolved by reference to days of the week and dates of the month in 1826 or 1827. Finally, it will become manifest that these years and the moon lore link the novel imaginatively with the Gondal poems.

A demonstration of the presence of three harvest moons in the novel makes a necessary beginning for this study. As a preliminary, it is helpful for us to review the characteristics of the harvest moon so that the clues which Emily Brontë provides may be recognized. The harvest moon, as popularly understood, is the full moon closest to the autumnal equinox, which is the twenty-second or twenty-third of September.[3] Primarily, then, it is a full moon at a particular point in the sun's yearly course on the ecliptic. Since the cycle between full moons completes itself every twenty-nine to thirty days, this full moon can reach its phase as late as October, though not in many years. But I assume here that common rural usage would attach the description to the first full moon in September, when the harvest was under way or ending.

It is important to note that every full moon rises as the sun sets and sets as the sun rises. Therefore, if the moon is described as rising at or near sunset, we must understand it as full or nearly so. At the height of its phase, then, the full moon will shine with maximum brilliance all night. But each twenty-four hours will find it rising roughly fifty minutes later than upon the night before, while its illuminated area wanes proportionately into the last quarter phase, at which point the moon, being twenty-two days old, rises at midnight and sets the following noon. But there is a marked difference between the ordinary full moon and the harvest full moon in this regard in the North Temperate Zone: at the autumnal equinox the full moon rises later each evening by only a few minutes. In short, moonrise occurs at about the same time, soon after sunset, for four or five evenings in succession.

Another feature of the harvest moon is its seemingly low path above the horizon. One consequence, as this moon rises, is the magnification of its apparent size, together with the apparent intensification of moonlight. Another is the harvest moon's richly glowing orange or golden color. Especially as seen over open country, the grandeur and brilliance of the harvest moon impress the beholder for several successive nights.

With these clues, one can recognize three harvest moons over the world of *Wuthering Heights*. The first coincides with the return of Heathcliff in Chapter x, on a "mellow evening in September" of 1783. The moon has risen, yet it is so low that it "looked over the high wall of the court" at such an angle with the horizon that the window panes "reflected a score of glittering moons." The light suffices to enable Ellen to recognize Heathcliff by his eyes and see, at a range of two miles, the valley of Gimmerton where

3. *The Columbia Encyclópedia*, ed. William Bridgwater and Seymour Kurtz, 3rd ed. (New York and London, 1963), p. 915, s.v. "harvest moon." Most popular handbooks on astronomy present the elementary lunar and solar information used in this study.

the moonlight makes "silvery vapour" of the line of mist rising from the sough and the beck. Therefore, it is in the light of an undoubted harvest moon that Heathcliff reappears after an absence of three years.

The second harvest moon manifests itself in Chapters xxviii and xxix. Under the aegis, so to speak, of this moon, Edgar Linton dies and Cathy Linton is abducted by Heathcliff and taken to Wuthering Heights. At 3 AM on the day of Edgar's death, Ellen goes downstairs to fetch a jug of water. A sharp knock calls her to the door. She opens it. "The harvest moon shone clear outside." Once again she recognizes by the light of the moon a familiar figure; this time it is Cathy.[4]

Chapter xxix opens on the evening after the funeral of Mr. Linton. Ellen and Cathy are sitting in the library at the Grange, "venturing conjectures as to the gloomy future," when Heathcliff arrives. Through Ellen's comments, Emily Brontë points out the similarities between the scene and that attending the return of Heathcliff in 1783. "It was the same room into which he had been ushered, as a guest, eighteen years before: the same moon shone through the window; and the same autumn landscape lay outside. We had not yet lighted a candle, but all the apartment was visible, even to the portraits on the wall—the splendid head of Mrs. Linton, and the graceful one of her husband." The identification of the two moons as being the same confirms our recognition of the earlier one as a harvest moon.

A striking parallel between this scene and Emily's poetry deserves noticing here. A similar detail appears in her poem "Written in Aspin Castle," where three portraits are seen in the light of "the moonbeam chill and blue," one a picture of "Lord Alfred's idol queen, / So loved, so worshipped long ago." Outside the hall where these portraits hang, "The harvest moon looks down . . . heaven smiles with love and light. . . . "[5] A cursory inspection of Emily's poetry reveals more than a score of allusions to the moon and moonlight. Several of them relate to the autumn season. The preference for scenes of night and dusk in the poetry has been remarked by critics. But to the best of my knowledge the significance of these features in relation to the novel has not received the study it deserves.

The third harvest moon illuminates the final scene of the novel, with its celebrated conclusion under a benign sky. The episode takes place in September 1802. Lockwood, having returned on an impulse to Thrushcross Grange, decides to walk up to Wuthering Heights, a distance of about four miles, or perhaps two hours' walking time. Lockwood sets out toward sunset: in his own words, "I . . . made my exit [from Thrushcross Grange], rambling leisurely along with the glow of a sinking sun behind, and the mild glory of a rising moon in front; one fading, and the other brightening, as I quitted the park, and climbed the stony by-road branching off to Mr. Heathcliff's dwelling." The fact that the moon is rising as the sun is sinking proves it to be a full moon, which in September can be taken to be a harvest moon.

4. To avoid confusion, "Cathy" identifies the daughter of Edgar Linton, and "Catherine" her mother, née Earnshaw.

5. *The Complete Poems of Emily Jane Brontë*, ed. C. W. Hatfield (New York, 1941). pp. 177–179.

Before Lockwood has rambled much farther than the two-mile or halfway point of his walk, the sun is well down, probably twelve degrees, more or less, below the horizon. Hence nautical evening twilight is ending, and (except in the west) the sunlight is too far faded out of the sky to show the pedestrian much of his path. Lockwood's description of the evening sky at this point exhibits unusually keen observation of the related light phenomena. "Before I arrived in sight of [Mr. Heathcliff's dwelling], all that remained of day was a beamless, amber light along the west; but I could see every pebble on the path, and every blade of grass by that splended moon." The lingering light of day is properly described as "beamless" because the sun has dipped below the horizon. The "amber" hue in the cloudless west marks a late stage in the transition of colors sometimes seen during a fine sunset, and one which terminates in a band or zone of yellowish light. In the passage cited, Lockwood presumably means by "amber" a transparent orange-yellow hue. Futhermore, in autumn the full moon, shining through the thick atmosphere of the horizon, can suffuse the landscape with rich orange or bronze-orange light and so replace the fading twilight.[6] Thus, later in the evening after Ellen has furnished the sequel of Heathcliff's history (almost three chapters long), there will still be ample moonlight to enable Lockwood to venture off the path to Thrushcross Grange and walk across the moor to see the kirk and the graveyard. In its luminosity he can make out the inscriptions on the three headstones, and see the moths fluttering among the heath and harebells. In the glow of this "splendid moon," the third harvest moon of the novel, the affairs of *Wuthering Heights* are charmed to rest.

Whatever other functions they may serve in the novel's symbolisms and structure, these moons afford dates for testing the novel's chronology, and therefore they can help to clear the ground for a systematic study of it. The harvest moon fell on the following dates[7] in the years specified by the novel.

---

6. Because it means a yellowish-brown, or a medium to dark or deep orange-yellow color, I take "amber" here to refer to that stage of twilight just following sunset when from the horizon upward the zones of color are brown, orange, and yellow. *OED* cites applications to sky light. The word appears in Emily Brontë's poetry in connection with the evening sky; see Hatfield, pp. 33 and 91 (l. 40). Cf. Gerard Manley Hopkins' descriptions of "yellow streaming" September sunsets in his *Journals and Papers*, ed. Humphrey House and Graham Storey (London, 1959), e.g., on the evening before the harvest moon, where he notes the light effect on the grass (as he also does, on a meadow at sunset in April). For the light effects peculiar to the different stages of sunset and the night sky, a useful treatise is M. Minnaert, *The Nature of Light and Colour in the Open Air*, trans. H. M. Kremer-Priest, rev. K. E.

Brian Jay (New York, 1954), esp. pp. 268–273.
7. The dates of phases of the moon for the years 1800 and after are found in Berenice L. Morrison, *Phases of the Moon 1800–1959*, U.S. Naval Observatory Circular No. 112 (Washington, D.C., 1966). Data for key week-days and the harvest moons before 1800 were supplied by Prof. G. M. Clemence, Yale University, and Prof. Owen Gingerich, Harvard University and Astrophysical Laboratory, Smithsonian Institution, who also furnished photocopies of the January pages of an almanac for 1784. I am indebted to my colleague Dr. Philip S. Riggs, Professor of Astronomy, for his advice. But for the application of these data to *Wuthering Heights* I am solely responsible. In my analysis I have tried to keep in mind the countryman's experience and use of these phenomena.

1783—Thursday, September 11
1801—Tuesday, September 22
1802—Saturday, September 11

In its context, the first of these dates raises no problem, but the second and third, as will be explained, cannot be reconciled with the associated dates in the episodes in which they occur. The second is hopelessly too late, the last appreciably too early. There is, then, a discrepancy between 1801 and 1802 in the novel and those same years in actual, historical fact. Much more obviously, the keystone date of the temporal span of the novel— Monday, March 20, 1784—does not in fact match the year, for in 1784 the twentieth of March fell not on Monday but on Saturday. Yet, apart from the year, this day and date is perfectly consistent with the calendar of events of the narrative where it figures. These facts suggest something odd, yet possibly explicable, about the construction of the chronology of *Wuthering Heights*.

Grounds exist for attempting a solution; the chronological data of the novel are notoriously abundant, even if not always very conspicuous. Most of them appear in five major narrative blocks or sequences in the novel. These sustained units are as follows:

1. The events of January, February, and March, "1784" (seven chapters, from xi into xvii).

2. Developments associated with Ellen's three-week illness, autumn, "1800" (Chapters xxii, xxiii, and xxiv).

3. Events preceding and immediately following Edgar Linton's death and burial, August and September, "1801" (four chapters, xxvi through xxix).

4. Ellen's sequel, covering affairs at the Heights from February to May, "1802" (Chapters xxxii through xxxiv).

5. The interesting hints and details of temporality in the account of Lockwood's return visit in September, "1802" (the opening of Chapter xxxii and the closing of Chapter xxxiv).

The calendars of these units are each inferrable from three kinds of data which the narrative incorporates. First, there are allusions to clock time, and to day of week, month and year. A second consists of the familiar and casual kind of references to the passage of time, such as to age or anniversary, to periods of the day or seasons of the year, or such colloquial dating as "a few days." The third gives a fascinating collection of lunation data, positive and negative, and notice of the sun, especially with respect to sunset. The correlation and cross-checking of these data will prove that Emily Brontë articulated them with calculating care into time sequences wholly consistent with the activities and the seasons they measure—consistent, that is, with themselves within their own fictive calendars, but inconsistent with the historical calendar years that the novel pretends to be observing.

Because Monday, March 20, 1784, provides the whole chronological system with its central date, I propose to begin by analyzing the temporal sequence which it climaxes. Throughout seven chapters this sequence of affairs follows an intricate calendar. Although not obtrusive—complete dates do not occur—the dates and time are deducible, sometimes even to the hour of a specified day, sometimes within the span of a few days or weeks.

In the aftermath of a violent scene at Thrushcross Grange on a Monday early in January 1784, Heathcliff having been expelled from the premises, Catherine locks herself in her bedroom and refuses to eat (Chapter xi). On the third evening she becomes delirious, and Ellen attends her. After midnight, they open the window: "There was no moon, and everything beneath lay in misty darkness." The time then, according to Ellen, is very early Friday morning. The sky is sufficiently clear for starlight to render the mist visible despite the absence of moonshine. But Friday, January 9, 1784, enjoys a full moon, only two days old; the following Friday, an unlikely choice, has a last-quarter moon rising, of course, at midnight. These phases of the moon eliminate 1784 as the source of Brontë's dates and weekdays.

Furthermore, as Sanger learned, Monday did not fall on March 20 in 1784. These discrepancies suggest a search for the year or years in which the phenomena do conform to the story. During Emily Brontë's lifetime— to narrow the search to almanacs reasonably available to her—Monday fell on March 20 in 1820, 1826, 1837, and 1843. In addition if one plots the coincidence with the years of her lifetime of definite dates and phases of the moon in *Wuthering Heights*, one finds the plotting pointing especially to two years, 1826 and 1827. The present sequence of dates, despite their assignment to fictive 1784, does in fact correlate with the almanac of 1826.

Returning to the story, we find that Isabella and Heathcliff elope about 2 AM that Friday morning when Catherine is delirious, and return to Wuthering Heights eight weeks later, a week before Catherine's death. The information supplied by Ellen on this matter indicates too that the Heathcliffs return on March 13 (or perhaps 14). Thus they had departed on or about January 13. In fact the corresponding date in 1826 is Friday, January 13— an appropriately ill-omened day and date for both Isabella's elopement and her sister's illness. In the almanac of 1826 the Monday of the violent quarrel (Chapter xi) is January 9.[8] What is even more convincing, in view of the odds against it, is the fact that the phase of the moon also fits the conditions for the night of January 12–13. On that night in 1826 the moon lacked three days of waxing into the first quarter. This means, of course, that it would have set before Catherine threw open the window on the dark and misty night. Even if one concedes the possibility that Brontë's imagined scene may have been overcast by a lowery sky, and Ellen made up the mist

9. Although "beautiful moonlight" could plausibly suffice for Hareton's making out sizable letters cut into stone, it is not bright enough to allow for distinguishing a change of color in the face. Perhaps by discerning a darkening of his features, Cathy correctly imagined the red blush. On the intensity of moonlight consult, for one, Minnaert, pp. 79–81.

out of total darkness, the moon of 1826 was in any case only a few days old.

Dating the narrative connected with Ellen's three-week illness in Chapters xxii, xxiii, and xxiv rests on two phases of the moon in the fall of the year, which, in the world of the novel, is 1800. These are a full (too late to be a harvest) moon and the next following first-quarter phase, some three weeks later. The action begins "on an afternoon in October, or the beginning of November" (a suitably conversational imprecision), when Heathcliff persuades Cathy to visit Linton at Wuthering Heights. The next day (Chapter xxiii) Ellen wets her feet walking to the Heights, with the result that, "On the succeeding morning, I was laid up; and during three weeks I remained incapacitated for attending to my duties. . . ." During this time Cathy takes advantage of her freedom from supervision to make almost nightly trips to Wuthering Heights. About nine o'clock on the evening of the third day of her recovery, Ellen, sitting in the dark by a window, detects Cathy returning home: "The moon shone bright; a sprinkling of snow covered the ground." Cathy, confessing her forbidden excursions to Wuthering Heights, describes in some detail her third visit to her cousin. She tells Ellen that "it was beautiful moonlight after tea." By this light Hareton Earnshaw tries to read the inscription over the door, meaning to impress Cathy by his newly acquired skill. But her scornful response hurts his feelings: "He reddened—I saw that by the moonlight—dropped his hand from the latch, and skulked off, a picture of mortified vanity."[9] The time of the incident is about half-past six, when, as she states, Cathy arrives each night at Wuthering Heights.

Cathy's account of this visit clearly establishes a full moon for "October, or the beginning of November." That of November 14, 1826, falls far too late. Turning, therefore, to 1827, which preliminary investigation had suggestively linked with 1826, one finds a full moon on Saturday, November 3. By the calendar of 1827 the "afternoon in October, or the beginning of November" is Tuesday, October 30, and Ellen's unfortunate walk in the wet is on Wednesday, October 31. On the next day, Thursday, November 1, Ellen being in bed suffering from her cold, Cathy pays her first surreptitious visit to Wuthering Heights.

In November 1827 the new moon rose on Monday the 19th and the first-quarter moon on Sunday the 25th. On Wednesday the 21st, Ellen leaves her sickroom, recovered from her three-week illness (opening of Chapter xxiv). On Friday she first sits up in the evening, and then and Saturday evening she finds Cathy an unwilling, even impatient companion. On Sunday, November 25, in moonlight augmented by reflection from the snow,[1] Ellen sees Cathy ride in from her latest secret jaunt to Wuthering Heights. All conditions, including the time of day—about nine o'clock—

---

1. Though the intensity of illumination would have been much less than that for a full moon, Emily evidently knew that half a moon reflecting on a snowy landscape gives as much useful light as does a full moon shining on a green landscape, and may even exceed it.

concur with the presence of a winter moon in its first-quarter phase.[2] "Last Sunday," Cathy is made to say on *this* Sunday, as she confesses her transgressions. To interpret her allusion in this sense is to grant it the only sense it has in the context: "a week ago today."

The death of Edgar Linton (Chapter xxviii) coincides with the second and central harvest moon in the novel. This moon furnishes the key to harmonizing the chronology of the narrative block, in which it is twice invoked. Edgar's death climaxes a series of actions that span two weeks and one or two days beginning on a Thursday in fictive August 1801. According to Chapter xxvi, "Summer was already past its prime. . . . It was a close, sultry day." The weather fits August; the bilberries (which Cathy searches for) ripen in August. In the course of a meeting with Linton Heathcliff on this day, Cathy promises to return "next Thursday" for another tryst. "Seven days glided away" (opening of Chapter xxvii) and Thursday came around, "a golden afternoon of August." With such statements the narrative verifies the first August Thursday, accounts for the passage of one week, and establishes the second August Thursday. The month remains August, but how closely the date approaches September remains to be inferred from clues in this chapter and in Chapter xxviii.

Following the rendezvous on the Thursday of the golden afternoon, Heathcliff kidnaps Cathy and Ellen, whom he locks up the next (Friday) morning in separate rooms at Wuthering Heights. Ellen is detained for five nights and four days. Therefore, she gains her release—the first night being Thursday—on Tuesday in the second week of this affair. At 3 AM on the following morning—Wednesday—a harvest moon, as she tells us, "shone clear outside." Consequently, Wednesday must fall in September, which puts the death of Edgar not later than September 6.

In actual 1801, as distinguished from the novel's "1801," the harvest moon occurred on Tuesday, September 22 (Wednesday being the autumnal equinox that year), a date which the narrative simply rules out. The almanac of 1827 matches the time scheme perfectly. It shows us the dates to be as follows:

> The first Thursday (Chapter xxvi), August 23
> The second Thursday (Chapter xxvii), August 30
> Tuesday of Ellen's release (Chapter xxviii), September 4
> Edgar's death (Chapter xxviii), Wednesday, September 5[3]

---

2. The first-quarter moon is a waxing half moon which rises at noon and is still fairly high in the sky at nine o'clock. With respect to the moon phases of this sequence, it should be noted that the almanac of 1800 also meets the chronological requirements. The full moon occurs on Saturday, Nov. 1, and the following first quarter on Sunday, Nov. 23, which is two days earlier than the 1827 month dates but still matching the phases with identical weekdays.

Nevertheless, the 1827 dates seem the likelier references, since 1827 also explains the chronology of the ensuing five chapters dealing with the abduction of Cathy and the death of Edgar Linton.

3. Here is an instance of where Sanger's conjectural dates can now be replaced with definite ones. According to Sanger, "Ellen is let out" in "August or September." (He recognized the problem, but lacked the key for solving it.) His

This inquiry into the chronology of *Wuthering Heights* may conclude for the present with an examination of the calendar governing the final year of the narrative, which is "1802." The calendar data in the last three chapters emphasize Emily's plotting of March and April, with a "fix" on Easter Monday, as Ellen tells Lockwood what has happened during his eight-month absence. She dates the kiss and currant-bush incidents on Easter Monday and Easter Tuesday, respectively. Not only is the season past Cathy's eighteenth birthday (March 20), but also a March Easter is unmistakably established. The timing and Emily's liking for symmetries invite an imaginative comparison with March 1784.

Two statements in the novel measure the passage of time immediately succeeding: Chapter xxxiv begins, "For some days after that evening," i.e., Easter Tuesday evening; a few lines later remarks, "We were in April then." But once again the fictive calendar does not agree with the historical calendar. In 1802 Easter fell very late, being in that year on April 18 (a fact easily ascertainable in a parsonage). A date after mid-April, 1802, cannot be reconciled with the narrative time-scheme. A calendar that does coincide with the latter, just as it plausibly matches the time-scheme of fictive 1784, is that of 1826. Emily's expression "for some days" can be construed to carry the story from Easter Tuesday on March 28, 1826, into the month of April that year. In short, the same almanac had supplied the author with her dates for events in "1802" as well as in "1784."

The story of Lockwood's return that autumn to revisit Thrushcross Grange and Wuthering Heights concludes the novel. Several unmistakable hints provide the means of calculating that final date of *Wuthering Heights*. The skill with which they are insinuated into the narrative bespeaks Emily Brontë's artistic concern with the chronology of the closing section of the novel.

Chapter xxxii opens, "1802.—This September." Lockwood's impulsive detour is firmly placed late, rather than early, in September. Suitable details allow for the testimony of the hosteler at a roadside public house to the lateness of the harvest at Gimmerton. The harvest there is always three weeks later than elsewhere; we remember from Chapter xxii that a really late harvest in that district can take us past Michaelmas.[4] Moreover, had he seen Gimmerton's delightful scenery "nearer August," Lockwood tells us, he might have spent a month at Thrushcross Grange. In fact, since his Michaelmas tenancy[5] began October 10, 1801, his remark implies clearly that his return to the Grange must be dated sometime after September 10, when his tenancy would have less than a month to run. Observation of that fact reduces the

next entry, "Edgar is dying; he sends for Mr. Green, the lawyer, who does not come," he dates uncertainly as "next Tuesday." We can now see that both incidents occur on one and the same day; this is true regardless of the calendar one uses. It is simply a datum of the narrative to which the calendar must conform, as does the calendar of 1827.

4. Cf. "In some places, if it has been what the country people call a forward summer, harvest has already commenced [in August], though it is more general about the beginning of [September], which heralds in autumn"; from Robert Chambers, *The Book of Days* (London and Edinburgh, 1864), II, 153.
5. Sanger identified the Michaelmas tenancy.

dating problem to the question of how long after the 10th he had returned.

The decisive detail in this pattern of circumstantiality is the harvest moon, so carefully featured at the beginning and end of this last section of the novel. Although such a moon, in Yorkshire's high latitude, rises nearly at sunset for several nights in succession, "that splendid moon" of Lockwood's description can only have just entered its phase.

In historical 1802 the harvest full-moon phase began on Saturday, September 11, a date which barely encroaches on the last month of Lockwood's tenancy, but hardly allows for stressing a late harvest, or, for that matter, on not having "seen [the delightful scenery] nearer August." Therefore, as was the case with Easter Week, the almanac of 1802 is out of step with the chronology required by the narrative. Furthermore, actual 1827, which had fitted perfectly elsewhere to the time-scheme of events, does not fit the circumstances demanded by data in this passage, because its harvest moon entered the phase as early as Wednesday, September 5—undeniably "nearer August" and enough so to have allowed for a month's occupancy thereafter. But the almanac of 1826 serves just as well for this period as it did for the Easter-week dates of fictive 1802. In actual 1826 the harvest moon entered its phase on Saturday, September 16; this day is quite acceptable on all counts as the last day of *Wuthering Heights*.

At this point multiple correspondences have been established between certain years of the novel and two actual historical years, namely 1826 and 1827. Days of the week, dates of the month, sunset times, the movable feast of Easter, and phases of the moon match with an accuracy that is statistically incomparable with mere coincidence in a realm combining so many variables. These two years relate to the years of the novel in this sequence:

$$1826 \text{ to } 1784$$
$$1827 \text{ to } 1800$$
$$1827 \text{ to } 1801$$
$$1826 \text{ to } 1802$$

The author's masterly handling of time in *Wuthering Heights* has long since commanded praise. Together with other forms of ordering in the novel, the insistent consciousness of time regulates and counterpoints the turbulence of the story at the same time that it authenticates the narrators' credibility as reliable witnesses—to some extent Lockwood's, but especially Ellen Dean's. Her manner of telling rests firmly on a technique of reminiscence and recall of the past; without a strong ordering sense of time, unobtrusive, yet pervasive, the narrative would lack its dramatic qualities of immediacy and change.

These are objective aritistic techniques, but the insistence, behind the scenes so to speak, on 1826 and 1827 suggests a subjective personal attachment to those years. One senses, for example, the author's private concern with time, perhaps equated with change, as threat and promise. The birthday notes, written by Emily and Anne to be opened four years from date, record details of the household scene presumably as data by which change could be retrospectively measured. Similar concerns are reflected in the opening of Chapter xxix, where the two women sit in the library "venturing conjectures as to the gloomy future" and agreeing on "the best destiny which could await Catherine." Miss Ratchford comments, "Each of the extant notes or papers signed by Emily and Anne ends with a similar straining into the future—always hopeful."[6]

Perhaps not surprisingly, one glimpses a trace of chronological ordering in Emily's poems, which are distillations of the chronicles of Gondal and Gaaldine. As noted above, one finds also in the poetry a number of instances of the moon motif, including the autumn moon. In these and other features parallels exist between the poems and *Wuthering Heights*. Internal dates in the poetry proved particularly suggestive in the course of the investigation reported in this paper. Miss Ratchford's comparison summarizes the point very well: "I had evidence . . . that, notwithstanding the growing and perhaps shifting nature of the Gondal creation, Emily was working out an over-all design comparable to the clear-cut blueprint of *Wuthering Heights*. Four of her poems, for instance, carry in their headings, along with dates of composition, internal plot dates indicating a well-established Gondal chronology, such as 'From a Dungeon Wall in the Southern College. J. B. [Julius Brenzaida], 1825'; 'From a D—W—in the N.C. A.G.A. Sept., 1826'; and 'Written on Returning to the P. of I. on the 10th of January, 1827.' "[7]

The internal plot dates invited investigation for two reasons: first, their application by Emily in creative work; second, the concurrence with dates in these years of selected day-of-week and lunar phenomena in the novel. In other words, it began to appear that 1825, 1826, and 1827, being "Gondal years," might hold a special significance in Emily's creative imagination. Furthermore, 1826, 1827, and 1828 were years associated in Emily's childhood with the Young Men's Play. In June 1826 the Reverend Patrick Brontë gave Branwell a new box of wooden soldiers. "Around the twelve wooden soldiers, designated as the Young Men, the four Brontë children created through the days, weeks, months, and years a saga of group games called collectively the Young Men's Play, which they carried on with mounting gusto until Charlotte's departure for Miss Wooler's school at Roe Head in January, 1831."[8] After that date the game continued under somewhat different alignments, Emily and Anne then inventing new imaginary kingdoms, Gondal and Gaaldine. A quotation from one of Charlotte Brontë's little manuscripts may serve to illustrate the relation of these years to Emily's juvenilia: "Our plays were established; *Young Men*, June, 1826; *Our Fellows*, July, 1827; *Islanders*, December, 1827. These are our three great plays, that

6. *Gondal's Queen*, by Emily Jane Brontë, arranged by Fannie E. Ratchford (New York, 1964), p. 188, n. 14. There is a fatalistic strain, however, as in Emily's "Time will show—" (p. 190).

7. Ratchford, *Gondal's Queen*, p. 23.
8. *Gondal's Queen*, p. 12.

are not kept secret. Emily's and my best plays were established in the 1st of December, 1827; the others March, 1828."[9]

Perhaps it is impossible to determine what these years, 1826 and 1827, meant to Emily Brontë that she seems to have used their clocks and moons, consciously or subconsciously, as the chronometers for navigating the worlds of her imagination. If we knew, it might explain a feature of her writing glanced at by E. M. Forster: "The author may dislike his clock. Emily Brontë in *Wuthering Heights* tried to hide hers."[1] Perhaps the present study will suggest a different interpretation of Emily Brontë's motives.

The hypothesis now offered is that Emily Brontë based the more intricate time sequences in *Wuthering Heights* on almanacs originally associated with the Young Men's Play. At some point, such as Charlotte's departure to Roe Head, Emily could have preserved two of these almanacs among her personal papers not only for their sentimental associations but also for convenience and accuracy in constructing elaborate time sequences for her narratives. At a glance she would have had days of the months, days of the week, Sundays and holidays, term days, the phases of the moon by day, hour, and minute, with other phenomena and information pertaining to each month. For the purposes of composition the almanacs of two years offer more advantages, of course, than does one. With her interests, she would have appreciated the remarks of Robert Louis Stevenson on the value to the writer of fiction of the map and the almanac.

> The author must know his countryside, whether real or imaginary, like his hand; the distances, the points of the compass, the place of the sun's rising, the behaviour of the moon, should all be beyond cavil. And how troublesome the moon is! I have come to grief over the moon in *Prince Otto*, and so soon as that was pointed out to me, adopted a precaution which I recommend to other men—I never write now without an almanack. With an almanack, and the map of the country, and the plan of every house, either actually plotted on paper or already and immediately apprehended in the mind, a man may hope to avoid some of the grossest possible blunders.[2]

A map of the country of *Wuthering Heights* can be plotted with considerable accuracy; by conforming to the rough triangulations afforded by the leading topographical features, one can measure out a surprisingly detailed graphical sketch of the terrain of the novel.[3] Even the place-names, richly connotative, evoke native attributes of the scene; the plain-spun name of Gimmerton places on these moors the young ewe past first shearing, the "gimmer."

In this firmly realized landscape, time consistently relates to space. Any

9. Extract from Charlotte Brontë's "The History of 1829," transcribed by Mrs. Gaskell and quoted by Margaret Lane, *The Brontë Story* (New York, 1953), p. 79.
1. *Aspects of the Novel* (London, 1927), p. 50.
2. Robert Louis Stevenson, "My First Book,"
quoted in Miriam Allott, *Novelists on the Novel* (New York and London, 1960), p. 303.
3. An excellent sketch appears in J. F. Goodridge, *Emily Brontë: Wuthering Heights*, Studies in English Literature No. 20 (London, 1964), p. 63.

attempt to compute the rate of movement of the characters, whether by horse or foot, quickly affirms Emily's grasp of the interplay of ground, light, and weather. Space readily converts into time: "the clock chimed twelve as I entered the house; and that gave exactly an hour for every mile of the usual way from Wuthering Heights." To an extraordinary degree, this novel consubstantiates space and time. Just as surely its author read the daily and seasonal changes measured by the sky, the sun, and the moon. Therefore, it is not surprising that the ancient measurer for mankind of the bonds between landscape and time, and growth and change—the familiar waxing and waning moon—should play its natural and symbolical roles in *Wuthering Heights*. Nor is it surprising that in the composition of the novel the author conjoined to the uncompromising physical setting of her "map" an equally rigorous control of the time schemes of its episodes, a careful adherence to almanacs.

What is remarkable is the concurrence of the intricately articulated movements in the chronology of the action with whole weeks or months, moon cycles, sunsets, and the movable feast of Easter with the almanacs of two years of Emily Brontë's childhood—1826 and 1827.

# A. STUART DALEY

## A Chronology of *Wuthering Heights*

This chronology both amplifies and silently corrects the 1926 chronology by C. P. Sanger. As I have explained in "The Moons and Almanacs of *Wuthering Heights*," the novel years 1784 and 1802 conform to the Easter, weekdays, and ephemeris of the calendar for 1826, and the novel years 1800 and 1801 conform to 1827. The source of calculation is the more than six hundred temporal allusions in the novel. Some day-dates may, however, be qualified as "on or about." Critics have placed Heathcliff's death variously between April and, even, June. But the reasons for taking April 15 as the latest possibility appear in my "The Date of Heathcliff's Death: April, 1802," *Brontë Society Transactions* 17 (1976): 15–17. The 1826 and 1827 "Almanack for Yorkshire, Durham, Northumberland, Westmorland, and Cumberland" were consulted for astronomical data and special days, e.g., the Quarter Sessions in West Riding.

| YEAR | SEASON/MONTH/DAY | EVENT (BY CHAPTER) |
|---|---|---|
| 1757 | Before September | Hindley Earnshaw born |
| 1762 | Before September | Edgar Linton born |
| c. 1764 | | Heathcliff born |
| 1765 | Summer | Catherine Earnshaw born |
| 1765 | Late in year | Isabella Linton born (6, 10) |

| | | |
|---|---|---|
| 1771 | September, start of harvest | Mr. Earnshaw brings Heathcliff home (4) |
| 1773 | Spring/early summer | Mrs. Earnshaw dies (4) |
| 1774 | October | Hindley Earnshaw sent to college (5) |
| 1777 | Before mid-September | Hindley Earnshaw marries (5) |
| 1777 | An October evening | Mr. Earnshaw dies (5); Hindley is master of the Heights (6) |
| 1777 | Sunday, November 19 | Catherine and Heathcliff rebel against Sabbath discipline (3); they are caught intruding at Thrushcross (6) |
| 1777 | Sunday, December 24 | Catherine returns from Thrushcross (7) |
| 1777 | Monday, December 25 | Earnshaws visit the Heights; Heathcliff excluded from the Christmas party (7) |
| 1778 | June, start of haying | Hareton Earnshaw born; later in year or in early 1779, Frances Earnshaw dies |
| 1780 | Two days in early summer, full moon | Major episode, beginning with Edgar Linton's visit, climaxed by Heathcliff's disappearance, and ending with Catherine's coming down with a fever (8–9) |
| 1780 | Autumn | Catherine convalesces at Thrushcross; senior Lintons catch her infection and die (9) |
| 1783 | Spring or early summer | Edgar and Catherine marry; Ellen joins Catherine at Thrushcross (9) |
| 1783 | Thursday, September 11, Harvest moon | Heathcliff returns (10) |
| 1783 | October | Isabella in love with Heathcliff (Edgar at Quarter Sessions sitting of October 24) (10) |
| 1783 | December/early January 1784 | Ellen sees Hareton; Heathcliff kisses Isabella (11) |
| 1784 | Monday, January 9, Plough Monday | Quarrel between Edgar and Heathcliff; Catherine locks herself in bedroom, refuses to eat (11) |
| 1784 | Friday, January 13 | Catherine delirious; at 2 A.M. Isabella elopes with Heathcliff (12) |
| 1784 | Monday, March 13 | The Heathcliffs return to the Heights (13) |
| 1784 | Wednesday, March 15 | Ellen brings letter from the Heights to Catherine (11) |
| 1784 | Sunday, March 19, Palm Sunday | Heathcliff visits Catherine; passionate leave-taking (15); |

| 1784 | Monday, March 20 | Catherine II born about midnight; 2 A.M., her mother dies (16, date given in 21) |
| 1784 | Tuesday, March 21, Vernal Equinox | Heathcliff puts lock of his hair in Catherine's locket (16) |
| 1784 | Friday, March 24, Good Friday | Catherine is buried (16); Hindley attempts to kill Heathcliff (17) |
| 1784 | Saturday, March 25, Lady Day | Isabella runs away (17) |
| 1784 | September | Linton Heathcliff born about eight months after his parents elope (17, 19) |
| 1784 | September | Hindley Earnshaw dies; Heathcliff acquires Heights (17, 19) |
| 1797 | July | Cathy Linton meets Hareton, who shows her around Penistone Crags (18) |
| 1797 | Beginning of August | Edgar brings Linton Heathcliff home following Isabella's death; Heathcliff takes Linton to Heights (19, 20) |
| 1800 | March 20 | Cathy Linton and Ellen meet Hareton and go to Heights to see Linton Heathcliff; Edgar forbids Cathy's correspondence with Linton (21) |
| 1800 | Tuesday, October 30 | Heathcliff induces Cathy to visit Linton at Heights (22) |
| 1800 | Wednesday, October 31, Almanack for 1827 forecasts "cold with rain" | Cathy and Ellen visit Linton; Ellen ill after getting wet (23) |
| 1800 | Thursday and Friday, November 1 and 2 | Cathy disobeys Edgar and sees Linton at Heights (29) |
| 1800 | Saturday, November 3, Full Moon | Hareton reads in moonlight the inscription above Heights entrance (29) |
| 1800 | Wednesday, November 21 | Ellen leaves her sickroom (24) |
| 1800 | Sunday, November 25, First Quarter moon, 6 P.M. | Ellen surprises Cathy returning from Heights at about 9 P.M. (24) |
| 1801 | February–June | Edgar in failing health (25) |
| 1801 | March 20 | Edgar too ill to keep remembrance vigil at Catherine's grave (25) |
| 1801 | Thursday, August 23 | Cathy and Ellen meet Linton (26) |
| 1801 | Thursday, August 30 | They meet again; Heathcliff confines Cathy and Ellen at Heights (27) |
| 1801 | Friday, August 31 | Marriage of Cathy and Linton (27) |
| 1801 | Tuesday, September 4 | Ellen released, returns to Thrushcross to find Edgar dying (28) |

| 1801 | Wednesday, September 5, Harvest Moon | Cathy escapes, reaches Thrushcross at 3 A.M.; Edgar dies before sunrise, intestate (28) |
| 1801 | September, "evening after the funeral" | Heathcliff takes Cathy to Heights (29) |
| 1801 | Autumn | Linton Heathcliff dies; Hareton friendly to Cathy (30) |
| 1801 | October 10, old Michaelmas, observed as a quarter day | Lockwood rents Thrushcross |
| 1801 | November | Lockwood calls at Heights (1) |
| 1801 | November, next day | Lockwood calls again, is snowbound, spends night at Heights (2, 3) |
| 1801 | November, next day | Lockwood takes ill and Ellen Dean begins her story (4) |
| 1801 | December, about the tenth and three weeks later | Heathcliff sends Lockwood the last grouse of the season (10) |
| 1801 | December, one week | Heathcliff calls (10) |
| 1802 | January, one week later | Lockwood continues Ellen's tale (15) |
| 1802 | January, second week | Before leaving next week, Lockwood calls at Heights (31) |
| 1802 | Beginning of February | Ellen moves to Heights (32) |
| 1802 | Early March | Hareton housebound after hunting accident (32) |
| 1802 | Monday, March 27, Easter Monday cattle fair at Haworth | Cathy kisses Hareton (32) |
| 1802 | Tuesday, March 28 | Heathcliff experiences "a strange change approaching" (33) |
| 1802 | Beginning of April | Heathcliff "swallows nothing for four days" (34) |
| 1802 | Before April 15 (for week of tenth, forecast for "Windy, with rain or sleet") | Heathcliff dies on windy, rainy night and is buried beside Catherine (34) |
| 1802 | Saturday, September 16, Splendid Harvest Moon | Lockwood returns and Ellen updates story; concluding scene in light of full moon (32–34) |
| 1802 | October 9, Michaelmas Quarter Day Eve | Last day of Lockwood's tenure of Thrushcross |
| 1803 | January 1 | Cathy and Hareton to marry (34) |

# CAROL JACOBS

## At the Threshold of Interpretation †

\* \* \* The entrance to *Wuthering Heights* is marked by the metaphor of the doorway. Passage through that threshold will generate a crisis both in the voice of the self and in the logic of the good text, for in *Wuthering Heights* one dreams of finding its center only to find that the center is a dream. We enter *Wuthering Heights* through the voice of Lockwood, who devotes the first three chapters of his narrative to what he twice calls the "repetition of my intrusion." These intrusions are, to be sure, the literal incursions he makes into the house of Wuthering Heights, but they function no less as attempts to penetrate *Wuthering Heights-as-text*. The outsider, conventional in language as well as understanding, makes repeated efforts to force his way to the penetralium. Yet one knocks vainly for admittance at these locked doors, and on his second visit, the intruder enters only by means of a violence that almost matches that of Wuthering Heights itself. He penetrates to the innermost chamber of the structure and to the enclosed oaken bed within, and here he experiences the very center of Wuthering Heights as a dream, or, more accurately, as a series of nightmares. This dream-troubled night rapidly results in Lockwood's excommunication from Wuthering Heights, for the illness brought on by these events confines him to Thrushcross Grange. At the same juncture Nelly Dean replaces Lockwood in his role as narrator, for Lockwood becomes the mere recorder of Nelly's story.

How are we to interpret this curious point of articulation between the first three chapters of the novel and the narrative that follows? Certainly not by taking Lockwood at his word. He organizes his explanation by suppressing all further mention of the dreams and by linking the subsequent events into a simplistic causal chain. A sleepless night and a difficult journey through the snow bring on a bad cold. The illness, in turn, incapacitates him, and so he calls in the housekeeper to entertain him with her tales. A fiction surely, for if we return to Chapter III, we find that the texts of the dreams dislocate the possibility of such explanation. The exclusion of Lockwood from the Heights and the displacement of Lockwood as direct narrator of the novel, his excommunication from Wuthering Heights both as a banishment from its community and as a relegation to a position outside of communication, are already the common, if oblique, themes of the dreams themselves. They mark the disjunction not only between Lockwood and Wuthering Heights but also between Lockwood and *Wuthering Heights-as-text*. For these passages offer a commentary on the nature of the fictional

† Reprinted from *Uncontainable Romanticism: Shelley, Brontë, Kleist* by Carol Jacobs by permission of The Johns Hopkins University Press. An earlier version appeared as "*Wuthering Heights*: At the Threshold of Interpretation," *Boundary II* (Spring 1979): 49–71.

space marked off as Nelly's narrative, a commentary made possible by setting off Lockwood as that which lies outside the fictional realm. The exact locus of this commentary will remain equivocal; for it lies somewhere between Lockwood's puzzlement and Nelly's explanation, and yet again at the heart of *Wuthering Heights*.

Finally closeted within the panelled bed, Lockwood imagines he has delineated a protective boundary between himself and the threatening realm without: "I slid back the panelled sides, got in with my light, pulled them together again, and felt secure against the vigilance of Heathcliff, and every one else." The diary records but two descriptive details of this apparently secure inner space: "a few mildewed books" lie piled in the corner of the window ledge, and the ledge itself is "covered with writing scratched on the paint." Having reached the very center of Wuthering Heights, Lockwood finds it inhabited by texts. And not just any texts. For the scratchings of Catherine and the books of her library, whose margins also contain her diary, figure most significantly in Lockwood's dreams. Each dream incorporates one of these three texts. In the first appear the specter-like letters etched on the sill. The second concerns the pious discourse of Jabes Branderham, which Lockwood had just begun reading. The third personifies the child Cathy, who speaks from the pages of her diary.

Lockwood's narrative elaborates a system of "careful causality"[1] to establish the relationship between text and dream. He describes himself reading Catherine's name and then dreaming of it. He wakes to find his candle burning one of the good books and so peruses them. He dreams once again of the text he has just been reading and is awakened by "a shower of loud taps on the boards of the pulpit, which responded so smartly that, at last, to my unspeakable relief, they woke me." He locates the dream-source in the title of Jabes's sermon, and its noisy conclusion is easily explained away by assigning it to a referent in the "real world," the branch of the fir tree: "And what was it that had suggested the tremendous tumult, what had played Jabes's part in the row? Merely the branch of a fir tree that touched my lattice, as the blast wailed by, and rattled its dry cones against the panes!" Lockwood attributes his last dream to the reading of Cathy's diary: " 'The truth is, sir, I passed the first part of the night in—' here, I stopped afresh—I was about to say 'perusing those old volumes;' then it would have revealed my knowledge of their written, as well as their printed contents."

Lockwood interprets his dreams by rooting them firmly in his waking world. In this manner he attempts to establish the ascendancy of reality over dream and to dispense with a merely fictional terror by rational explication. Yet the terror of fiction is otherwise. The "reality" by means of which Lockwood claims deliverance is, after all, rather a series of texts. And looking to the dreams themselves, we find they give those texts quite another inter-

---

1. The phrase is Edgar F. Shannon's in "Lockwood's Dreams and the Exegesis of *Wuthering Heights*," *Nineteenth-Century Fiction*, 14 (September 1959), 99. Shannon's essay assumes Lockwood's reasoning in its insistence on the causal relationship between "reality" and dream.

pretation. In each of the dreams the dreamer is engaged in a violent struggle, and it is precisely those apparently innocuous texts that function as his vicious adversaries.

The waking Lockwood imagines himself victorious in these conflicts, but the dreams themselves tell the story of a different mastery. First the glaring letters of Catherine's name swarm at Lockwood; then it is quite literally the text of Jabes Branderham's sermon that assaults him; and finally he struggles unsuccessfully with a figure arisen from Cathy's diary, or "an impression which personified itself" out of the name Catherine Linton.

In his second dream Lockwood is condemned to endure the endless sermon of Jabes Branderham. With each division of the sermon, Lockwood rises to go, but is forced each time to resume his seat. The forgiveness demanded of Lockwood strangely figures as forgiveness of the discourse itself rather than of the sins the text names. The length of the text and especially the repetitive nature of its structure make its textuality more prevalent than its content:

> "Sir," I exclaimed, "sitting here, within these four walls, at one stretch, I have endured and forgiven the four hundred and ninety heads of your discourse. Seventy times seven have I plucked up my hat and been about to depart—Seventy times seven times have you preposterously forced me to resume my seat. The four hundred and ninety-first is too much."

The four hundred and ninety-first attempt to deny the text, this time by destroying Jabes Branderham, the refusal to forgive the four hundred and ninety-first head of the discourse is the sin for which Lockwood cannot be forgiven. As anticipated, the sentence of excommunication is handed down:

> "*Thou art the Man!*" cried Jabes, after a solemn pause, leaning over his cushion. "Seventy times seven times didst thou gapingly contort thy visage—seventy times seven did I take counsel with my soul—Lo, this is human weakness; this also may be absolved! The First of the Seventy-First is come. Brethren, execute upon him the judgment written! such honour have all His saints!"

Although its violence is initially masked, it is ultimately the endless text that wields the power to destroy Lockwood.

Lockwood's last dream displays a similar pattern. Here, too, he must struggle with a textual emanation, a figure from the diary passage just read. The child-specter clasps his hand, and Lockwood attempts to disengage himself by pulling the child's wrist along the broken window pane. Finally he beguiles her into letting go, and yet, as in his other dreams, his struggle is never definitively won. Neither the piling of the books before him as a barrier nor the stopping of his ears can rid him of the terrifying child's voice.

The waking, rational Lockwood thinks to master this violence by reestablishing the reality of certain texts, but his nightmares mock him. They mimic the structure of his relationship to those same texts and reverse the apparent order of ascendancy.

Lockwood dreams of the texts that lie at the center of Wuthering Heights and in this manner confronts the text of *Wuthering Heights*,[2] the actual narrative begun in Chapter IV. Or is it quite the reverse? Perhaps, after all, it is *Wuthering Heights* that dreams here, dreaming of a violent struggle with its other, Lockwood, in order to define a space for its own fiction. Whatever the pattern of confrontation, Chapter III (its dreams, its texts, its description of Lockwood's coming and going) anticipates all that takes place in the pages that follow. And yet it does not merely anticipate what takes place there *as event*.[3] If Chapter III is a pre-figuration of the narrative to come, it operates as that which literally comes before the figure. It is the image of the figure: *avant la lettre*, it transforms what might otherwise seem to be simple narrative content into the fiction's continual commentary on its own figuration. * * *

No one has written more suggestively on this relationship between dream and narrative than Frank Kermode. In his provocative essay "A Modern Way with the Classic,"[4] Kermode uses the multiple inscriptions of Catherine's names to account elegantly for the movement of events in the novel.

> When you have processed all the information you have been waiting for, you see the point of the order of the scribbled names, as Lockwood gives them: *Catherine Earnshaw, Catherine Heathcliff, Catherine Linton*. Read from left to right they recapitulate Catherine Earnshaw's story; read from right to left, the story of her daughter, Catherine Linton.

To be sure, it is the permutation of names in *Wuthering Heights* that generates the movement of the text. But is that generation really quite as ordered as Kermode would have us believe? He quite correctly ascribes the linear ordering of the names to Lockwood: "you see the point of the order of the scribbled names, as *Lockwood gives them*" (italics mine) from Catherine Earnshaw, to Heathcliff, to Linton. And yet those same names, as they appear first on the window ledge and then in the dream, elude the reification that Lockwood imposes. On the window ledge they are simply varied here and there from one name to the next: "This writing, however, was nothing but a name repeated in all kinds of characters, large and small— *Catherine Earnshaw*, here and there varied to *Catherine Heathcliff*, and then again to *Catherin Linton*." In the nightmare as well the names swarm at Lockwood in no apparent order.

2. This question of the text, which forms the crux of this essay, plays the central role in Robert McKibben's article "The Image of the Book in *Wuthering Heights*," *Nineteenth-Century Fiction*, 15 (September 1960), 159–69. McKibben reads the novel literally in search for books. At the Grange books are misused to "reflect a shrinking from reality" (1620)—at the Heights they are equally misused, for they are subordinated to the creation of reality (162)—but at the novel's conclusion they function as the stabilizing force that resolves the apparently insurmountable tension between these two alternatives (168). In order to restore the misused book to its "proper duty," McKibben must dance rather gingerly over the texts in Lockwood's dream (161).

3. This is the limited thrust, for example, of Ronald E. Fine's reading, "Lockwood's Dreams and the Key to *Wuthering Heights*," *Nineteenth-Century Fiction*, 24 (June 1969), 16–30. In this context see also William A. Madden's "*Wuthering Heights*: The Binding of Passion," *Nineteenth-Century Fiction*, 27 (September 1972), 127–54.

4. Frank Kermode, "A Modern Way with the Classic," *New Literary History*, 5 (Spring 1974), 415–34, hereafter cited as MW.

Kermode's interpretation, as radical as it often is, operates in strange complicity with Lockwood. We have already seen the fundamental disparity between the text and dreams at the center of *Wuthering Heights* on the one hand, and Lockwood's account of them on the other. Kermode here chooses Lockwood's version—and he has his own good reason. Such a version allows him to assume the stance of a linear reading not only of the novel's plot "from left to right," from beginning to end, but also of the interpretative experience from the " 'hermeneutic' promise" of an early inscription to the fulfillment of that promise (MW, 418–420). His reading functions as a processing of information from an indeterminancy of meaning to "the repair of indeterminancy" and "to the generation of meaning" (MW, 419, 426).

The linear reading of events gives the sense of a closed, happy ending (although no one understands the ironical implications of such a reading better than Kermode himself).[5] For Kermode speaks of the "restoration" of true names and of "inheritance restored" that bring about the emergence of "a more rational culture" (MW, 418, 419, 421). This restoration operates, of course, as a metaphor for Kermode's own hermeneutic enterprise, for the solution of the dream-rebus given above appears precisely in terms of restoring names rationally to their proper place. * * *

If we look to the actual functioning of names within the text, the uncanny dearth of names may permit linear trajectories for each of the Catherines, but it also fabricates interrelations between other characters that are hardly reducible to linearity. Others, too, change and gain their identities through the combinatory dance of names in which all major characters take part. The assumption of another's name functions less to advance the plot line than to elaborate complex patterns of differentiation that govern the entire text. Thus the second Catherine Linton can take her mother's name only at the price of distinction:

> It was named Catherine, but he [Edgar] never called it the name in full, as he had never called the first Catherine short, probably because Heathcliff had a habit of doing so. The little one was always Cathy; it formed to him a distinction from the mother, and yet, a connection with her. . . .

If the text plays upon the imperfect repetition of names, it plays no less on the imperfect repetition[6] of personality and feature, for just as Cathy fails to resemble her mother, so Linton Heathcliff only partially resembles his uncle. * * *

The paradox in this realm of dislocated identities is that characters nevertheless relate to one another as images of those they only half resemble.

5. In his long meditation *The Sense of an Ending* (London: Oxford University Press, 1966), he repeatedly concludes: "Men, like poets, 'rush into the middest,' *in medias res*, when they are born; they also die *in mediis rebus*, and to make sense of their span they need fictive concords with origins and ends, such as give meaning to lives and poems" (7).

6. Inga-Stina Ewbank, in *Their Proper Sphere: A Study of the Brontë Sisters as Early-Victorian Female Novelists* (Cambridge: Harvard University Press, 1966), admirably outlines the functioning of repetition with a difference as a structural device in the plot of the novel.

Edgar Linton's attachment to his daughter "sprang from its relation to" her mother. Isabella and Linton are metaphors in Heathcliff's eye for Edgar Linton, and Hareton for his own youth: "Five minutes ago, Hareton seemed a personification of my youth, not a human being." Everything in Heathcliff's final world swarms as endless signs for Cathy:

> For what is not connected with her to me? and what does not recall her? I cannot look down to this floor, but her features are shaped on the flags! In every cloud, in every tree—filling the air at night, and caught by glimpses in every object by day, I am surrounded with her image! The most ordinary faces of men and women—my own features—mock me with a resemblance. The entire world is a dreadful collection of memoranda that she did exist, and that I have lost her!

In a realm in which all has become pure image, here then is the function of names. Throughout *Wuthering Heights* they resemble that to which they refer only to mark its absence. Surely this betokens something closer to insanity rather than rationality restored. * * *

It is this same function of names that the pattern of inheritance repeatedly traces. For inheritance in *Wuthering Heights* takes place as a series of usurpations. The family name, once inextricably bound to its property (that of Earnshaw to Wuthering Heights and Linton to Thrushcross Grange), can no longer guarantee possession. On the contrary, the earliest episode of Nelly's tale, the arrival of the parentless, originless child, threatens disjunction between name and property. Heathcliff, never granted the family name, named rather for that which does not exist, a dead child, enters speaking an incomprehensible "gibberish" to dislocate name from referent. This agency of usurpation governs the text, then, from the very beginning.

On what is this relentless will to usurpation based? It figures less as desire for possession[7] than as a bizarre imitation. The object of imitation would seem to be the previous master in the chain of usurpations. * * * And yet, because it is the unwillingness to forgive past infractions which motivates these usurpations, they operate less as imitations of a person than of the gesture of violation, less as the attempt to replace a fixed identity than as the repetition of displacement. * * *

Hardly a major character eludes the violence of this displacement. * * * The ultimate figure of homelessness is, of course, the first Cathy, for it is she who creates her exile as a conscious act of the imagination:

> "If I were in heaven, Nelly, I should be extremely miserable." . . . . "I dreamt, once, that I was there." . . . . "Heaven did not seem to be my home; and I broke my heart with weeping to come back to earth; and the angels were so angry that they flung me out, into the middle of the heath on the top of Wuthering Heights; where I woke sobbing for joy.

---

7. The desire for possession as such paradoxically comes into play only well after the moment of usurpation. It operates as the foredoomed struggle to close the gap between property and possessor, to render the one present to the other, to establish a definitive mastery.

> That will do to explain my secret, as well as the other. I've no more
> business to marry Edgar Linton than I have to be in heaven. . . ."

The marriage to Edgar fulfills this prophecy of homelessness from which
only death promises a respite. Yet Cathy's death, in turn, is yet another
self-imposed exile. Lockwood encounters her as the ghostly child-waif who
has been wandering for twenty years. * * *

The text casts us back here to Lockwood's dreams, where it is no coincidence that the ultimate figure of homelessness should first have appeared.
The entire episode of Lockwood's visit is an allegory of homelessness and
excommunication, an allegory that reads and is read by the narrative that
follows. As soon as he enters Wuthering Heights, Lockwood senses his exile.
* * * He is then forced even deeper into darkness as he enters the inner
chamber of the house. He imagines he has located a haven in what proves
to be the very center of dislocation. Lockwood dreams of, and on waking
experiences, excommunication. This, at least, is the tale of the second
nightmare.

* * *

What is the nature of this fundamental estrangement that *Wuthering
Heights* imposes on narrator and characteres alike? The path that finally
returns Lockwood to his residence, the space that marks the untraversable
distance between Wuthering Heights and home, tells the tale:

> The whole hill-back was one billowy, white ocean, the swells and falls
> not indicating corresponding rises and depressions in the ground: many
> pits, at least, were filled to a level; and entire ranges of mounds, the refuse
> of the quarries, blotted from the chart which my yesterday's walk left
> pictured in my mind.

The nature of this fundamental estrangement is that between signs and
meaning, an impasse of interpretation. For in this remarkable snowscape
there is no correspondence between surface and ground. The risk here is a
potential loss of life; but more significantly it is also the loss that has of
necessity already taken place, a loss of reason, of the potential to re-mark,
that which the above passage calls a blotting of the chart of the mind.
Lockwood continues:

> I had remarked on one side of the road, at intervals of six or seven yards,
> a line of upright stones, continued through the whole length of the barren:
> these were erected, and daubed with lime, on purpose to serve as guides
> in the dark, and also, when a fall, like the present, confounded the deep
> swamps on either hand with the firmer path: but, excepting a dirty dot
> pointing up here and there, all traces of their existence had vanished. . . .

The homelessness imposed by *Wuthering Heights* is that of the trace. The
trace of existence, and the trace *as existence*, has vanished, for it no longer
functions as a substantial sign *of* something, no longer serves as guide, but
as a random "dirty dot pointing up here and there" and leading nowhere.

Where, then, are we in *Wuthering Heights*? The theater of naming that governs the text stages a series of tyrannical displacements of the namesake. The pattern of inheritance displays a disjunction of name and property, for property is handed on through usurpation, a gesture that is less one of appropriation than an almost-repetition of the dislocating gesture that preceded it. Little wonder, then, that the problematics of naming and inheritance are paralleled by that of perpetual exile, and that this homelessness figures also as the homelessness of the trace, which has lost its powers to identify its referent.

Perhaps this enables us to reread in *Wuthering Heights* that one last refuge of identity, the passion between Catherine and Heathcliff, for this relationship defines itself in terms of those themes of disjunction it would seem to transcend. Passion, as Cathy describes it, is a self-imposed usurpation, willed dispossession of self-unity.[8] Heathcliff is the way in which she names herself: "I *am* Heathcliff." He is an existence of Cathy beyond herself, in her mind as her own being and is more Cathy's self than she is. He provides a path of mediation to Cathy's self that at the same time marks the impossibility of coincidence with that self. Passion becomes a mode of self-naming, a self-reflection that is necessarily self-sundering. This is why, when Cathy finally states her love for Heathcliff, she must in the same breath declare her decision not to marry him. Her declaration of love signals their disunion: "It would degrade me to marry Heathcliff now; so he shall never know how I love him." The pause between the two phrases is, of course, also the juncture at which Heathcliff leaves Wuthering Heights, the critical severance of Cathy and Heathcliff.

From the very first mention of this passion (in Chapter III), it appears as separation as well as union, since the passage from Catherine's diary marks the first but definitive break between Heathcliff and herself. The passage is written as two separate entries. The first describes a rainy Sunday afternoon at the Heights shortly after the death of Earnshaw—a long sermon by Joseph, the beginning of Cathy and Heathcliff's rebellion by the destruction of good books, the writing of Cathy's diary in the back-kitchen, and a proposed scamper on the moors. Here there is a break in the text. And when Cathy writes again, the crucial first separation between her and Heathcliff has already taken place. The separation she writes of is that imposed by Hindley. * * * The first actual break between the child-lovers occurs at the gap in the diary text—for this gap marks their scamper to Thrushcross Grange, Cathy's first wandering away from Wuthering Heights, her initial encounter with Edgar Linton, and thus the beginning of the split in Cathy herself. * * *

If the text that Lockwood discovers introduces Cathy's passion, it does so only in terms of separation, and it also specifically prefigures the other two gestures of self-exile, death and marriage. The diary entry prefigures her death, because at the height of her fatal illness Cathy longs to return to the

8. See J. Hillis Miller's subtle elaboration of this paradox of passion, *The Disappearance of God* (Cambridge: Harvard University Press, 1963), 173–76.

bed in which Lockwood had read her text, and she recalls the moment described in the second passage of her diary. At the same time, she likens this moment to when she was wrenched from Wuthering Heights on marrying Edgar. * * *

Cathy's diary first introduces the tale of *Wuthering Heights* that Nelly will go on to narrate. The tale, then, doesn't begin at the beginning but opens by marking the initial break in the only relationship that approaches perfect identity. At the same time it sets up the central pattern of violent severance that organizes the novel. Strange that this diary which stresses disjunction and rebellion should be found within the covers of "good books." Cathy's diary has been penned as an interpretation of the religious books of her library, an interpretation that contributes to their dilapidation:

> Catherine's library was select, and its state of dilapidation proved it to have been well used, though not altogether for a legitimate purpose; scarcely one chapter had escaped pen and ink commentary—at least, the appearance of one—covering every morsel of blank that the printer had left.

Perhaps not so coincidentally, this diary which devours the textual margin also relates the initial step of Cathy's rebellion as the destruction of the good books that Joseph forces her and Heathcliff to read.

> "Saying this, he compelled us so to square our positions that we might receive . . . a dull ray to show us the text. . . .
>
> "I could not bear the employment. I took my dingy volume by the scroop, and hurled it into the dog-kennel, vowing I hated a good book."

On being banished to the back-kitchen, Cathy continues her rebellion by writing her diary alongside Jabes Branderham's pious discourse, and thus destroying the "good book."

Cathy wishes to destroy Jabes's pious writing, yet the text which Cathy comments on, or at least the only version we have of it (that given in Lockwood's dream), rather than being destroyed by the interpretation seems strangely to enter into the spirit of Cathy's world of non-forgiveness and revenge. The text that one expects to preach the turning of the other cheek ultimately demands an eye for an eye and a tooth for a tooth. When Lockwood finally fails to forgive the text by refusing to listen further, when he accuses the text and demands the annihilation of its source, Branderham accuses Lockwood in return and demands the narrator's annihilation.

Jabes Branderham's sermon, like Cathy's diary, is itself a commentary on a "good book." The discourse, entitled "Seventy Times Seven, and the First of the Seventy-First," interprets a passage from the New Testament. Although Branderham's comments seem at first to violate the text they interpret (for surely, here in the holiest of texts, one expects to find a call to forgiveness),[9] in fact Matthew 18:21–35 already contains its own dislocations.

---

9. See Vereen M. Bell, "*Wuthering Heights* and the Unforgivable Sin," *Nineteenth-Century Fiction* 17 (September 1962), 188–91.

In the earlier verses, Jesus apparently preaches unending forgiveness:

> [21]Then came Peter to him, and said, Lord, how oft shall my brother sin against me, and I forgive him? till seven times?
> [22]Jesus saith unto him, I say not unto thee, Until seven times: but, Until seventy times seven.

Yet when Jesus relates a parable to illustrate God's limitless capacity for forgiveness, it culminates rather with the refusal to forgive. The lord who represents God in the parable forgives his servant his debt, but only until the servant himself fails to forgive his debtor. When the servant commits this sin (the first of the seventy-first), the lord demands an eye for an eye and a tooth for a tooth:

> [32]Then his lord, after that he had called him, said unto him, O thou wicked servant, I forgave thee all that debt, because thou desiredst me:
> [33]Shouldest not thou also have had compassion on thy fellow-servant, even as I had pity on thee?
> [34]And his lord was wroth, and delivered him to the tormentors, till he should pay all that was due unto him.
> [35]So likewise shall my heavenly Father do also unto you, if ye from your hearts forgive not every one his brother their trespasses.

The biblical text pretends to preach unending forgiveness, yet God himself pays back sins in kind.[1] Thus both Cathy's seemingly destructive commentary on Branderham and Branderham's on Matthew are already contained in the good books they interpret.

The complicated relationship between Lockwood's narrative and the tale of *Wuthering Heights* is rather the reverse of these commentary-text relationships. Whereas both Cathy and Branderham comment destructively on apparently pious texts, Lockwood tries to convert a disturbingly menacing tale into a "good book." He wishes to regard Nelly's tale as benign entertainment. Just as he speaks of his dreams as superstition and uncontrolled imagination, he repeatedly hints at the merely fictional and formal nature of the story. * * *

As we have seen, the language of *Wuthering Heights* insists upon irresolvable disjunction, yet for Lockwood Nelly's language functions as the means for uniting people, as a form of sociability. Even when Lockwood begins to sense that *Wuthering Heights* is not quite the unambiguous amusement he sought, he continues to convert the ominous into the beneficial: "Dree, and dreary! I reflected . . . and not exactly of the kind which I should have chosen to amuse me. But never mind! I'll extract wholesome medicines from Mrs. Dean's bitter herbs."

Lockwood makes clear this tendency to extract wholesome medicine from bitter herbs when (in Chapter III) he attempts to protect himself from the

---

1. This is precisely what takes place in Lockwood's dream. Jabes reads an apparently interminable list of forgivable sins—yet just when Lockwood refuses to forgive, Jabes, like the lord in the parable, refuses to forgive Lockwood.

ghost-child of his last dream by throwing up a barrier of texts. "The fingers relaxed, I snatched mine through the hole, hurriedly piled the books up in pyramid against it." These are, to be sure, *good* books, and Lockwood expects the good text to exorcise an evil that he perceives as coming from the other side of the windowpane—from without. He all but forgets that the terrifying figure of the ghost-child emanates rather from within the margins of those same texts.

Lockwood closes his narration as he began it, by extracting a benevolent resolution from a text that is at best duplicitous. In his last journey from Wuthering Heights to Thrushcross Grange, the narrator makes a diversion in the direction of the kirk, the same path taken in the second of his dreams. Here he seeks out the graves of Edgar, Cathy, and Heathcliff. Despite Nelly's report that Heathcliff and Cathy have been known to "walk," Lockwood chooses to imagine peaceful slumbers for the two lovers: "I lingered round them, under that benign sky; watched the moths fluttering among the heath and hare-bells; listened to the soft wind breathing through the grass; and wondered how any one could ever imagine unquiet slumbers for the sleepers in that quiet earth." Just as he once struggled to free himself from Cathy's ghost and tried to dispel her specter-like name, so now Lockwood chooses to believe that the menacing supernatural lies at rest. In this manner the "good book" of *Wuthering Heights* concludes, a tale enclosed within the covers of Lockwood's reassuring narrative and therefore mediated by his interpretation.

\*   \*   \*

What is in question here is not only a particular ending to the tale of *Wuthering Heights* but the sense of an ending altogether, which is to say an ending with sense, one that puts to rest all wandering and all generation of contradictory forces. We have already seen Lockwood's determination to fix the boundaries of textuality in his second dream. There the dreamer was able to forgive exactly seven times seventy heads of Branderham's sermon. The first of the seventy-first is the moment of crisis precisely because in exceeding the definitive and literal limits set on the discourse, Branderham's text can no longer be controlled. The "ending" that Lockwood imposes on *Wuthering Heights* is a gesture of the same kind.

However benignly Lockwood closes his interpretive narration of *Wuthering Heights*, the text itself always counters his conclusions. Within the good book that Lockwood narrates is the story of the fictional nature of his textual posture, an interpretation of its interpreter. Which, then, is the narrator and which the narrated? As the tale begins in Chapter III and as it ends in Chapter XXXIV, Lockwood desperately tries to keep the menacing text under his control.[2] The excommunication that results from his first

---

2. It is at this juncture that I can best delineate what separates this reading from that of Dorothy Van Ghent in *The English Novel: Form* and *Function* (New York: Rinehart, 1953), 153–170. Van Ghent's essay proceeds from an incisive and promising declaration that *Wuth-*

struggles with the text is also the result of his last attempts to suppress the supernatural by setting limits to the narrative. Lockwood is once again silenced and displaced as narrator. His position is usurped by a text that, because founded on disjunctive self-reading, repeatedly ironizes itself as "good book." Lockwood's conception of literature is one fiction among many that the novel narrates. It creates this fiction in order to excommunicate it, in order to define itself over and against that which it is not.

*Wuthering Heights* is an annunciation of excommunication, both a fabrication in language of the real world—of that which is outside language (ex-communication)—and then again an expulsion of the heretic from its own textuality. The outsider from that "real world" who enters the closed space of Wuthering Heights is peremptorily banished. Yet this excommunication of Lockwood is not simply an expulsion to a position so distant that he no longer threatens what one is tempted to conceive of as the true inside nature of fiction. Excommunication is also incorporation of what the text posits to be its other. Rather than allowing Lockwood to separate himself, it holds him in a relationship to itself of violent difference. It risks itself by allowing Lockwood's conception of fiction its apparent victory.

*Wuthering Heights* is (about) this struggle between fiction and non-fiction. The fictional space is not a home for fiction, securely bound off from the threats of a world that calls itself real. Fiction is always in exile from itself. It involves the elaboration of and repeated struggle with this other realm, a continual marking of the discrepancy between itself and that which claims to lie outside. At the same time that fiction defines itself as this disjunction, it renounces the possibility of absolute self-definition, not only because it can "define" itself only through its other but also because no delineating boundary can then be drawn—no limits set to the voracious realm of fiction. It is perhaps after all, not mere superstition that causes Lockwood to struggle against the dream-texts, for as the fictional work marks the discrepancy between itself and that which lies outside, it paradoxically threatens to incorporate all that is within its reach, to assimilate the "real" into its own fiction. Lockwood is genuinely at stake and this is indicated by the increasingly violent relationship of Lockwood and text in the course of his three dreams. His dreams go through him like wine through water: they write him and his language into their fiction.

The fabrication of Lockwood is the means by which *Wuthering Heights* speaks of its own textuality, and the relationship between Lockwood and the

---

*ering Heights* is "of all English novels, the most treacherous for the analytical understanding" (153). And she develops a cogent argument throughout her essay for placing this treachery on one side of an axis that defines *Wuthering Heights* variously as a tension between mythical imagination and civilization, between excess and limitation, between outside and inside, between otherness and consciousness. Although Van Ghent sees these "two kinds of reality" (165) intersecting in each of the characters, she is unwilling to extend this "breaking-through of a separating medium" (165) to the final outcome of the novel. On the contrary: she undermines the radicality first by reinscribing the text under the protective aegis of Lockwood's reassuring "dream-rejecting reason" (155) and lastly, in her closing passage, by maintaining that this boundary between excess and limitation had never actually been violated. Here this violation takes place such that limitation is inscribed within excess.

tale of Wuthering Heights is in turn the gap that makes a certian critical language possible—a gap here generated, perhaps only to close. But what does this alternate generation and closure imply? The implications are critical in several senses. The gesture of generating the disparity between Lockwood as narrator and the narrative fiction, of criticizing Lockwood's naiveté, necessarily falls prey to the very illusions it pretends to disparage. Although Lockwood's conception of language is a fiction created by the novel, one is forced, from a certain point of view, to take Lockwood literally, to pose at least the imaginative possibility of a language that means what it says and refers to a realm outside the insanity of its own self-reflection. Critical rhetoric depends on temporarily forgetting the madness copresent with the "knowledge" that all is language. This forgetfulness gives free play to a referent, that itself, after all, has pretensions to discursive truth. No less than Lockwood's, then, any reading is at stake in the novel's textuality. The enterprise becomes critical in yet another sense of the word—which brings us to the crisis of interpretation in the question of closure. In elaborating a commentary whose theoretical stance implicitly insists on remaining within the enclosure of *Wuthering Heights*, how does such a text fit it? Perhaps, too well. For such supplemental discourse may disrupt the limits of Lockwood's narration, but it is of necessity already accounted for as yet another fiction that the novel itself continues to fabricate.

# NANCY ARMSTRONG

# Emily Brontë In and Out of Her Time†

Although she wrote but one novel, Emily Brontë continues to carry on a precarious relationship with a nineteenth-century intellectual tradition that consistently endorsed humanistic values, either by advancing the claims of the individual, or by maintaining those of the community. The temptation for readers is to stabilize this relationship either by seeing Brontë as a Romantic reactionary who rejected the kind of fiction coming into vogue during the 1840's or by aligning her work with the utilitarian tradition that gave rise to literary realism. In attempting to pin down the genre of *Wuthering Heights*, however, the problem has not been resolved. It has only become more apparent: if, as Terry Eagleton claims, a drably spiritless form of realism displaces the " 'pre-industrial' imaginative creativity" in Brontë's fiction, it is also true that "the real world" is eclipsed by an earlier Romantic form of the imagination, as J. Hillis Miller maintains.[1] How such politically and

† *Genre* XV (Fall 1982), 243–264. Copyright (c) 1982 by The University of Oklahoma. Reprinted by permission.

1. Terry Eagleton, *Myths of Power: A Marxist Study of the Brontës* (London: Macmillan, 1975), p. 12, and J. Hillis Miller, *The Disappearance of God* (Cambridge: Harvard U.P., 1963), p. 160. Also see Marilyn Butler's *Romantics, Rebels and Reactionaries* (London: Oxford U.P., 1981), pp. 178–88, for an informative description of the Romantic counter-revolution to Enlightenment individualism during the 1820's.

philosophically hostile positions can coexist in her sister's novel is the very question Charlotte Brontë tried—and with no little success—to defer in her preface to the 1850 edition of *Wuthering Heights*. By describing the author as one who combined the skills of a budding regional novelist with the powers of a full-blown visionary artist, Charlotte made Emily's novel, in effect, *sui generis*, the interaction of a remote social milieu with a unique personal vision. From the earliest to some of the more recent of Brontë's readers, then, the effort has been to resolve the problem and not to clarify it.

Any attempt to classify the novel, even if this entails making it a kind unto itself, rests upon Heathcliff and how one describes his character. Most often such attempts proceed on the ground that he is full of meaning and that by finding the key to decode him one will also discover what familiar set of nineteenth-century categories makes the novel a coherent whole. To see Heathcliff in this way is to see him as a conventional mediator, however, and, if nothing else, the history of failed attempts at resolving the debate over the genre of *Wuthering Heights* testifies to the fact that this is precisely what Heathcliff is *not*. True, he calls forth and appears to validate both modes of Enlightenment thinking, those which continue to make themselves felt on into the nineteenth century in the conflict between utilitarianism and Romanticism, to name but one such manifestation. But in doing so, Heathcliff actually problematizes the literary categories that depend upon these oppositions, namely, the distinction between romance and realism. Thus it is due to the breakdown of such primary cultural differences in Brontë's fiction that the whole question of its genre arises.

\* \* \*

\* \* \* Through at least half of her novel, Heathcliff's rise into power dramatizes the apotheosis of the Romantic hero, his intrusion into and transformation of a convention-bound world. But at some point it becomes clear that Romantic conventions will no longer do as a way of negotiating the text and of understanding the world to which it refers. By making them manifest in an energetic new form, Heathcliff actually cancels out Romantic possibilities and reduces that system of belief to mere superstition. From this point on, not surprisingly, the novel proceeds according to norms and expectations that are much more characteristic of Victorian realism. The meaning of Heathcliff's desire for Catherine Earnshaw changes so as to place such desire beyond the bounds of middle-class thinking and therefore outside the discourse of domestic fiction. But just as certain as her awareness of change is Brontë's unwillingness to see this change as an improvement or gain rather than as a kind of trade-off, an exchange of psycho-sexual power for economic power in which each calls the value of the other into question.

By taking the conventions of an earlier literature as the subject matter of a new kind of fiction, she demonstrates that fiction could no longer be written from the Romantic viewpoint and still be considered a novel. At the same time, the alternative offered to her as a novelist could not represent the totality of personal experience as she saw it. Out of this dilemma, we might imagine, came Heathcliff, who, in participating in both literary traditions, actually reveals the limitations of each. This is why he remains an enigma to readers, then, not because he is both noble savage and entrepreneur, but because he is ultimately neither. He only prefigures a time and discourse in which the boundary between self and society is no longer so necessary to the making of fiction.

\* \* \*

\* \* \* When he is thrust upon the Earnshaws "as a gift of God, though its dark almost as if it came from the devil," when Nelly tells Heathcliff "he's fit for a prince in disguise," or when Catherine Earnshaw declares him to be "more myself that I am," the possibility is created for Heathcliff to become one of the Earnshaws in the manner of his heroic prototypes. But this is only because the Romantic assumptions are kept in play that he is—figuratively speaking—an aristocrat concealed beneath a barbarous exterior, that his desire has all the force of nature behind it, and that such a noble savage can eventually redeem the community by making manifest his desires within it.

But Heathcliff's character includes features besides those of a Romantic hero. These have an economic and political logic all of their own and acquire their rhetorical force from the association between gypsies and the laboring classes, a conception of man that stubbornly resists idealization. We should recall that *Wuthering Heights* was written against the background of swelling industrial centers and Chartist uprisings that had reached alarming proportions by the forties, as had the hoards of migrant workers who were newly arrived on the English social scene. Against such a background Heathcliff's Napoleonic features set him in direct opposition to the vested interests of the readership who would hardly be well served by any unleashing of popular energy or further democratizing of social authority. Simply by giving his character a particular point of origin in the slums of a major industrial city rather than leaving the matter open to more romantic possibilities, Brontë made her protagonist capable of acquiring whatever negative meaning adhered to such a potentially hostile social element. In a realistic schema it follows, therefore, that father Earnshaw is not humane but demented for picking up a child, "starving, and houseless, and as good as dumb in the streets of Liverpool" and taking it into his family. Heathcliff proves true to the worst implications of the type, furthermore, by enchanting the master's daughter, supplanting the legitimate son in the father's affections, and so breeding dissension in the family for a generation to come.

Brontë defers these obvious and timely possibilities for meaning, however, and allows her reader to sympathize with this character in defiance of middle-class norms. The novel begins by designating the year of its telling as 1801, which is to move the events of the story backwards by several decades into the previous century. Moreover, the story of the family's dissolution and restoration unfolds, as Charlotte reminds us in her preface, on the "wild moors of the north of England." Much like Scott's settings, this remote landscape endows a contemporary crisis with all the trappings of an archaic one and summons up a context in which Heathcliff's insurgency seems to justify the emergence of middle-class power. One finds, for example, the Earnshaws exercising power over the hapless orphan in a manner reminiscent of the villainous aristocrats in earlier fiction. If old man Earnshaw's policies seem rather capricious ("A Nothing vexed him, and suspected slights of his authority nearly threw him into fits"), the next generation is clearly perverse. Hindley Earnshaw exercises power out of class anger, fraternal rivalry, and thwarted sexual desire. His aim is to obstruct legitimate desires, those to which one is entitled by nature rather than rank, and he succeeds in twisting Heathcliff's spontaneous desire for Catherine into a lust for vengeance. At Thrushcross Grange, on the other hand, one finds the other half of Brontë's fictional world governed by a conspicuously genteel breed, the man of sensibility. But the very refinement that makes both Lockwood and the Lintons before him so much at home in the parlor and library proves utterly useless, even debilitating, and just as destructive as open tyranny in dealing with the crises generated by Heathcliff's desire. Heathcliff may be relatively powerless without the cultural accountrements of a gentleman, but it is also true that men with little more than their education and good manners to fall back on founder stupidly amidst the social and emotional turbulence at Wuthering Heights. That such characters are virtually out of their element in the novel itself is demonstrated on more than one occasion, by Lockwood's pratfall in the Earnshaw's threshold, for instance, or by his failure to ac-knowledge his own desire for the young Catherine Earnshaw as well as the truth in his dream of her mother. The Lintons demonstrate this same order of false consciousness whenever events require them to restrain their emo-tions humanely or to respond with genuine compassion.

It is important to note that between them the heads of these families possess all the features necessary for a benevolent patriarchy that could reward natural merit while preserving established traditions. The problem lies in combining the features of the Lintons and Earnshaws to make such a har-monious whole. When broken down into the components of a brutal tyrant and ineffectual gentleman, the socio-economic data of the novel create the double-bind situation that tears Catherine Earnshaw asunder. "Did it never occur to you," she explains to Nelly, "that if Heathcliff and I were married, we should be beggars? whereas, if I marry Linton, I can aid Heathcliff to rise, and place him out of my brother's power." Should she dare to enjoy immediate gratification, then Catherine would cut herself off from economic power. To acquire that power, however, she must forgo her desire for Heathcliff. An extraordinary act of sublimation or displacement of desire is therefore the precondition for entering into relationships at the Grange. Such a conspicuous lack of a narrative means for harnessing desire and exhausting it productively within a domestic framework is all we are given to sustain the belief that Heathcliff alone can reconstitute the family along more tolerable lines. By the end of the century, to be sure, Freud would have formulated the narrative model for substitution and sublimation that could resolve this dilemma. But in the absence of the narrative logic for bridging this gap between intolerable cultural alternatives we are left with the Romantic doctrine which says that a poor and uneducated individual may "conceal depths of benevolence beneath a stern exterior."

But the Romantic critique of rigidly hierarchical thinking can itself become subject to a critique, especially when its logic unfolds within the structure of a novel. There is the irony that Heathcliff can retain his role as the hero of the tale so long as he remains virtually powerless, the unwitting object of pathos. This in itself constitutes a departure from Romantic prototypes whose rebellion appears to advance the general good and bring about social reform. There is the further irony as well that even as an object of pathos Heathcliff is ruthlessly cur-like and therefore incapable of submitting to paternal authority. (The more primitive fear of separation from the maternal figure is what ultimately regulates his desire.) Nelly cautions him that this antisocial nature of his must be concealed if he hopes to succeed in bettering his position. "Don't get the expression of a vicious cur that appears to know that the kicks it gets are its deserts, and yet hates all the world, as well as the kicker, for what it suffers," she tells him. That he can possess these bestial qualities while still serving as the protagonist through at least half of the novel—through all of the novel, according to some—is also what differentiates this character from historically later counterparts, the entrepreneurs of Dickens's and Thackeray's fiction, for instance.

Heathcliff can no longer serve as the mediator if the novel has redefined the problem that needs mediation. Originally, this problem is clearly a matter of how to satisfy the claims of the individual within the categories of the existing social order. Heathcliff's acquisition of power can indicate neither the triumph of the individual nor the affirmation of the community, however, much less some reconciliation of the conflict between the two, for these become historically discontinuous viewpoints as the history of his rise into power unfolds. The impedance of the individual's claims for the sake of preserving class boundaries only seems to be the central conflict which the narrative needs to resolve. Once competition has been injected into the system and power has emerged from below, value shifts immediately to those institutions that have been dismantled in the process, as well as to the fictions swept away by the harsh facts of the economic struggle his rise entails. What once served as the novelist's answer to problems posed by her cultural milieu has evidently become the problem itself, and having been redefined, the problem must now be resolved by some other means. It is no longer a matter of how to gratify the individual in the face of social constraints; it has become a matter of how to maintain the values of the community in a competitive world.

In the second half of the novel, nature remains the repository of the authentic self and the constituent element in Heathcliff's character, but nature no longer serves as a source of benign possibilities. It resembles nothing quite so much as the inhuman battleground mapped out in Darwin's biology, the source of one's most perverse impulses as well as his will to power. As nature bares its teeth and claws at this point in the novel, the social order undergoes a corresponding change. A competitive principle rooted in the accumulation of capital provides the transforming agency that moves Heathcliff from the margins of society to its very center. Once there, he displays all the vices that have accompanied political power, the Lintons' sophistication, their veneer of civility, as well as the Earnshaws' brutality. It is money alone that empowers him to infiltrate the timeless institutions of marriage, inheritance, and property ownership and to shape these institutions to serve his own interests. Upon gaining possession of both the Heights and the Grange, Heathcliff initiates a new form of tyranny that undoes all former systems of kinship and erases the boundaries between class as well as between family lines.

Out of this dissolution of boundaries, however, a new division emerges. Catherine regards the change in Heathcliff as a splitting away of his socioeconomic features from his emotions, a division that has drained away all his sensuality and lent a spiritual quality to their passion. "That is not Heathcliff," she insists, "I shall love mine yet; and take him with me—he's in my soul." Whenever it is that one finally makes the equation between Heathcliff's sexual desires and his worldly ambition, between his ambition and gross bestiality, it is then that the romance of individualism is punctured, the essentially competitive nature of Brontë's protagonist demystified, and the politics underlying sexual desire in the novel exposed. Accordingly, Heathcliff becomes the opponent and not the proponent of middle-class values. What residue still clings to him of earlier prototypes—noble savages, fiery rebels, and plucky rogues alike—is abruptly placed in the past or relegated to the realm of memory and fiction. This is none other than the bewildering situation into which Lockwood stumbles at the beginning of the novel, one where character cannot be understood unless one has the history of relationships that Nelly's gossip provides.

The kind of world that will come into being under Heathcliff's domination is what Catherine Earnshaw tries to make the bedazzled Isabel Linton recognize:

> "Tell her what Heathcliff is—an unreclaimed creature, without cultivation; an arid wilderness of furze and whinstone. I'd as soon put that little canary into the park on a winter's day as recommend you to bestow your heart on him! It is deplorable ignorance of his character, child, and nothing else, which makes that dream enter your head. Pray don't imagine

that he conceals depths of benevolence and affection beneath a stern exterior. He's not a rough diamond—a pearl-containing oyster of a rustic—he's a fierce, pitiless, wolfish man. . . . I know he couldn't love a Linton; and yet he'd be quite capable of marrying your fortune and expectations. Avarice is growing with him a besetting sin."

In no uncertain terms does Brontë equate the Romantic doctrine of presence with "ignorance," a view of character which says that surface features point to meaning beyond the material manifestations of the self. The kind of fiction arising from this older notion of language, the self, and the world seems to fall into oblivion at this point in the novel, leaving the reader with a tangible sense of what the world is like with no spirituality in it. * * * This failure of Romantic conventions to represent adequately the relationships comprising her narrative is Brontë's way of acknowledging the fact that fiction could no longer be written from a Romantic viewpoint and still be considered a novel.

So it is that in the second half of the novel, the conventions of earlier literature, thus dismantled, become the subject matter of a new kind of fiction. The structure of social relationships erected from the ruins of the old calls forth a cast of characters much more in line with Victorian norms and expectations. Not unlike those of Dickens and Thackeray, for that matter, Brontë's fictional world fast becomes a veritable bestiary of predators and victims wherein only the latter retain some vestige of their humanity. Conventionalized behavior rather than impulse or desire seems to be the true mark of one's character. Capitalism replaces a belated feudalism as the chief source of villainy, and competition is treated as a fact of life that converts sentient beings into objects in the marketplace. At the same time, an idealized notion of the long-banished aristocracy, still conveniently remote from a society operating according to the *laissez-faire* principle, comes to serve as the repository of ethical value. But Dickens and Thackeray do not change from one historical frame of reference to another. For all the inconsistencies swarming about in their cultural milieu, they operate consistently from within Victorian categories and paradigms. Brontë's novel, on the other hand, appears to fall into their world from another of necessity, as the idealist categories of Romantic discourse break down. Out of the pieces of earlier fiction then comes a new kind of narrative art where value no longer resides in the claims of the individual but rather in the reconstitution of the family. The result is that problems are posed and questions asked in one set of literary conventions that cannot be answered by the other, which is to say what most critical readings strive to deny, that this is an essentially disjunctive novel.

* * *

It is not true that one manner of distributing wealth amends or complements the other in this novel. Quite the contrary, when brought together in Linton Heathcliff, these forms of social authority prove mutually un-dercutting, contradictions surface, and the literary machinery that once reconciled them is thoroughly dismantled. We find, for example, that all the Gothic devices of abduction, rape, incest, and necrophilia enabling Linton to marry his cousin against her will are engineered by common law and empowered by acquired wealth. This is to foreclose any possibility of sweeping away the injustices of a degenerate aristocracy by the coming in of a new social order. A version of the middle-class hegemony itself is what perverts established traditions in the second half of Brontë's novel and brings Gothic devices to the service of realism instead of romance.

To turn the contemporary world into such a nightmare is to invert the procedures of earlier Gothic Fiction and anticipate the sensation novels that came into fashion during the 1860's. By developing the character of Hareton Earnshaw, however, Brontë hit upon what may be considered a typically Victorian way out of the dilemma of a world thrown open to competition. Heathcliff's aggressive individualism plays itself out in a psychotic nightmare and historical cul-de-sac, but, as this becomes apparent, the story of an upward aspiring hero begins anew in an epicycle of the plot that originally brought Heathcliff into power. The second time around the emergence of power from below, so to speak, bears with it no traces of rebellion against paternal authority. Rather than unleashing popular energy, this protagonist's rise entails the harnessing and exhaustion of subversive forms of desire. Hareton Earnshaw is quite literally a noble savage, for one thing, and although he, like Heathcliff, originally occupies a servile position, his rude-ness cannot be construed as the gross sensuality of the laboring classes. It is the natural vigor of "the ancient stock." Much like the boy heroes spawned by Thomas Hughes's *Tom Brown*, Hareton's rough and readiness lends itself readily to acculturation through the persuasive power of a pretty girl and the influence of the written word. His mastery of the two houses and not Heathcliff's, significantly, signals an amalgamation of the ruling classes where there had been grave division (all their intermarriages having proved fatal). Nor does this unification entail any dissolution of social boundaries, but rather a situation, as Joseph calls it, where "the lawful master and the ancient stock had been restored to their rights." While Hareton's rise into power does represent the reform of an intolerably authoritarian society along more humanitarian lines, this reform is accomplished by means of a return to the past which restores the lines of inheritance and reconstitutes the family as it was prior to Heathcliff's intervention.

This kind of narrative resolution obviously won the immense popularity it did during the 1850's because it revised the fictional struggle between the bourgeoisie and the old aristocracy to accommodate later Victorian norms. The same middle-class interests could no longer be served by a fable in which the ruling class was defeated in the course of an industrial revolution. Quite the contrary, the struggle must now be represented as that of an entrenched middle class allied with the old aristocracy and beleaguered by the barbarians who were clambering to get in. The benevolent patriarchy towards which Brontë's narrative moves by reshuffling the features of character, reversing the relationships among individuals, and playing their story backwards and forwards ultimately denies the optimistic individualism that first set it in motion.

In contrast with the other characters in the novel, it is Heathcliff who embodies the contradiction produced as the novel shifts its frame of reference from one side of some historical faultline to the other. Once we dissolve the text back into this large context, it becomes clear why he seems to be several characters even though his name and competitive nature never vary. Against the background of a too rigid class structure where the individual appears to be radically undervalued, even such negative terms for the gypsy as "imp," "fiend," or "devil" can only recall his Romantic prototypes and lend him a positive value. By the 1840's, however, middle-class intellectuals were giving up on the individual as the guarantee of a reality superior to that designated by material facts. As Heathcliff's triumph over the institutions which had been oppressing him turns into something on the order of a reign of terror, it seems clear that the individual's desire has been overvalued to the detriment of the community. Desire loses its salutary power, value is reinvested in traditions that bind family and class, and Heathcliff's demonic features, as the factor disrupting these traditions, take on an ominously literal meaning. A resolution for the novel is grounded on revisionary principles where love is no longer to be equated with natural desire, nor the community with nature itself:

> The intimacy between Hareton and young Cathy, thus commenced, grew rapidly, though it encountered temporary interruptions. Earnshaw was not to be civilized with a wish; and my young lady was no philosopher and no paragon of patience; but both their minds tending to the same point—one loving and desiring to esteem, and the other loving and desiring to be esteemed—they contrived in the end to reach it.

If this were truly the mediation and final note it seems to be, however, it is difficult to imagine readers having all that much trouble placing *Wuthering Heights* squarely within the mainstream of Victorian literature. After all it is not that unusual for the protagonist of a novel to violate social boundaries as Heathcliff does. What is more, the social climbers of the fiction of the thirties and forties tend to differ from their earlier counterparts in this significant respect: lacking a pedigree, they cannot penetrate the old squirarchy without destroying it. Thus Heathcliff joins ranks with such characters as Dickens's Oliver Twist, Charlotte Brontë's Jane Eyre, Mrs. Gaskell's Mary Barton, and Thackeray's Becky Sharp in this respect. For they also threaten to become usurpers, criminals, or tyrants in their own rights by pursuing individualistic goals, and their demonic features must also be neutralized before the social tensions in these novels can convincingly give way to social cohesion.

\* \* \* *Wuthering Heights* was caught in the same shifting winds of history as other major novels of the period. It is easy to see how, on the one hand, novels that played out a fantasy of upward mobility provided the middle-class readership with a fable of its own emergence into power as Ian Watt has suggested. During the thirties and forties, however, when the obvious evils of industrialism made that power seem less the stuff of utopian fantasy and more of a fact to be defended, aggressive individualism begins to play a villainous role in history and "tradition" becomes an exalted thing to be preserved at any cost. \* \* \*

\* \* \*

How *Wuthering Heights* ultimately evades the kind of literary determinism I have been proposing becomes evident when the text has been mapped out against this background. Only then can we see how Brontë took issue with a public opinion that suppressed certain kinds of fantasy in order to sanction others as realistic. Even while playing to the expectations of her contem-poraries, this novel, we find, maintains the relative independence of artistic play from the fluctuations of social history. This is not to say that *Wuthering Heights* transcends the limits of her materials or the whole set of suppositions that made it possible for one to think and write novelistically at her moment in history, yet Brontë does make it clear that in insisting on her freedom to imagine, she felt those very constraints. All the images of breaking out and of renewed confinement that characterize not only her work but Charlotte's as well may serve as metaphors for the self in a tradition-bound world, but they also function on a quite different level, as a way of acknowledging the problem in writing that arises when the conventions for representing the self in opposition to society will no longer do. The division of the semantic universe into parlor and heath, male and female, past and present, real and fictive obstructs the narrative process which depends upon making something new of all these deadlocks, and continuing the story therefore requires periodic acts of violence.

More telling, paradoxically, than what *can* be said are the seams and joints, chinks in the armor of realistic narration, that the author refuses to seal even by some violent conjunction. The omission of the one event on which hinge all changes of fortune in the novel gives us a clear indication of her departure from literary norms. We are told that during a three-year's absence Heathcliff miraculously changed and then reappeared, still savage at heart, bearing all the outward and visible signs of a gentleman. Yet this change itself must take place outside the province of literature. "Like a planet revolving around an absent sun," the novel reminds us, "an ideology is made of what it does not mention; it exists because there are things which must not be spoken of." And what may not be brought into the open, in this case, is the very transformation that makes other novels so gratifying, the Napoleonic moment where the ruthless acquisitor and pretender to power becomes the redeemer and rightful claimant, a benevolent patriarch. Even though Brontë excludes the moment where this radical inversion of meaning takes place, the absence itself points to the discontinuity within the materials of her chosen genre as manifest in the character of the protagonist whose "development" usually smooths them away. It also points to the consistently competitive element in Heathcliff that is the more disturbing for the lack of a rational cause.

We are likely to become aware of this problem first as a rupture in the narrative flow. Nelly breaks off her story at the point where Heathcliff disappears, in response to which Lockwood implores, "With all my heart! Don't interrupt me. Come and take your seat here . . . now continue the history of Mr. Heathcliff from where you left off, to the present day." This hunger for intelligibility is only whetted by the interruption in the story. It is never entirely satisfied. Even after the telling of the tale resumes, there remains a disturbing break in the chain of events comprising what Lockwood calls "the history of Mr. Heathcliff." Significantly, Lockwood endeavors to mend the break by drawing upon a repertoire of novelistic devices meant just for this purpose but which must now be couched in the interrogative: "Did he finish his education on the continent? or escape to America, and earn honors by drawing blood from his foster country? or make a fortune more promptly, on the English highways?" By cataloguing the permissible explanations for a rise in social position such as Heathcliff enjoys, Brontë makes her reader only too aware that the truth is neither in the novel nor among the conventions novelists use for diverting power into the hands of ordinary individuals. Implying a kind of ironic self-consciousness on the order of that permeating a work like *Tristram Shandy* or even *Bouvard et Pécuchet*, the very arbitrariness of the novelist's catalogue drains away its explanatory power, leaving behind the mere husks of words for us to play with. By giving voice to the novel reader's expectations through Lockwood's relatively naive commentary, Brontë raises the questions such conventions were supposed to answer but in answering actually suppressed.

There is not only Heathcliff's strange disappearance from the text to deal with but also his strange refusal to do so. The persistance of forms of Romantic supernaturalism in the novel disturbs the otherwise conventional ending and further separates the author's viewpoint from the beliefs and values she ascribes to the reader. In death Heathcliff becomes part of nature and, as such, continues to compete with Edgar Linton for possession of Catherine Earnshaw, only now for the privilege of mingling with her corpse through the process of their physical decomposition. Such demonstrated perversity notwithstanding, Brontë maintains nature's superiority to culture in certain respects, and she has Heathcliff pursue his desires through to their own sort of resolution. Counter to the beliefs of what Lockwood calls "the busy world," Heathcliff demonstrates the primacy of man's essential nature over and against a more modern notion of character that trusts to familiar roles and places material limits on the self. He has a "conviction" that spirits "can, and do exist, among us" and feels Catherine's ghostly presence as "certainly as you perceive a substantial body in the dark." That this is something more than a delusion on his part is indicated by Lockwood's similar encounter with her ghost, by Heathcliff's "frightful, life-like gaze of exultation" on his deathbed, and by Nelly's testimony that "country folk, if you asked them, would swear on their Bible that he *walks*." Heathcliff's apotheosis as the demon lover of folklore and superstition exactly inverts the assumption of scientific thinking that nature remains securely locked within its rational categories. Contrary to Heathcliff's magical thinking, Lockwood's empiricism merely flattens characters into stereotypes and suppresses the desires that alone can revitalize a rigidly endogamous society. Essentially hostile to social categories of any kind, these aspects of character remain in the novel as the signs of absent desire. As such, they comprise a separate world of romance, a fantasy of power that is both obsolete and imminently threatening.

Viewed from this perspective, the process of domestication allowing the characters to fall more in line with familiar social roles in the manner of domestic realism does not constitute a mediation of the conflict between self and society so much as a contraction and fragmentation of the novel's original fantasy materials, a process of displacement that is the more sophisticated for baring its own devices. Like the Romantic poet, Brontë seems to locate value in the natural aspects of the self and conceive social roles as confining, but she also accepts a materialistic view of nature as the ultimate reality, never retreating as Keats did, for example, from a world "where every maw / The greater on the lesser feeds evermore."[2] In confronting the Victorian dilemma of man's identification with this depraved nature, she refuses to soften the harsh facts of competition underlying human history or to countenance the possibility of amelioration by such means. Nature's utter hostility to humanistic values locates her fiction within a later Victorian context, that is clear. In maintaining sympathy for what is more primal in the self than rules whose business it is to constrain the individual, the author casts in her lot with artists of an earlier age.

In this way her writing carries on a precarious relationship with a nineteenth-century intellectual tradition that continuously endorsed humanistic values either by advancing the claims of the individual or by maintaining those of the community. The first metamorphosis of Heathcliff from a "gipsy brat" into someone who is "in dress and manners a gentleman" tells us that the Romantic tradition fails to answer adequately the questions posed by an industrialized world. But the second metamorphosis of Heathcliff from the social interloper, a *nouveau riche*, into the bogeyman of popular lore and superstition reveals that this is precisely what the novel must hide if it is to remain a novel: the subversive desire at the origins of middle-class power, hence the history of the discourse in which the novel itself participates. The second change in the rules governing the formation of character in the novel reroots economic power within a domestic world whose function is to harness

2. "Epistle to John Hamilton Reynolds," ll. 94–95.

competitive energy and convert desire into the means for some ulterior end. The presence of the supernatural is dangerous, in turn, because it antedates science and undermines the rational categories that domestic realism affirms. If Heathcliff's first metamorphosis tells us something cannot be spoken if the novel is to remain a novel, then the second uncovers the act of repression that has enabled Victorian fiction to emerge. With the division of the protagonist in two, the ascension of Hareton, and the return of Heathcliff as a ghost, the boundaries between romance and realism are reestablished in the novel, but the philosophically hostile positions of Enlightenment thinking achieve a disturbing kind of equivalence there as well.

Under circumstances such as these it becomes rather evident that the author of the novel, as Foucault would say, "is not simply an element of speech . . . Its presence is functional in that it serves as a means of classification. A name," he explains, "can group together a number of texts and thus differentiate them from others. A name also establishes different forms of relationships among texts."[3] By situating her sister's name in circumstances that might explain away the peculiar discontinuities shaping *Wuthering Heights*, Charlotte's biographical sketch and preface to the second edition perform this classificatory function where neither the novel itself nor Emily's pseudonym apparently could. It was Charlotte Brontë who separated *Wuthering Heights* from her own fiction and Anne's, with which it was initially confused. It was Charlotte who cautioned the readership that "an interpreter ought always to have stood between her [sister] and the world" and thereby implied that Emily's was an essentially private language. Most criticism has followed in the path cut by this first attempt to detach *Wuthering Heights* from the literary categories of the 1840's, by placing the author backwards or even forwards in history but rarely within her own moment in time. Nevertheless, these biographical constructions themselves must incorporate the paradox of male and female features of discourse, those of budding novelist, full-blown visionary and even the weary skeptic inscribed within her technique, as well as the biographical material for both a classic instance of hysteria and a case of aesthetic martyrdom on the order of Keats's. We should not be too surprised consequently to discover that despite the biographical mythology still clinging to the text its boundaries remain unstable and shifting, the viewpoints within it comprising the sort of discontinuities that emerge only from a series of texts, reversible and capable of speaking from several perpectives at once. In resisting our categories, however, *Wuthering Heights* allows one to see not only the transformations giving rise to a distinctively Victorian fiction, but also the radical act of forgetting that enables such discourse to exist.

3. Michel Foucault, "What is an Author?," *Language, Counter-Memory, Practice*, ed. Donald F. Bouchard, trans. Donald F. Bouchard and Sherry Simon (Ithaca: Cornell Univ. Press, 1977), p. 123.

# J. HILLIS MILLER

# *Wuthering Heights*: Repetition and the "Uncanny"†

"I don't care—I will get in!"
Emily Brontë, *Wuthering Heights*

Lockwood's "ejaculation," as Brontë calls it, when he tries to get back into the Heights a second time, might be taken as an emblem of the situation of the critic of *Wuthering Heights*. This novel has been a strong enticement for readers. It exerts great power over its readers in its own violence, and in its presentation of striking psychological, sociological, and natural detail. It absorbs the reader, making him enwrapped or enrapt by the story. In spite of its many peculiarities of narrative technique and theme, it is, in its extreme vividness of circumstantial detail, a masterwork of "realistic" fiction. It obeys most of the conventions of Victorian realism, though no reader can miss the fact that it gives these conventions a twist. The reader is persuaded that the novel is an accurate picture of the material and sociological conditions of life in Yorkshire in the early nineteenth century. The novel to an unusual degree gives that pleasure appropriate to realistic fiction, the pleasure of yielding to the illusion that one is entering into a real world by way of the words on the page.

Another way the novel entices the reader is by presenting abundant material inviting interpretation. Like *Lord Jim*, it overtly invites the reader to believe that there is some secret explanation which will allow him to understand the novel wholly. Such an interpretation would integrate all the details perspicuously. It is in this way chiefly that the first, grounded form of repetition is present in this novel. The details, the reader is led to believe, are the repetition of a hidden explanatory source. They are signs of it. By "materials inviting interpretation" I mean all those passages in the novel which present something evidently meaning more than what is simply present. The surface of "literal representation" is rippled throughout not only by overtly figurative language but also by things literally represented which at the same time are signs of something else or can be taken as such signs. Examples would be the three gravestones by which Lockwood stands at the end of the novel, or the "moths fluttering among the heath, and hare-bells" and the "soft wind breathing through the grass" as he stands there. Such things are evidently emblematic, but of what? Passages of this sort lead the reader further and further into the novel in his attempt to get in, to reach the inside of the inside where a full retrospective explanation of all the

† Excerpted by permission of the author and publishers from pp. 42–29, 50–53, 60–68, and 70–72 of *Fiction and Repetition: Seven English Novels*, by J. Hillis Miller, Cambridge, Massachusetts: Harvard University Press, 1. See Robert C. McKibben, "The Image of the Book in *Wuthering Heights*," *Nineteenth-Century Fiction*, 15 (1960), 159–169.

enigmatic details will be possible. Nor is this feature of style intermittent. Once the reader catches sight of this wavering away from the literal in one detail, he becomes suspicious of every detail. He must reinterrogate the whole, like a detective of life or of literature on whom nothing is lost. The text itself, in its presentation of enigmas in the absence of patent totalizing explanation, turns him into such a detective.

The reader is also coaxed into taking the position of an interpreting spectator by the presentation in the novel of so many models of this activity. Lockwood, the timid and civilized outsider, who "shrunk icily into [himself], like a snail" at the first sign of warm response demanding warmth from him, is the reader's delegate in the novel. He is that familiar feature of realistic fiction, the naive and unreliable narrator. Like the first readers of the novel, like modern readers, in spite of all the help they get from the critics, Lockwood is confronted with a mass of fascinating but confusing data which he must try to piece together to make a coherent pattern. I say "must" not only because this is what we as readers have been taught to do with a text, but also because there are so many examples in the novel, besides Lockwood, of texts with interpretation or commentary, or of the situation of someone who is attempting to make sense of events by narrating them.

Lockwood establishes the situation of many characters in the novel and of its readers as interpreting witnesses in a passage near the start of the novel. He first boasts of his ability to understand Heathcliff instinctively, and then withdraws this to say he may be merely projecting his own nature: "I know, by instinct, his reserve springs from an aversion to show displays of feeling— to manifestations of mutual kindliness . . . —No, I'm running on too fast— I bestow my own attributes over liberally on him. Mr Heathcliff may have entirely dissimilar reasons for keeping his hand out of the way, when he meets a would be acquaintance, to those which actuate me." The second chapter gives additional examples of Lockwood's ineptness as a reader of signs or as a gatherer of details into a pattern. He mistakes a heap of dead rabbits for cats, thinks Catherine Linton is Mrs. Heathcliff, and so on. His errors are a warning to the over-confident reader.

Lockwood is of course by no means the only interpreter or reader in the novel. Catherine's diary is described by Lockwood as "a pen and ink commentary—at least, the appearance of one—covering every morsel of blank that the printer had left" in all the books of her "select" library. That library includes a Testament and the printed sermon of the Reverend Jabes Branderham. Catherine's diary is written in the margin of the latter. Branderham's sermon is an interpretation of a text in the New Testament. That text is itself an interpretation by Jesus of his injunction to forgiveness as well as a reading of certain Old Testament phrases which are echoed, just as Jesus's interpretation (or that of the Gospel-maker) comes accompanied, characteristically, by a parable. A parable is an interpretation by means of a story "thrown beside" that which is to be interpreted, as in fact all of *Wuthering*

*Heights* might be said to be, since Lockwood's narration is adjacent to or at the margin of the enigmatic events he attempts to understand. Branderham's sermon is "interpreted" by Lockwood's dream of the battle in the chapel, in which "every man's hand [is] against his neighbor." The sound of rapping in the dream, in turn, is rationally "read," when Lockwood wakes, as the fir-branch scratching against the window, like a pen scratching on paper. That scratching is reinterpreted once more, in Lockwood's next dream, as the sound of Catherine's ghost trying to get through the window. Lockwood, when he wakens again, and Heathcliff, when he comes running in response to Lockwood's yell, of course interpret the dream differently. Lockwood sees Heathcliff's frantic calling out the window to Catherine (" 'Come in! come in!' he sobbed. 'Cathy, do come.' ") as "a piece of superstition."

These few pages present a sequence of interpretations and of interpretations within interpretations. This chain establishes, at the beginning, the situation of the reader as one of gradual penetration from text to text, just as Lockwood moves from room to room of the house, each inside the other, until he reaches the paneled bed inside Catherine's old room. There he finds himself confronting the Chinese boxes of texts within texts I have just described. The reader of *Wuthering Heights* must thread his or her way from one interpretative narrative to another—from Lockwood's narrative to Nelly's long retelling (which is also a rationalizing and conventionally religious explanation), to Isabella's letter, or to Catherine's dream of being thrown out of heaven, to her interpretation of this in the "I am Heathcliff" speech, and so on.

The novel keeps before the reader emblems of his own situation by showing so many characters besides Lockwood reading or learning to read.[1] The mystery Lockwood tries to understand is the "same" mystery as that which confronts the reader of the novel: How have things got the way they are at Wuthering Heights when Lockwood first goes there? What is the original cause lying behind this sad disappearance of civility? Why is it that the novel so resists satisfactory reasonable explanation? Lockwood, at the point of his deepest penetration spatially into the house and temporally back near the "beginning," encounters not an event or a presence open to his gaze, but Catherine's diary, another text to read. Catherine and Heathcliff, in their turns, are shown, in the diary, condemned to read two religious pamphlets, "The Helmet of Salvation" and "The Broad Way to Destruction," on the "awful Sunday" when they escape for their "scamper on the moors" under the dairy-woman's cloak. Edgar Linton reads in his study while Catherine is willing her own death. He tries to keep her in life by enticing her to read: "A book lay spread on the sill before her, and the scarcely perceptible wind fluttered its leaves at intervals. I believe Linton had laid it there, for she never endeavoured to divert herself with reading, or occupation of any kind." Much later, the taming of Hareton is signaled by his patiently learning to

1. See Robert C. McKibben, "The Image of the Book in *Wuthering Heights*," *Nineteenth-Century Fiction*, 15 (1960), 159–169.

read under the second Catherine's tutelage. Reading seems to be opposed to the wind on the moors, to death, and to sexual experience. Yet all the readers, in the novel and of the novel, can have as a means of access to these is a book, or some other mediating emblem.

Brontë's problem, once she had agreed with her sisters to try her hand at a novel, was to bend the vision she had been expressing more directly and privately in the Gondal poems to the conventions of nineteenth-century fiction, or to bend those conventions to accommodate the vision. Each technical device contributing to the celebrated complexity of narration in *Wuthering Heights* has its precedents in modern fictional practice from Cervantes down to novelists contemporary with Brontë. The time shifts, the multiplication of narrators and narrators within narrators, the double plot, the effacement of the author, and the absence of any trustworthy and knowing narrator who clearly speaks for the author are used strategically in *Wuthering Heights* to frustrate the expectations of a reader such as Lockwood. They are used to invite the reader to move step by step, by way of a gradual unveiling, room by room, into the "penetralium" of Brontë's strange vision of life.

The first who accepted this invitation was Brontë's sister Charlotte, or rather one should say almost the first, since the first reviews of *Wuthering Heights* precede Charlotte's essay. Charlotte Brontë's two prefaces, the "Biographical Notice of Ellis and Acton Bell" and the "Editor's Preface to the New [1850] Edition of *Wuthering Heights*," are often the first thing the modern reader of the novel encounters, with the exception of some twentieth-century critic's introductory essay. The novel comes to the reader wrapped in layers of prefatory material. It is difficult to be sure where the margin of the introductions ends and where the novel "proper" begins. Where does the reader step over the threshold into the novel itself? If the modern critical essay is definitely outside, a kind of alien presence within the covers of the book, Charlotte's prefaces would seem to have privileged access to the house. They seem to be the last layer before entrance, the inside outside, or perhaps the first region actually within, the outside inside, an entrance room. Perhaps they should be thought of as liminal, as the threshold itself. In any case, the language of Charlotte's prefaces is often continuous with Emily's language, for example in its use of figures of speech drawn from Yorkshire scenery, though whether or not Charlotte's language distorts Emily's language by misusing it is another question.

Charlotte's prefaces establish the rhetorical stance which has been characteristic of criticism of this novel. This stance involves dismissing most previous critics and claiming one has oneself solved the enigma, cracked the code. Charlotte's prefaces also establish the situation of a reader confronting an enigmatic text as the appropriate emblem for those both inside and outside the novel:

> Too often do reviewers remind us of the mob of Astrologers, Chaldeans, and Soothsayers gathered before the "writing on the wall," and unable

to read the characters or make known the interpretation. We have a right to rejoice when a true seer comes at last, some man in whom is an excellent spirit, to whom have been given light, wisdom, and understanding; who can accurately read the "Mene, Mene, Tekel, Upharsin" of an original mind (however unripe, however inefficiently cultured and partially expanded that mind may be); and who can say, with confidence, "This is the interpretation thereof."

Charlotte is here ostensibly praising the one previous review of which she approves, that by Sydney Dobell in the *Palladium* for September 1850. Dobell was persuaded that Charlotte Brontë had written *Wuthering Heights*. His review is by no means unintelligent, for example in what he says of Catherine Earnshaw: "in the very arms of her lover we dare not doubt her purity." In the end, however, Dobell only restates the enigma rather than solving it: "one looks back at the whole story as to a world of brilliant figures in an atmosphere of mist; shapes that come out upon the eye, and burn their colours into the brain, and depart into the enveloping fog. It is the unformed writing of a giant's hand; the 'large utterance' of a baby god." Charlotte, in spite of her praise of Dobell, means to present herself as the first genuine reader of this "unformed writing," the first true interpreter of the "Mene, Mene, Tekel, Upharsin."

Charlotte's preface of 1850 confidently tells the reader, before he has even read the novel, what the text is to mean. The difficulty is that she presents in fact at least four incompatible readings, citing chapter and verse for each interpretation she proposes, without apparent awareness that they differ from one another. Her readings, moreover, function to throw the reader off the track. They attempt to shift the blame for the novel away from Emily by reducing its meaning to something Charlotte imagines Victorian readers will accept.

Emily Brontë was in *Wuthering Heights*, says Charlotte in the first reading she proposes, simply following nature. She was warbling her native woodnotes wild. The novel is not Emily speaking, but nature speaking through her. The novel "is rustic all through. It is moorish, and wild, and knotty as a root of heath. Nor was it natural that it should be otherwise; the author being herself a native and nursling of the moors."

This reading is immediately qualified and replaced by a new one. The true source of the novel, says Charlotte now, is the actual wild way of life of the peasants of Yorkshire. The novel is sociologically accurate. Emily is merely the innocent transcriber of fact: "She knew them; knew their ways, their language, their family histories; she could hear of them with interest, and talk of them with detail, minute, graphic, and accurate . . . Her imagination, which was a spirit more sombre than sunny, more powerful than sportive, found in such traits material whence it wrought creations like Heathcliff, like Earnshaw, like Catherine. Having formed these beings, she did not know what she had done."

No, after all, this is not it either, Charlotte in effect says in proposing yet another reading. In fact Emily Brontë was a Christian. The novel is a religious allegory, with Heathcliff, for example, an incarnation of the Devil: "Heathcliff, indeed, stands unredeemed; never once swerving in his arrow-straight course to perdition." His love for Catherine is "a passion such as might boil and glow in the bad essence of some evil genius; a fire that might form the tormented centre—the ever-suffering soul of a magnate of the infernal world: and by its quenchless and ceaseless ravage effect the execution of the decree which dooms him to carry Hell with him wherever he wanders."

No, says Charlotte finally, this is not the true explanation or excuse. In fact, whatever the nature of the work, Emily is not to be blamed for it because she was not responsible for it. She was the passive medium through which something or someone else spoke, just as, for Rimbaud, in "les lettres du voyant," the metal is not to blame if it finds itself a trumpet ("Je est un autre."); and just as the speaker in some of Brontë's poems is subject to a "God of visions" who speaks through her without her volition. "But this, I know," says Charlotte; "the writer who possesses the creative gift owns something of which he is not always master—something that at times strangely wills and works for itself . . . Be the work grim or glorious, dread or divine, you have little choice left but quiescent adoption. As for you—the nominal artist—your share in it has been to work passively under dictates you neither delivered nor could question—that would not be uttered at your prayer, nor suppressed nor changed at your caprice."

Charlotte's prefaces, with their multiple interpretations, each based on some aspect of the actual text of *Wuthering Heights*, establish a program for all the hundreds of essays and books on *Wuthering Heights* which were to follow. They do this both in the sense that most readings could be lined up under one or another of Charlotte's four readings. They do it also in the sense that all these books and essays are also empirically based on the text. Each tends to be plausible, but demonstrably partial, though each also, like Charlotte's prefaces, tends to be presented with confident certainty. Each critic presents himself as the Daniel who can at last decipher the writing on the wall. Though the many essays on the novel do not exist on a common axis of judgment, that is, though they do not even raise the same questions about the novel, much less give the same answers, each critic tends to claim that he has found something of importance which will indicate the right way to read the novel as a whole.

\* \* \*

\* \* \* The literature on *Wuthering Heights* is abundant and its incoherence striking. Even more than some other great works of literature this novel seems to have an inexhaustible power to call forth commentary and more commentary. All literary criticism tends to be the presentation of what claims to be the definitive rational explanation of the text in question. The criticism of *Wuthering Heights* is characterized by the unusual degree of incoherence among the various explanations and by the way each takes some one element in the novel and extrapolates it toward a total explanation. The essays tend not to build on one another according to some ideal of progressive elucidation. Each is exclusive.

All these interpretations are, I believe, wrong. This is not because each does not illuminate something in *Wuthering Heights*. Each brings something to light, even though it covers something else up in the act of doing so. * * *

My argument is not that criticism is a free-for-all in which one reading is as good as another. No doubt there would be large areas of agreement among competent readers even of this manifestly controversial novel. It is possible to present a reading of *Wuthering Heights* which is demonstrably wrong, not even partially right, though I believe all the readings listed above are in one way or another partially right. They are right because they arise from responses determined by the text. The error lies in the assumption that the meaning is going to be single, unified, and logically coherent. My argument is that the best readings will be the ones which best account for the heterogeneity of the text, its presentation of a definite group of possible meanings which are systematically interconnected, determined by the text, but logically incompatible. The clear and rational expression of such a system of meanings is difficult, perhaps impossible. The fault of premature closure is intrinsic to criticism. The essays on *Wuthering Heights* I have cited seem to me insufficient, not because what they say is demonstrably mistaken, but rather because there is an error in the assumption that there *is* a single secret truth about *Wuthering Heights*. This secret truth would be something formulable as a univocal principle of explanation which would account for everything in the novel. The secret truth about *Wuthering Heights*, rather, is that there is no secret truth which criticism might formulate in this way. No hidden identifiable ordering principle which will account for everything stands at the head of the chain or at the back of the back. Any formulation of such a principle is visibly reductive. It leaves something important still unaccounted for. This is a remnant of opacity which keeps the interpreter dissatisfied, the novel still open, the process of interpretation still able to continue. One form or another of this openness may characterize all works of literature, but * * * this resistance to a single definitive reading takes different forms in different works. In *Wuthering Heights* this special form is the invitation to believe that there is a supernatural transcendent "cause" for all events, while certain identification of this cause, or even assurance of its existence, is impossible.

*Wuthering Heights* produces its effect on its reader through the way it is made up of repetitions of the same in the other which permanently resist rational reduction to some satisfying principle of explanation. The reader has the experience, in struggling to understand the novel, that a certain number of the elements which present themselves for explanation can be reduced to order. This act of interpretation always leaves something over, something just at the edge of the circle of theoretical vision which that vision does not encompass. This something left out is clearly a significant detail. There are always in fact a group of such significant details which have been left out of any reduction to order. The text is over-rich.

This resistance to theoretical domination, both in the sense of clear-seeing and in the sense of conceptual formulation, is not accidental, nor is it without significance. It is not a result of Brontë's inexperience or of the fact that she overloaded her novel with elements which can be taken as having meaning beyond their realistic references. The novel is not incoherent, confused, or flawed. It is a triumph of the novelist's art. It uses the full resources of that art against the normal assumptions about character and about human life which are built into the conventions of realistic fiction. The difficulties of interpreting *Wuthering Heights* and the superabundance of possible (and actual) interpretations do not mean that the reader is free to make the novel mean anything he wants to make it mean. The fact that no demonstrable single meaning or principle of meaningfulness can be identified does not mean that all meanings are equally good. Each good reader of *Wuthering Heights* is subject to the text, coerced by it. The best readings, it may be, are those, like Charlotte Brontë's, which repeat in their own alogic the text's failure to satisfy the mind's desire for logical order with a demonstrable base. *Wuthering Heights* incorporates the reader in the process of understanding which the text mimes in Lockwood's narration. It forces him to repeat in his own way an effort of understanding that the text expresses, and to repeat also the baffling of that effort.

＊　＊　＊

The celebrated circumstantiality of *Wuthering Heights* is the circumstantiality of this constant encounter with new signs. The reader of *Wuthering Heights*, like the narrator, is led deeper and deeper into the text by the expectation that sooner or later the last veil will be removed. He will then find himself face to face not with the emblem of something missing but with the right real thing at last. This will be truly original, the bona fide starting place. It will therefore be possessed of full explanatory power over the whole network of signs which it has generated and which it controls, giving each sign its deferred meaning. Through this labyrinth of linkages the reader has to thread his way. He is led from one to another in the expectation of reaching a goal, as Heathcliff leads Lockwood from marker to marker down that snowcovered road.

A further feature of this web of signs behind signs is that they tend to be presented in paired oppositions. Each element of these pairs is not so much the opposite of its mate as another form of it. It is a differentiated form, born of some division within the same, as the different Catherines in the passage discussed above are forms of the same Catherine; or as Heathcliff and Lockwood are similar in their exclusion from the place where Catherine is, as well as opposite in temperament, sexual power, and power of volition; or as Cathy says of Heathcliff not that he is her opposite, other than she is, but that "He's more myself than I am"; or as, in the passage describing the three graves, Edgar on one side of Catherine or Heathcliff on the other each represents one aspect of her double nature. The novel everywhere organizes itself according to such patterns of sameness and difference, as in the opposition between stormy weather and calm weather; or between the roughness of the Heights and the civilized restraint of Thrushcross Grange, or between inside and outside, domestic interior and wild nature outside, beyond the window or over the wall; or between the stories of the two Catherines, or between those who read and those who scorn books as weak intermediaries, or between people of strong will like Heathcliff, who is "a fierce, pitiless, wolfish man" and people of weak will like Lockwood.

These apparently clear oppositions have two further properties. The reader is nowhere given access to the generative unity from which the pairs are derived. The reader never sees directly, for example, the moment in childhood when Cathy and Heathcliff slept in the same bed and were joined in a union which was prior to sexual differentiation. This union was prior to any sense of separate selfhood, prior even to language, figurative or conceptual, which might express that union. As soon as Cathy can say, "I am Heathcliff," or "My love for Heathcliff resembles the eternal rocks beneath," they are already divided. This division has always already occurred as soon as there is consciousness and the possibility of retrospective storytelling. Storytelling is always after the fact, and it is always constructed over a loss. What is lost in the case of *Wuthering Heights* is the "origin" which would explain everything.

Another characteristic of the oppositions follows from this loss of the explanatory source. The separated pairs, differentiations of the same rather than true opposites, have a tendency to divide further, and then subdivide again, endlessly proliferating into various nuances and subsets. Once the "primal" division has occurred, and for Brontë as soon as there is a story to tell it has already occurred, there seems to be no stopping a further division. Once this primitive cell is self-divided it divides and subdivides perpetually in an effort to achieve reunification which only multiplies it in new further-divided life cells.

The sequence of generations in *Wuthering Heights*, for example, began long before the three presented in the novel. The name Hareton Earnshaw and the date 1500 carved in stone above the front door of the Heights testify to that. The marriage of the second Cathy and the new Hareton at the end of the novel will initiate a new generation. The deaths of Heathcliff, Edgar Linton, and the first Catherine have by no means put a stop to the reproductive power of the two families. This force finds its analogue in the power of the story to reproduce itself. It is told over and over by the sequence of narrators, and it is reproduced again in each critical essay, or each time it is followed through by a new reader. The words on the page act like a genetic pattern able to program the minds of those who encounter it. It induces them to take, for a time at least, the pattern of the experience of those long-dead imaginary protagonists. The emblem for this might be that concluding scene in which Lockwood stands by the triple grave prolonging the lives of Edgar, Catherine, and Heathcliff by his meditation on the names inscribed on their tombstones. In this act and in the narration generated by it he prevents them from dying wholly. Many Victorian novels stress this double form of repetitive extension beyond the deaths of the protagonists, for example *Tess of the d'Urbervilles*. *Wuthering Heights* gives this familiar pattern a special form by relating it to the question of whether Cathy and Heathcliff are to be thought of as surviving their deaths or whether they survive only in the narrations of those who have survived them.

Any of the oppositions which may be taken as a means of interpreting *Wuthering Heights* has this property of reproducing itself in proliferating divisions and subdivisions. Just as, for example, the name of the maiden Catherine caught between her two possible married names becomes an air "swarming" with Catherines, so the neat opposition within Christianity between good and evil, salvation and damnation, "The Helmet of Salvation" and "The Broad Way to Destruction," becomes the separation of sins into seven distinctions, and this in turn, in the Reverend Jabes Branderham's sermon, becomes a monstrous division and subdivision of sins, a dividing of the text, as Protestantism has multiplied sects and set each man's hand against his neighbor. Two becomes seven becomes seventy times seven, in a grotesque parody of a sermon: "he preached—good God! what a sermon: divided into *four hundred and ninety* parts—each fully equal to an ordinary address from the pulpit—and each discussing a separate sin!"

*Wuthering Heights* is perhaps best read by taking one or more of its emblematic oppositions as an interpretative hypothesis and pushing it to the point where the initial distinction no longer clearly holds. Only by this following of a track as far as possible, until it peters out into the trackless snow, can the reader get inside this strange text and begin to understand why he cannot ever lucidly understand it or ever have rational mastery over it. The limitation of many critical essays on the novel lies not in any error in the initial interpretative hypothesis (that storm and calm are opposed in the novel, or that windows, walls, and doors are used emblematically, for example). The limitation lies rather in the failure to push the given schematic hypothesis far enough. It must be pushed to the point where it fails to hypothecate the full accounting for the novel which is demanded in the critical contract. At that point the mortgage on *Wuthering Heights* is fore-closed and the reader, it may be, confronts his mortality as reader, that vanishing of lucid understanding which his critical reason, the reason that divides and discriminates in order to master, has done everything to evade.

Why is it that, with this novel, the logical mind so conspicuously fails? What does this have to do with the gage or promissory note that both holds off death and risks death, puts one's death on the line, as a kind of mortgage insurance? Why is it that an interpretative origin, *logos* in the sense of ground, measure, chief word, or accounting reason, cannot be identified for *Wuthering Heights*? If such an origin could be found, all obscurity could be cleared up. Everything could be brought out in the open where it might be clearly seen, added up, paid off, and evened out. What forbids this accounting?

An economic metaphor of course pervades *Wuthering Heights*. Heathcliff uses his mysteriously acquired wealth to take possession of the Heights and the Grange. He takes possession of them because each thing and person in each household reminds him of Catherine. By appropriating all and then destroying them, he can take revenge on the enemies who have stood between him and Catherine. At the same time he can reach Catherine through them, in their demolition. This is a violently incarnated way to experience a paradoxical logic of signs:

> "What is not connected with her to me? and what does not recall her? I cannot look down to this floor, but her features are shaped on the flags! In every cloud, in every tree—filling the air at night, and caught by glimpses in every object by day, I am surrounded with her image! The most ordinary faces of men and women—my own features mock me with a resemblance. The entire world is a dreadful collection of memoranda that she did exist, and that I have lost her!"

In this strange numismatics, each thing is stamped with the same image, the face of the person who is Queen to Heathcliff's Jack. In this novel no man is King or Ace. The Queen's countenance makes everything have value and pass current. There are problems with this coinage, however. For one thing, no one of these stamped images has a distinct number which indicates its worth in relation to other images or its exchange value in relation to goods or services. No orderly economic system of substitution and circulation is set up by this mint. Neither Heathcliff, nor Lockwood, nor the reader can buy anything with this money. There is, in fact, nothing left to buy, since there is nothing which is not coin stamped with the same image, of infinite value and so of no value.

The entire world is a dreadful collection of memoranda. Memoranda of what? Here is the second problem with this coinage. Each thing stands not for the presence of Catherine as the substance behind the coin, the standard guaranteeing its value, the thing both outside the money system and dispersed everywhere in delegated form within it. In this case, each thing stands rather for the absence of Catherine. All things are memoranda, written or inscribed memorials, like a note I write myself to remind me of something. They are memoranda that she did exist and that Heathcliff has lost her, that she is dead, vanished from the face of the earth. Everything in the world is a sign indicating Catherine, but also indicating, by its existence, his failure to possess her and the fact that she is dead. Each sign is both an avenue to the desired unity with her and also the barrier standing in the way of it.

From this follows the double bind of Heathcliff's relation to Hareton and to the second Cathy, both of whom he detests and loves because they look so much like the first Catherine. From this also follows the double bind of his relation to the Heights and to the Grange. He has taken much trouble to obtain them, manipulating the property laws of Yorkshire to do this as C. P. Sanger has shown. If he possesses the two households, he can take possession of Catherine through them, since they are her property, stamped with her image, proper to her, as much hers as her proper name. But to possess her image, like appropriating her by uttering her name ("Cathy, do come. Oh do—*once* more! Oh! my heart's darling! hear me *this* time—Catherine, at last!") is to possess only a sign for her, not Catherine herself. He must therefore destroy the things he has made his own in order to reach what they signify. He must destroy Hareton and the second Cathy, as well as the two houses. If he destroys them, however, he will of course reach not Catherine but her absence, the vacancy which stands behind every sign that she once existed and that he has lost her. In the same way, his goal of "dissolving with her, and being more happy still!" is blocked, in the coffin-opening scene, by the vision of Catherine's spirit not in the grave, "not under me, but on the earth." To merge with her body, like merging with his new possessions by destroying them, is to join only a sign and to destroy its function as sign. When Heathcliff recognizes this, he abandons his goal of destroying the Heights and the Grange. This leaves him as far from his goal as ever. He will be an infinite distance from it as long as he is alive:

> "It is a poor conclusion, is it not," he observed, having brooded a while on the scene he had just witnessed [the second Catherine and Hareton reading a book together, a sign of their growing intimacy]. "An absurd termination to my violent exertions? I get levers and mattocks to demolish the two houses, and train myself to be capable of working like Hercules, and when everything is ready, and in my power, I find the will to lift a slate off either roof has vanished! My old enemies have not beaten me—now would be the precise time to revenge myself on their representatives—I could do it; and none could hinder me—But where is the use? I don't care for striking, I can't take the trouble to raise my hand! . . . I have lost the faculty of enjoying their destruction, and I am too idle to destroy for nothing.

"But where is the use?" This extraordinary passage defines a complex economy of substitution and exchange which has broken down in an infinite inflation which has made the money worthless. The manipulation of the system is therefore of no use. Each element in this system is now without value either in relation to other elements it "represents" or in relation to what it stands for outside the system, since the standard behind the system has vanished, leaving it supported by nothing. It is like a paper currency which has no gold or silver, or no more credit, behind it, and so becomes again mere paper. The two houses and their land have represented Heathcliff's enemies. His enemies are those who stood between him and Catherine, forbidding their union. To destroy the houses is to destroy the enemies. His enemies, Hindley, Earnshaw, and Edgar Linton, are now dead. He must get at them through their living representatives, Hareton and the second Catherine, the scions of the two families, last of each stock. What these have always stood for is Catherine herself. To put this more exactly, they have stood for the infinite distance between Heathcliff and Catherine. This distance always exists as long as there are still signs for her. Everything resembles her, even Heathcliff's own features, but this resemblance is the sign that she is gone. To leave these signs in existence is to be tormented by the absence they all point to, but of which they also block the filling. To destroy them is to be left with nothing, not even with any signs of the fact that Cathy once existed and that he has lost her. There is no "use" in either destroying or not destroying. Within that situation Heathcliff remains poised, destroying himself in the tension of it, so that breathing or doing any slightest act is for him "like bending back a stiff spring."

The critic's conceptual or figurative scheme of interpretation, including my own here, is up against the same blank wall as the totalizing emblems within the novel, or up against the same impasse that blocks Heathcliff's enterprise of reaching Cathy by taking possession of everything that carries her image and then destroying it. If "something" is incompatible with any sign, if it cannot be seen, signified, or theorized about, it is, in our tradition, no "thing." It is nothing. The trace of such an absence therefore retraces nothing. It can refer only to another trace, in that relation of incongruity which leads the reader of *Wuthering Heights* from one such emblematic design to another. Each passage stands for another passage, in the way Branderham's sermon, as I have said, is a commentary on Jesus's words, themselves a commentary on an Old Testament passage, and so on. Such a movement is a constant passage from one place to another without ever finding the original literal text of which the others are all figures. This missing center is the head referent which would still the wandering movement from emblem to emblem, from story to story, from generation to generation, from Catherine to Catherine, from Hareton to Hareton, from narrator to narrator. There is no way to see or name this head referent because it cannot exist as present event, as a past which once was present, or as a future which will be present. It is something which has always already occurred and been forgotten. It has become immemorial, remembered only veiled in figure, however far back one goes. In the other temporal direction, it is always about to occur, as an end which never quite comes, or when it comes comes to another, leaving only another dead sign, like the corpse of Heathcliff at the end of the novel with its "frightful, life-like gaze of exultation." "It" leaps suddenly from the always not yet of the future to the always already of the unremembered past. This loss leaves the theorizing spectator once more standing in meditation by a grave reading an epitaph, impelled again to tell another story, which will once more fail to bring the explanatory cause into the open. Each emblematic passage in the novel is both a seeming avenue to the desired unity and also a barrier forbidding access to it. Each means the death of experience, of consciousness, of seeing, and of theory by naming the "state" or "place" that lies always outside the words of the novel and therefore can never be experienced as such, and at the same time, in itself and in its intrinsic tendency to repeat itself, each emblematic passage holds off that death.

This "death" may be called an "it" in order not to prejudge the question of whether it is a thing, a place, a person, a state, a relationship, or a supernatural being. The various narrations and emblematic schemas of the novel presuppose an original state of unity. This ghostly glimpse is a projection outward of a oneness from a state of twoness within. This duality is within the self, within the relation of the self to another, within nature, within society, and within language. The sense that there must at some time have been an original state of unity is generated by the state of division as a haunting insight, always at the corner or at the blind center of vision, where sight fails. This insight can never be adequately expressed in language or in other signs, nor can it be "experienced directly," since experience, language, and signs exist only in one thing set against another, one thing divided from another. The insight nevertheless exists for us only in language. The sense of "something missing" is an effect of the text itself, and of the critical texts which add themselves to the primary text. This means it may be a performative effect of language, not a referential object of language. The language of narration in *Wuthering Heights* is this originating performative enacted by Lockwood, Nelly, and the rest. This narrative creates both the intuition of unitary origin and the clues, in the unresolvable heterogeneity of the narration, to the fact that the origin may be an effect of language, not some preexisting state or some "place" in or out of the world. The illusion is created by figures of one sort or another—substitutions, equivalences, representative displacements, synecdoches, emblematic invitations to totalization. The narrative sequence, in its failure ever to become transparent, in the incongruities of its not-quite-matching repetitions, demonstrates the inadequacy of any one of those figures.

\* \* \*

\* \* \* The situation of the reader of *Wuthering Heights* is inscribed within the novel in the situations of all those characters who are readers, tellers of tales, most elaborately in Lockwood. The lesson for the reader is to make him aware that he has by reading the novel incurred a responsibility like that of the other spectator-interpreters.

"Thou art the man!"—this applies as much to the reader as to Lockwood or to the other narrators. The double guilt of Lockwood's narration as of any critic's discourse is the following. If he does not penetrate all the way to the innermost core of the story he tells, he keeps the story going, repeating itself interminably in its incompletion. This is like the guilt of the one who keeps a grave open, or like the guilt of a sexual failure. On the other hand, to pierce all the way in is to be guilty of the desecration of a grave, to be guilty, like Heathcliff when he opens Cathy's grave, of necrophilia. The punishment for that is to be condemned to go where the vanished protagonists are. Really to penetrate, to get inside the events, rather than seeing them safely from the outside, would be to join Cathy and Heathcliff wherever they now are. The reader's sense of guilt is systematically connected to the swarm of other emotions aroused in any good reader of *Wuthering Heights* as he makes his way through the book: affection for the two Catherines, though in a different way for each, and mixed with some fear of her intransigence in the case of the first Catherine; scorn for Lockwood, but some pity for his limitations; awe of Heathcliff's suffering; and so on.

The line of witnesses who feel one or another form of this complex of emotions goes from the reader-critic to Charlotte Brontë to Emily Brontë to that pseudonymous author "Ellis Bell" to Lockwood to Nelly to Heathcliff to Cathy, the inside of the inside, or it moves the other way around, from Cathy out to the reader. The reader is the last surviving consciousness enveloping all these other consciousnesses, one inside the other. The reader is condemned, like all the others, to be caught by a double contradictory demand: to bring it all out in the open and at the same time to give it decent burial, to keep the book open and at the same time to close its covers once and for all, so it may be forgotten, or so it may be read once more, this time definitively. The guilt of the reader is the impossibility of doing either of these things, once he has opened the book and begun to read: "1801— I have just returned from a visit to my landlord."

The reading of the first present-tense words of the novel performs a multiple act of resurrection, an opening of graves or a raising of ghosts. In reading those first words and then all the ones that follow to the end, the reader brings back from the grave first the fictive "I" who is supposed to have written them or spoken them, that Lockwood who has and had no existence outside the covers of the book. With that "I" the reader brings back also the moment in the fall of 1801 when his "I have just returned" is supposed to have been written or spoken. By way of that first "I" and first present moment the reader then resurrects from the dead, with Lockwood's help, in one direction Hindley, Nelly, Joseph, Hareton, the two Catherines, Heathcliff, and the rest, so that they walk the moors once again and live once again at the Heights and the Grange. In the other direction are also evoked first Ellis Bell, the pseudonymous author, who functions as a ghostly name on the title page. Ellis Bell is a male name veiling the female author, but it is also the name of a character in the book: someone who has survived Lockwood, an "editor" into whose hands Lockwood's diary has fallen and who presents it to the public, or, more likely, the consciousness surrounding Lockwood's consciousness, overhearing what he says to himself, what he thinks, feels, sees, and presenting it again to the reader as though it were entirely the words of Lockwood. In doing this Ellis Bell effaces himself, but he is present as a ghostly necessity of the narrative behind Lockwood's words. The name Ellis Bell functions to name a spectator outside Lockwood, who is the primary spectator. Ellis Bell is another representative of the reader, overhearing, overseeing, overthinking, and overfeeling what Lockwood says, sees, thinks, feels, and writing it down so we can in our turns evoke Lockwood again and raise also that thin and almost invisible ghost, effaced presupposition of the words of the novel, Ellis Bell himself. Behind Ellis Bell, finally, is Brontë, who, the reader knows, actually wrote down those words, "1801—I have just returned . . ." at Haworth on some day probably in 1846. Brontë too, in however indirect fashion, is brought back to life in the act of reading.

If in Lockwood's dream the air swarms with Catherines, so does this book swarm with ghosts who walk the Yorkshire moors inside the covers of any copy of *Wuthering Heights*, waiting to be brought back from the grave by anyone who chances to open the book and read. The most powerful form of repetition in fiction, it may be, is not the echoes of one part of the book by another, but the way even the simplest, most representational words in a novel ("1801—I have just returned . . .") present themselves as already a murmuring repetition, something which has been repeating itself incessantly there in the words on the page waiting for me to bring it back to life as the meaning of the words forms itself in my mind. Fiction is possible only because of an intrinsic capacity possessed by ordinary words in grammatical order. Words no different from those we use in everyday life, "I have just returned," may detach themselves or be detached from any present moment, any living "I," any immediate perception of reality, and go on functioning as the creators of the fictive world repeated into existence, to use the verb transitively, whenever the act of reading those words is performed. The words themselves, there on the page, both presuppose the deaths of that long line of personages and at the same time keep them from dying wholly, as long as a single copy of *Wuthering Heights* survives to be reread.

# Selected Bibliography

Materials reprinted in this edition are not included.

## EMILY BRONTË

Allott, Mariam, ed. *The Brontës: The Critical Heritage*. London: Routledge & Kegan Paul, 1974.
Barclay, Janet M. *Emily Brontë Criticism, 1900–1982: An Annotated Checklist*. Westport: Meckler, 1984.
Benvenuto, Richard. *Emily Brontë*. Boston: Twayne, 1982.
Gérin, Winifred. *Emily Brontë: A Biography*. Oxford: Clarendon Press, 1971.
Hatfield, C. W., ed. *The Complete Poems of Emily Jane Brontë*. New York: Columbia UP, 1941.
Ratchford, Fannie E. *The Brontës' Web of Childhood*. New York: Columbia UP, 1941.
———. *Gondal's Queen: A Novel in Verse by Emily Jane Brontë*. Austin: U of Texas, 1954.
Wise, Thomas J. and Symington, J. A., eds. *The Brontës: Their Lives, Friendships, and Correspondence*. 4 vols. Oxford: Basil Blackwell, 1932.

## WUTHERING HEIGHTS

Bell, Vereen M. "*Wuthering Heights* and the Unforgivable Sin." *Nineteenth-Century Fiction* 17 (1962): 188–91.
Cecil, David. "Emily Brontë and *Wuthering Heights*." *Victorian Novelists: Essays in Revaluation*. Chicago: U of Chicago P, 1958. 136–82.
Dunn, Richard J. "The Feeling of *Wuthering Heights*." *Research Studies* 45 (1977): 160–67.
Eagleton, Terry. "*Wuthering Heights*." *Myths of Power: A Marxist Study of the Brontës*. London: Macmillan, 1975. 97–121.
Fine, Ronald E. "Lockwood's Dreams and the Key of *Wuthering Heights*." *Nineteenth-Century Fiction* 24 (1969): 16–30.
Gilbert, Sandra M. "Looking Oppositely: Emily Brontë's Bible of Hell." *The Madwoman in the Attic: The Woman Writer and the Nineteenth-Century Literary Imagination*. New Haven: Yale UP, 1979. 248–308.
Homans, Margaret. *Women Writers and Poetic Identity: Dorothy Wordsworth, Emily Brontë, and Emily Dickinson*. Princeton: Princeton UP, 1980.
Kermode, Frank. "A Modern Way with the Classic." *New Literary History* 5 (1974): 415–34.
Kiely, Robert. "*Wuthering Heights*: Emily Brontë." *The Romantic Novel in England*. Cambridge: Harvard UP, 1972. 233–51.
Leavis, Q. D. "A Fresh Approach to *Wuthering Heights*." *Lectures in America*. New York: Pantheon Books, 1969. 85–138.
Madden, William A. "*Wuthering Heights* and the Binding of Passion." *Nineteenth-Century Fiction* 27 (1972): 127–54.
Mathison, John K. "Nelly Dean and the Power of *Wuthering Heights*." *Nineteenth-Century Fiction* 11 (1956): 106–29.
McCarthy, Terrence. "The Incompetent Narrator of *Wuthering Heights*." *Modern Language Quarterly* 42 (1981): 48–64.
McKibben, Robert. "The Image of the Book in *Wuthering Heights*." *Nineteenth-Century Fiction* 15 (1960): 159–69.
Miller, J. Hillis. "Emily Brontë." *The Disappearance of God: Five Nineteenth-Century Writers*. Cambridge: Harvard UP, 1963. 157–211.
Sabol, Ruth C. *A Concordance to Brontë's* Wuthering Heights. New York: Garland, 1984.
Shannon, Edgar F. "Lockwood's Dreams and the Exegesis of *Wuthering Heights*." *Nineteenth-Century Fiction* 14 (1959): 95–109.
Sonstroem, David. "*Wuthering Heights* and the Limits of Vision." *PMLA* 86 (1971): 51–62.
Van Ghent, Dorothy. "On *Wuthering Heights*." *The English Novel: Form and Function*. New York: Rinehart, 1953. 153–70.
Watson, Melvin R. "*Wuthering Heights* and the Critics." *The Trollopian* 3 (1948): 243–63.
Woodring, Carl R. "The Narrators of *Wuthering Heights*." *Nineteenth-Century Fiction* 20 (1957): 298–305.

# NORTON CRITICAL EDITIONS

ANDERSON *Winesburg, Ohio* edited by Charles E. Modlin and Ray Lewis White
AQUINAS *St. Thomas Aquinas on Politics and Ethics* translated and edited by
Paul E. Sigmund
AUSTEN *Emma* edited by Stephen M. Parrish *Third Edition*
AUSTEN *Mansfield Park* edited by Claudia L. Johnson
AUSTEN *Persuasion* edited by Patricia Meyer Spacks
AUSTEN *Pride and Prejudice* edited by Donald Gray *Second Edition*
BALZAC *Père Goriot* translated by Burton Raffel, edited by Peter Brooks
BEHN *Oroonoko* edited by Joanna Lipking
*Beowulf* (the Donaldson translation) edited by Joseph F. Tuso
BLAKE *Blake's Poetry and Designs* selected and edited by Mary Lynn Johnson and
John E. Grant
BOCCACCIO *The Decameron* selected, translated, and edited by Mark Musa and
Peter E. Bondanella
BRONTË, CHARLOTTE *Jane Eyre* edited by Richard J. Dunn *Second Edition*
BRONTË, EMILY *Wuthering Heights* edited by William M. Sale, Jr., and Richard Dunn
*Third Edition*
BROWNING, ELIZABETH BARRETT *Aurora Leigh* edited by Margaret Reynolds
BROWNING, ROBERT *Browning's Poetry* selected and edited by James F. Loucks
BURNEY *Evelina* edited by Stewart J. Cooke
BYRON *Byron's Poetry* selected and edited by Frank D. McConnell
CARROLL *Alice in Wonderland* edited by Donald J. Gray *Second Edition*
CERVANTES *Don Quijote* translated by Burton Raffel, edited by Diana de Armas Wilson
CHAUCER *The Canterbury Tales: Nine Tales and the General Prologue* edited by
V. A. Kolve and Glending Olson
CHEKHOV *Anton Chekhov's Plays* translated and edited by Eugene K. Bristow
CHEKHOV *Anton Chekhov's Short Stories* selected and edited by Ralph E. Matlaw
CHOPIN *The Awakening* edited by Margo Culley *Second Edition*
*The Classic Fairy Tales* edited by Maria Tatar
CONRAD *Heart of Darkness* edited by Robert Kimbrough *Third Edition*
CONRAD *Lord Jim* edited by Thomas C. Moser *Second Edition*
CONRAD *The Nigger of the "Narcissus"* edited by Robert Kimbrough
CRANE *Maggie: A Girl of the Streets* edited by Thomas A. Gullason
CRANE *The Red Badge of Courage* edited by Donald Pizer *Third Edition*
DARWIN *Darwin* selected and edited by Philip Appleman *Second Edition*
DEFOE *A Journal of the Plague Year* edited by Paula R. Backscheider
DEFOE *Moll Flanders* edited by Edward Kelly
DEFOE *Robinson Crusoe* edited by Michael Shinagel *Second Edition*
DE PIZAN *The Selected Writings of Christine de Pizan* translated by Renate
Blumenfeld-Kosinski and Kevin Brownlee, edited by Renate Blumenfeld-Kosinski
DICKENS *Bleak House* edited by George Ford and Sylvère Monod
DICKENS *David Copperfield* edited by Jerome H. Buckley
DICKENS *Great Expectations* edited by Edgar Rosenberg
DICKENS *Hard Times* edited by George Ford and Sylvère Monod *Second Edition*
DICKENS *Oliver Twist* edited by Fred Kaplan
DONNE *John Donne's Poetry* selected and edited by Arthur L. Clements *Second Edition*
DOSTOEVSKY *The Brothers Karamazov* (the Garnett translation) edited by Ralph E. Matlaw
DOSTOEVSKY *Crime and Punishment* (the Coulson translation) edited by George Gibian
*Third Edition*
DOSTOEVSKY *Notes from Underground* translated and edited by Michael R. Katz

DOUGLASS *Narrative of the Life of Frederick Douglass, an American Slave, Written by Himself* edited by William L. Andrews and William S. McFeely

DREISER *Sister Carrie* edited by Donald Pizer *Second Edition*

*Eight Modern Plays* edited by Anthony Caputi

DU BOIS *The Souls of Black Folk* edited by Henry Louis Gates Jr. and Terri Oliver

ELIOT *Middlemarch* edited by Bert G. Hornback

ELIOT *The Mill on the Floss* edited by Carol T. Christ

ERASMUS *The Praise of Folly and Other Writings* translated and edited by Robert M. Adams

FAULKNER *The Sound and the Fury* edited by David Minter *Second Edition*

FIELDING *Joseph Andrews with Shamela and Related Writings* edited by Homer Goldberg

FIELDING *Tom Jones* edited by Sheridan Baker *Second Edition*

FLAUBERT *Madame Bovary* edited with a substantially new translation by Paul de Man

FORD *The Good Soldier* edited by Martin Stannard

FORSTER *Howards End* edited by Paul B. Armstrong

FRANKLIN *Benjamin Franklin's Autobiography* edited by J. A. Leo Lemay and P. M. Zall

FULLER *Woman in the Nineteenth Century* edited by Larry J. Reynolds

GOETHE *Faust* translated by Walter Arndt, edited by Cyrus Hamlin

GOGOL *Dead Souls* (the Reavey translation) edited by George Gibian

HARDY *Far from the Madding Crowd* edited by Robert C. Schweik

HARDY *Jude the Obscure* edited by Norman Page *Second Edition*

HARDY *The Mayor of Casterbridge* edited by James K. Robinson

HARDY *The Return of the Native* edited by James Gindin

HARDY *Tess of the d'Urbervilles* edited by Scott Elledge *Third Edition*

HAWTHORNE *The Blithedale Romance* edited by Seymour Gross and Rosalie Murphy

HAWTHORNE *The House of the Seven Gables* edited by Seymour Gross

HAWTHORNE *Nathaniel Hawthorne's Tales* edited by James McIntosh

HAWTHORNE *The Scarlet Letter* edited by Seymour Gross, Sculley Bradley, Richmond Croom Beatty, and E. Hudson Long *Third Edition*

HERBERT *George Herbert and the Seventeenth-Century Religious Poets* selected and edited by Mario A. DiCesare

HERODOTUS *The Histories* translated and selected by Walter E. Blanco, edited by Walter E. Blanco and Jennifer Roberts

HOBBES *Leviathan* edited by Richard E. Flathman and David Johnston

HOMER *The Odyssey* translated and edited by Albert Cook *Second Edition*

HOWELLS *The Rise of Silas Lapham* edited by Don L. Cook

IBSEN *The Wild Duck* translated and edited by Dounia B. Christiani

JAMES *The Ambassadors* edited by S. P. Rosenbaum *Second Edition*

JAMES *The American* edited by James W. Tuttleton

JAMES *The Portrait of a Lady* edited by Robert D. Bamberg *Second Edition*

JAMES *Tales of Henry James* edited by Christof Wegelin

JAMES *The Turn of the Screw* edited by Deborah Esch and Jonathan Warren *Second Edition*

JAMES *The Wings of the Dove* edited by J. Donald Crowley and Richard A. Hocks

JONSON *Ben Jonson and the Cavalier Poets* selected and edited by Hugh Maclean

JONSON *Ben Jonson's Plays and Masques* selected and edited by Robert M. Adams

KAFKA *The Metamorphosis* translated and edited by Stanley Corngold

LAFAYETTE *The Princess of Clèves* edited and with a revised translation by John D. Lyons

MACHIAVELLI *The Prince* translated and edited by Robert M. Adams *Second Edition*

MALTHUS *An Essay on the Principle of Population* edited by Philip Appleman

MANN *Death in Venice* translated and edited by Clayton Koelb

MARX *The Communist Manifesto* edited by Frederic L. Bender

MELVILLE *The Confidence-Man* edited by Hershel Parker

MELVILLE *Moby-Dick* edited by Harrison Hayford and Hershel Parker

MEREDITH *The Egoist* edited by Robert M. Adams

*Middle English Lyrics* selected and edited by Maxwell S. Luria and Richard L. Hoffman

*Middle English Romances* selected and edited by Stephen H. A. Shepherd

MILL *Mill: The Spirit of the Age, On Liberty, The Subjection of Women* selected and edited by Alan Ryan

MILTON *Paradise Lost* edited by Scott Elledge *Second Edition*

*Modern Irish Drama* edited by John P. Harrington

MORE *Utopia* translated and edited by Robert M. Adams *Second Edition*

NEWMAN *Apologia Pro Vita Sua* edited by David J. DeLaura

NEWTON *Newton* edited by I. Bernard Cohen and Richard S. Westfall

NORRIS *McTeague* edited by Donald Pizer *Second Edition*

*Restoration and Eighteenth-Century Comedy* edited by Scott McMillin *Second Edition*

RHYS *Wide Sargasso Sea* edited by Judith L. Raiskin

RICH *Adrienne Rich's Poetry and Prose* edited by Barbara Charlesworth Gelpi and Albert Gelpi

ROUSSEAU *Rousseau's Political Writings* edited by Alan Ritter, translated by Julia Conaway Bondanella

ST. PAUL *The Writings of St. Paul* edited by Wayne A. Meeks

SHAKESPEARE *Hamlet* edited by Cyrus Hoy *Second Edition*

SHAKESPEARE *Henry IV, Part I* edited by James L. Sanderson *Second Edition*

SHAW *Bernard Shaw's Plays* edited by Warren Sylvester Smith

SHELLEY, MARY *Frankenstein* edited by J. Paul Hunter

SHELLEY, PERCY BYSSHE *Shelley's Poetry and Prose* selected and edited by Donald H. Reiman and Sharon B. Powers

SMOLLETT *Humphry Clinker* edited by James L. Thorson

SOPHOCLES *Oedipus Tyrannus* translated and edited by Luci Berkowitz and Theodore F. Brunner

SPENSER *Edmund Spenser's Poetry* selected and edited by Hugh Maclean and Anne Lake Prescott *Third Edition*

STENDHAL *Red and Black* translated and edited by Robert M. Adams

STERNE *Tristram Shandy* edited by Howard Anderson

STOKER *Dracula* edited by Nina Auerbach and David Skal

STOWE *Uncle Tom's Cabin* edited by Elizabeth Ammons

SWIFT *Gulliver's Travels* edited by Robert A. Greenberg *Second Edition*

SWIFT *The Writings of Jonathan Swift* edited by Robert A. Greenberg and William B. Piper

TENNYSON *In Memoriam* edited by Robert H. Ross

TENNYSON *Tennyson's Poetry* selected and edited by Robert W. Hill, Jr. *Second Edition*

THACKERAY *Vanity Fair* edited by Peter Shillingsburg

THOREAU *Walden and Resistance to Civil Government* edited by William Rossi *Second Edition*

THUCYDIDES *The Peloponnesian War* translated by Walter Blanco, edited by Walter Blanco and Jennifer Tolbert Roberts

TOLSTOY *Anna Karenina* edited and with a revised translation by George Gibian *Second Edition*

TOLSTOY *Tolstoy's Short Fiction* edited and with revised translations by Michael R. Katz

TOLSTOY *War and Peace* (the Maude translation) edited by George Gibian *Second Edition*

TOOMER *Cane* edited by Darwin T. Turner

TURGENEV *Fathers and Sons* translated and edited by Michael R. Katz

TWAIN *Adventures of Huckleberry Finn* edited by Thomas Cooley *Third Edition*

TWAIN *A Connecticut Yankee in King Arthur's Court* edited by Allison R. Ensor

TWAIN *Pudd'nhead Wilson and Those Extraordinary Twins* edited by Sidney E. Berger

VOLTAIRE *Candide* translated and edited by Robert M. Adams *Second Edition*

WASHINGTON *Up From Slavery* edited by William L. Andrews

WATSON *The Double Helix: A Personal Account of the Discovery of the Structure of DNA* edited by Gunther S. Stent

WHARTON *Ethan Frome* edited by Kristin O. Lauer and Cynthia Griffin Wolff

WHARTON *The House of Mirth* edited by Elizabeth Ammons

WHITMAN *Leaves of Grass* edited by Sculley Bradley and Harold W. Blodgett

WILDE *The Picture of Dorian Gray* edited by Donald L. Lawler

WOLLSTONECRAFT *A Vindication of the Rights of Woman* edited by Carol H. Poston *Second Edition*

WORDSWORTH *The Prelude: 1799, 1805, 1850* edited by Jonathan Wordsworth, M. H. Abrams, and Stephen Gill